LIBRARY OF HEBREW BIBLE/
OLD TESTAMENT STUDIES

553

Formerly Journal for the Study of the Old Testament Supplement Series

THE ONE WHO READS MAY RUN

Essays in Honour of Edgar W. Conrad

edited by

Roland Boer,
Michael Carden
&
Julie Kelso

t&t clark

Published by T & T Clark International
A Continuum imprint
80 Maiden Lane, New York, NY 10038
The Tower Building, 11 York Road, London SE1 7NX

www.continuumbooks.com

Visit the T & T Clark blog at www.tandtclarkblog.com

Library of Congress Cataloging-in-Publication Data
A catalog record for this book is available from the Library of Congress.

ISBN: HB: 978-0-567-60217-6 (hardback)

Typeset and copy-edited by Forthcoming Publications Ltd. (www.forthpub.com)
Printed and bound in the United States of America

CONTENTS

Part III
ENGAGED READINGS

ABBREVIATIONS

AB	Anchor Bible
ABGTS	Asia Baptist Graduate Theological Seminary
AGAJU	Arbeiten zur Geschicte des antiken Judentums und des Urchristentums
ARSR	*Australian Religion Studies Review*
BDAG	Bauer, W., F. W. Danker, W. F. Arndt, and F. W. Gingrich. *Greek–English Lexicon of the New Testament and Other Early Christian Literature*. 3d ed. Chicago, 1999
BZAW	Beihefte zur *ZAW*
CBQ	*Catholic Biblical Quarterly*
EEWC	Evangelical & Ecumenical Women's Caucus
HSM	Harvard Semitic Monographs
ICC	International Critical Commentary
ISBE	*International Standard Bible Encyclopedia*. Rev. ed. G. W. Bromiley. 4 vols. Grand Rapids, 1979–88
JBL	*Journal of Biblical Literature*
JBS	*Journal of Bible Sarangbang*
JQR	*Jewish Quarterly Review*
JSOT	*Journal for the Study of the Old Testament*
JSOTSup	Journal for the Study of the Old Testament: Supplement Series
MECW	Marx Engels Collected Works
NIBC	New International Biblical Commentary
NIDB	*New Interpreter's Dictionary of the Bible*. Edited K. D. Sakenfeld et al. 5 vols. Nashville, 2006–2009
NRSV	New Revised Standard Version
OBT	Overtures to Biblical Theology
OCB	*The Oxford Companion to the Bible*. Edited by Bruce M. Metzger and Michael D. Coogan. Oxford, 1993
OTL	Old Testament Library
RSV	Revised Standard Version
SBL	Society of Biblical Literature
SCS	Septuagint Commentary Series
StTh	Studia Theologica
VT	*Vetus Tetamentum*
VTSup	Vetus Tetamentum Supplements
WBC	Word Bible Commentary
ZAH	*Zeitschrift für Althebräistik*
ZAW	*Zeitschrift für die altetestamentliche Wissenschaft*

CONTRIBUTORS

George Aichele, Adrian College, Michigan, USA

Roland Boer, University of Newcastle, Australia

Michael Carden, University of Queensland, Brisbane, Australia

Philip R. Davies, University of Sheffield, England

Norman Habel, University of South Australia, Adelaide, Australia

Jione Havea, United Theological College and Charles Sturt University, Sydney, Australia

Se-Hoon Jang, KukJe Theological Seminary and University, Seoul, South Korea

Julie Kelso, Bond University, Gold Coast, Australia

Francis Landy, University of Alberta, Edmonton, Canada

Johnson Lim, Asia Baptist Graduate Theological Seminary, Kowloon, Hong Kong, China

Judith McKinlay, University of Otago, Dunedin, New Zealand

Paul Morris, Victoria University of Wellington, New Zealand

Katherine Stott, Gorgias Press, Orange, Australia

Elaine Wainwright, University of Auckland, New Zealand

EDGAR W. CONRAD:
A BIOGRAPHY

—with thanks to Linda Conrad

Ed was born in 1942 in rural Lancaster County, Pennsylvania, well known for its large Amish community and the "Pennsylvania Dutch" people. His father came from a Mennonite family. Growing up in the small village of West Willow, Ed spoke with a Pennsylvania Dutch accent and used colloquial vocabulary such as "schusslich" (nervous) and "dopplich" (clumsy). There was one church in the town, the West Willow Evangelical United Brethren Church, and the Christianity encountered was conservative and pious. The EUB denomination (itself a merger of the United Brethren and the Evangelical Churches) was the first mainstream denomination to have its origin in America. Essentially a German-speaking Methodist Church, merger with the Methodist Church was discussed, but Wesley maintained that the future of the Church was with speakers of English, not German. The present "United Methodist Church" in the U.S. is the result of the union of the EUB and Methodist denominations in 1968. Ed's family, like most of the community, was active in the local church, which was a focal point for community life.

In spite of his parents' lack of opportunity for further education, Ed's parents encouraged him and his brother, J. Richard, to study and had high hopes for their children's success, supporting them in every way possible. Ed began school in a one-room school house, Columbus School, with one teacher responsible for eight grades. At the end of Ed's fifth grade, the school district constructed a new consolidated school, Pequea Township Elementary School. Then a move to Penn Manor High School opened up new perspectives. Millersville University was located in the same town as the high school. Here rural students were integrated with students from homes of professional, university and business people, and student teachers from the nearby University made further education seem attainable. At this time Ed began to think seriously about studying to be a minister in the Evangelical United Brethren church, in which he was active, with a plan to go to college for his B.A. and seminary for his M.Div. "To go to college" as they say in the States was a leap into the unknown. At that time, no one except the minister in West Willow had a higher degree.

In 1960 Ed chose to go to Lebanon Valley College in Annville, Pa., a private, church-related college, established in 1867, typical of relatively small degree-granting institutions in the U.S. and noted for the quality of its higher education. Although Ed did receive a small scholarship from the church, a substantial proportion of the cost was not covered. Ed had saved money from a number of jobs. The money he managed to save was gone with the first check to pay tuition. While he was in college he also had part-time jobs, both during the academic year and in the summers.

In the college religion courses he attended, Ed felt liberated by the notion that reading the Bible historically and critically could facilitate understanding. The course he took on introduction to the Old Testament used the first edition of Bernhard W. Anderson's well-known textbook, *Understanding the Old Testament*. Little did he realize that he would become the editorial assistant for the third edition of that book 14 years later.

When Linda Slonaker arrived the following year in 1961, Ed met her at an off-campus picnic. Linda returned to campus in Ed's car with a number of friends. Afterward Ed discovered that she had left her dink (a cap required to be worn by first-year students) in the car. Returning the dink led to their first date. From that day on they were together continually, and a life-time partnership began. They were inseparable, even studying together, except for the summers when Ed went home to his family in West Willow and Linda attended summer sessions at the University of North Carolina. Because Linda attended the maximum number of summer sessions over a two-year period, she was able to finish her B.A. in three years, and Ed took delight in the fact that she graduated *summa cum laude* in the same year that he was awarded his B.A.

Ed and Linda were married by Linda's father in the Winchester First EUB Church a few days after Linda returned with her mother from summer school at UNC and after Ed had completed a final summer of work. Immediately after the wedding they set out for Dayton, Ohio where Ed had enrolled for an M.Div. degree at United Theological Seminary. Linda had won a scholarship to do an M.A. at Miami University in Oxford, Ohio.

At first they struggled to support themselves. Ed took a position as the minister of a Society of Friends Church, and Linda decided to study part-time and teach freshman English composition at Miami University. Since Linda travelled about 100 miles round trip to Oxford, Ohio and came home late in the day, Ed decided that he would cook the evening meals. Each night he selected a recipe from *The Joy of Cooking*, a wedding present, and prepared dinner. From that point on Ed found what has become his lifetime passion. He says that cooking the evening meal is the best way to relax at the end of a hectic day. Later Linda took up public school teaching full-time to maximize income but continued to take evening classes toward her M.A.

Life at the seminary was busy but exciting. Ed committed himself fully to study, concentrating primarily on biblical studies, especially the Old Testament. At the time of his graduation he was awarded the Bert V. Flinchbaugh award for the study of the Old Testament in Hebrew and was beginning to think about further study. He can remember spending an afternoon reading an article by Bernhard W. Anderson that introduced the main ideas of Gerhard von Rad's theology. The emphasis on God's intervention in history presented in the biblical text as *Heilsgeschichte* was exhilarating and matched his interest in social action. During his period of study he participated in street marches and demonstrations in Dayton and Washington protesting the Vietnam War and supporting civil rights for Afro-Americans. Planning to march with the garbage workers, he arrived in Memphis, Tennessee the day after Martin Luther King was assassinated. He has said that during Ralph Abernathy's sermon, in which Abernathy likened the march through the streets of Memphis to the biblical exodus, he decided to do a Ph.D. in Old Testament.

In order to make a final decision between the parish and postgraduate study, Ed spent one year doing an internship as an assistant minister at the Beverley EUB church in the Appalachian Mountains in Kentucky. While Ed found this experience rewarding, on his return to the seminary for the last year of study he gradually decided to pursue further academic study. At that time he envisaged his ministry as teaching theological students. He applied, and was accepted, at Princeton Theological Seminary. Having finished the M.Div. in 1968, he moved with Linda to Princeton to begin a Th.M. In 1968, when Ed commenced his study at PTS, Barney Anderson was beginning his first year as professor of Old Testament there. Linda withdrew from pursuing further academic study and was offered a position by Educational Testing Service. She began by writing items for the SAT, GRE, and other examinations and eventually was appointed as Associate Program Director for the Graduate Record Examinations; but she always had the time and interest to review Ed's papers, respond to his ideas, and make suggestions.

Ed was awarded the Th.M. in the spring of 1968 and applied for the Ph.D. This was a propitious year to commence the degree, although it was not evident at the time. In the fall of that year James Muilenburg gave his well-known presidential address to the Society of Biblical Literature, "Form Criticism and Beyond." Barney Anderson, himself a student of Muilenburg, encouraged his students to think about the future of biblical studies beyond the existing assumptions by focusing on rhetorical criticism as represented by Muilenburg's commentary on Second Isaiah in the *Interpreter's Bible* series. This advice from Barney led, many years later, and in ways that went beyond Muilenburg's assumptions, to Ed's publication of *Reading Isaiah.* Barney once told Ed that he was the shyest student he had ever had. Nevertheless, in the two years of seminar work in the Ph.D. program, Ed was appointed as a tutor. He loved teaching and research and knew that he had made the right career move.

In a seminar on the Pentateuch, Ed gave a paper on Gen 15 and concentrated on the אל תירא ("fear not") pericope in the first verse. The paper was well received and was the launch for Ed's dissertation, "Patriarchal Traditions in Second Isaiah," later books *Fear Not Warrior: A Study of 'al tira' Pericopes in the Hebrew Scriptures* and *Reading Isaiah,* and numerous articles. After two years of seminars, thirty-six hours of examination, including an oral examination, and three years of research followed again by an oral examination on the research, he was awarded the Ph.D. *magna cum laude* in early 1974. Immediately after graduation, Ed worked as the editorial assistant for the third edition of *Understanding the Old Testament.*

When taking a part-time teaching position at Rutgers University in religious studies during completion of his degree, Ed had become convinced that the best future academic position for him would be in religion, not in theology. However, his opportunities were limited if he stayed in the Princeton area, where Linda was successfully employed. Even though Princeton is roughly equidistant from New York City and Philadelphia, where numerous colleges and universities were located, the prospects of finding a job in religion rather than theology in that geographical area were daunting.

Unexpectedly, Ed was offered a position in the religion department of LaSalle College in Philadelphia. His name had been spotted in *Openings*, the SBL publication in which new graduates could advertise themselves for employment. Ed was offered a one-year appointment. The next year he accepted a Mellon Postdoctoral Fellowship at the University of Rochester. Like an increasing number of professional couples, Ed and Linda lived apart, visiting each other on weekends. During the post-doctoral program, Ed applied for a position at a large state university. Even though Ed had received a letter of offer, was contacted by the Head of Department concerning the course he was to teach, and had received and returned a request from the bookstore for information on books and other resources for the proposed courses, he subsequently received a letter from the Dean saying his position had been eliminated.

After this setback, Ed decided to seek an alternative career direction. He took a job as director of the data dictionary at Mathematica, a social policy research center in Princeton Junction. Ed and Linda bought a house in Pennington, a beautiful little town close to Princeton, and decided to settle down.

Soon thereafter, Ed received a telephone call at work informing him that he was short-listed for a position at the University of Queensland in Brisbane, Australia. He reluctantly went to the interview that took place in Princeton, firmly committed, he thought, to continuing a new career path. An offer came a few months later. The first reaction was laughter at the absurdity of the situation. Such a move half-way around the world was certainly not possible! Yet, the more Ed and Linda talked about it, the more appealing the job appeared to be. A period of time in another country would be an exciting and broadening experience. The University of Queensland was discontinuing a Bachelor of Divinity program staffed mainly by lecturers from the theological colleges hired part-time and was replacing it with a religion department based in the Arts Faculty with full-time tenured staff. The situation was ideal for someone contemplating a move from theology to religion. They decided to rent their newly purchased house, and Linda was given a year's leave of absence from ETS in case the new appointment was not what it seemed.

Over thirty-four years later, Ed has retired; Linda was awarded her Ph.D. from the University of Queensland, later joining the faculty at Griffith University. She retired as Deputy Director of the Griffith Institute for Higher Education. Both have become dual citizens of Australia and the U.S. While Ed's Pennsylvania accent is no longer noticeable, most people in Australia recognize his accent as North American. Lancaster County colloquialisms have been replaced with phrases such as "fair dinkum" and "she'll be right, mate."

The move to Australia was ideal for Ed professionally, but initially less so for Linda. For both, the distance from family and friends was formidable, without the possibility of instant communication that is now possible over the internet. The distance meant that they could not return even for the funerals of beloved family members: Linda's mother and their nephew, Matthew. Relationships with family could only be maintained through occasional visits and letters. However, Ed and Linda decided to stay. The house in Pennington was sold. Eventually, during study leaves and especially in retirement, it would be possible to visit family and friends in America more frequently and for longer periods.

The University of Queensland, when Ed arrived in 1977, was a strong research institution, aggressively advancing its research programs. Since then there has been continual construction, renovation, expansion and establishment of new research institutes, with the student population growing from 17,000 to over 45,000. The University of Queensland in Ed's early years provided young academics with time to develop as teachers and researchers. Research money made it possible to attend international conferences, invite established academics as visiting professors, and take a fully funded six-month study leave every three years. In addition, employers gave long-service leave, six months of full paid holiday every ten years. However, it was expected that university work would be done during the summers as well as during the normal academic year.

The new situation allowed Ed to reflect on the difference between teaching and research in a state university department of religion and a theological institution. He wrote his early reflections on this matter in an article, "Changing Context: The Bible and the Study of Religion." In this new situation, collegial contact with colleagues in other Arts departments provided the situation for re-evaluating the historical-critical approach more clearly from a meta-critical position. The new criticism in English literature, post-structuralism, reader-response criticism, the new historicism and other dimensions of critical theory enabled him to see that biblical studies had atrophied. The historical-critical study of the Bible that had looked like a raging torrent at the beginning of the nineteenth century began to look like a "frozen waterfall".[1] Furthermore, both undergraduate and postgraduate students represented a far greater diversity than those interested solely in Christian theology. Conservative and liberal Christians, atheists, Jews, Muslims, Buddhists and students from other backgrounds were in the classroom. In this environment Ed began to see that biblical studies had authorized a particular set of reading strategies that adapted to make the Bible fit the modern world of the theological interpreter, with the supposedly disinterested intention of determining what biblical texts meant at the time of their origin. In this context Ed wrote *Reading Isaiah* and the two books that succeeded it: *Zechariah* and *Reading the Latter Prophets*.

---

1.   Emil Brunner (1943, 31) first used this simile in describing the age after the energizing intellectual developments of the Reformation: "the Age of Orthodoxy appears like a frozen waterfall, mighty shapes of movement, but no movement."

Ed's early publications—including *Fear Not Warrior: A Study of 'al tira' Pericopes in the Hebrew Scriptures* (1985), and two articles "Second Isaiah and the Priestly Oracle of Salvation" (*ZAW* 93 [1981]: 234–46) and "The Fear Not Oracles in Second Isaiah" (*VT* 34 [1984]: 129–52)—reflected the mandate in Muilenburg's 1968 article that biblical scholarship continue to do form criticism, but considering larger literary features of the text. In these early studies, Ed paid close attention to the literary settings of a *Gattung*, the *Sitz im Text*, rather than a reconstructed *Sitz im Leben* supposedly located in the world out of which it emerged. In particular, he critiqued Begrich's thesis that the "fear not" oracles in Second Isaiah had their original setting in the cult as the priestly response to lament. While the Psalter does contain the priestly response to lament, none of these responses follows the structure of the "fear not" oracles in Second Isaiah. What was beginning to trouble Ed at this time was the way historical-critical scholarship was projecting onto the ancient world interpretations that reflected the world of the critic. For example, Begrich's priestly oracle of salvation was akin to the words of assurance that follow the call to confession in Christian worship services.

Ed found it bewildering that critical scholarship dismissed certain parts of biblical narrative as unhistorical while using much of that narrative itself in historical reconstruction. Scholarship also treated the historical narrative in prophetic books as a reliable portrayal of prophetic figures while simultaneously dismissing much of the material in prophetic books as secondary, later additions.

Coupled with unease about the practice of historical criticism was Ed's continued concern about social injustice, which had led him to study Old Testament prophecy. Increasingly, he began to notice social injustice in the hallways of learning; it was not confined to the streets. The rise of feminist criticism, black theology, and liberation theology among others made manifest the academy's repression of the voice of the Other in order to serve the power and authority of the privileged few. Historical criticism, whatever assessment is made of it at the time of its origin, in its stagnated form at the end of the twentieth century was confidently endorsing authoritative meaning for a powerful community of readers rather than celebrating the rich plurality of meaning emerging from other communities with different perspectives and strategies for assessing meaning.

Ed's dissatisfaction with traditional biblical studies began to coalesce into a new perspective in 1986 when, in the course of preparing lectures on the prophets, he read Stephen Moore's article, "Negative Hermeneutics, Insubstantial Texts: Stanley Fish and the Biblical Interpreter," which appeared in *JAAR*. Ed began to read reader-response criticism, beginning with Stanley Fish, whose work had already been influential in the study of literature in English. Fish argued that readers play an active role in the construction of meaning and that, furthermore, readers create meaning as members of interpretive communities, governed by shared interpretive strategies. Ed understood biblical studies in the academy to be just such a community. Historical-critical technologies had restricted the way biblical texts were read. Reading needed to be freed from the constraints of historical-critical interpretive strategies of imagining the unknowable—what the author's or authors' intentions, or the redactors' and editors' intentions were—and to examine the received text, whatever its disparate source, in interaction with readers in a particular time and place. Breaking away from the normative approach, Ed began to read Isaiah as an entirety, without reference to the previous divisions of the text into First Isaiah, Second Isaiah, Third Isaiah and even Fourth (or more). The strong impact of feminist readings, third world readings, indigenous readings, and readings of the Bible by many different communities underscored for him the wisdom of Fish's arguments and highlighted the historical-critical exclusion of such voices that were articulating alternative approaches, including unorthodox literary approaches to textual meaning.

Reading Isaiah was recognized by the editor of the series in which it was published as being a "remarkable achievement, well-written, thoughtful, irenic while daring…a major marker in the new season of Isaiah interpretation" (Brueggemann, Editor's Foreword, *Reading Isaiah*, p. ix) and by Melugin as making "a significant contribution to a postmodern approach to the prophetic book" (*Interpretation* [1993]: 78–79). Later Ed was invited to write a commentary on Zechariah for the series, *Readings: A New Biblical Commentary*. In *Zechariah* he continued to pursue his interest in presenting a reading of a biblical book as it stands rather than attempting to recreate an imagined literary history. In particular, he saw a link between Haggai's "the messenger of the LORD" (Hag 1:13) and "the messenger of the LORD" who speaks to Zechariah. In making this connection, he argued against the traditional way of reading Zechariah as having strange visions and suggested instead that a messenger is explaining to Zechariah the symbolism of the temple under construction. Ed did not claim to have done a definitive reading, but to be offering an alternative to traditional historical-critical excursions "behind" the text.

In his later *Reading the Latter Prophets*, Ed drew on the semiotic insights of Umberto Eco. His focus was on the openings of prophetic books and their implications for the way each prophetic book is to be read. "The vision of," "the words of" and "and it happened" are distinctive beginnings of the Major Prophets, with parallels in the Minor Prophets. He understood these as signs a reader can use in reading the book that follows. *Reading the Latter Prophets* has led to Ed's current scholarly interest in "vision" in the Old Testament.

This new perspective also helped Ed assess the significance of doing research on the Bible in a University funded by the government where students were drawn from a wide variety of backgrounds. This changed outlook was clearly reflected in the range of students pursuing Ph.D. study and other advanced degrees. Ed has supervised 18 Ph.D. students to completion and over 30 Masters and Honours theses. In 2002 he received the Award for Excellence in Research Higher Degree Supervision from the University of Queensland, partly based on innovative group and peer supervision. Ed developed a regular meeting of his students, which the students dubbed "Ed's Group." Members of this group shared their research in informal gatherings in Ed's home. The group, averaging from 10 to 15 students at any given time, comprised people from widely different backgrounds: men and women; young and mature aged; Australian, Asian, American; Christians from a wide variety of backgrounds; Buddhists; atheists and agnostics; and people with varying sexual orientations. In spite of these broad differences, this group, in which the majority focused on the study of the Hebrew Bible, became supportive of one another not only in the group meetings but also in their daily lives of doing research. Ed's Group contained a broad mixture of readers belonging to a diversity of interpretive communities. In a sense, the group was a microcosm of the broader world in which Ed envisaged the future for the academic study of the Bible.

Ed viewed postgraduate supervision or advisement as an opportunity for both the student and supervisor to learn from one another. He did not want his students to become his academic clones. He encouraged them to pursue their research by drawing on their individual backgrounds and particular interests. Ed learned a vast amount from his students: queer theory, French literary theory, Korean culture, semiotics, historical methodology, theories of leadership, media studies, and contemporary Catholic theology among others. The relationships with his students have been, and continue to be, both intellectually and personally rewarding.

Ed's Group also included students with whom Ed shared supervision with colleagues from other departments: English, Sociology, Philosophy, and Social Work. These students pursued research in medieval literature, spirituality and hospice care, mothering, feminist studies, and Australian Catholics. While these students, unlike most of the members of the group, were not focused on the Bible, their presence indicated that biblical research shared commonalities with a broad spectrum of research in the university.

Toward the end of Ed's career he has become more interested in doing research on the Bible in contemporary culture. This interest grew partly out of courses he was teaching, such as "Gods and Goddesses: Past and Present," and a popular course, "Controversies in Biblical Interpretation," which focused on contemporary controversies concerning the Bible as highlighted in news articles. He is currently working on a research project on the Bible and the News, which at this time has produced one article, "From Jefferson's Bible to Judge Moore's Ten Commandment Monument: Secularizing the Bible in the USA."

While he served for a period of time as Head of Studies in Religion, and frequently as Acting Head, Ed's major administrative responsibilities have been in postgraduate administration. For many years he was director of postgraduate (or using U.S. terminology, graduate) studies in the department. He has also represented the Arts Faculty on the central postgraduate committee. As the arts representative he revamped the Faculty of Arts postgraduate coursework awards and introduced a series of seminars designed to orient new Ph.D. students to research. He has also been the recipient of an Australian Research Large Grant (1997) and was elected as Fellow of the Institute for Advanced Study in the Humanities, The University of Edinburgh.

The story of Abraham in Gen 12 is one of Ed's favorites, with its theme of unfulfilled hopes and unexpected destinations. At the beginning of Gen 12, the LORD promises Abraham land, a great posterity and a destiny of blessing to the nations. By the end of the chapter, the very opposite has occurred: he has moved through the Promised Land to Egypt, his wife is in the Pharaoh's harem because of his lie to Pharaoh that Sarai was his sister, and plagues, not blessings, have ensued. Although Ed has never claimed any parallels in his life to the biblical story, the promises imagined about his future often turned out to be quite different from those he had anticipated. Ultimately, he found professional fulfillment beyond his dreams in research, teaching, and collegial relationships at the University of Queensland and internationally.

PUBLICATIONS BY EDGAR W. CONRAD

Ed has published both articles and books in North America, Europe (including the UK), Asia and Australia. His works have been cited and/or reviewed in publications in England, France, Germany, Belgium, the Netherlands, Sweden, Italy, the United States, Canada, Australia, India, Korea and Singapore. Sources of reviews and citations include some of the most prestigious journals and presses in Studies in Religion as well as the most reputable scholars in the field.

Books

The Bible in the News. Work in Progress.

Zechariah. Readings: A New Biblical Commentary. Sheffield: Sheffield Phoenix, 2009 (Republication of the 1999 volume by a new press.)

Reading the Latter Prophets: Toward a New Canonical Criticism. JSOTSup 376. London: T&T Clark International, 2003.

Reading Isaiah. Eugene, Oregon: Wipf & Stock, 2002 (Reissue of the 1991 volume, negotiated by Fortress and Wipf & Stock.)

Korean translation of *Reading Isaiah*. Translated by Se-Hoon Jang. Seoul: CLC, 2002.

Zechariah. Readings: A New Biblical Commentary. Sheffield: Sheffield Academic, 1999.

Reading Isaiah. Overtures to Biblical Theology. Minneapolis: Fortress, 1991.

Fear Not Warrior: A Study of 'al tira' Pericopes in the Hebrew Scriptures. Brown Judaic Studies 75. Chico: Scholars Press, 1985.

Patriarchal Traditions in Second Isaiah. Ph.D. dissertation. (Available through University Microfilms. The dissertation has been cited in English and German by scholars such as Westermann, Merendino, Gitay and Watts.)

Edited Books

Redirected Travel: Alternative Journeys and Places in Biblical Studies. Ed. R. Boer and E. W. Conrad. JSOTSup 382. London: T&T Clark International, 2003.

Perspectives on Language and Text: Essays and Poems on Francis I. Andersen's Sixtieth Birthday, July 18, 1985. Ed. E. W. Conrad and E. G. Newing. Winona Lake: Eisenbrauns, 1987.

Understanding the Word: Essays in Honor of Bernhard W. Anderson. Ed. J. Butler, E. W. Conrad and B. Ollenburger. JSOTSup 37. Sheffield: JSOT, 1985.

Articles (Periodicals)

"The Bible and Culture: The Role of the Bible in Interpretation." *Canon and Culture* 1 (2007): 43–69. (Korean)

"Yehoshua Gitay: 'What is *He* Doing?'" *JSOT* 27 (2002): 237–41.

"The Bible and Culture: The Role of the Text in Interpretation." *Pacific Journal of Theology* 3 (2000): 3–16.

"The Present State of Biblical Studies." *Journal of the Australasian Universities Language and Literature Association* 94 (2000): 109–18.

"Messengers in Isaiah and the Twelve: Implications for Reading Prophetic Books." *JSOT* 91 (2000): 83–97.

"Reading Zechariah in the Context of the Scroll of the Twelve Minor Prophets." *Journal of the Korean Old Testament Society*, forthcoming.

"Reading Isaiah: Window or Mirror." *JBS* 12 (2000): 90–101. (In Korean, translated by Kim Joong Woo.)

"Reading the Old Testament: Response and Responsibility." *JBS* 11 (2000): 57–65. (In Korean, translated by Se-Hoon Jang.)

"The Bible, Religion and Multiculturalism." *Theology and Religion: The Forum of the Australia–Korea Theological Society* 2 (1999): 1–12.

"The End of Prophecy and the Appearance of Angels in the Book of the Twelve." *JSOT* 73 (1997): 65–79.

"Reflections on Biblical Reflections." *ARSR* 8 (1995): 1–7.

"Heard But Not Seen: The Representation of Books in the Old Testament." *JSOT* 54 (1992): 45–59.

"The Bible and the Reader." *Colloquium* 23 (1991): 49–56. Also appeared in the *JBS* 8 (1999): 70–75. (In Korean, translated by Se-Hoon Jang.)

"The 'Other' Side of the Bible." *Trinity Occasional Papers* 9/10 (1991): 44–49.

"The Royal Narratives and the Structure of the Book of Isaiah." *JSOT* 41 (1988): 67–81.

"Isaiah and the Abraham Connection." *Asia Journal of Theology* 2 (1988): 382–93.

"The Annunciation of Birth and the Birth of the Messiah." *CBQ* 47 (1985): 656–53.

"The Fear Not Oracles in Second Isaiah." *VT* 34 (1984): 126–52.

"Prophets and Prophetic Books." *East Asia Journal of Theology* (1988): 63–70.

"Second Isaiah and the Priestly Oracle of Salvation." *ZAW* 93 (1981): 234–46.

Articles (In Books)

"From Jefferson's Bible to Judge Moore's Ten Commandment Monument: Secularizing the Bible in the USA." *The Bible and Secularization*. London. Ed. R. Boer. London and Oakville: Equinox, 2010.

"Looking into Vision: See-Sawing in Prophetic Books" *Voyages in Uncharted Waters: Essays on the Theory and Practice of Biblical Interpretation in Honor of David Jobling*. Ed. W. E. Bergen and A. Siedlecki. Hebrew Monographs 13. Sheffield: Sheffield Phoenix, 2006.

"Semiotics, Scribes and Prophetic Books." *Redirected Travel: Alternative Journeys and Places in Biblical Studies*. Ed. R. Boer and E. W. Conrad JSOTSup 382. London: T&T Clark International, 2003. (pp. 42–51) (Essays at the International Meeting of the Bible and Critical Theory Seminar, Melbourne, July 2001.)

"Forming the Twelve and Forming Canon." *Thematic Themes in the Book of the Twelve.* Ed. Paul Redditt and Aaron Schart. BZAW 325; Berlin: de Gruyter, 2003. (pp. 90–103) (Essays in the Formation of the Twelve Seminar, the Society of Biblical Literature, Toronto, November 2002)

"How the Bible Was Colonised" *Scripture, Community and Mission: Essays in Honor of D. Preman Niles.* Ed. Philip L. Wickeri. Hong Kong: The Christian Conference of Asia, 2002. (Essays delivered at a seminar in Chennai, India sponsored by Cambridge University and the University of Madras, January 2002).

"Messengers in the Sky." *Readings from the Perspective of Earth.* Ed. Norman Habel. The Earth Bible 1. Sheffield: Sheffield Academic and Cleveland: Pilgrim Press, 2000 (pp. 86–95).

"Reading Isaiah and the Twelve as Prophetic Books." *Writing and Reading the Scroll of Isaiah: Studies of an Interpretive Tradition.* Ed. C. C. Broyles and C. A. Evans. VTSup 70. Leiden: Brill, 1997 (pp. 3–17).

"Prophet, Redactor and Audience: Reforming the Notion of Isaiah's Formation." *New Visions of the Book of Isaiah.* Ed. R. Melugin and M. Sweeney. JSOTSup 214. Sheffield: Sheffield Academic, 1996 (pp. 306–25). (Essays delivered to the Isaiah Seminar of the Society of Biblical Literature, 1991–95).

"Re-reading the Bible in a Multicultural World." *Religion and Multiculturalism in Australia: Essays in Honour of Victor Hayes.* Ed. N. C. Habel. Special Studies in Religion Series 7. Adelaide: AASR, 1992 (pp. 324–35).

"Changing Context: The Bible and the Study of Religion." *Perspectives on Language and Text: Essays in Honor of Francis I. Andersen's Sixtieth Birthday July 28 1985.* Ed. E. W. Conrad and T. G. Newing. Winona Lake: Eisenbrauns, 1986 (pp. 393–402).

"The People as King in Second Isaiah." *Understanding the Word: Essays in Honor of Bernhard W. Anderson.* Ed. J. Butler, E. W. Conrad and B. Ollenburger. JSOTSup 37. Sheffield: JSOT, 1985 (pp. 99–111).

"Classifying Ritual Forms." *A Resource Book for the Study of Religion.* Ed. J. Pippin; Sydney: Australian Association of Religious Education, 1984 (pp. 69–76).

Articles (Encyclopedias)

These articles discuss uses of Hebrew, Greek and Aramaic words in original texts and their renderings in contemporary English translations of the Bible.

New Interpreter's Dictionary of the Bible, Abingdon Press, 2010.
"Ararat." 1:231.
"Destroyer, Destroyers." 2:105–6.
"King, God As." 3:504–5.
"Remnant." 4:761–62.
"Satan." 5:112–16.

The Oxford Companion to the Bible, Ed. Bruce M. Metzger and Michael D. Coogan. Oxford: Oxford University Press, 1993.
"Ban." 73.
"Curse." 144–45.
"Drunkenness." 171–72.
"Vine and Vineyard." 789.

International Standard Bible Encyclopedia. Rev. ed. G. W. Bromiley. 2 vols. Grand Rapids: Eerdmans, 1979–82.
"Calamity." 1:572–73.
"Complain, Complaint." 1:755–56.
"Deliver." 1:915–16.
"Destroyer." 1:933.
"Doom." 1:983.
"Enemy, Foe." 2:81.
"Filth, Filthiness, Filthy." 2:303.
"Force." 2:334–35.
"Foreigner." 2:336.
"Frame." 2:359–60.
"Garland." 2:401.
"Generation." 2:411.
"Grief, Grieve." 2:574–75.
"Guard." 2:578.
"Guide." 2:579–80.

Book Reviews

Review of Roland Boer's *Novel Histories: The Fiction of Biblical Criticism* (Playing the Texts, 2; Sheffield: Sheffield Academic, 1997) in *ARSR* 12 (1999): 87–88.

Review of Petersen, D. L. *Zechariah 9–14 and Malachi: A Commentary* in *JSOT* 76 (1997): 127–28.

Review of Roland Boer's *Jameson and Jeroboam* in *ARSR* 10 (1997): 102–3.

Review of Norman Habel's *The Land is Mine: Six Biblical Land Ideologies* in *ARSR* 10 (1997): 103–5.

Review of Christopher Seitz's *Isaiah 1–39* in *Interpretation* 49 (1995): 305.

Review of Yehoshua Gitay's *Isaiah and His Audience: The Structure and Meaning of Isaiah 1–12* in *Hebrew Studies* 35 (1994): 141–43.

Review of S. H. Widyapranawa's *Isaiah 1–39: The Lord is Savior: Faith in National Crisis* in *Horizons in Biblical Theology* 13 (1991): 175–76.

Papers Read at Conferences

August 1977. "Second Isaiah and the Priestly Oracle of Salvation." Australian Association for the Study of Religions (AASR), Brisbane

May 1978. "Second Isaiah and the Priestly Oracle of Salvation." The Nineteenth Congress of The Australian Language and Literature Association, Brisbane

August 1979. "Moses at the Altar." AASR, Sydney

August 1981. "Prophets and Prophetic Books." AASR, Adelaide

August 1981. "Biblical Studies and a Department of Studies in Religion." AASR, Adelaide

September 1986. "Intention, Convention and the Unity of the Book of Isaiah." AASR, Adelaide

June 1982. "Second Isaiah and the Language of War." Canadian Biblical Association (CSBA), Ottawa

August 1982. "Jonah: A Social Perspective." AASR, Melbourne

August 1983. "Fear Not Oracles in Second Isaiah." AASR, Brisbane

September 1985. "The Annunciation of Birth and the Birth of the Messiah." International Association for the History of Religion (IAHR), Sydney

August, 1987. "The Royal Narratives and the Structure of the Book of Isaiah." AASR, Melbourne

September 1988. "Who Are 'We' in Isaiah?" AASR, Brisbane

July 1990. "The Reader and the Bible." ANZATS, Brisbane

September 1990. "Heard But Not Seen: The Representation of Books in the Hebrew Scriptures." AASR Conference, Canberra

November 1992. "Response to Gerald T. Sheppard for the Isaiah Seminar." SBL, San Francisco

July 1993. "Three in One: An Isaian Unity." AASR, Armidale

July 1994. "The End of Prophecy and the Appearance of Angels/Messengers in the Book of the Twelve." AASR, Adelaide

July 1994. "The Biblical Text: Window or Mirror." AASR, Adelaide

July 1996. "Reading Isaiah and the Twelve as Prophetic Books." AASR/NZAR, Lincoln, New Zealand

July 1998. "Reading Isaiah and the Twelve as Prophetic Books." Bible and Critical Theory Seminar (BCT), Melbourne

June 1999. "Messengers in the Sky." Bible and Critical Theory Seminar (BCT), St. Albans, New South Wales

June 2000. "Reading Prophetic Books: The Role of the Text in Interpretation." Bible and Critical Theory Seminary (BCT), Monash University, Melbourne, Victoria

June 2001. "Semiotics, Scribes and Prophetic Books." Bible and Critical Theory Seminary (BCT), Monash University, Melbourne, Victoria

November 2002. "Forming the Twelve and Forming Canon." Society of Biblical Literature, Toronto, Canada

July 2005. "Looking into Vision: See-Sawing in Prophetic Books." Society of Old Testament Studies, University of Edinburgh

Seminars (International)

October 1986. "Isaiah and the Abraham Connection." Alttestamentlichen Societät, Heidelberg, Germany

November 1990. "Prophet, Audience and Redactor: The Reception of the Book of Isaiah." Society of Biblical Literature (SBL) Formation of the Book of Isaiah Consultation, New Orleans

November 1991. "Response to Rolf Rendtorff's 'The Book of Isaiah: A Complex Unity. Synchronic and Diachronic Reading'." SBL Formation of the Book of Isaiah Consultation, Kansas City

January 1997. "Reforming the Notion of Isaiah's Formation: A Critique of Redactional and Canonical Criticism." Centre for Bible and Theology, Biblical Studies, The University of Sheffield

March 1997. "Reading Zechariah as a Prophetic Book." Staff Student Seminar, Biblical Studies, The University of Sheffield

January 2001. "Transcoding Prophetic Books: Semiotics and the Limits of Interpretation." Seminar of Hebrew Bible and the New Testament, New College, The University of Edinburgh

February 2001. "Missing Books and the Rhetoric of the Hebrew Bible." Institute for Advanced Studies in the Humanities, The University of Edinburgh

INTRODUCTION

In 1976 the University of Queensland offered a young American biblical scholar named Edgar W. Conrad his first full-time academic position in what was then the Department of Religious Studies (later changed to the Department of Studies in Religion). After much thought about what it would mean for them personally to accept this offer, Ed and his wife Linda, also a scholar, moved half-way across the world. What appealed to Ed at that time was the department's shift away from theological training toward a more historical and literary focus, specifically in regard to the research and teaching of sacred texts. Those of us in Australia lucky enough to have been taught by Ed and/or who became familiar with him and his work though conferences, seminars and such like now reflect on the importance of the decisions of that selection committee, of that young scholar and of his wife. That young scholar would go on to become one of the most important voices in Australian biblical studies, probably contributing more to the paradigmatic shifts that were taking place in biblical studies than any of his contemporaries.

Apart from Ed's own innovative approaches to reading biblical literature, and his persistent reappraisal and implementation of pedagogical issues concerned with the tertiary setting in which the Bible was taught, he was instrumental in establishing, with Roland Boer, the Bible and Critical Theory Seminar, now in its fourteenth year. This seminar was set up to enable the (geographically) marginalized voices of biblical scholars in Australia and New Zealand, especially, to meet and present their research every year. It also encouraged a strong collegiality among those of us working with the Bible using non-traditional methodologies and interpretive frameworks, such work itself somewhat marginalized in Australian biblical studies at that time. Indeed, it is a dramatic understatement to say that the face of biblical studies in Australia changed for the better because of those decisions made in 1976, and with this volume, published in the seventieth year of Ed's life, we seek to honour and thank him in some small way.

The contributors to this volume, colleagues and former students of Ed, represent a richly diverse range of perspectives and methodologies, but this diversity, nevertheless, reflects important aspects of Ed's own scholarship and teaching. Three such aspects, reading prophetic literature, reading the Bible as literature, and engaged readings of the Bible, have been used to group the essays into three sections respectively and thus highlight, despite their diversity, the shared points of reference with Ed's work.

The greater part of Ed's research and writing has concerned the biblical prophets, in particular, Isaiah and The Twelve (most notably Zechariah). Thus Part I, "Reading Prophets," appropriately leads off the collection with essays addressing a range of prophetic texts and figures. The section begins with two essays on prophetic figures other than Isaiah and the Twelve. Philip Davies writes on the prophet Jeremiah. While he is quite prepared to accept the existence of a historical Jeremiah as the most plausible explanation for the initiation of such a scroll, he considers it neither knowable nor important whether the hero of the scroll conforms to any historical profile. Davies' main interest is in the literary figure of Jeremiah who is the central component of the book's "message." No modern reading can avoid confronting the centrality of that figure and yet both the book and the character seem incoherent, even contradictory. Davies argues that it is possible to overcome this apparent failure to read by accepting that the incoherence lies in the way the scroll has been constructed, that the prophet is the voice of two different writers whose voices in the book use conflicting language. One Jeremiah had a thoroughly anti-Jerusalem and anti-Davidic voice, a figure who, by the other Jeremiah, was made to recant his prognostications and repent of the zeal with which he uttered his denunciations. That Jeremiah is now remembered as the prophet who lamented to an extraordinary degree is due to the book remastering a stern voice into a sorrowful one.

Prophets are generally remembered as male figures, but female ones are remembered too. Judith McKinlay is not interested in a writing prophet but in the female prophet Huldah, found in 2 Kings and 2 Chronicles. Her essay draws on Ed Conrad's insights in *Reading Isaiah*, that "a myriad of readers may engage with the text, which has an endless depth of meaning" (Conrad 1991, 166), and that "there can be no detached interpretation of the biblical texts, no textual meaning independent of the present reception of the biblical text" (Conrad 1991, 164), and argues that readings of the prophet Huldah demonstrate the validity of these observations. In her essay, McKinlay explores a number of readers, from both early and contemporary traditions, many of them theologians rather than biblical scholars *per se*, and discusses not only how they view Huldah, but also the way they draw her into their own quite particular debates and worldviews, far removed in time and place from her textual location.

The other essays in the Reading Prophets section address Isaiah, the book and the prophet, and acknowledge the impact of Ed Conrad's own *Reading Isaiah*. Francis Landy discusses a range of issues arising from Isaiah's commission in 6:9–10, which he regards as a paradox: the prophet fulfils his mission by failing to fulfil it, communication is non-communication. He identifies three ethical and exegetical problems arising from the commission. One problem is the relationship of the prophet and God, since the prophet, as well as being God's emissary, has a human voice. Second, there is the conflict between God's malevolence and his desire to send the prophet. Third, there is the problem of the limit to the period of incomprehension and the apparent clarity of much of the text. He argues that these problems may be resolved diachronically, through source-critical analysis, the retrojection hypothesis, the proposal that Isaiah introduces a theopolitical revolution, or mystically, as for example in Elliot Wolfson's discussions of mystical language (2005). Landy develops these approaches to consider the relationship of the *mysterium tremendum* to death, and to an apprehension of meaninglessness at the heart of life and the poem, one which contradicts the entire prophetic metanarrative, the comforting trajectory through exile and death to utopian restoration. Exile is everywhere and nowhere. The transition from the seraphim's celebration of God's glory in 6:3 to the commission in 6:9–10 marks that from ontology to ethics, from fullness to desolation, and to the ascesis of responsibility of Levinas and Derrida. Reading Isaiah as a unity was Ed Conrad's groundbreaking move. Se-Hoon Jang is interested in how this text achieves a unity and he examines the scholarly consensus that Isa 1 and 65–66 form an *inclusio* to give shape to the book of Isaiah. Rather than attempting to situate Isa 1 and 65–66 in a historical context (e.g. post-Babylonian), he is interested in a synchronic approach that concentrates on the coincident occurrence of the phrase, "Hear the word of God!" in Isa 1 and 65–66. He argues that hearing the word of God in Isa 1 and 65–66 plays a pivotal role in reading the book of Isaiah as a whole. Finally, Norman Habel considers how the classic oracles of Isaiah would sound if expressed in traditional form but addressed to the people of today's world who are polluting the planet with greenhouse gases? His contribution is, however, not a traditional essay, but a series of poetic oracles expressed in the language and imagery of Isaiah. These modern oracles address the current global warming crisis yet reflect much of the imagery of the original text. Habel's piece both closes this section and anticipates the engaged readings in the third section of the book.

Ed Conrad has always highlighted the role of readers and their reading strategies in giving meaning to texts. The essays in Part II, "Reading Literarily", address issues of reading and interpretation and the role of reading communities in the reception of texts. Johnson Lim uses a text-centred reading strategy augmented by intratextual and intertextual evidence in conversation with the work of James Barr and Walter Moberly as conversational partners to examine the hermeneutical Rubik's cube that is Gen 2:16–17. At issue is the fact that God warns the couple in the Garden of Eden that they would die the instant they eat the forbidden fruit. However, they do not die, which might suggest, on a literal reading, that God lied. Consequently, scholars who are troubled by such an interpretation prefer more metaphorical readings. Lim challenges this move asking whether a literal reading must lead to a conclusion of divine duplicity at all and questions whether there is any textual warrant for a metaphorical reading in the first place. Roland Boer's "The Anomaly of Interpretation" is a critical survey of intersections between Marxism, Marxist readers and the Bible. Boer's essay has three sections, although there are myriad overlaps between them: he begins with various uses Marxists have made and continue to make of the Bible, the underlying motive being the search for political insights and models. From there he considers the contributions various Marxist studies have made or, in fact, have the potential to make to biblical studies (and there is some work that needs to be done here). Finally, he tracks, somewhat critically, the uses biblical critics have made of Marxist methods in dealing both with ancient literary texts and the political and economic context of those texts.

Katie Stott is interested in the trope of "lost manuscripts" in the Bible as found in the book of Ezra, which contains a number of references to written documents. She considers two such texts, the well-known Hebrew edict of Cyrus, permitting the Jews to return from their captivity (Ezra 2–4), and the Aramaic decree of Cyrus, said to have been found in Ecbatana in the time of Darius (Ezra 6:2–5). In the past, there has been much debate about these two ordinances, particularly over their relationship and authenticity. The most widely held view is to regard the Aramaic document as an authentic decree, but the one in Hebrew as a literary invention. However, not everyone agrees. On one end of the spectrum, the authenticity of both ordinances has been defended by some. At the other end of the spectrum, it has recently been suggested that both could be literary inventions. In this context, Stott proposes the discussion be moved in a different direction by considering not whether these documents were genuine, but what purpose they serve in their narrative context. Her analysis of the literary function of the documents mentioned in Ezra is informed by comparative examination of classical stories about lost and found books. Such comparison provides literary support for her proposition that the Ezra documents perform a rhetorical function in the book, regardless of whether or not they are based on actual documentation. While Stott examines the role of documents cited within biblical texts, George Aichele focuses on the way biblical texts themselves are transformed into larger documents by canonical processes. His essay explores postmodern semiotics in relation to the Bible and Christian theology through the correlated concepts of unlimited semiosis and intertextuality. He argues that, in light of these concepts, the biblical canon appears as an intertextual mechanism that controls and limits the flows of semiosis in relation to biblical texts, thus making the canon a profoundly ideological structure. This fact has various consequences and possibilities for semiotic study of the Bible. These include the growing importance of the canon in relation to contemporary readings of the Bible, the significance of variations among ancient Bible manuscripts, the transformations of signifiers as the texts are first printed and then digitized and otherwise transformed by various electronic media, and the ideological significance of translation. He concludes by reflecting on some theological consequences of a greater awareness of the Bible as semiotic mechanism.

As noted above, Ed Conrad has advocated strongly against the notion of the detached reading and interpretation of biblical texts. Readers come to the text with a variety of concerns and their readings are shaped by the shared reading conventions of the particular reading communities to which they belong. For the greater part of the last two centuries the goal of biblical scholarship was to attain an "objective" detached reading of the biblical text. However, the recent paradigm shift in biblical studies, of which Ed has been an important part, challenged those notions and highlighted the way such detached "objective" readings remained unconscious of their own subjectivity and the agendas and assumptions that were brought to the text. The paradigm shift to which Ed Conrad contributed has undermined this interpretive monopoly over the biblical text, enabling the engagement of a greater diversity of interpretive communities and hermeneutical concerns. Part III of our collection, "Engaged Readings," acknowledges this shift bringing together a range of essays from a variety of concerns and interpretive perspectives.

Four essays typify the new hermeneutic concerns and approaches responding to contemporary political and cultural debates. Elaine Wainwright seeks resources from the Gospel narratives to address the most significant challenge facing the peoples of our planet at the beginning of the twenty-first century, the ecological crisis currently impacting (and that will continue to impact) on the lives of all earth's citizens. She takes as her starting point Lorraine Code's ground-breaking work, *Ecological Thinking* (2006), in which Code develops an ecologically reconfigured epistemology to construct a responsive-responsible theory of knowledge and subjectivity. Wainwright explores the significance of Code's notion of *habitat* as a place to know as well as a place from which to know and the way this might function in a responsible-responsive ecological reading of biblical texts. Wainwright takes as her focal texts the agrarian parables of Matt 13 and allows the full significance of *habitat* to function in the Matthean text. She does so by moving beyond the metaphorical implications of the agricultural or agrarian imagery of seeds, soil, sower and related imagery to search out the ways these function to make meaning when account is taken of their constituting habitat within the socio-political, economic and cultural contexts of first-century Galilee within imperial Rome. She uses the term inter-con/text-uality to describe this approach within an ecological reading of the text. In contrast, Michael Carden discusses intertextual recontextualizing processes in biblical reception. His "Getting to Know You: Reformation Marriage Ideologies and Contemporary Debates on Same-Sex Marriage" examines the arguments surrounding the meaning of the word "know" in Gen 19:5 in debates over homosexuality. Over fifty years ago, Derrick Sherwin Bailey (1955) broke from long-established Christian tradition by arguing that, when the Sodomites declared that they wanted to "know" Lot's guests, they were not actually declaring a sexual intent but were instead wanting to check their *bona fides*. Bailey argued that the homophobic interpretation of the Sodom story was based on a misinterpretation of this word "know" as conveying a sexual intent on the part of the Sodomites. Opponents of Bailey argued that his interpretation was naïve and flew in the face of a weighty, hence credible, tradition. However, Carden points out that Bailey's interpretation of "know" was not a novel one. In fact, the Geneva Reformer, John Calvin, also broke with tradition and argued that the Sodomites were demanding to check the credentials of Lot's visitors. Unlike Bailey, who wanted to break down the homophobic interpretation of the Sodom story, Calvin believed that the Sodomites were masking their true erotic intentions to trick Lot into handing over his guests. Thus, unlike modern anti-homophobic interpreters, Calvin's reading is designed to demonstrate how dangerous same-sex desire can be. Carden explores the dynamics of Calvin's argument and, further, how it provides a basis for a theology of the closet that would serve as a structuring social ideology central to current debates about same-sex marriage in the United States. While Carden draws on queer theory to address issues of homosexuality, Julie Kelso responds to moves to deploy queer theory to reconfigure feminist debates around female desire and empowerment. She criticizes recent queer-pornographic readings of the Song of Song's "beating scene" (5:2–7), especially, Virginia Burrus and Stephen Moore's essay, "Unsafe Sex: Feminism, Pornography, and the Song of Songs," in which they argue that we need to take seriously the idea that a woman might desire a good beating and that this idea is subversive. Challenging their idea that a woman's desire for contractually agreed-upon pain is subversive, Kelso contends that "woman" is precluded from the place of the subject in the formation of contract and thus cannot actually agree to anything unless she assumes a masculine subjective stance. Consequently, feminism does not ultimately profit from a queering of erotics, or specifically from understanding female masochistic fantasies to be subversive, as Burrus and Moore suggest. Instead, Kelso draws upon the work of Luce Irigaray, and argues the need to take seriously the idea that sexual difference has only an "unthought" status in Western cultures, to contend that a feminist reading of the Song needs to think this through. She concludes with a few suggestions to be taken up by future feminist work. Jione Havea writes as a foreigner to Australia—a nation of several countries of Aborigines, the First People of this southern land—to invite himself to the conversation on "minority biblical criticism" (Bailey, Liew and Segovia 2009) with a reading of Jonah that privileges the First people, the people of the land, the people of Nineveh. He reads Jonah in solidarity with first peoples, their faces, tongues, ways and interests, from Nineveh, and from Oceania.

In his work on the prophets of Israel, Ed Conrad advocates readings of our inherited and "alien" texts that challenge the implicit assumptions of the changing fashions of biblical scholarship and the ways in which the ancient is rendered contemporary (Conrad 1991, 1999, 2003). The theological assumptions of implied audiences are often powerful determinants of how these meanings may be generated and he cautions us wisely against premature biblical theologies. Paul Morris draws on these insights to raise significant issues of how the Bible is being read, interpreted and applied in the contemporary world to underline the importance of the link between academic biblical research and present interpretative communities. Recognizing that the biblical prophets were intensely concerned, as were biblical authors more generally, with justice/righteousness, Morris explores one current notion of justice, restorative or transformative justice, and in particular, the discourse that supports it on biblical grounds. He explores the implicit elements in definitions of this sort of justice and how they relate to particular historical, theological positions. He attends not to the mass of arguments and evidence for the efficacy or otherwise of restorative justice, but rather on the ways in which the Bible is utilized to support this concept and the frameworks for these understandings. He concludes by reflecting on the demand made by Christian proponents of restorative justice that we urgently need to re-consider the relationships and responsibilities of citizens, their communities and the state, and that the Bible has an absolutely central role to play in this. In a second contribution, "A Web of Fascination: Marxism and the Bible," Roland Boer analyses how the text can give rise to different interpretive communities. Crucial, for Boer, is the role of anomaly—that which causes a problem, which causes a disturbance in the narrative or poetic scheme—in biblical interpretation. He argues that the fact of anomaly lies at the heart of each approach taken to the Bible; anomaly functions as a trigger for those approaches. Without anomaly, interpretation would not exist. To investigate this thesis, Boer explores in detail the intersections between allegorical biblical interpretation and the work of Fredric Jameson. From there, he considers historical criticism and the range of approaches that have arisen since historical criticism lost its brief hegemony: feminist, psychoanalytical, literary, Marxist, and so on. All of this, Boer argues, leaves us with a curious final twist: anomaly may be ubiquitous in texts, and each approach may respond to anomalies in very different ways, but they also create those different anomalies in the act of interpretation.

The collection concludes with another essay by Michael Carden, "Dying to Bring Heaven Down to Earth: The Mother of Melchizedek and Miraculous, Messianic Mothers in the Bible," drawing again on queer and feminist theory, in which the subject of prophetic literature returns. However, Carden, considers a very different, and extra-biblical prophetic text, *2 Enoch*, and its closing narrative of the miraculous conception and birth of Melchizedek. Melchizedek has only a brief walk-on part in Genesis and yet he becomes an important figure in the Hebrew Bible, the New Testament and extra-biblically. In some of these later texts, Melchizedek is a type of heavenly being, without mother or father, in others he is an ordinary human born in the usual way. In the *2 Enoch* account, however, Melchizedek is the product of a miraculous, asexual conception and his birth is also an extraordinary, morbidly bizarre, prodigy. In this narrative, he is the son of Sothanim/Sopanim, wife to Nir, the brother of Noah. Despite her sterility, she conceives miraculously in her old age. However, when accused of immorality by her husband she drops dead on the spot. Melchizedek is subsequently born from her corpse, to become the heavenly archetype for a line of royal priests. According to Beverly Bow (2000, 35), of "the five barren women in the Hebrew Bible, Sopanim most resembles Sarah" who herself is a type of miraculous mother. Melchizedek himself first appears textually in the Abraham/ Sarah stories in Genesis. Thus his scriptural debut is framed by the accounts of Sarah, the miraculous mother, and mothers whose pregnancies are disreputable (Lot's daughters and possibly Hagar). In conversation with Luce Irigaray, Carden explores the ways Sopanim, Sarah, the daughters of Lot and their mother are connected through these tropes of miraculous and disreputable motherhood. Carden reflects upon the ways patterns of sexual transgression and the repression/appropriation of the maternal body are interwoven with the themes of miraculous (messianic) motherhood to disrupt and even expose the patriarchal dynamics of the narrative.

This project began in 2007 and was in response to Ed's retirement at the beginning of 2006. It was meant as a way of expressing our appreciation and gratitude for his work, but, being published in the year of Ed's 70th birthday, it is also a gift marking a landmark year in Ed's life, too. We know that Ed will not consider this as some small token. Even in retirement, his lifelong fascination with the Bible (or Bibles, more correctly) and his sharp and critical interest in the work of his peers continues. We know that Ed will devour this volume, appreciating its rich diversity, to keep thinking, keep learning and keep challenging. And we hope, dear reader, that you will do so too.

Roland Boer, Michael Carden, Julie Kelso
May 2011

Part I

READING PROPHETS

READING JEREMIAH

Philip R. Davies

Much of Ed Conrad's research has been devoted to the reading of prophetic books (see bibliography) and it is a pleasure to contribute to this volume some observations on this topic.

Conrad is sceptical of the use of the biblical text as a source for the history of ancient Israel and Judah, even for the history of its literature. We agree that prophetic books are with few exceptions the product of much rewriting and that detailed literary-historical reconstructions, especially of a historical "prophet," are unproductive: it is a false beginning to assign the "authorship" of any prophetic book to the prophet whose name it bears: prophets do not write books. I also share his dislike of the historical critic who does not *read* the book but instead dismantles it for the purpose of assembling another kind of "book." Where I want to hesitate is over his censure of getting behind the message of the *text* to the message of the *sender* (Conrad 2003, 5–30). It would be enjoyable to debate this matter over several beers on his porch in Brisbane, and I rather hope he will read this in that setting (really or virtually) as a conversation about history and about the reading process, which are both more complicated than the drinking process.

The book of Jeremiah has proved a happy hunting ground for the reconstruction of an authorial biography. Many commentators still ascribe much of the book to his secretary Baruch, leaving it as a largely contemporary record of late seventh- and early sixth-century Judah (especially Holladay 1986, 1989; Lundbom 1999, 2004). Some others see the book (and its prophetic persona) as the outcome of a "rolling corpus" (McKane 1986, 1996) and others (Carroll 1986) see the prophet as entirely a literary creation. Ed Conrad's own reading of Jeremiah as "war-prophet" (Conrad 2003, 92–160), of course, addresses this literary figure and not any historical person. But the book does have authors, however anonymous, and the literary figure of Jeremiah is their creation. I am personally quite happy to accept the existence of an historical

Jeremiah as the most plausible explanation for the initiation of such a scroll, but how far the hero of the scroll conforms to any historical profile is neither knowable nor important. The historian of the period may wish to include a Jeremiah among the *dramatic personae* of life in Judah at the end of the seventh and beginning of the sixth centuries B.C.E., but our knowledge of this person can only be deduced from the literary one. But the figure of Jeremiah is the central component of the book's "message," and the creators of this figure are the "senders" of that message. No modern reading can avoid confronting the centrality of that figure (as one can with many of the other prophets).

If it is the reader's responsibility to try and make sense of a text as a whole (which perhaps cannot always be done: see Mark Love [1999] on Zechariah), the challenge is to make sense of the figure of the prophet himself. But both the book and the character seem incoherent, even contradictory—at least to this reader. This could be the reader's fault, though my wife tells me I always avoid blaming myself if possible, and I fear she is right. But it is possible to overcome this apparent failure to read by accepting that the incoherence lies in the way the scroll has been constructed. There are, of course, two major editions of the Jeremiah scroll, preserved in the Masoretic and Septuagint texts (and among the Qumran manuscripts), meaning that is has no definitive shape. However, each edition displays the same features of incoherence, which I will shortly explain.

But how was the scroll of Jeremiah constructed? We have its own account in ch. 36, which claims that the deity dictated words to Jeremiah during his lifetime, which he intended to recite publicly at the Jerusalem temple. But being prevented from entering its precincts, he recited instead to Baruch, who was to read it out. The story is revealing in many ways: the implication is that the book was an accidental outcome and that Jeremiah intended to reveal its entire contents just once in a single address. It also asserts that the contents consist of an accurate transcription of divinely dictated messages, as the Qur'an also claims. But the story also claims that the scroll we have is not that scroll but another (the parallels with Moses' production of the Law are so striking than only an incompetent reader [there have been several] will think of treating this story as a sober historical record). We do not in fact know the authors of this scroll any more than those of any other scroll in the Hebrew Bible. We do, though, know something of the history in which the texts were produced and how texts were written and read, and this reader, at any rate, is unable to bracket that knowledge out of his reading. Yet there is no single answer to how prophetic books were written and read: the implied reader of Jeremiah is not the implied reader of the little story of Jonah. I doubt, for instance, that Jeremiah was intended to be read as a whole (despite the implication of ch. 36), either at one time or in successive episodes. Parts of the book clearly *do* require to be read through, notably the narrative sections, but much of the rest looks like anthology (the existence of the two editions suggests that the contents do not entail a particular structure). Ancient readers would therefore have read it like most moderns, in bits. However, being professionally literate like modern biblical scholars, they would have read it intertextually, earning Ed Conrad's approval on the second score if not on the first.

Even if the authors or first readers of either editions of the Jeremiah scroll bother about coherence, about "reading" in our modern sense, contemporary readings strive for it by perceiving a unifying literary or structural thread or characteristic. As I have already remarked, however, coherence may be sought in the form of a narrative about the construction of the scroll, a kind of "Just-So" story about how it came to be the way it is, especially when that way seems not to be very coherent. This, it seems to me, is what historical-critical readings do. But, like any "literary" reading, these cannot, or should not, claim to be more than "competent": they do not offer definitive accounts, but only the kind of explanation that makes sense; sometimes historians forget that they are really only telling stories to make sense of a past that has no intrinsic meaning.

The incoherence I find in Jeremiah can be expressed, and explained, in terms of its central theme: the character of the prophet. The scroll places him in an historical context at the very outset; like most of the prophetic writings, it dates his prophet's activity (for a fuller account see Davies 2007). As in Isaiah and Ezekiel, the narrative passages integrate the prophetic character with a contemporary history that suggests a context for the oracles too. The reader is drawn into a specific world in which the prophetic figure spoke and acted: in the case of Jeremiah (and Isaiah) there is an overt intertextual relationship with the books of Kings. The once-popular scholarly view that sought to identify the historical message of the prophet as the kernel is faithful to the prompting of the scrolls themselves, though not as faithful to good critical methodology nor to the canonical implication that the prophets deliver a single timeless divine message.

This canonical view suggests that the prophet is the dummy and the deity the ventriloquist. The modern scholar might well see it the other way round, of course: the deity can only say what the prophet makes him say. But in both cases the ventriloquist and the puppet are only constructions. The prophet is the puppet of his creator, a device for the conveying of the message of invisible authors ("Heard But Not Seen," Conrad 1992). These authors we do not know, but we can hear their voice, both in the words that Jeremiah speaks and in the way these words are staged and the puppet described.

We can describe the character Jeremiah better than most of his prophetic companions. His hometown is given as Anathoth (1:1; 11:21–23; 29:27)[1] where he is also described as buying some property from his cousin (32:7–9). He is thus a Benjaminite. He attacks the Judean ruling house (chs. 21–22; 36) and predicts the destruction of the temple in Jerusalem (chs. 7; 26), warning that Nebuchadnezzar will destroy the city, in accordance with the divine will (20:1–6; 21:1–10; 25; 27). Hence, he calls upon the rulers not to resist the divine will and on his fellow Benjaminites to get out of Judah so as to avoid the coming devastation (6:1). He is persecuted for his activities but saved by a group of apparently influential people, including a certain Gedaliah ben Ahikam. This Gedaliah (and perhaps all of Jeremiah's protectors) is also apparently a Benjaminite, since after the fall of Jerusalem he is appointed to rule the province from the Benjaminite city of Mizpah, to which Jeremiah accompanies him.

Whose voice does this prophet Jeremiah speak, whose meaning does he convey? By whom was he created and remembered? A Benjaminite who was not deported but went to live in Mizpah along with his patron, a vociferous opponent of the Judean monarchy and the Jerusalem temple, an advocate of surrender to the Babylonians—Jeremiah is surely the voice of the new Benjaminite regime, and so it is almost certain that his scroll began to take shape in Mizpah. The attitude of patriotic Judeans is quite different (41:1–3, also related in 2 Kgs 25:25): Gedaliah—and those with him—was assassinated by a supporter of the Davidic dynasty, a reaction in line with the Judean king's action (ch. 36) in having the original scroll of the prophet's words torn up and burnt. And just to make it quite clear that the prophet and his scroll stand with Mizpah and against Jerusalem, the original text of a letter that Jeremiah is said to write to deported Judeans (29:1–9) counsels them to settle down in Babylonia, since they are not going to be returning.

Even the oracles addressed to Samaria as "Israel" (e.g. 3:18; 5:11; 11:10, 17; 13:11; cf. 31:27, 31; 33:14) fit, because concern with the province of Samaria might be expected of a Benjaminite, but hardly of Judean deportees for whom the "kingdom of Israel" was probably regarded as a difficult neighbour now long gone. Jeremiah's bond with

---

1. Verse references apply to the Masoretic edition of the book (i.e. as found in modern English Bibles).

Samaria/Israel is also shown in his reference to the destruction of Israelite Shiloh (7:12, 14; 26:6, 9; 41:5) as a premonition of what will happen to Jerusalem.

So far the character and the book read coherently as a celebration and vindication of the fall of Jerusalem. The new government in Mizpah, who could now replace the patronage of Jerusalem's elite with their own, with all the personal and family benefits that such patronage inevitably brings, create a prophetic scroll that justifies the turn of events, not only in the words of denunciation but in the stories of Jeremiah's harsh reception in Jerusalem. The prophet and his book exist because of this purposeful creation: they *commemorate* the fall of Jerusalem, and not in tones of sympathy or condolence but *Schadenfreude*.

But such coherence is achieved only at the expense of what Ed Conrad would criticize as the creating of another book in place of the one we have—by selecting those bits that fit and discarding those that do not. For Jeremiah has another voice, one that protests, resists what he is being told to say, and laments the pain of his mission. This voice turns on the Babylonian patrons of his Benjaminite creators and wishes terrible revenge on them for what they did to the city and the temple that he himself had attacked (ch. 50). The letter to the deportees now contains (vv. 10–14) a rosy picture of their (or their descendants') return and Jerusalem as once again the "throne of Yahweh" (3:17). In short, he adopts the voice of a patriotic Judean—the kind of person who would willingly have thrown him into a pit or torn up his scroll.

We therefore have to abandon the person of the prophet as a stable centre for a reading of the scroll. The best we can do in retaining his integrity is to assume that he is schizophrenic (a solution that works better with Ezekiel). But literary figures do not have an unconscious to be analyzed: their whole identity is on the surface: they are two-dimensional. Hence an alternative explanation: the prophet is the voice of different writers. Indeed, the two voices in Jeremiah use different language. The prophet can do poetry or prose, and in his prosaic voice he can manage a nice impression of the narrator of Moses speaking on the plains of Moab (a rather boring sermonizer). All scholarly readers of the book of Jeremiah recognize this voice and use the word "Deuteronomistic," defining a rhetorical style that celebrates Jerusalem, David, covenant and Torah—a long way from the voice of Mizpah.

The creators of this voice clearly speak *for* Jerusalem. But where *from*? The majority of commentators are drawn to the Babylonian exile. This, though, seems unlikely. The deported elite, however, are unlikely to have wanted to develop a literary character like the Jeremiah from

Mizpah, and certainly unlikely to have had any knowledge of the character created there. More probably, we are looking at a voice from Jerusalem after it had regained its capital status from Mizpah. Exactly how
and when this occurred we do not know (the biblical sources pretend it
was immediate). But it did happen: the former dynasty was not restored,
but the city and its temple were. Moving capitals about is cumbersome.
In the European Union the Parliament meets for plenary sessions in
Strasbourg, but for committee meetings in Brussels; in South Africa the
seat of government is in Pretoria while Parliament sits in Cape Town.
These arrangements represent political compromises and modern travel
makes it possible. But Judah could not so easily have two capitals. When
Jerusalem became the capital of Judah, Mizpah ceased to, and presumably all the trappings of administration, including documents, were transferred. In the religious sphere, the cult centre was now located on the site
of the old royal sanctuary.

Among the many pieces moved from the palace library in Mizpah—
or possibly the temple library in Bethel—were some prophetic scrolls,
including Amos and Hosea, and also Jeremiah. Unlike the other two
which were originally critical of Israel/Samaria, and so could more easily
be amended by supplying oracles relating to Judah, Jeremiah had a
thoroughly anti-Jerusalem and anti-Davidic figure whose joy at Jerusalem's demise had not evaporated. Burning it was no longer an option:
its memory could not be so easily erased among the *literati* at least.
Recantation has often been thought a better way of dealing with heretics.
So Jeremiah was made to recant his prognostications and repent of the
zeal with which he uttered his denunciations. Jeremiah is now remembered as the prophet who lamented to an extraordinary degree (and
credited with a book of Lamentations over Jerusalem). He now cries out
in pain at what he is forced to say, as one truly loyal to Jerusalem would.
This image of Jeremiah has not effaced the other, but has placed it in a
context of a past disaster that is now over and remastered a stern voice as
a sorrowful one. It is not a bad effort at unifying the prophetic persona
(and has certainly had a remarkable success in the reception of the
prophet). It presumably satisfied the ancient reader. But it does not
satisfy the modern literary reader. Or at least not *this* one.

Perhaps Ed Conrad, reclining on his Brisbane porch will be asking me
(soaking in the hot tub) "Why should any modern reader be bothered
with recovering a hidden voice, one that contradicts the ideology of the
book as it now stands?" I might begin by teasing him that he sounds like
Brevard Childs (Childs 1979)—why try and reverse the "canonical
intention," the "final form" (or "forms"). This would be cheap: he is by
no means a canonical critic. I might simply repeat that this is the only

way I can read Jeremiah coherently, by means of telling a story of how the prophet was first put together and then given a makeover. I would probably assert that only one voice fits the historical context that the scroll itself gives to the prophet. And if all this fails to persuade, I would declare that where I have a choice, I will always read against the text— and then ask for another beer.

FILLING THE GAPS AND PUTTING HULDAH TO USE

Judith E. McKinlay

I read Ed Conrad's *Reading Isaiah* soon after it appeared in 1991. Walter Brueggemann described it as "an act of considerable methodological courage" (1991, vii); just as Isaiah came freshly alive in Ed's reading, so did the enterprise of discovering meaning in these ancient texts. Readers were important and readers read differently: "the getting of a biblical text...can never be complete or definitive. A myriad of readers may engage with the text, which has an endless depth of meaning" (Conrad 1991, 166). This brief study follows Ed's insistence that "there can be no detached interpretation of the biblical texts, no textual meaning independent of the present reception of the biblical text" (1991, 164). I am interested in how some readers, many of them theologians rather than biblical scholars *per se*, have not only viewed the prophet Huldah but drawn her into their own debates and worldviews, far removed from hers in time and place. I have warm memories of standing in the sun at St Albans, at the 1999 meeting of the Bible and Critical Theory Seminar, talking with Ed about Huldah.

Huldah appears, quite unexpectedly, in one small biblical clip in 2 Kgs 22:14–20, repeated in 2 Chr 34:22–28. The discovery of a long-lost law-book during a maintenance check to the Temple shatters the calm of the king to such an extent that he calls for a verification of its fateful words. This is Huldah's entry, with a prophetic judgment that, according to the 2 Kings account, sets in action a radical Yahwistic cleansing.[1] The major focus is, of course, upon Josiah, the good and righteous king, forever famed for this reform, but behind the figure of Josiah stands the prophet Huldah, the woman consulted as the deliverer of the divine judgment, the woman who declares the Deuteronomistic programme of one god worshipped in one centre as the divine Word, the woman bearer of the Deuteronomistic Word. My interest lies in how this figure, originally employed as a tool in the hands of theologically determined scribes,

---

1. The chronology is notably different in the Chronicler's account, where the reform has already taken place.

continued to be read and employed in other theological debates. I look at her with some amazement and, as a twenty-first-century woman, admit to an ambivalence. This is indeed a woman prophet legitimizing Scripture, an unexpected find in a document both written and edited by male scribes, but I also wonder at her role in the destruction of the Asherah. For, as the text in 2 Kings reads, this is the woman who provides the justification for what is supposedly the final eradication of the Asherah, Israel's one physical symbol of the divine feminine.[2] I wonder, too, what later writers have made of this, just as I would also ask, with Judith Plaskow, "why we know nothing else of a prophet who was sufficiently well-known and respected that the king's servant would turn to her at this critical juncture" and "why is there no book of Huldah along with the books of the other prophets." Plaskow's view is that traditions about women were seen as either threatening or unimportant, so their roles were "downplayed and obscured." And maybe this is the situation from the beginning, that even in Huldah's own day, it was "because she was a woman that she left no school to record her prophecies and pass them on to succeeding generations" (Plaskow 1990, 39–40).[3] As it is, the silence remains. Not that this hinders readers filling in the gaps! For, to quote Renita Weems, "the less detail given about a character, the more readers impute significance to the few details that are offered, the more they are inclined to draw on their own experiences to help make the character come alive and gain significance in the narrative" (Weems 2003, 331). I warm to the picture Weems herself paints: "a woman sitting at her desk in the middle of the day hunched over a dusty manuscript, peering intently down at its contents, consumed with deciphering the meaning hidden in the script" (2003, 322—owning that "Huldah soon became my secret role model"): Huldah the scholar, painstakingly at the task, a picture that leaps over the centuries encouraging all of us who work as women scholars. Of course, there is a question whether Huldah was responsible for the words attributed to her.

2. That Asherah worship existed alongside that of YHWH has been confirmed by the archaeological discoveries of inscriptions, which have been variously interpreted as referring to a goddess or as a cultic object associated with the goddess. The many terracotta figurines depicting a nude female figure may also be Asherah figures.

3. Praetorius (2006, 89) charges the canonization process for deliberately omitting the prophecies of women, leaving only a few names: "Miriam, Noadiah, Deborah, Huldah and a few nameless female prophets... [T]heir words were not included in the canon, or were included under men's names." Praetorius notes Klara Butting, *Prophetinnen gefragt. Die Bedeutung der Prophetinnen im Kanon aus Tora und Prophetie* (Knesebeck: Erev Rav, 2002), who suggests that some prophecies by women may have been recorded under the names of male prophets.

Some time ago I wrote a script for a Deuteronomist (2005a, n.p.), imagining him scoffing:

> Just listen to her! She thinks she really was a prophet! I suppose that's somewhat our fault—we did decide to use the phrase *daras 'et-yhwh* which implies a prophetic response. Perhaps she also thinks she has the gift of Jeremiah—what supreme arrogance! When I think of the care I took choosing the phrases with their resounding echoes of Jeremiah.[4]

Diana Edelman suggests "a late, post-exilic editor...wrote the prophecy ... He imitated the prophetic style of the book of Jeremiah, making Huldah à female alter ego for the latter prophet" (1994, 248). Whether either of these scenarios was so or not, Huldah remains the prophet in the text and readers have continued to fill the gaps in this so-called history. Huldah, the scholar, is already present in *Targum Jonathan*, written sometime before 135 C.E., pronouncing her oracle and instructing the king's male officials from her place in the "the house of instruction," although this scholarly promotion is, perhaps, due to a textual happenstance, this being the meaning of the word in post-biblical Hebrew. I whimsically wonder if it is the benefit of study that makes her divine judgment sharper and more specific: Judah has "offered up sweet spices to the idols of the nations" in a deliberate act of provocation (Harrington and Saldarini 1987, 309)—although in the Septuagint she had already accused the people of acting purposefully to provoke YHWH (v. 17). Of Huldah's connection with the Asherah destruction there is no trace. Asherah's tree connection has changed her quite literally into a Septuagintal grove.

Josephus can hardly leave Huldah out of his history; although he generally portrays women negatively: women's testimony is inadmissible because of their levity and the boldness of their sex (*Ant.* 4.219). But Huldah is a prophet, and Josephus has a high regard for prophets (Brown 1992, 76). Is this why he, too, enlarges her brief? She is not only to verify the document but to intercede, "to propitiate God and try to make him benevolent." Josephus's Huldah, however, is more assertive: she refuses. God had already decided on the divine course of action, therefore such a decision was irrevocable. Her words heighten the consequences: the Deity will "annihilate the people, expel them from their country, and deprive them of all the good things that were now present." (*Ant.* 10.59–60). The people have not listened and judgment follows, spoken through the prophets, which happens here to be Huldah. Josephus,

---

4. The Jeremiah parallels are well noted. For details see Edelman (1994, 231) and Knoppers (1994, 146).

however, makes a further change: Huldah's husband, Shallum, is now a man "distinguished on account of his noble birth" (*Ant.* 10.59) and no longer a minor temple official. Josephus's Huldah is an aristocrat. Is he a little hesitant about a woman in such a significant role, so this makes her more acceptable? He, too, is not concerned about the Asherah; she has been namelessly subsumed under the category of foreign gods or idols.

The rabbis, however, were puzzled: Why was Huldah approached by Hilkiah and the others and not Jeremiah? Their answer? "Hulda was a near relative of Jeremiah, and he did not object to her doing so" (*b. Meg.* 14b). So Huldah had Jeremiah's permission! But "how could Josiah himself pass over Jeremiah and send to her?" The school of R. Shila suggested this was because "women are tender-hearted": Josiah was apprehensive about what Jeremiah might say. R. Johanan closed the debate: "Jeremiah was not there, as he had gone to bring back the ten tribes." Huldah here is simply the Jeremiah substitute. No more than that.

If R. Shila thought her tender-hearted, R. Nahman saw her otherwise. A few paragraphs later he declares, "haughtiness does not befit women. There were two haughty women, and their names are hateful, one being called a hornet [Deborah, usually translated as 'bee'] and the other a weasel [the literal meaning of Huldah]" (*b. Meg.* 14b). Why haughty? Because she said "say to the man," instead of the more respectful "say to the king" (2 Kgs 22:15). Or was it that a woman who stepped up into a Jeremiah-like role must necessarily have been haughty and proud? Yet, in some typically midrashic gap-filling, R. Nahman declares her a descendent of Joshua, through Tikvah's father Harhas, although R. Judah counters this, insisting she is a descendent of Rahab, the harlot.[5] This time it is R. Nahman who resolves the matter: "the truth can be found by combining my statement and yours. We must suppose that she (i.e. Rahab) became a proselyte and Joshua married her." Not only was Rahab highly esteemed by the rabbis, she was also extremely beautiful, one of "the four women of surpassing beauty in the world" along with Sarah, Abigail and Esther or Vashti (*b. Meg.* 15a). Huldah now not only has a high-born husband, she has a significant ancestor.[6]

5. R. Nahman's midrashic link here is with Judg 2:9, which has Joshua buried in Timnath-heres, which is interpreted as Timnath belonging to Heres, who here is identified with Harhas. R. Judah links *tikvah*, the name of Shallum's father, with the crimson cord that Rahab ties to the window in Josh 2:18. *Ruth Rab.* 2.1 made the same connection, listing "ten priests who were also prophets descended from Rahab the harlot...some add that Huldah the prophet was also a descendent of Rahab the harlot."

6. Cf. *Mekhilta 'Amalek* 3; *Deut. Rab.* 2.26–27; *Num. Rab.* 8.9; *Pesiq. Rab.* 40.3.

Well connected, tender-hearted as well as haughty, acting in place of Jeremiah, but did the rabbis recognize her as a scholar, for the biblical Huldah had clearly been charged with reading and studying Torah? While the Tosefta implies women could read "from the Torah, the Prophets and the Writings, and study mishnah, halakhot, and aggadot" (*t. Ber.* 2.12), the Babylonian Talmud sees things differently. There is a problem: "women are a separate people…whatever is fit for a man is not fit for a woman, and whatever is fit for a woman is not fit for a man" (*b. Shab.* 62a). Men are to study Torah, and women are to carry out their own work in their own areas.[7] Besides, women are inherently lascivious: as R. Joshua warns, "do not converse much with women, as this will ultimately lead you to unchastity" (*b. Ned.* 20a). The *Megilla* passage in which Huldah's ancestry is discussed is immediately followed by the statement that "our Rabbis taught: Rahab inspired lust by her name" and R. Isaac declares, "whoever says, Rahab, Rahab, at once has an issue." When R. Nahman says that when he says Rahab, Rahab, nothing happens to him, R. Isaac replies, "I was speaking of one who knows her and is intimate with her." Beauty paired with lust; so often in these texts men's fear of the arousal it might bring in its wake follows any talk of women's beauty. Yet the Talmud preserves the tradition of Beruriah, famed for her Torah study, even learning "three hundred laws from three hundred teachers in one day" (*b. Pesah.* 62b). The *Pesikta Rabbati* (ch. 26) has a solution: Jeremiah prophesied in the streets of Jerusalem, Zephaniah in the synagogues, while Huldah had a school for women, where she taught the divine Words that women should know. Huldah may be teaching torah, but only the portions deemed suitable for women, and suitably sequestered away from male sight. Louis Ginzberg has a reference to a mystical twelfth-century work where Huldah is one of nine women heading seven divisions in the women's section of Paradise (1998, 33). The arithmetic may be a little at odds but this is certainly promotion for Huldah, even if confined to the women's quarters. Rashi provides a different solution again: linking the Targum reference to her study with the Mishnah's note of two southern Temple gates named the Huldah Gates (*Tractate Middot* 1.3), he grants her an academy right there in the Temple, next to this gate, but while it was open on one side, it was closed toward the Sanhedrin, because of modesty. There, however, she teaches

7.   Boyarin (1993, 196) argues that the concern is that a Torah student or scholar might not fulfill the very positive and essential roles of wife and birth-giver: "[t]he Torah and the wife are structural allomorphs and separated realms…both normatively to be highly valued but also to be kept separate."

the Oral Law to the elders of the generation.[8] Nor was she forgotten; despite predicting disaster upon Jerusalem her bones remain there, as the Tosefta claims:

> they do not set up graves in it (i.e. Jerusalem), except for the graves of the house of David and the grave of Huldah, the prophetess, which were there from the days of the former prophets. (*t. Neg.* 6.2.1)

Huldah alongside the Davidic family—she is exceptional indeed!

The Christian Testament has no need of her. Women prophets are not a problem initially; Peter, at Pentecost, quotes Joel's prophesy about sons and daughters prophesying and Acts 21:9 does not hesitate in recording the four daughters of Philip each having the gift of prophecy. While the women prophets in Corinth were clearly a worry to Paul, his concern may have been about interpretation and manner rather than gender (Wire 1990). If Christianity began as a charismatic movement, a more extreme version followed. Not that the followers of the "New Prophecy" or Montanist movement (mid-second century C.E.) saw themselves as extreme; they simply believed themselves filled with the same Spirit as the biblical prophets. Not so, thundered Eusebius; "they cannot point to a single one of the prophets under either the Old Covenant or the New who was moved by the Spirit in this way" (*Church History* 5.17). Men and women freely prophesying alongside each other, outside the strict confines of a claimed "orthodoxy," was definitely unacceptable. Whether this opposition was fuelled by theology or politics might be debated. Barbara Rossing sees Christianity faced with the choice: to oppose the power of Rome or accommodate itself to the imperium. Gender roles and women's behaviour are a factor: Is charismatic gender equality in the New Jerusalem compatible with Empire? (2005, 284).[9] Or was such equality simply out of touch with a theology that saw the Fall and Eve's punishment as prescriptive?

Tertullian a few years later, opposing the Gnostics, is equally appalled: "[a]s for the women of the heretics, how forward they are! They have the impudence to teach, to argue" (*Praescr.* 41).[10] What was Huldah doing?

---

8. See Rashi's commentaries to 2 Kgs 22:14; 2 Chr 34:22 and *b. Meg.* 14. Linking *mishneh* with "two" in his commentary on Kings, he also has her expounding publicly on everything in Deuteronomy that is repeated twice.

9. "At the very same time that the New Prophets were enthusiastically announcing their vision of the New Jerusalem established in Phrygia and urging martyrdom for God's cause, orthodox apologists were trying to persuade the Empire that Christianity posed no threat to the established imperial order" (Rossing 2005, 284).

10. Although in *de anima* 9.4 Tertullian writes approvingly of a sister "amongst us" who sees and hears "mysterious communications" and who "is in the regular

He does not mention her, but Origen supplies an answer, including her in a list of biblical women, known as prophets, but never so presumptuous as to speak out in public. Her address was solely "to an individual man who had come to her home seeking her out."[11] Origen's view is clear: if Titus 2:3–4 allows women to teach right behaviour, they should not do this "in such a way that men are seated and listening to women, as though there were not enough men capable of mediating the word of God." And then the final cut: "even if she utters marvellous things, holy things, the fact remains that all of it is only coming from the mouth of a woman." Gender roles are clearly an issue at the end of the second century. Huldah has become useful in setting limits; she is shrinking before my eyes.

She appears again, but alongside Sophonias and Jeremiah in a summary of biblical history written by Clement of Alexandria, with variations, in the late second century C.E.:

> Then Chelkias the priest, the father of the prophet Jeremiah, having fallen in with the book of the law that had been laid up in the temple, read it and died. And in his days Olda prophesied, and Sophonias, and Jeremiah. (*Strom.* 1.21)

Yet in the same chapter he writes, "let us direct our wives to that which is good…let them show forth the sincere disposition of meekness." Did he see Huldah as a model of meekness? He does, however, note in a later chapter (1.55) that "[m]any women also, being strengthened by the grace of God, have performed numerous manly exploits," naming "the blessed" Judith and Esther. Why manly? This already has a long history; Aristotle, Philo and the *Gospel of Thomas* have all laid the foundations. Women, as women, were not as spiritual or as capable as men, in the roles thought appropriate for men. If, however, unexpectedly, they prove capable, they must have transcended the limitations of their gender and become man-like. Accept the first premise and the logic flows naturally (Jantzen 1995, 43–58).

What seems to exercise the minds of many of the writers of the early Christian centuries is the matter of the godliness, or otherwise, of the prophets. It concerns the writer of *The Constitutions of the Holy Apostles*, thought to have been written in the fourth century C.E.: "neither is every

habit of reporting to us whatever things she may have seen in vision." Her authenticity is not in doubt, "for her witness there was God."

11.   Origen, *Commentarium in Iᵃᵐ epist. ad Corinthios* 14: 34–35 in Codex Vat. gr, 762, quoted by Coyle (1978, 73–74). 1 Cor 14:35 and 1 Tim 2:12 are used to settle the matter.

one who prophesies holy… It is manifest…that the ungodly, although they prophesy, do not by their prophesying cover their own impiety." True prophecies "are wrought in holy man by the inspiration of God." Women too! He acknowledges that "women prophesied also," and lists Miriam, Deborah, Huldah and Judith, followed by Mary, Elizabeth and Anna and the daughters of Philip. "[Y]et were not these elated against their husbands, but preserved their own measures." That not all of these are known to have had husbands seems not to matter. He concludes, "[w]herefore if any among you also there be a man or a woman, and such a one obtains any gift, let him be humble, that God may be pleased with him." A quote from Isa 66:2b underlines the point (viii. i. ii). If women show godly humility there is no problem about their holding office, at least the office of deaconess, limited to assisting the male presbyters, particularly in the baptism of women, "for reasons of decency." Ironically, the prayer for the ordination of a woman deacon names Miriam, Deborah, Anna and Huldah as warrant of divine legitimation for this limited office:

> O Eternal God, the Father of our Lord Jesus Christ, the Creator of man and of woman, who didst replenish with the Spirit Miriam, and Deborah, and Anna, and Huldah…do Thou now also look down upon this Thy servant, who is to be ordained to the office of a deaconess, and grant her Thy Holy Spirit, and cleanse her from all filthiness of flesh and Spirit, that she may worthily discharge the work which is committed to her to Thy glory, and the praise of Thy Christ, with whom glory and adoration be to Thee and the Holy Spirit for ever. Amen. (viii. iii. xx)

Jerome, also writing in the fourth century, resolves the problem of Huldah's role:

> Nor need we wonder that Huldah, the prophetess, and wife of Shallum, was consulted by Josiah, King of Judah, when the captivity was approaching and the wrath of the Lord was falling upon Jerusalem: since it is the rule of Scripture when holy men fail, to praise women to the reproach of men. (*Jov.* 1.25)

The implication is clear: prophecy is indeed a man's role. Only when men abdicate their responsibility is it appropriate for a woman to act, and then specifically as a reproach. Huldah has a new role. Jerome includes the detail "wife of Shallum," although the writer of the fourth-century Codex Vaticanus curiously changes this so that Huldah becomes Shallum's mother, not his wife.

Yet women continued to prophesy and teach throughout the Middle Ages, and continued to meet opposition. The reasons are well rehearsed. Jacques de Vitry (1160–1240 ᴄ.ᴇ.) who, in fact, encouraged women, had learned well from Augustine: "because man is made in God's image, he has stronger intellectual powers than woman" (Muessig 1998, 146). The Dominican preacher, Humbert of Roman (d. 1277 C.E.) provides a list: "First is lack of judgment, for a woman has less than a man… Third, if she were to preach, her appearance would provoke lascivious thoughts… Fourth, in remembrance of the foolishness of the first woman" (*De eruditione praedicatorum*; Muessig 1998, 154). Even Hildegard of Bingen (1098–1179 C.E.), who recorded God calling out to her, "O human…cry out and speak of the origin of pure salvation until those people are instructed," adds that she is to do this until "they who now think you contemptible because of Eve's transgression are stirred up by the flood of your irrigation" (*Scivias*; 1990, 59). Eve, so often called upon to block women's active roles in the Church! But if men are offended "because in these times the Lord deigns to show His mercy most gloriously in the weak sex," they should recognize that "holy women" such as "Olda, Deborah, Judith, Jahel and other women" were "filled with the Spirit of God" to prophesy and act. So writes St. Elizabeth of Schönau (1129–1165) in her Book of Visions. But the women did this because "the men were given over to sluggishness." It is Jerome's see-saw argument again: women are only up if the men are down. It is a good example of the way in which women accepted and internalized the views of male theologians and clerics (Jantzen 1995, 49). Yet, Alfonso of Jaén, writing in the fourteenth century to the ecclesiastical authorities in support of Bridget of Sweden's credibility as visionary and prophet, uses Huldah in his argument, without qualification. If Huldah was a prophet who advised the king, then so was Bridget (Voaden 1999, 82). Once again Huldah is a useful tool.

She is more of a problem for Luther. He may have radicalized church order, but his view of women as different and inferior to men is remarkably similar to that of the earlier church fathers.[12] Where he differs he is also inconsistent. For while "in no part, neither in body nor in soul, was Eve inferior to her husband Adam" before being deceived by the serpent and falling into sin,[13] Satan made his approach to her because "Satan…

12. Augustine (fifth century) and Aquinas (thirteenth century) were particularly influential. As Luther writes on Gen 1:27 in his 1535 commentary, "although Eve was…similar to Adam so far as the image of God is concerned…she was nevertheless a woman… As the sun is more excellent than the moon…so the woman, although she was a most beautiful work of God, nevertheless was not equal of the male in glory and prestige" (Luther 1958a, 68–69).

13. Luther further comments (1958a, 203), "[i]f Eve had persisted in the truth… she herself would also have been a partner in the rule which is now entirely the concern of males."

attacks the weak part of the human nature, Eve the woman, not Adam the man. Although both were created equally righteous, nevertheless…in the perfect nature the male somewhat excelled the female" (Luther 1958a, 185, 151). Now, post-Fall, however, there is no question. Women are to stay at home, "like a nail driven into the wall," while the man "rules the home and the state, wages wars, defends his possessions, tills the soil, builds, plants, etc." Women "cannot perform the functions of men, teach, rule etc. In procreation and in feeding and nurturing their offspring they are masters. In this way Eve is punished" (1958a, 202–3).[14] So Huldah? She appears in a lecture, not on Genesis but on 1 Timothy. Discussing 2:11, Luther fully agrees that in the public assembly of the church a woman must be "completely quiet," a "hearer and not a teacher." Acknowledging that Huldah, Deborah and Jael "have been very good at management,"[15] he then asks rhetorically: "[w]hy, then, does Paul say here that he deprives them of the administration of the Word as well as of work?" To which, of course, he has his answer ready: understanding that v. 12 refers to wives, he declares, "where men and women have been joined together, there the men, not the women, ought to have authority." How, then, to account for Huldah? "An exceptional example is the case where they are without husbands, like Huldah and Deborah, who had no authority over husbands" (1973, 276). What has happened to Shallum? Or is Luther using the Codex Vaticanus, with Huldah as Shallum's mother? Huldah and Deborah are then joined by the woman of Abel-maacah (2 Sam 20:14–21) and the four daughters of Philip (Acts 21:9), allowing that "[w]here there is no man, Paul has allowed that they can do this, because it happens by a man's command… Where there are men, she should neither teach nor rule." Huldah is once again the man's substitute. Luther, the husband, concludes:

14. See Douglas (2003, 87): the implication of the Fall theology was that "God's express punishment of women…must endure till the end of time"; there is nothing that can be done to change it: women, as they now are, are indeed subordinate to men. Yet if all Christians are called to the priestly office, as Luther argues in 1522, in "Misuse of the Mass" (Luther 1959, 151–52), then this must apply to both sexes, and must include preaching, but, and one can almost anticipate the but, "one should not use any person for this task…unless he is better fitted than the others." Naturally men are better fitted as "more skilled." 2 Tim 2:2 is the text, and Gen 3:16 the warrant.

15. The original here is "quod mulieres optime adminstrarunt res" (WA 26. 46/16), which as Peter Matheson, in personal correspondence, points out, better translates as "that women handle/deal with/manage matters extremely well."

> There would be a disturbance if some woman wished to argue against the doctrine that is being taught by a man... That subjection of women and domination of men have not been taken away, have they? No. The penalty remains. (1973, 276–77, 279–80)

Then, surprisingly, at the end of a long section on childbearing and childraising, Luther returns to Huldah: "If the Lord were to raise up a woman for us to listen to, we would allow her to rule like Huldah." As Jane Dempsey Douglas comments, "[o]ne wonders how Luther would recognize that she had been raised up by God" (2003, 86)!

Luther returns to the subject of Huldah and others in a letter written in 1532 to Eberhard von der Tannen, where he is virulently opposing the spread of the Anabaptists, "these emissaries of the devil," and "murderers of souls, blasphemers, and enemies of Christ and his churches" (1958b, 383–84). He declares himself "astonished" that "in their spiritual wisdom they haven't learned to adduce examples of how women have prophesied and thereby attained rule over men, land, and people" (1958b, 390). For there they are, women, recorded in the canon as exercising their prophetic roles: Deborah, the wise woman of 2 Sam 20, and Huldah, followed by Sarah, Anna and the Virgin Mary. It seems the Anabaptists are debating various readings and challenging the Lutheran preachers, and, as Luther concedes, 1 Cor 14:31 might seem to encourage anyone able to prophesy. No! This applies only to the prophets, and not to the people. Just imagine!

> The women too would claim the right of...telling the men to be silent. Then one woman silencing the other—oh, what a beautiful holiday, auction, and carnival that would be! What pig sties could compare in goings-on with such churches? (1958b, 388)

What, then, of the women prophets he has mentioned? It seems he does not want to deal with this: "We shall for the present not be concerned about the right of these women of the Old Testament to teach and rule" (1958b, 390). Why did he bring them into the discussion in the first place? Yet he seems to be reluctant to leave it unaddressed:

> But surely they did not act as the infiltrators do, unauthorized, and out of superior piety and wisdom. For then God would not have confirmed their ministry and worked by miracles and great deeds. (1958b, 390)

It is a theological balancing act. The tension is clear: it is quite out of the question, quite ridiculous, for women to presume to teach or preach, and yet Huldah was specifically named as a prophet, and recorded as acting prophetically, and that is an office that Luther holds in the highest esteem. This is a problematic Huldah.

Yet there were women speaking out, or, in Argula von Grumbach's case, doing this in writing. In a letter of 1523, in which she challenges the trial and forced recanting of a young student by the University of Ingolstadt, she justifies herself on the grounds that she is "constrained" by Matt 10:30–33. "Now that I cannot see any man who is up to it, who is either willing or able to speak," it is she who must do so, adding "[w]hat I have written to you is no woman's chit-chat, but the Word of God" (Matheson 1995, 79, 90). This seems to be the Jerome see-saw once again. Balthasar Hubmaier accepts both the reasoning and the prophetic Word, adding her name to the list of biblical women cited in his theses against Eck:

> where the men are afraid and have become women, then the women should speak up and become manly, like Deborah, Hulda, Anna the prophetess, the four daughters of the evangelist Philip, and in our own times Argula. (Hubmaier 1989, 56)

Women are to become "manly" because the men have become "womanly." Haughty or tender-hearted, Huldah, acting as one prophet among many, on equal standing with the men, remains anomalous, acceptable only as "manly." Even so, she provides a precedent; she is useful.

This is the Huldah legacy, handed down mainly by male clerics, their perspective even internalized by women. It would, of course, be different today? I wonder, and begin a search, deciding to start with Elizabeth Cady Stanton's late nineteenth-century *The Woman's Bible*, since for many of us, influenced by the feminist movement, this is now iconic. So is her Huldah, not only "residing in the college in Jerusalem," where the Targum had placed her, but now "a statesman...doubtless a professor jurisprudence, or of languages." Her gap-filling continues: why was Huldah consulted? "It is fair to suppose that there was not a man at court who could read the book." Especially not Shallum! "While Huldah was pondering great questions of State and Ecclesiastical Law, her husband was probably arranging the royal buttons and buckles." I am mindful again of Ed's statement that there is "no detached interpretation of the biblical texts, no textual meaning independent of the present reception of the biblical text" (Conrad 1991, 164). Stanton's agenda cannot be mistaken. If the clergy "had read of the dignity accorded to Huldah" women would not "have had such a struggle...to open the college doors." And, she adds, "[i]magine the moral hardihood of the reverend gentlemen who should dare to reject such women as Deborah, Huldah and Vashti as delegates to a Methodist conference, and claim the approval of God for such an indignity" (Stanton 1898, 81–83). Lucretia Mott

(1793–1880) and Sarah Grimké (1792–1873), both friends of Stanton and writers in their own right, also drew Huldah into their strong pro-women stands, Grimké, arguing in one of her letters for the *New England Spectator*, that women should be accepted as prophets and ministers, along with men, seeing that the biblical prophets had included women such as Huldah, Miriam and Deborah.[16] Lucretia Mott, arguing against Richard Henry Dana, an opponent of equal rights for women, cited Huldah, along with Deborah, Miriam and Jael, as women exercising public roles alongside men (noted by Selvidge 1996, 54–59).[17] Catherine Booth's agenda is clearly stated in the title of her 1895 pamphlet, *Female Ministry; or, Woman's Right to Preach the Gospel*. Huldah, the prophet-ess, carries "authority and dignity," not "that trembling diffidence or abject servility which some persons seem to think should characterise the religious exercises of woman" (MacHaffie 1992, 143).

And today? Interestingly Huldah was the cause of a "heated debate" by the Canadian Anglican bishops in 2000, over whether she was to be included in a eucharistic prayer in a new Book of Alternative Services. It was not so much a question of her importance as a prophet, but the fact that she had virtually been forgotten that won the day: "we are making a point when we name a woman who has been ignored."[18] Renita Weems recalls Patrick Miller's comment to a class that "[d]espite the role she played in inspiring the canon [Huldah] is one of the most overlooked figures in the Bible" (2003, 321). Rachel Montagu notes Abraham Heschel's silence: "to him, she is invisible" (1994, 52). Why this neglect, this invisibility? In the academy, it seems that Josiah almost completely overshadows her, as lecturers follow the clue inserted by the ancient scribes, allotting Huldah only these few verses.

And in the Church? Ruth Fox, noting the "disproportionate number of passages about women of the Bible" that have been omitted, suggests it is the selective nature of the Church's Lectionary; when 2 Kgs 22:8–13; 23:1–3 are read, the verses referring to Huldah "are neatly sliced out of the middle." There is no use made *of* her as there is no use *for* her; the silence is "to reinforce what some believe to be the weaknesses or proper roles of women" (1996, n.p.). This does not mean Huldah is found in churches not bound to the Lectionary; "in all my years as a fundamental-ist attending four church services a week, I never once heard mention of her," writes Virginia Ramey Mollenkott (2000, n.p.). Her reasoning? "Huldah was so threatening to male supremacy."

16. Grimké (1838, 102), noted by Selvidge (1996, 52).
17. The address, delivered in 1849, was titled "Discourse on Woman."
18. Bishop Ann Tottenham, quoted in De Santis (2000).

Yet websites from conservative faith communities show that far from being forgotten Huldah continues to provide sharp ammunition. Why was her place away from the Temple? This allows the writer of a Tribute to the Apostolic Women of the Apostolic Messianic Fellowship of Tampa, Florida, to assert she "never went to the Tabernacle to demand assignment to duties or to receive the anointing and ordination into the Ministry… Fact is, Huldah prophesied, she did not preach." The writer shows his colours more vividly as he continues: "[s]he did not parade up and down on a platform or swish her skirt-tale up and down a Church isle [*sic*]…she did not use her gift of prophecy to belittle her husband " Huldah can, however, be a model for those who "possess the gifts of the Spirit, and use them under the direct authority of the Pastor, down out of the pulpit."[19] This in a Tribute dedicated to the writer's mother, wife and daughters, et al.

Titus 2 Men and Women allows that Huldah spoke the word of God, providing a model for those knowing the word to speak up "when the Holy Spirit gives us opportunity." Yet the writer is reluctant to grant her any recognized position. Some interesting gap-filling continues: if, somehow, she was at a college or school, then she must have been there as cook or housekeeper, and so "able to hear the students discussing the law of God…[and then] made comments at some time that caused the students and staff to recognize her ability to rightly divide [*sic*] the word of truth" (Neevel 1988). The writer on another website concedes that Huldah "may have been a true prophetess. However"—and this is a significant "however"—"it is more likely that she was the librarian" working in the college, which was "not the place to get a direct word from God." The Targum's legacy has seemingly posed both a problem and solution. Since "searchers for a stand up, speak out role for women may have found a librarian rather than a revealer of the Word of God," they cannot, therefore, claim her as "an authority for the feminist move on the church." What Huldah's librarian role does allow is that "women may be the best preservers of the Word (conservative) *as it has been written*."[20] The question remains: How to accommodate this Huldah, who was both a woman and a biblically recognized prophet? The search for solutions is never ending, although the conclusions are sometimes remarkably ancient. Renita Weems's suggestion that the point being made was, if "[e]ven a woman could see…that the kingdom was doomed

19. Online: www.jesus-messiah.com/w-preach/wp-ot-7.html, n.p. [cited 22 July 2008].

20. Online: www.piney.com/Huldah.html, n.p. [cited 22 July 2008], emphasis in original).

to disaster, why couldn't the leading men see the same thing?" (2003, 335), already has a long history, as noted above. Mary Joan Winn Leith's suggestion that Huldah may have been acceptable because she was post-menopausal may sound remarkably modern, but it draws on the ancient fear of women's sexuality.[21]

Second-wave feminism sent women looking for those who had been forgotten and overlooked, in the Bible as elsewhere. Huldah was waiting to be found, and put to use once more. She might have been surprised at the number of different Huldahs brought to light from the text's "end-less depth of meaning," although admittedly the complexities of her prophetic words already allowed for this. Rachel Neiman, for example, takes vv. 18–20 as revealing Huldah's compassion: although any true prophet, male or female, would have had to deliver the same message from God, a prophet "is at liberty to alter the tone of his or her message." Huldah chooses to show a "compassion that is the heritage of every Jewish woman" (2008, n.p.). For Leila Leah Bronner, this is motherly compassion. There may be no mention at all of Huldah as a mother in the texts but that does not matter: Huldah is metaphorically a mother, "because she offers comfort to a royal figure, King Josiah…mothering him in a time of national crisis." Nor was this private domestic mother-ing; Huldah acted as the "national mother…consulted on behalf of an entire nation." There is no contradiction with the role of prophet: both mothers and prophets "hail from the hand of God" and "are divinely given occupation." Why did Josiah consult her? Here imaginative gap-filling supplies an unexpected answer: Josiah was influenced by his godly mother Jedidah (2004, 87–89). For Virginia Ramey Mollenkott, it is Huldah speaking out God's Word, "calling for justice…challenging the ways things are, and bringing hope that a way can be found where there is no way." So, for her, Huldah "is the foremother of those daugh-ters called to prophesy within the ministry or as educators" (2000, n.p.). Similarly for Rachel Montagu, for women rabbis Huldah is 'a role model of a woman who hears the word of God and conveys it in words they can accept" (1994, 52). Brenner has Huldah herself say that she sees herself as "a forerunner" in the move for women "to officiate as rabbis and singers," although "not because I was a prophet, but because I had an office in the temple" (2005, 161).

---

21. So Mary Joan Winn Leith (2001, 328): "The prophets Deborah and Huldah were married women; perhaps they should be compared to post-menopausal women in other countries who become religious functionaries."

Women scholars are more concerned with Huldah as the interpreter of Scripture. Bronner, in a final paragraph, not only refers to Huldah as "the first and only person within the Bible who interprets a scroll found in the temple," but suggests that in doing this, she "issues in a new phase of textual analysis" (2004, 87–89). Phyllis Trible subtitled her article, "Huldah's Holy Writ, On Women and Biblical Authority"; on a canonically ordered reading, Huldah's oracle provides an answer to the question posed by Miriam: Has YHWH spoken only through Moses? While Huldah may be the Bible's first canoniser, Miriam had already protested, but she too is remembered as a prophet, so Trible's call here, as always, is "to liberate scripture from the confines of patriarchy and thereby claim its authority anew." In a rounding conclusion, she both warns and encourages: "prophets expect trouble and do not let it deter them. Surrounded by a cloud of witness, including Eve, Miriam, and Huldah, they pursue with joy the task that lies before them" (1985, 6–13). Claudia Camp's Huldah is very much embroiled in these issues of authority and interpretation. In the very act of verifying the lost book as the Word of God, she not only "authorized" Scripture, but, as prophet, authorized it to speak to the politics of her own day. She is, in effect, the prophetic contextual theologian, "speak[ing] Yahweh into powerful existence" for that time and place, with an "authority that rests in the interaction of the text and its interpreter" (1987, 100–101). If Adrien Janis Bledstein's suggestion were to be taken seriously, Huldah might even be a writer of Scripture as well as its authorizer and interpreter: "[r]ead as a woman's satirical narrative, the book of Judges is a trenchant criticism of human (most often male) arrogance. We might imagine Huldah designing this scroll to admonish the young monarch Josiah: 'Beware of he-who-would-be-God'" (1993, 54).

So far, I note no mention of the Asherah connection. Athalya Brenner has an imagined Huldah saying, "I myself served and loved the Asherah cult because it was so peaceful and family oriented" (2005, 156). In an earlier presentation in 2005, I tried to highlight the Asherah issue by having an Asherah-worshipping Huldah caught in the tension:

> I felt honoured when the notice came that Hilkiah the high priest and some other high ranking officials were about to bring this new book for me to read. I soon got the message there was an expectation that I would say in no uncertain terms that this was a genuine Word of God. I hadn't got too far through when I found myself reading that God's people were not to worship Him on the hills or under trees and that they were to burn the Asherah poles and any altars that had been built in those places, because they were signs of a worship of other gods. All this because God loved us,

set His heart on us and wanted us as His treasured possession (Deut 7:5–
8). What was I to do? I had been out to our local Asherah shrine just a few
days before—a whole group of us had gone there with Miriam who is
eight months pregnant and needed to pray for a safe delivery. What could I
say? What else could I do? The book itself was clear.

It is Diana Edelman who most imaginatively fills the Asherah gap:
Huldah may have been a prophet of Asherah rather than YHWH. Josiah
may have hesitated to inquire directly from YHWH and so chose the
female partner. This is the tender-hearted side of the divine, rather than
the tender-hearted prophet. But if Huldah was Asherah's prophet, how
could she then have pronounced the judgment that led to the goddess'
removal and destruction? Edelman smartly dismisses any problem: the
Deuteronomistic words were written in for her, at the time a later post-
exilic writer "made Huldah a spokesperson for the sole ruler of heaven,
Yahweh" (1994, 250).

While Edelman's Huldah is exonerated, the Deuteronomist's Huldah
remains disturbing. For, in the final form of 2 Kings, it is she who sets in
place the destruction of the Asherah. According to Jer 44, if the Queen of
Heaven can be assumed to be Asherah, she was not entirely successful,
but this is not the point. As it is written, her judgment regarding the
divine Word is responsible for the so-called reform that follows immediately in the next chapter. If this has an historical base, then, as John
Collins states, it "immediately…changed the nature of Israelite religion"
(2004, 166). Whether this was so or not, this is the way the biblical
account presents it. So, too, biblical references would imply that Asherah
was particularly associated with women.[22] The resulting account in
2 Kings thus presents her as a woman caught in the position of ruling
against women's interest. It was this I had in mind in a paper I wrote
comparing the Deuteronomistic ploy of using Huldah to voice their own
theological "orthodoxy" with a political move in my own context of
Aotearoa New Zealand (2005b).[23] Once again this was "no detached

22.   One notes women weaving vestments for Asherah in the Jerusalem Temple
(2 Kgs 23:7) and Maʿacah, the queen mother, having "an abominable image" made
for her (1 Kgs 15:13).

23.   This was a case of cultural interest rather than gender, although it did involve
women, but the strategy was remarkably similar: three Maori women members of
parliament were being pressured to vote against their own cultural understandings in
a bill concerning ownership of the seabed and foreshore. One of the women, Tariana
Turia, left the party, stayed in parliament as an independent and went on to form a
new Maori Party, committed to repeal the ensuing ruling. At the time of writing a
committee has been set up by the present government to review the Seabed and
Foreshore Act.

interpretation." Perhaps it was not interpretation at all, but simply taking a text out of its own world and putting it to use in another. Perhaps I was simply following the Deuteronomists, who employed, if not created, a Huldah for their own purposes.

This brief, and selective, overview has revealed a host of readers who have found in Huldah either an ally or a problem for their own theologically desired "orthodoxies" or their own interests as biblical readers and teachers. Her world has been filled with details that would have amazed and surprised her, while her tasks have been reduced or expanded according to the needs of those who have followed in the steps of Josiah and employed her once again. Away from the Temple and overshadowed by Josiah she may been, yet a myriad of readers have not only visited the Deuteronomists' Huldah, but have reshaped and reused her for their own purposes, time and time again over the centuries. Huldah remains in use indeed.

Paradoxes of Prophetic Language in Isaiah[*]

Francis Landy

> But prophetic speech announces an impossible future.
> —Maurice Blanchot

> Hear intently, but do not understand;
> See attentively, but do not perceive;
> Make fat the heart of this people, make its ears heavy,
> Glaze over its eyes/make its eyes gaze;
> Lest it see with its eyes, and hear with its ears,
> And its heart understands, and it turn and be healed. (Isa 6:9–10)

> My strategy in this study has been to preserve both the presence and the
> remoteness of the Book of Isaiah.
> —Edgar Conrad

My reading of Isaiah is, at first sight, very different from Ed Conrad's. Ed divides the book into two parts: the Vision (chs. 6–39) and the Book (chs. 1–5; 40–66), the latter of which decodes the former. If the primary audience was meant to be baffled by the vision, subsequent readers, who had before them the entire book, were intended to understand it. "The occasion for reading the vision of Isaiah is the renewed command to read in 40:6, when the vision of Isaiah can be read aloud to a receptive audience" (Conrad 1991, 156). But then for contemporary readers, such as Conrad himself, it is once again "alien," since it comes from a remote past, whose literary conventions are strange and not entirely known to us (158). Moreover, there never was an original audience, or any one that can be identified (156). And while Conrad rejects a theory of absolute textual indeterminacy (164),[1] he does acknowledge that for us the Bible has "a plurality of meanings" (168).

* The original version of this study was delivered at the International SBL Meeting in Auckland in July 2008. I think of it as my Antipodean study in more senses than one. Thanks are due to the Support for the Advancement of Scholarship program at the University of Alberta for facilitating travel to the conference.

1. Conrad (1991, 158–59) identifies this approach with that of Derrida. However, that is to misunderstand Derrida. Derrida, indeed, is distinguished by extremely

On the other hand, Conrad (1991, 132–33) acknowledges that the vision is repeatedly associated with the book, for instance in 29:11 and 30:8. One cannot separate the two so easily, and I find the neat division between the vision and the book to be too categorical. Vision and book are synonymous, as the first verse tells us,[2] and antithetical; the text translates the vision into a book, and leads us from the book to the vision. Similarly, vision and audition are metaphors for each other, as well as referring to different domains of sensory experience, since what is seen is something heard: "Hear, O heavens, and give ear, O earth."[3]

But I also find the concept of the book to be too unquestioned. In its massiveness and totality the book of Isaiah exerts an extraordinary gravitational force upon its reader, whom it persuades of the unity of the vision through such ploys as the correspondence of the first and last chapter, and even more by its presence as a book. Of course, two or more centuries of critical endeavour have sought to dissect that unity, just as recent redaction criticism has tried to show that the book is the result of a conscious editorial process. Nonetheless, the book as a self-contained, aesthetic whole, and as an expression of the unity and comprehensibility of the world, is an achievement which is both partial and wish-fulfilling. We want the book to make sense. But to make sense, in any way that is not trivial, it has to confront the particularity and contingency of the world, and the failure of metanarratives, notably the metanarrative of Israelite election in the wake of catastrophe. To go from destruction to exile to restoration, to dream of the impossible future, to quote Blanchot (2003, 79), means that the book is an aspiration, something of which our book is a fragmentary and imperfect forerunner. Hence the images of the ideal book within the book.[4]

The tension between the vision and the book, and the possibility of finding an adequate language for the prophetic experience, is encapsulated in my other epigraph, and indeed in the chapter of which it is part

precise readings of texts. That Derrida does not believe that there is any single, ultimate truth does not mean that he thinks that all interpretations are valid. For the influence of Derrida on biblical studies, see especially Sherwood 2004.

2. "Vision" is used as a title for prophetic books in Obad 1 and Nah 1. Some think it is a dead metaphor, e.g., Ben Zvi (1996, 12) and the long discussion by Williamson (2005, 18–19). For the view that it is a poetic symbol, see Melugin (2009, 9) and Miscall (1993, 12, 22).

3. See in particular my article, "Vision and Voice in Isaiah" (Landy 2000; 2001, 371–91), and Carroll 1997.

4. Examples include 29:11–12 and 34:16. I discuss this topic at length in my 2011 article, "The Book that Cannot Be Read."

(Conrad 1991, esp. 160), with its account of Isaiah's initiatory vision and vocation:[5]

> Hear intently, but do not understand;
> See attentively, but do not perceive;
> Make fat the heart of this people, make its ears heavy,
> Glaze over its eyes/make its eyes gaze;
> Lest it see with its eyes, and hear with its ears,
> And its heart understands, and it turn and be healed.

These verses are among the most famous and the most puzzling in the book. They constitute what one may call a "metapoetics" of the book, in other words a statement on the book's own status as poetry.[6] It is a key to how to read or not to read the book, to the author's intentions, and to the primal encounter, whether one of opposition or of congruity, between the prophet and God. Since it is introduced at the very beginning of the prophet's mission, as indicated by the words, "Go, say to this people"—whether or not it is chronologically his first prophecy—it conditions all the subsequent discourse. However, it results in a double bind: the prophet is sent to communicate and not to communicate at the same time. If the prophet's role is that of a divine emissary, charged with transmitting the divine word to the people so as to lead them to act in accordance with the divine will, the prophet thereby becomes an anti-prophet, who negates the very *raison d'être* of prophecy. To the extent that he does communicate, in poetry of extraordinary intensity and urgency, he is in contravention of the divine will, or at least has failed to adequately obfuscate his message.

---

5.   There is some scholarly discussion about the genre of ch. 6, which need not concern us here. For a summary of views, see Sweeney 1996, 136. The question is whether this is in fact Isaiah's initiatory vision, corresponding to Jer 1 and Ezek 1–3, and if so, why it is displaced from the beginning of the book. Some scholars, such as Milgrom (1964), believe that it was chronologically preceded by chs. 1–5. There is no reason, however, to think that the literary structure of the book corresponds to the sequence of its composition, at least in any mechanical way, and much reason not to. There is a well-known rabbinic principle of *'ein muqdam ume'uḥar batorah*: "there is no before or after in the Torah." Vermeylen (1977, 191–92) notes that the dating formula is evidence of its initiatory status. Whatever its position in Isaiah's literary career, its vocational character is clear. For imaginative, fictional accounts of the scene, see Magonet (1991, 92–97) and my own pseudo-autobiography of Isaiah, "Ghostwriting Isaiah" (2001, 392–413; 2002).

6.   The concept of the metalinguistic function of language comes from Jakobson. For its application to biblical prophecy, see Ben Zvi (2003), who argues that Jonah is a metaprophetic book, which comments on all other prophetic books and the institution of prophecy itself. See also Ben Zvi (2009b, 95). An interesting study of Job as metaprophecy is James Harding (2010).

The prophet's double bind is matched by an equally exigent one on the part of the people: "Hear intently, but do not understand; see attentively, but do not perceive." Whatever will they have to repent and be healed will be manifested by their failure to repent and be healed. If they faithfully understand the divine command and thus do not understand, they have understood; correspondingly, they may understand through failing or refusing to heed the injunction, and thus have not understood. Moreover, we might not understand what it is to understand, hear, and see. If the people are instructed to hear and see with the utmost intensity, and not to understand and perceive, then their hearing and seeing becomes a non-hearing and non-seeing. Prophetic vision and audition is then a deconstruction of normal or conventional sight and sound. In other words, everything seen and heard in ch. 6, and by implication the entire book, despite its rhetorical persuasiveness, is rendered incomprehensible.

The problem is compounded by v. 10. There the prophet is commanded to work on the consciousness of the people to prevent their understanding: "Make fat the heart of this people, make its ears heavy, glaze its eyes…" The people only apparently have the capacity faithfully not to understand or perceive, since their will is preempted by the prophet and God. God instructs them to understand not to understand, and makes it impossible for them to do so. In that case, every word carries an implicit rider: this does not mean what it says, it may be a ruse to deceive us. But that might also be true of these verses themselves, each of whose familiar words may have radically different meanings.[7]

There are a number of interpretative problems. The first is the relationship of the prophet and God. The prophet, as a person, has a human allegiance. The prophet's will might not conform to the divine will, and as such he might be the site of resistance. Throughout the book Isaiah is focalized as an independent personality, if only through such annotations as "This I heard" (e.g. 21:10; 28:22).[8] In ch. 6, in particular, we experience him seeing, listening, and responding, and are invited to imagine his consciousness. Many years ago, Peter Ackroyd (1978) argued that Isaiah

---

7.   Schenker (1986, esp. 586) explores the contradiction between the commission to deceive the people and the communication of that commission, which leads to a version of the paradox of the Cretan liar.

8.   I am including under the label "Isaiah" all the prophetic voices in the book. Several critics think that the first person voices in Deutero- and Trito-Isaiah are modelled on that of Isaiah e.g. for Trito-Isaiah, Berges (2008, 91); Childs (2001, 296); Goldingay (2005, 6); and Zapff (2006). Sommer (1998), on the contrary, holds that the most important antecedent for Deutero-Isaiah (to whom he also attributes Trito-Isaiah) is Jeremiah. Baltzer (2001, 20–22) thinks that the Servant in Deutero-Isaiah is based on Moses.

in chs. 1–12 is a fictive character, created as an ideal or representative prophet; the success of the portrait accounts for that of the book, to which more and more material was attached.[9] Unlike Moses, Amos and Jeremiah, he does not have an overtly intercessory function.[10] However, he expresses grief over the destruction, both of his own people (e.g. 22:3) and of the nations condemned through his words (e.g. chs. 16, 21) as well as anticipatory joy (e.g. 12:1). He acts,[11] speaks, claims various roles for himself,[12] constructs an intermittent biography, whether in the first or third person. We do not know whether and when his words faithfully transmit the divine speech, whether there is room for divergence and interpretation. At any rate, the prophet's interposition between God and the people makes us aware of his complex origins, as a messenger of God and a human person, of potentially divided loyalties. We cannot but be aware, too, that it is Isaiah who reports his experience, including his commission, perhaps giving it his own twist.

Second, there is the relationship of God with himself. God, in this text, is apparently utterly malevolent; on the other hand, he does wish to send someone, according to 6:8 ("whom shall I send? who will go for us?), even if only with a message of despair, and he does reveal, to us as well as to the prophet and to "this people,"[13] the desire to obstruct meaning. If you wish to instil incomprehension, what is the point of disclosing this wish? The split in the prophet's personality would then be duplicated by one in God, between, for instance, his commitment to humanity and Israel and his rage against them.[14] These imperil both the unitary vision of the divine and the possibility of a happy ending for the book.[15]

9.   See also Ackroyd (1982), who extends the argument to chs. 36–39, which are consciously modelled on the encounter, with Ahaz in ch. 7. See also the discussion in Conrad (1991, 34–46) on the relationship of the two narratives. However, I disagree with Conrad that "As a character…Isaiah plays an insignificant background role throughout the Book of Isaiah" (1991, 35).

10.   For the intercessory function of prophets, see, e.g., Exod 32–34; Amos 7–8; Jer 4:9–10. Jeremiah is prohibited from interceding on the people's behalf, implying that is a normal prophetic role (14:10–11). See further Muffs (1992, 9–48).

11.   For instance, he has intercourse with "the prophetess" (8:3), walks naked for three years (ch. 20), and heals a king (38:21, 22)

12.   For example, he claims to be a "sign" (8:18), "a light to nations" (42:6; 49:6, 8), and a comforter (61:3).

13.   Many scholars remark that "this people" indicates alienation. See, for example, Kaiser (1983, 131) and Clements (1980, 76). Conrad (1991, 132) notes that "the community incapable of receiving the vision of Isaiah is referred to as 'this people'."

14.   Similarly, Nielsen (1986, 6) remarks that, rather than a conflict between YHWH and Isaiah or between them and the people, Isa 6 presents an internal drama, both within YHWH and the prophet, and between the will to communicate and the

Third, there is a limit to the period of incomprehension, even if it is projected beyond the end of the book. Chapter 6, for instance, ends with an answer to Isaiah's question in 6:11, "How long, my Lord?," with the return or repentance of the survivors in 6:13, even if it is indefinitely deferred.[16] Many scholars think that Deutero- and Trito-Isaiah systematically reverse the language and imagery of Proto-Isaiah, and portend an age of clarity and understanding.[17] However, these too may be subject to the interdict, and may be a lure set to destroy us.

Fourth, there are the innumerable passages in Isaiah which are relatively clear, such as those in which God looks for justice and righteousness and imagines ideal worlds. Are they too subject to the prohibition and injunction? These could be evidence of the prophet's failure or refusal to carry out the divine decree,[18] or alternatively, of divine reluctance to be bound by it. Then it would be a sign of intra-divine dialogue. On the other hand, it may be that these passages are misleading in their very clarity. Then the critical task would become impossible, because the book refers to the impossible future, entirely discontinuous with our world, and because we are the intended audience, or at least identify with the intended audience, and thus must not understand, even if we are capable of it.

There are various ways of attempting to resolve these problems, all of which are productive of insight, though each leaves some intractable issues. One approach is diachronic. For example, Hanna Liss, in her recent book *Die Unerhöhrte Prophetie*, argues that the people do not understand, because the prophet comes from and signifies a different reality. All he can do is to tell them that they cannot understand, that nothing is as it seems; to understand, and thus to pass from this age to the next, would mean undoing all the structures of knowledge in order to start afresh. Liss (2002, 19, 281) says that this is a mark of immense respect for the audience, who are challenged to attempt to understand

desire not to: "both Yhwh and Isaiah emerge as characters distinguished by deep inner tensions."

15.   In later Jewish thought this is articulated in the bifurcation between the aspects of justice (*middat haddin*) and compassion (*middat harahamim*).

16.   Isa 6:13 is multiply ambiguous (Landy 1999, 76–79). Conrad calls Isaiah "the first of the survivors" (1991, 110–13).

17.   There are many variations of this approach. See Clements (1982, 1985) and Laato (1998). For a detailed case that ch. 6 was introduced as a preface and antithesis to Deutero-Isaiah, see Williamson (1994, 30–56).

18.   For instance, Tsevat (1980, 171–74) argues that insofar as Isaiah's prophecies are intelligible and directed towards repentance, they are in opposition to God's will, and that thereby Isaiah shows himself paradoxically "loyal to his master" (174).

even as they know that they may be preconditioned not to understand, and that they are prohibited from understanding despite the intensity with which they listen and look. The imperative "Hear intently" is as important as "do not understand." The secret is a temptation, since once they know that there is a secret hidden in the words they will attempt to unveil it. Once they know it is a panacea—that it will bring them healing and avert disaster, and that repentance will compel God to retract—its denial will make it the object of forbidden desire, even if they faithfully avert their eyes from it. She divides ch. 6 into two parts: the Vision (6:1–8) and the Commission (6:9–13). The second negates the first. Whereas the vision draws upon the imagery of the Jerusalem Temple to communicate an entirely traditional theophany, the commission subverts all the expectations associated with it.[19] According to Liss, the trajectory from the affirmation that the plenitude of the world is, or is the manifestation of, the divine glory,[20] to the desolation predicted in vv. 11–12, marks that from a locative to a utopian theology, to borrow Jonathan Z. Smith's terminology for the moment.[21] Through the course of her book, she shows how metaphors, biographical anecdotes, and prophetic signs serve as agents of defamiliarization,[22] since they are used to destabilize the symbolic world they constitute, for example, when Isaiah parodies the language of Assyrian imperial propaganda.

What Isaiah introduces, Liss argues, is a "theopolitical revolution" (2002, 270–89), through which God is detached from national history and ideology and becomes universal. The message of the prophet, and with it that of Judaism, does not depend on state power, and thus, unlike Assur,

19. For a book-length study of this imagery as well as its subversion, see Hartenstein (1997). Other exemplary studies are by Williamson (2006), Müller (1992), and Keel (1977, 46–123).

20. Most contemporary scholars take מְלֹא in 6:3 to be a noun, "plenitude," rather than the more traditional adjective, "full" (cf. Williamson 2006). This, however, does not accord with the use of the word in vv. 1 and 4, where it is clearly adjectival.

21. One of Jonathan Smith's most productive ideas is the contrast between "locative" religions, which are founded on a sense of sacred space, and "utopian" ones, which transcend space, developed in his collection *Map is Not Territory* (1978), especially in his essay "The Wobbling Pivot" (1978, 88–103). A valuable discussion and critique of the dichotomy in the light of later developments in Smith's thought is Parrish (2010).

22. A good summary for English readers is to be found in Liss's 2002 article "Undisclosed Speech: Patterns of Communication in Book of Isaiah," which focuses on the rhetorical techniques whereby defamiliarization is accomplished. The term "defamiliarization" is derived from the Russian Formalists and was popularized in the West by Structuralist poetics, for which deviation from conventional language characterized poetry.

God will survive the demise of the Israelite kingdoms. The "theopolitical revolution," in fact, consists entirely of the prophet's language and his impact on world history. Thus, Liss (2002, 69–70) radically separates the political and social aspects of Isaiah's thought. For her, the command to block understanding applies solely to Isaiah's interventions in politics, which is why it occurs in ch. 6, as an introduction to the *Denkschrift* of chs. 6–8, which primarily concern the Syro-Ephraimite crisis.[23]

A second approach to the problem might be termed "mystical." Isaiah's vision in ch. 6, and indeed the whole book, is typical of mystical discourse, which attempts to translate the experience of the ineffable into human language. Hence the paradoxes of a poetic/prophetic language which seeks to express what cannot be said. The problem is compounded by the transgressive implications of the metaphor of being "impure of lips" (6:5), which renders human speech sacrilegious. Not only is it impossible to communicate the vision, it may also be prohibited. Yet Isaiah must do so.

Elliot Wolfson, in his book *Language, Eros, Being*, writes that in mystical texts the concealed is revealed, but only as the concealed in the revealed.[24] The revelation of the secret embeds it further, since the revelation discloses a mystery that may be the subject of infinite interpretation and reveiling. The mystery is unknown, or else it is known and no longer a mystery. If the secret is that Israel will be destroyed, and that the path to avoid it is through justice and righteousness, then it is divulged in 6:11–12, and indeed from the very beginning of the book. The secret is no secret at all. If it is something else, then it is a hidden supplement to the words of the book and the vision from which it emanates. In other words, the words of the book point back to an experience whose meaning is unknown, and which threatens to destroy us.

Isaiah 6 is a classic instance of what Rudolf Otto called the *mysterium tremendum et fascinans*, as the basis of the idea of the holy.[25] The

---

23. Liss attributes this shift to later redaction, rather than chronological priority of the first five chapters, unlike Milgrom (1964) and Kaplan (1926). She notes that the expression העם הזה, "this people," is found exclusively in political contexts. For the somewhat eccentric view that Isaiah's social criticism is in fact an allegory for his politics (and the even more eccentric view that the Syro-Ephraimite crisis is an allegory of the Assyrian one!) see Bäckersten (2008) and the review by Kim (2010).

24. "The secret necessarily exemplifies (a) double bind, for the secret can be a secret only to the extent that it is hidden, but the secret can be hidden only to the extent that it is revealed" (Wolfson 2005, 164). The book is full of such apothegms.

25. "If a man does not *feel* what the numinous is, when he reads the sixth chapter of Isaiah, then no 'preaching, singing, telling' can avail him" (Otto 1923, 63). Otto insists that the experience of the holy cannot be rationally communicated.

seraphim call, "Holy, holy, holy is YHWH of Hosts, the whole earth is full of his glory" (6:3), but Isaiah reacts with horror: "Woe is me, for I am destroyed/silenced…for the king, YHWH of Hosts, my eyes have seen" (6:5).[26] To see the face of God is to die, according to a well-established tradition.[27] There is then a gap between the inaugural vision and the word and world that emanate from it, between the death Isaiah's gaze portends and the fullness of existence the seraphim celebrate. The vision is both fascinating (*fascinans*), since it is the creative centre of the book, and something to be avoided at all costs.[28] This ambivalence is typical of many mystical traditions; the mystical quest is dangerous, because it can lead to death. But this is also true of poetry. Hélène Cixous (1993, 59) writes, after quoting Kafka, that reading "should wake us up with a blow to the head," that "whoever wants to write must be able to reach this lightening region that takes your breath away." For Cixous, writing is, first of all, the confrontation with death.[29] For her, in contrast to Isaiah— but also with him—"what we hope for…is to look straight at the face of God, *which is none other than my own face…*" (italics original).

Then the mystery—that which makes us tremble, as Jacques Derrida says, and is the hidden reference of the seraphim's triple "holy," whose piling on indicates indescribability—is of death in the midst of life, of prophecy and history as a lethal trap for Israel.[30] So on the one hand, we have the mystery, with its absorption and annihilation of the prophet's gaze, and on the other the possibility that there is no mystery at all, nothing at all, the abyss of meaninglessness and despair that is the hidden voice of Isaiah. To put it differently, Isaiah denies the exile and is an all-encompassing poem of exile.[31]

---

26. For the ambiguity of כי נדמיתי, "for I am destroyed/silenced," see Roberts 1992, 44–46.

27. See, for example, Exod 33:20: "No human can see me and live." There are two stories which assume the fatal consequences of seeing the divine: Gen 32:31, after Jacob's struggle at Peniel, and Judg 13:22–23, in Samson's annunciation narrative. In 1 Sam 6:19, the very sight of the Ark of the Covenant causes the death of the inhabitants of Beth-Shemesh.

28. In my article "Strategies of Concentration and Diffusion in Isaiah 6" (1999), I analyzed the techniques whereby the description deflects the gaze through synecdoche and metonymy. We never actually see what Isaiah sees. Instead our attention is redirected to his skirts, the seraphim, their wings, their voices, and so on.

29. The first part of *Three Steps on the Ladder of Writing* is called "The School of the Dead."

30. This is a frequent motif in eighth-century prophecy. See Amos 3:3–8; Hos 7:12; 9:8; and Isa 8:13–14 and 28:13. (On Hosea, see Landy 1995, 15, 116–17.)

31. On this, see Landy (2010).

Another, rather widespread, explication of the strange commission is psychological, the *Rückprojizierungsthese* or retrojection hypothesis, which goes back to Mordechai Kaplan (1926) in Anglophone scholarship and Franz Hesse (1955) in the German tradition.[32] According to this thesis, Isaiah retrospectively imputed the command to God, so as to account for the failure of his mission. This approach is similar to the diachronic one, in that the comprehension is deferred, except that the process of understanding and justification is held to take place in the prophet rather than the reader. The prophet is the first interpreter, or reader, of his experience. Clearly it depends on more or less fictional reconstructions of the prophet's biography. Exponents differ as to whether the period of incomprehension is limited to the so-called *Denkschrift*, Isaiah's Memoir of the Syro-Ephraimite crisis in chs. 6–8, or covers his entire career.[33] The reference to sealing the instruction in "my disciples" in 8:16 differentiates the receptive and non-receptive audiences, as well as the time of fulfilment from that of latency. The prophet "waits" and "hopes" for YHWH, who "hides his face from the house of Jacob" (8:17). According to the *Rückprojizierungsthese*, this first record of the prophecy is the nucleus of the book.[34] The prophet writes it down, for his disciples, until it should become comprehensible, and as evidence for his authenticity.

There are many things wrong with this hypothesis. For one thing, Isaiah uniquely among the prophets does not present himself as a failure. Second, it does not solve any problems. The command to block understanding and the prohibition of doing so is as baffling whether we attribute it to God or Isaiah. It merely saves God from theological absurdity by transferring it to the prophet. But it does point to something very important. That is, as Barthel (1997, 115–17) says, every account of an experience, especially of mystical experience, is a process of interpretation, revision, and transmission. It translates the ineffable into language. We are always explaining ourselves to ourselves and to others.

When will the "witness" (תעודה) be realized? It might be very short term indeed, if the reference is to the overthrow of Aram and Israel, as

32. Gruber (2004) traces Kaplan's view to medieval Jewish sources and contrasts it with Heschel's insistence on Isaiah's empathetic response to the vision.

33. Barthel (1997, 106–11), for instance, thinks that the commission only applied to the *Denkschrift*, while Blum (1996/97) argues that it was composed, together with most of chs. 2–11, late in his career.

34. For recent discussions, see Barthel (1997, 233–36); Blenkinsopp (2000, 243–44); and Beuken (2003, 231). Carr (2005, 60) does not think תעודה need refer to written testimony; see, however, Blum (1997, 27), who adduces 8:1–2, where the witness is clearly written, and Clements (2000).

the narrative of the birth of Maher-Shallal-Hash-Baz suggests. Or it may be infinitely protracted. Several scholars have argued that, once written, the text of Isaiah tended to attract esoteric interpretations.[35] Far from being an agent of clarification, it becomes one of mystification. The *Rückprojizierungsthese* is here turned on its head. The "strange command" of 6:9–10 is no longer composed in order to account for the discrepancy between the vision and the disappointment of the prophet's expectations. Instead it becomes part of the vision, poetically articulated to amplify its strangeness. In other words, the prophet sets us a puzzle, like a *koan*, we can never resolve, for instance through pervasive ambiguity.[36]

Another approach is ethical. Isaiah's vision is ontological and aesthetic: the glory fills the earth, corresponds to the plenitude of existence, and emanates from God who is its transcendent origin. On the other hand, the command is ethical: this is the way you must speak to and act toward the people, and tell them how to respond, in order paradoxically that they should not respond, return, and be healed. Then what the chapter inscribes is the passage from ontology to ethics. This is close to the philosophy of Emmanuel Levinas, for whom Isaiah's "Here I am, send me" in 6:8 is the prototype of the ethical relation (1998, 146), characterized by the openness of *Le Dire*, a pre-originary responsiveness to everything that God will call upon him to say. This accords with Levinas's watchword "ethics as first philosophy" (1989; see also Peperzak 1995), and the view that the prophets primarily teach ethical responsibility for the Other, for the poor and destitute.[37] For Levinas, the divine glory consists precisely in ethical responsibility, which is also a self-abnegation on the part of God, since the passivity of God is the precondition of absolute human freedom, on which ethical responsibility is founded (1998, 140–52). Glory is the opposite of the glory of the divine pleroma the seraphim celebrate, or at least it is to be understood differently.

---

35.   Blenkinsopp has devoted a monograph to this subject (Blenkinsopp 2006). See also Sonnet (1992, 234–35), who suggests that the openness to further interpretation is a sign of a rejection of the determinacy of apocalyptic, and Ferry (2008, 34–35).

36.   For the pervasive ambiguities of 6:9–10, see, in particular, Landy (1999, 71–72). I have tried to communicate the double meaning of שעע/השעע, which may mean either "to look" or "to smear over (the eyes)" in my translation above, "Glaze over the eyes/make the eyes gaze."

37.   A favourite if grotesque image of Levinas's is of offering the bread from one's own mouth (e.g. 1998, 74). Levinas cites one's duty to the naked and homeless in Isa 58.

This approach has some similarity to that of Hanna Liss, and likewise draws upon Jewish tradition.[38] However, while Liss sees the transition as being primarily political, for Levinas it is ethical and social. For Levinas, indeed, politics and the demands of social justice pertain to the reciprocity of social relations, posterior to the immediacy of *me voici* ("Here I am"), the unconditioned readiness of the ethical encounter.

Then the "strange command" of 6:9–10 points not only to a language of the future, but the irreducibility of any speech to a message that can be communicated. *Le Dire*, in Levinas's thought, is opposed to *Le Dit*, the totality of all that has been and can be said (1998, 5–8). To speak in any way comprehensible to the audience, for instance in the language of myth and ontology, would be to turn God into an object, a "theme," something that can be said (1998, 149–50). For Levinas, this is idolatry. Of course, it cannot be avoided. For example, ch. 6 is a story, with a beginning, middle, and end. However, it is a story which is about the disruption of every unity, every narrative, by the call of the Other.

The two parts of the chapter correlate and intersect, exemplifying the transfers and shifts of meaning. The word כבוד, "glory," recurs in הכבד את עיניו, "make its ears heavy" in 6:10, an image that suggests not only deafness or perhaps drowsiness, but also a self-glorification that precludes recognition of the divine glory.[39] Analogously, in 3:8, the strange expression למרות עני כבודו, "to rebel against the eyes of his glory," evokes a refusal of God's gaze, manifested in his care for the poor, YHWH's vineyard. Another example is the motif of seeing and hearing. Isaiah "sees" YHWH in v. 1; he describes the seraphim; we imagine the scene of his initiation. Similarly, he hears the voice of the seraphim, and YHWH speaking in v. 8. At the same time, both "seeing" and "hearing" are ambivalent. The Temple quakes from the sound of the seraphim (6:4); Isaiah's vision incurs the fear of death. This ambivalence, compounded by ambiguity, is transposed to the repeated occurrences of "seeing" and "hearing" in the commission. Whatever else might be said about the doubling of ראו ראו, literally "seeing, see," and שמעו שמוע, "hearing, hear," it suggests something other than normal hearing and seeing, corresponding, for instance, to the ideal ruler of ch. 11, who judges "not according to the appearance of the eyes" or "the hearing of the ears" (11:3).

---

38. For a detailed study of Levinas's Jewish sources, see Ajzenstat (2001).

39. See Magonet (1985, 94), who sees it as an instance of irony, and Sonnet (1992, 223).

Chapter 6, as I have mentioned, is disseminated throughout the book, and there have been several studies devoted to its permutations.[40] It would not be possible to pursue them here. The various approaches I have mentioned—mystical, theopolitical, diachronic, ethical—are likewise projected and amplified in the book, as are the problems to which they respond. One may note, for instance, the democratization of the Davidic covenant in Deutero-Isaiah (esp. 55:3), and the disappearance of the international stage in Trito-Isaiah as evidence of the "theopolitical" revolution; or the blind servant in Deutero-Isaiah, whose task it is to bring illumination to the world (42:19; 42:6–7; 49:6, 8). More generally, the trajectory from the vision to the book comprises a process of revision, retrojection, and explication, through which the vision is accommodated in human thought.

Nonetheless, none of the problems disappear. At the end of the book, the apparently godfearing community complains to God, who has deliberately led them astray (63:17; 64:4). The last chapters are dominated by "the sense of the ending," and the inability to conclude.[41]

But is closure possible? If the command is given to a fictive historical Isaiah, does it apply to his successors? Then the speech is attributed to others, disciples or bystanders, at any rate the audience, as well as to God. The "vision" of Isaiah implicitly includes all subsequent visions in the book, so that "Isaiah" sees, speaks for, and authorizes his remote intellectual posterity. We can then go back to Liss's theory, according to which the book, especially as writing, is a provocation (2002, 203–9), that arouses an expectation of meaning and calls the audience into being, as well as to the retrojection hypothesis, in particular if we give it a twist, following A. J. Heschel, enabling insight into God's thoughts and feelings (however we imagine God).[42] Then we are left with proliferating interpretations of Isa 6, which transpose and displace it, put it into a new context, apperceiving it—in accordance with the instructions in 6:10—and gazing intensely through it.

40.   In addition to the work of Williamson (1994, 30–56), one should note the formative study of Rendtorff (1993). Sweeney (1996, 136), following Melugin (1976, 83–84), describes ch. 6 as "a paradigm for Isaiah's entire prophetic career." See also Aitken (1993) and the monograph of Evans (1989), which focuses on its post-biblical history.

41.   Unpacking this statement would require a separate article. On the difficulty of ending in Isaiah, see Clements (2002).

42.   Gruber (2004), in particular, contrasts Kaplan's projection theory with Heschel's empathetic one, which he relates to transpersonal psychology. See especially Heschel (2001, 285–98).

HEARING THE WORD OF GOD IN ISAIAH 1 AND 65–66:
A SYNCHRONIC APPROACH

Se-Hoon Jang

Introduction

Recent decades have seen a major paradigm shift taking place in Isaiah studies. This shift has moved away from reading the book of Isaiah as coming from different sources to interpreting it as a unitary whole.[1] It is worth noting that many biblical scholars have not been satisfied with historical-critical methods that tend to divide the book of Isaiah into three or more documents and have sought to find an alternative way of reading it as a coherent entity. Particular attention has been paid to several key factors for the unity of the book of Isaiah. One method focuses attention on the intention of a redactor(s) who is responsible for shaping the book as a whole (see Clements 1996 and Sweeney 1996). It is claimed that the book of Isaiah was editorially designed as one book by the final redactor.

Some insist that the book of Isaiah be read as it stands, since only its final form is authoritative for the Church (e.g. Childs 2001; Rendtorff 1993; Seitz 1991, 1998). The final-form of Isaiah is seen to be a starting point for reading it as a canonical whole. Unlike canonical critics, however, several biblical commentators espouse various literary approaches committed to reading the book of Isaiah as a unified text (Conrad 1991; Darr 1994; Watts 2005; Webb 1990). They avoid reconstructing the underlying sources of the book of Isaiah such as First, Second and Third Isaiahs and the historical background of each of these documents. Rather, they adhere to a synchronic reading based on literary indicators of the unity of the book of Isaiah such as repetition in vocabulary, recurring motifs, rhetorical patterns and so on.

---

1. For a full discussion of recent studies on the book of Isaiah, see Williamson (2009). See also Tate (1996) and Williamson (1994). For a helpful discussion of the unity of the book of Isaiah, see Conrad (1991). See also Melugin and Sweeney 1996.

It is commonly agreed, furthermore, that Isa 1 and 65–66 play a particularly key role in understanding the book of Isaiah as a whole. It is interesting to note that a deep division between the righteous and the wicked coincidently appears at the beginning and the end of the book of Isaiah. It should be taken into account that in these sections the two conflicting parties' future is dependent on how they respond to the Torah, the word of God. It is assumed that the importance of hearing the word of God in Isa 1 and 65–66 has to do with the overall message of the book of Isaiah. The purpose of this article is to show a concise overview of recent studies on Isa 1 and 65–66 and focus on a sharp conflict between the two opposing sides in these chapters. Special emphasis is placed on the different responses to the word of God that are illustrated in chs. 7 and 36–39 (the royal narratives), where two kings (Ahaz and Hezekiah) are confronted by the prophet Isaiah, who delivers the word of God.

Isaiah 1 and 65–66 in Recent Study

Though the sections (Isa 1 and 65–66) have been dealt with by many scholars, it was Liebreich (1955–56) who paved a new avenue for studying these texts.[2] He concludes that terminological parallels between Isa 1 and 65–66 form an inclusion for the whole book of Isaiah. In his 1973 paper, Lack (1973, 139–42) treads in Liebreich's footsteps by looking at the two sections. He agrees with Liebreich that both Isa 1 and 65–66 uncover serious problems in Judah such as corrupted rites and idolatry (1:29–31; 66:17), which result in a sharp separation between the righteous who receive a new name (65:15) and the impious who will be put to shame (1:29; 66:5) and burned with an unquenchable fire (1:31; 66:24). However, close attention is drawn to some important differences between Isa 1 and 65–66. Given the fact that several themes in Isa 65–66, such as the cosmic order centered on the holy mountain (65:25), the incredible fertility of the people (66:7–9) and the worldwide revelation of God's glory (66:23), are not set forth in Isa 1, considerable dissimilarities between the two sections are undeniable.[3]

---

2. For a helpful discussion of Liebreich's approach to Isa 1 and 65–66, see Carr (1996).

3. Sweeney points out that Lack's approach to Isa 1 is problematic due to the lack of a full discussion on Isa 1:29–31 which is an integral part of Isa 1. His criticism of Lack is that Lack has dismissed the fact that the writer(s) of Isa 65–66 utilized Isa 1:29–31 in order to describe the judgment against the apostates and the triumph for the righteous. For an analysis of the relationship between Isa 1:29–31 and Isa 65–66, see Sweeney (1988, 22–23).

It goes without saying that the studies on Isa 1 and 65–66 by Liebreich and Lack made a considerable impact on Isaiah studies. The fruitful result of their research on Isa 1 and 65–66 has been advanced by further investigations (see Beuken 1991; Sweeney 1988, 21–24). Contemporary scholars, including Sweeney, Carr and Conrad, maintain that these two sections form a literary envelope that ties the entire book together. It is interesting to note, however, that each of them employs a somewhat different interpretive methodology. Thus, it is of vital significance to articulate these various strategies and to elucidate the differences between them.

By consolidating Lack's approach to Isa 1 and 65–66, Sweeney is mainly concerned with the thematic connection between the beginning and the end of the book of Isaiah (Sweeney 1997).[4] He points out that both Isa 1 and 65–66 hold several issues in common: the abuse of cultic sacrifice, the distinction between the righteous and the wicked and the demise of the wicked. He goes on to assert that the thematic correspondence between these two parts is reinforced by a number of lexical connections. In other words, Isa 65–66 tends to take up a great deal of the vocabulary of Isa 1.

For instance, the phrase, "those who abandon YHWH" (עזבי ה) in Isa 65:11 clearly echoes the language of Isa 1:4, "they have abandoned YHWH" (עזבו את ה), and 1:28, "and those who abandon YHWH will perish" (ועזבי ה יכלו). The expression of Isa 65:2, "rebellious people" (עם סורר), is reminiscent of the language of 1:4, "a people heavy with sin" (עם כבד עון), and 1:5, "they continue rebellion" (תוסיפו סרה). The references to the people's acts that YHWH abhors in Isa 65:12 and 66:4, "and in what I did not delight you have chosen/they have chosen" (חפצתי בחרתם בהרו ובאשר לא), undeniably reiterate the expression of Isa 1:11, "I did not delight" (לא־חפצתי), and 1:29, "which you have chosen" (אשר בחרתם). The statements in Isa 65:3, "sacrificing in the gardens," and 66:17, "those who sanctify themselves and purify themselves unto the gardens," undoubtedly recall the references to the people sacrificing in the gardens in Isa 1:11, "why multiply to me your sacrifices?" (למה־לי רב־זבחיכם), and 1:29, "and you were embarrassed by the gardens" (ותחפרו מהגנות).

It needs to be pointed out, moreover, that the statements in Isa 65:13, 66:5 and 66:17, which refer to the shame of the apostates, correspond to the language of 1:29 and that the reference to the destruction of the

---

4. In this article, Sweeney calls our attention to the role of Isa 65–66 in the whole book of Isaiah by demonstrating the fact that Isa 65–66 serves as the conclusion for the entire book of Isaiah.

apostates in 66:17 recalls the expression of Isa 1:28 and 1:31. The reference to the fire that consumes the wicked in Isa 66:24 also appears in 1:31. In this regards, Sweeney concludes:

> These observations demonstrate that the imagery of Isa 1:29–31 permeates all of 65–66 and indicate that the writers of Isa 65–66 employed the imagery and language of this oracle in presenting their views on the coming punishment of the apostates and triumph of the elect. The considerations presented above indicate that Isa 1 and 65–66 form an inclusion which is intended to unite the entire book of Isaiah. (1988, 23–24)

His conviction is that the redactor(s) of the book of Isaiah intended to address his/their own generation with the message of the prophet Isaiah. He suggests that Isa 1 and 65–66 were editorially composed in the early Persian period. Emphasis is placed upon several features that function as clues for reading the book of Isaiah in the context of the early Persian period, particularly the time of Ezra and Nehemiah (mid- to late fifth century).

Sweeney is initially concerned with the reward and punishment scheme set forth in Isa 1 and 65–66, which is characteristic of the Deuteronomistic literature from the early Persian period. His attention is also drawn to the separation between the righteous and the wicked, which he considers typical of the early apocalyptic literature in the fifth century. Sweeney maintains that both Isa 1 and 65–66 apply the reward–punishment scheme to the two opposing groups, the righteous, who deserve God's reward, and the impious, upon whom God's judgment will come. He points to the fact that this application of the reward–punishment scheme to these two conflicting parties is evidently marked by Ezra's and Nehemiah's reforms. He concludes that "these two blocks of material (Isa 1 and 65–66) form a redactional envelope for the final fifth-century edition of the book of Isaiah" (1996, 69). In his judgment, this redaction was intended to support Ezra's and Nehemiah's reforms that concentrated on purging the city of the impious and reestablishing the covenant that requires moral justice.

Still, one may question whether the whole book of Isaiah, including Isa 1 and 65–66, was intentionally shaped in the time of Ezra's and Nehemiah's reforms. It can be argued that Sweeney's historical reconstruction of Isa 1 and 65–66 is not so much a reconstruction as a construction inspired by his own interpretive presupposition. In other words, the dates and the process of editing of Isa 1 and 65–66 that Sweeney proposes are based on his own historical reconstruction. Conrad is correct when he observes that "the redactors' intentions are no more inherent in the text than those of the prophet. His [a redactional critic] own interpretive strategies, imposed from outside the text, have shaped the text and have yielded intentions" (1991, 20). It is clear, therefore, that Sweeney does not discover the intentions of the redactor(s). Rather he creates them by utilizing his own interpretive strategies, which are imposed from outside the text.

By presenting a detailed survey of various approaches to both Isa 1 and 65–66, Carr (1996) tends to focus on the contrast between Isa 1 and 65–66. Interestingly, his textual analysis of these chapters differs from conventional critical approaches to them. When Carr deals with Isa 1, he does not accommodate the traditional way of dividing it into the two parts (1:1–20 and 1:21–31), but attempts to show a divergent treatment of this material in which Isa 1 is defined as 1:2–9; 1:10–17 and 1:18–31.

Notably, 1:10–17, marked by "the call to repentance," is placed at the center of the material (1:2–31). This position indicates that the wicked are urged to repent so that they can escape a devastating punishment. On the other hand, Carr's meticulous analysis of Isa 65–66 comes to the conclusion that the exhortation for repentance in Isa 1 is in no way explicit in Isa 65–66. Carr understands that unlike Isa 1, Isa 65–66 indicates that the destinies of the wicked and the righteous have already been determined. This argument is supported by his thorough treatment of the structure of Isa 65–66, which he divides into two major sections (65:1–66:4; 66:5–24). His textual study of Isa 65–66 leads him to argue that the purpose of the message of Isa 65–66 is to provide the righteous with comfort and to announce sinners' future without explicit exhortations for repentance. In his judgment, therefore, unlike Isa 1 that urges the unrighteous to repent, Isa 65–66 on no account leaves room for the possibility of repentance for the wicked (Carr 1996, 204).

Despite his provocative argument about the determined future for the sinners in Isa 65–66, I am reluctant to agree with his conclusion. My judgment is that Carr somewhat overstates the sinners' irreversible destiny and the inevitability of consequences for them in Isa 65–66. Though Isa 65–66 presents the portrayal of the different destinies of the wicked and the righteous, different behavioral choices that would result in the different consequences can still be made. It is noteworthy that several earlier passages (including 44:22; 55:6–7; 58:6–14) in the book of Isaiah make it clear that the nature of the future is dependent upon decisions about behavior. These texts presume that righteous deeds will result in favorable consequences, while unrighteous behavior will lead to punishment if such deeds are chosen. In particular, Isa 64:7–11 pays attention to the prayer for forgiveness of the community, a fact that indicates that the destinies of the two groups have not been determined.

What is more, Carr's judgment that a redactor has taken the conception of Isa 65–66 and placed it into the call to repentance in Isa 1 is not convincing. He observes that "here a redactor has taken the very part of the conceptual world of Isaiah 65–66 which is most diametrically opposed to a call to repentance—the proclamation of irreversible judgment to evildoers–and inserted it into the call to repentance in Isaiah 1" (1996, 215). Nevertheless, there is no way of knowing whether a redactor had such need for revising the section of Isa 1 by inserting the part of Isa 65–66 focused on the proclamation of irreversible judgment of evildoers into ch. 1. More correctly, Carr's attempt to reconstruct the process of redactional modification of Isa 1 is nothing less than the outcome of a sophisticated but presumptive hypothesis.

Conrad is regarded as a leading advocate of the synchronic approach, which is committed to reading the book of Isaiah as a literary whole. Since Duhm's seminal 1892 work, historical critics conclude that the book of Isaiah is to be dealt with as a composite work containing at least three independent sources: First Isaiah, Second Isaiah (known as the Deutero-Isaiah) and Third Isaiah (called Trito-Isaiah), each of which originated in a different historical context. As a consequence, since the early twentieth century, the theory of the three independent sources has dominated Isaiah studies. Over the past decades, historical criticism has faced a growing criticism among a host of biblical scholars.[5] Conrad (1991) embraces the literary approach that seeks to read the book of Isaiah as a literary whole, not as the three independent sources that historical critics propose. His approach to the book of Isaiah provides a new starting point for Isaiah research.

His particular emphasis is placed upon the interrelation between Isa 1 and 65–66 that functions as a crucial marker for reading the book of

---

5. One of the major problems with historical criticism is that its hermeneutical position is so imperialistic that it has been dealt with as a single way in which the meaning of the text is available. David M. Gunn and Danna Nolan Fewell (1993, 8) point out: "In the same vein, but perhaps even more important, was the assumption that what was being expounded by the historical critic was, if not the correct meaning of the text, at least a step towards the correct meaning. There are two questions here. One is whether critics (readers) think of texts as having ultimately only a single right meaning. The other is whether critics think that there is a single right method of interpretation. For most historical critics the answer to both questions was, yes. The critic was seeking the right meaning, and historical criticism was the correct method by which to seek it. Historical criticism, indeed, was the summit of the interpretational pyramid. All those layers below were merely relics of bygone mistakes, centuries of wrong interpretations. (The arrogance of this position is, of course, breathtaking, but recognizably Western.)"

Isaiah as a whole. He makes an insightful observation about what he calls "the implied audience" who appears as "we" in these sections, a first person plural voice that serves as a clue for understanding the relationship between the beginning and the end of the book. He argues that

> what the "we" implies about itself in the two passages toward the end of the book parallels what the LORD says about the community toward the beginning of the book. The self-description of the "we" at the beginning and end of the book, with its counterpoint in the LORD's description of the community, provides further evidence about the structure of the book as a whole. (1991, 83)

According to Conrad, the simultaneous appearance of the expression "we" in both Isa 1 and 65–66 is quite important. The two sections are also concerned with the present context in which the division between the implied audience (the righteous) and its rivals (the unrighteous) has been made. The situation in these passages indicates that the implied audience marked by "we" has met with great setbacks to its aspiration that include unsocial behaviors, including unjust oppression in which its opponents are actively involved. Therefore, in the beginning and the end of the book, the "we," the righteous, exhort their rivals to hear the word of God, all the while anticipating the ultimate fulfillment of what is intended by Yahweh who will punish sinners, who obstinately refuse to repent like the burning worms of Isa 66:24 and who will renew Zion.

My Synchronic Approach to Isaiah 1 and 65–66

So far I have emphasized three primary interpretive methodologies that relate Isa 1 and 65–66. While each of the three scholars noted above utilizes a somewhat different strategy for interpreting Isa 1 and 65–66, each fails to be entirely divorced from a socio-historical reconstruction of the text. Among the options presented above, I am inclined to agree with Conrad, since I find his understanding of the implied audience in Isa 1 and 65–66 persuasive. I endorse his thesis that the appearance of the first person plural voice in 1:9–10 alludes to a deep and longstanding chasm between the implied audience of survivors and their rivals in the community. Still, I am reluctant to accommodate his conclusion that the implied audience as "we" in Isa 1 and 65–66 has already experienced a devastating punishment of God against Babylon (Conrad 1991, 102, 116). It seems to me that his attempt to situate Isa 1 and 65–66 in a post Babylonian context is dependent on a socio-historical reconstruction of the text grounded in his own sophisticated hypothesis.

Undoubtedly, I am adamant that historical research is meaningful and Isa 1 and 65–66 are clearly bound up with history. It ought to be emphasized, however, that contemporary readers have no ability to recover the original historical settings of texts like Isa 1 and 65–66. Melugin is right when he remarks:

> Let me be clear: I am not arguing that historical inquiry has no value. Indeed, Isaiah 1 has very much to do with history. The prophet exhibits an intense concern with what was happening in the history which lies behind the text's figurative language. But I am profoundly skeptical of our ability to recover with much precision the history which lies behind the text. (1996, 284)

It is misguided for an interpreter to believe him-/herself independent of all metaphysical or theoretical presuppositions. For that reason, it is inappropriate to privilege historical reconstruction in interpretation.

My interest is to read the text as it stands rather than to reshape the original socio-historical world of the text. My attention is focused on the literary context in front of contemporary readers, which needs no historical reconstruction whatsoever. Apart from identifying the implied audience as the "we" and their original socio-historical situation in Isa 1 and 65–66, my concern is to concentrate on the phrase, "Hear the word of God!" This is because this expression is simultaneously found in the texts and plays a central role in understanding the book of Isaiah as a whole. Significantly, the beginning and the end of the book of Isaiah are concerned with an exhortation to hear the word of God addressed to those who are involved in carrying out sacrifices against God and engaged in the shedding of innocent blood.

> Hear the word of the LORD,
> you rulers of Sodom!
> Listen to the law of our God,
> you people of Gomorrah! (Isa 1:10)

> Hear the word of the LORD,
> you who tremble at his word:
> "Your brothers who hate you,
> and exclude you because of my name, have said,
> Let the LORD be glorified, that we may see your joy!";
> yet they will be put to shame. (Isa 66:5)

As Conrad observes, the coincident occurrence of the phrase, "Hear the word of God!" in Isa 1 and 65–66 suggests the importance of hearing the word of God for understanding the overall message of the book of Isaiah. To put it another way, the intended location of this expression at the beginning (1:10) and the end (66:5) of the book points to the fact that the future for a people of God marked by "we" is solely dependent on hearing God's word.

On the other hand, in these two passages, God's word serves as a negative word of judgment against evildoers who are engaged in hypocritical sacrifice that lacks social justice and righteousness. These passages confront those people with a call to repentance. I want now to concentrate on the significance of the phrase, "Hear the word of God!" in Isa 1 and 65–66 and how hearing the word of God in the royal narratives plays a pivotal role in the overall message of the book of Isaiah.

A War of Words in the Hezekiah Narrative

During the past two decades, several commentators, including Sweeney, the late Childs, and Conrad have examined the royal narratives, especially Isa 36–39, believing they function as a key indicator for the literary coherence of the book of Isaiah. In other words, they have no doubt that Isa 36–39 play a significant role in the transition from the "Assyrian" first half of the book to the "Babylonian" second half. Yet it is important to note that each of them employs a different strategy for interpreting these chapters. Sweeney (1988, 11–25) insists that Isa 36–39 serves as a clue for the redactional unity of the book of Isaiah. His chief preoccupation is with differences between the portrayal of Hezekiah in Isa 36–39 and in 2 Kgs 18–20. He presupposes that Isa 36–39 is a modified version of the earlier narrative in 2 Kings and avers that the description of Hezekiah in Isa 36–39 is more idealized than in 2 Kgs 18–20.[6] He maintains that Isa 36–39 was editorially designed to depict Hezekiah as an ideal model of God's people for the communities in chs. 40–55. He is adamant that the idealization of Hezekiah in Isa 36–39 resulted from the intentions of the final redactor, who shaped the whole book of Isaiah in the late sixth century.

Childs (2001, 159–266), having analyzed Ackroyd's treatment of Isa 36–39, somewhat sympathizes with Ackroyd but gives short shrift to his attempt to reconstruct the dates and the process of editing these chapters. He has been disillusioned with redaction criticism due to its failure to deal with the book of Isaiah as a canonical whole that presents a coherent

---

6. Sweeney remarks that "Modifications to the text of 2 Kings 18–20 have changed its generic character. These modifications include both the removal of the narrative framework pertaining to the reign of Hezekiah in 2 Kgs 18:1–12 and 20:20–21 and the removal of alteration of various elements in 2 Kgs 18:13–20:19, resulting in an idealized portrayal of Hezekiah in the Isaiah version of the narrative" (1996, 456).

theological witness in its final received form. Childs's primary goal is to elaborate how the three Isaiahs may be read as a canonical book by concentrating on its final form. According to Childs, when the various materials of the text are placed into a larger canonical context, the significance of its historical context is minimized, while the overall theological context of a text is maximized. In this sense, the wider canonical context of the biblical text makes it possible for a collection of prophetic sources to be isolated from their original historical settings in order to address a new theological message of a text. He suggests that Isa 36–39 plays a central role in forming a literary bridge between the Assyrian and Babylonian sections in the book of Isaiah and that its incorporation into the larger framework of the book leads to a new theological intention of the final canonical form of the text. Childs concludes that the placement of Isa 36–39 between Isa 1–35 and 40–66 leads to a new canonical context beyond any specific historical background and that "this present non-historical setting into which the canon has placed these traditions is a highly reflective, theological context" (2001, 325).

In contrast, Conrad responds with a clear voice to a canonical approach to the book of Isaiah. He seeks to make a sharp distinction between his interpretive method and the canonical criticism that Childs strongly espouses. Conrad forcefully resists Childs's adoption of biblical critics' historical reconstruction of a text. Rather he finds it essential to articulate the role of Isa 36–39 from a literary perspective devoid of any attempt to reconstruct the original setting of the texts. His initial attention is given to the royal narratives and their accompanying war oracles. It can be seen that the royal narrative in Isa 36–39, followed by the war oracles containing the formula "fear not" in Isa 41, 43, and 44, clearly reminds readers of the royal narrative in Isa 7 accompanied by a war oracle in 10:24–27. It needs to be considered that the war oracle in 10:24–27, which promises deliverance from the Assyrians, is fulfilled in the Hezekiah narrative. It is interesting to note that the fulfillment of this promise in this narrative makes it possible to look forward to the fulfillment of the fall of the Babylonians that is promised in Isa 41, 43 and 44 in which the formula "fear not" appears often.

To put it another way, "the fulfillment of this promise provides the basis for the hope in the fulfillment of the war oracles addressed to the people following the announcement of Babylonian devastation at the end of the Hezekiah narrative" (Conrad 1991, 49). In Conrad's judgment, the strategic location of the Hezekiah narrative in the book of Isaiah makes it evident that this narrative has a transitional role in the book by pointing back to the Ahaz narrative and forward to the future deliverance from the

Babylonians. Indeed, Conrad's scrupulous analysis of the transitional role of Isa 36–39 sheds light on how to read the book of Isaiah as a literary whole.

My interest is on the significance of hearing the word of God in Isa 7 and 36–39. The theme of hearing the word of God in the royal narratives plays a crucial role in understanding the overall message of the book of Isaiah. Close attention should be given to Ahaz's response to the prophet Isaiah's call for simple trust in Yahweh, a response that stands in stark contrast to that of Hezekiah. It is noteworthy that the testimony that Isaiah witnessed is to be seen as the Torah, the word of God in Isa 8:16, a fact that indicates that Isaiah's prophetic word delivered to Ahaz is nothing less than the word of God.

Significantly Ahaz's response of fake piety to the giving of the sign indicates that he gives little attention to Isaiah's message that Jerusalem's future is solely dependent on hearing the word of Yahweh, who promises deliverance from the alliance of the Syrian and Israelite kings. His response makes it clear that Ahaz's resistance to Isaiah's message means his rejection of the word of God. There is no doubt, in this sense, that the Ahaz narrative clearly identifies him as a deaf king who fails to cling to the word of God. Instead he commits his future to a pagan king. The portrayal of Ahaz as a deaf king is effectively designed to describe the faithless king as a characteristic figure representing deaf Israel in Isaiah's days who hears but never understands (6:9).

By contrast, the Hezekiah narrative, especially Isa 36–37, strategically portrays Hezekiah as an ideal model of Zion, who adheres to the word of God in a tumultuous time similar to the Israelite-Syrian attack on Jerusalem when Ahaz reigned. The Hezekiah narrative throws the king's response to Isaiah's comforting oracle containing the "fear not" formula into clear relief. Reminiscent of Isaiah's message to Ahaz in which the "fear not" formula appears, the prophet Isaiah also delivers a comforting oracle in which the expression "fear not" is strategically associated with Hezekiah. In particular, Isa 36–37 is concerned with hearing the word of God, a theme that plays a vital role in the book of Isaiah as a whole.

At the outset in the Hezekiah narrative, the Assyrian king poses a threat to Jerusalem. He sends his commander from Lachish to Jerusalem with a large force to quell the city (36:1–2). Interestingly, the Assyrian commander does not focus his attention on military assaults but on a persuasive speech to destroy the city. As is set forth in 36:5–10, the Assyrian officer's message to servants from Hezekiah shows a parallel structure in which the uselessness of trust in three options (the Judean king, Egypt and Yahweh) is respectively set forth:

A.   The uselessness of trust in Hezekiah (36:5)
  B.   The uselessness of trust in Egypt (36:6)
    C.   The uselessness of trust in Yahweh (36:7)
A'.   The uselessness of trust in Hezekiah (36:8)
  B'.   The uselessness of trust in Egypt (36:9)
    C'.   The uselessness of trust in Yahweh (36:10)

In this speech, the Assyrian officer's words mock the Israelites' trust in their king, in Egyptian assistance and ultimately in Yahweh as ridiculous. It is interesting to note that the Assyrian commander is at pains to reiterate the expressions, "words of the king" or "the king says" (cf. 36:4, 13, 14, 16). As is shown in 36:13, he emphatically calls out, "Hear the words of the great king, the king of Assyria!" The point he makes in the whole speech is that the Judean people must not cling to the word of God. They must listen to the words of the Assyrian king. Ironically the commander mocks the people of the city for resting on the word of God, while he himself is fighting only with words. The commander never focuses on any military action in Jerusalem but only on persuasive speech. In other words, it is not a military war, but a war of words. Whose words will be heard? The commander is adamant that survival or failure is dependent on hearing the words of the Assyrian king.

After receiving a message from the Assyrian commander, Hezekiah repents for what he has done by not trusting in Yahweh.[7] Reminding us of the comforting oracle containing the words "fear not" delivered to Ahaz, Isaiah's message is communicated through his servants and reassures the desperate but penitent king. Significantly, as is set forth in 37:6 where the formula "fear not" is characteristically shown, the prophet Isaiah strongly stresses the word of God that promises deliverance from the hands of the Assyrian army and predicts its fatal destruction. On the contrary, the commander continually invites Hezekiah to hear the words of the Assyrian king who guarantees Zion's survival and her fertility.

---

7. It should be noted that the two ways of interpreting Isa 37:3 deserve careful attention. One interpretation understands that Isa 37:3, which plays as a penitent confession of a fragile monarch, indicates that Hezekiah feels remorse for relying on Egyptian assistance implied in the commander's speech. On the other hand, scholars such as Seitz (1991, 73) claim that since the commander's charge of reliance on Egypt is nothing more than a groundless curse, this verse has nothing to do with Hezekiah's foreign alliances with Egypt. My sympathy, however, is with Darr who observes that Isa 37:1–3 "function as the confession of a now powerless monarch who, in violation of the expressed policy of Yahweh's prophet, has willfully chosen to rely on his own strength and that of his allies" (1994, 243). It can be seen that the commander's charges of Egyptian alliance appear to be grounded in fact, and Hezekiah's penitence seems to have to do with his foreign policy, especially his foreign alliance with Egypt.

Given this situation, Hezekiah finds himself in a fix. For him there are only two options. Either he ought to hear the words of the Assyrian king delivered through the commander, or he should listen to the word of God spoken through the prophet Isaiah. To whose words shall he listen? Refusing to tread in the footsteps of his predecessor, Hezekiah is unshakably willing to hear the word of God who promises that Zion will survive notwithstanding the fact that the present situation seems to be one of despair. It is his conviction that there is no other way of enduring a national crisis besides trusting in Yahweh whose words are to be heard. The language of 37:36–37 makes it clear that what God has said about the destruction of the Assyrian army relayed by the prophet Isaiah has dramatically been fulfilled. It should also certainly be borne in mind that Hezekiah is described in Isa 36–37 as a model of the righteous who hear the word of God.

Hearing the Word of God in Isaiah 1 and 65–66

The significance of hearing the word of God is also brought into prominence in Isa 1 and 65–66. As noted earlier, Isa 1 and 65–66 are strategically placed to be read as the introduction and the conclusion to the entire book of Isaiah. It is indicated in these passages, furthermore, that the deep chasm between the righteous and the impious is internecine. Interestingly, both chapters show an exhortation to hear the word of God (1:10; 66:5) and the identification of such groups has to do with each different response to the call to hear the word of God. Special attention ought to be drawn to the literary context of these passages to shed light on how the responses of the two groups to the word of God are diametrically opposed.

As was noted above, though Isa 1 has been reconstructed by a number of scholars, no consensus has been reached.[8] Most agree, however, that the best way to deal with this text is to read it as a prologue for the entire book of Isaiah since it anticipates the central conceptions set forth throughout the book.[9] Significantly, the chiastic parallel presentation of ch. 1 deserves careful consideration:

---

8.   Traditionally form-critical studies have tended to deal with Isa 1 as a compositional collage which is divided into five or six sections based on different historical settings. For an excellent study of the interpretation of Isa 1, see Melugin (1996).

9.   For instance, it is said that vv. 7–9 may have to do with the campaigns of Sennacherib against Judah in Isa 36–37 since these verses allude to the time when only Jerusalem was spared while many cities were destroyed. Moreover, Zion's ransom in 1:27 may anticipate a time when those who were taken into exile by the Babylonians will return to Zion. Also, the emphasis upon the restoration of Zion in

A.   The present situation of the rebellious Israel (vv. 2–4)
   B.   Israel has already been punished for her sins (vv. 5–9)
      C.   An indictment against murderers involved in hypocritical practices (vv. 10–15)
         D.   An exhortation for repentance (vv. 16–20)
      C'.   An indictment against murderers who lack social justice (vv. 21–23)
   B'.   Israel would be punished again if no repentance is shown (vv. 24–27)
A'.   The future situation of the rebellious Israel (vv. 28–31)

This literary structure focuses on a religious crisis when the hypocrite Israel is actively involved in social injustice. It warns that she would be doomed to face a harsh chastisement again if she shows lack of true penitence. Notably, in Isa 1:10–17 two groups respond to the word of God in diametrically opposed ways. Specifically, in Isa 1:10, a remnant group marked by "we/our" urges their opponents, who appear as "you," to listen to the word of God:

A.   Hear the word of the LORD,
   B.   You rulers of Sodom;
A'.   Give ear to the teaching of our God,
   B'.   You people of Gomorrah:

This striking parallel between the word (דבר) of the LORD and the teaching (תורה) of God suggests that תורה is on a par with the word of Yahweh. In this verse, the Hebrew word, תורה, has often been construed as the Mosaic Law, while it can also be dealt with as the prophetic Torah delivered to a contemporary audience (Sweeney 1996, 80).[10] The meaning of תורה here should not be confined to the strict sense of Mosaic formulation. Instead, the Hebrew word ought to be defined as "a highly existential application of the divine will that had long since been revealed to Israel, and now delivered with a fresh poignancy to a corrupt, complacent, and self-righteous population" (Childs 2001, 20).

What is more, v. 10 alludes to the fact that there is a serious division between two opposing circles, the righteous and the wicked. The juxtaposition of "our God" with "you people" indicates that the internal dissension between the survivors referred to as "we" and the opponents

v. 27 reemerges throughout chs. 40–55 or even chs. 56–66. In addition, the motif of idolatry in vv. 28–31 may resonate with the charge about inappropriate worship made in chs. 56–66, especially in 57:5 and 66:17. For a detailed discussion of the relationship between ch. 1 and the rest of the book of Isaiah, see Melugin (1996, 296–301).
   10.   For a full treatment of the use of the Torah in Isa 1–39, see Clements (2007).

called "you" comes to a head. The latter is portrayed as those who are involved in social sins that are "like scarlet" and "red like crimson" (1:18). Though they stretch out their hands with the blood of sacrifice, this practice is abominable to Yahweh since they have the blood of innocent people on their hands. As a consequence, this wicked group is faced with a call to hear the word of God, a point that suggests that their actions ignore the word and ways of God. The gloomy depiction of this bigoted group uncommitted to the word of God has an affinity with that of Ahaz who is portrayed as a deaf king who abandons the message of Isaiah that urges the disobedient king to return to God. On the contrary, the pious who are described as "we/our" invite their opponents to listen to the word of God. This group unshakably adheres to it. The remarkable description of the pious as a group clinging to the word of God unquestionably resonates with that of Hezekiah, who not only resists the words of the Assyrian king but firmly depends on the word of God. In this respect, what is made manifest in Isa 1 is that, for Zion, judgment or restoration entirely depends upon hearing the word of God.

Interestingly, the significance of hearing the word of God re-emerges at the end of the book of Isaiah. Here the deep chasm between the righteous and the wicked is more conspicuous than in Isa 1. When scholars examine Isa 65–66, it seems their preoccupation is with identifying who the addressee in these texts is. This matter has been investigated by a number of scholars but no agreement has been reached. Sweeney observes that Isa 65–66 is to be divided into three subsections (65:1–7; 65:8–25; 66:1–24), that the wicked as the addressee dominates in Isa 65, and the righteous largely appear as the addressee in Isa 66 (1997, 461–64). Carr contends that Isa 65–66 may be divided into the two smaller portions (65:1–66:4 and 66:5–24) and that the addressee in 65:1–66:4 is the wicked (1996, 211–212).[11] Sweeney tends to identify the addressee in the section of 66:1–4 as the righteous, while Carr regards those who are addressed in it as the impious.

This debate over determining the exact identification of the addressees in those texts is less important than often supposed. Instead, it needs to be noted that the portrayals of the two groups are contrasted throughout Isa 65–66. More importantly, the two themes, the judgment of the wicked and the restoration of the righteous, interchangeably occur in Isa 65–66 in which the former is repeatedly followed by the latter and finally concludes the two chapters. As a result, Isa 65–66 may be set forth as a chiastic unit focused on the two themes:

11. For a detailed discussion of the structure of Isa 65–66, see Childs (2001, 526–42).

A.   The judgment of the wicked (65:1–16)
  B.   The restoration of the righteous (65:17–25)
    C.   The judgment of the wicked (66:1–6)
      D′.   The restoration of the righteous (66:7–14)
    C′.   The judgment of the wicked (66:15–17)
  B′.   The restoration of the righteous (66:18–21)
A′.   The judgment of the wicked (66:22–24)

Indeed, this literary presentation of Isa 65–66 calls our attention to the different descriptions of the two circles hostile to each other. Some contend that the opponents of the righteous appear to be from within Israel's community, whereas several scholars argue that the enemies are from outside the community (see Childs 2001, 339–40). Given the fact that the enemies are referred to as a second person plural pronoun ("you") in Isa 65, the former seems to be more persuasive. Notably, the enemies called "you" in 65:1–12 are to be identified as those who are referred to as "they" in 66:1–6 since the references to the wicked in 65:1–12 largely correspond to those in 66:1–6. For instance, several Hebrew verbs, such as קרא, ענה, דבר, and שמע, simultaneously appear in both 65:12 and 66:4:

> I will destine you to the sword, and all of you shall bow down to the
>   slaughter;
> because, when I called (קראתי), you did not answer (לא עניתם),
> when I spoke (דברתי), you did not listen (לא שמעתם),
> but you did what was evil (עשו הרע) in my sight (בעיני),
> and chose (בחרתם) what I did not delight in (לא חפצתי).

> I also will choose to mock them, and bring upon them what they fear;
> because, when I called (קראתי), no one answered (אין עונה),
> when I spoke (דברתי), they did not listen (לא שמעו);
> but they did what was evil (עשו הרע) in my sight (בעיני),
> and chose (בחרו) what did not please me (לא חפצתי).

It needs to be noted that in both passages the unrighteous are urged to listen to what God has spoken to them, but they obstinately resist the word of God. The image of the unrighteous who repudiate the word of God in these passages reminds us of the royal narratives, especially the Ahaz narrative, in which the faithless king is depicted as a deaf king who pays no attention to the word of God, but trusts instead in the Assyrian king.

In particular, Isa 66:1–6 deserves careful consideration since this section offers a further description of the separation of the righteous and the wicked in relation to their different responses to the word of God. In other words, this section provides a rhetorical pattern marked by several key words which parallel each other. Specifically, the Hebrew noun for a dwelling place, מנוחה, in v. 1 is paralleled by the word for a temple, היכל, in v. 6. Also the word for "tremble," חרד, in v. 2 reappears as a plural form, חרדים, in v. 5 and the two words, בחר and חפץ, repeatedly occur in vv. 3 and 4. As a consequence, the repetition of these words unmistakably plays a central role in creating a chiastic unit:

A.   The heaven and the earth as the LORD's resting place (מנוחה) (v. 1)
  B.   Who trembles (חרד) at the word of the LORD (v. 2)
    C.   Those who have chosen (בהרו) their own ways (v. 3)
    C'.   Those who chose (בהרו) what did not please the LORD (v. 4)
  B'.   Who tremble (חרדים) at the word of the LORD (v. 5)
A'.   The voice of the LORD from the temple (היכל) (v. 6)

Moreover, this structure indicates that there is a deep chasm between the two groups, since it shows the two types of responses to the word of God. In other words, one group responds with humility to the word of God and even trembles at it, while another group is so stubborn that it persistently resists the word of God. These sinners not only abandon what God has spoken to them, but also are actively involved in persecuting the pious who tremble at the word of God. However, the pious are urged to focus on the call to hear the word of God since the enemies are doomed to experience the day of retribution for their sins. Though the righteous despair due to their enemies' persecution, they have no doubt that the persecutors will ultimately suffer from divine punishment since what God says about their future will be fulfilled. The way they show their trust is to hear the word of God and look for its fulfillment (66:6).

Conclusion

It has been argued that the intended location of the expression, "Hear the word of God!" at the beginning (1:10) and the end (66:5) of the book of Isaiah indicates the importance of hearing the word of God in the midst of a severe time. Also this phrase reminds us of the royal narratives in which hearing the word of God plays a crucial role in ensuring the protection of Judah from invaders like Assyria and the survival of Jerusalem. In this sense, Isa 1 and 65–66 make it clear that Zion's future hinges on hearing the word of God no matter what difficulties it faces. As Hezekiah and the righteous fall in each crisis, they are invited to focus on hearing the word of God, who alone can deliver his people from the hands of their enemies.

There is no doubt that the word of God has never receded into the past, unavailable for contemporary readers. Instead, the teaching of Yahweh,

Torah, is not only accessible to ancient Israel, but also continuously available for today's churches. Like Hezekiah or the pious in Isa 1 and 66, contemporary communities also face a variety of crises. As a member of the Korean Church, I have been alarmed at tensions between South Korea and North Korea. Recently, it was announced that a South Korean naval ship called "Cheonan" had been sunk. South Korea claims that North Korea planted an underwater mine to make the South Korean warship sink based on evidence recovered after the sinking, whereas North Korea has repeatedly denied any responsibility in the sinking. Most recently, I just heard that North Korea fired dozens of artillery shells onto one of the South Korean-controlled islands called Yeonpyeongdo just south of Northern Limit Line (NLL) in the Yellow Sea to the west of the peninsula. It was reported that North Korea fired as many as 200 rounds, some of which struck the island, killing two South Korean soldiers and two civilians, injuring at least ten South Korean soldiers, damaging buildings and setting fire to a mountainside. South Korea responded by firing some 80 shells of its own toward North Korea, and dispatching F-16 fighter jets to the area. It appears to me that ideological conflicts have been a constant part of history and humans are hardly capable of establishing a peaceful world devoid of political struggles. The prophet anticipates, nevertheless, that in the latter days, those who shall receive the word of God going out from Zion will not engage themselves in hostilities but enjoy a transformed life in a new era (Isa 66:20–22). Indeed, it is envisaged that in the last day the word of God will play an exclusive role in causing people to eliminate all dissension. I imagine that one day, people in both South Korea and North Korea will participate in a peaceful epoch with one accord due to their enthusiastic commitment to the word of God. Let us pray for this peaceful Korea.

ISAIAH *REDIVIVUS*

Norman Habel

To honour Ed Conrad, who imbibed the spirit of Isaiah in deep measure, I have chosen to imagine Isaiah *redivivus*, speaking in contemporary terms, especially those relevant to the environmental crisis facing our planet.

The Call of Isaiah

In the days of Barak Obama
When America was still mighty on Earth,
I was singing in God's presence,
Chanting with the seraphim:
"Holy, holy, holy is the Lord of hosts,
The whole Earth is full of his glory."
     And I heard Earth groaning,
Crying aloud to the heavens,
"Woe is me! I am unclean,
Filled with the pollutions of humanity!"
     Then I heard the Lord cry,
"Whom shall I send?
Who will go for me?
Who will return to Earth
And interpret her cry of woe?"
 And I replied, "Lord, my God,
I would like to go again,
But who will understand?
Who will listen to my word?
The people see but do not understand?
They listen but do not comprehend?
Earth is becoming desolate
And emptiness is everywhere.

Where is there a holy seed,
A harbinger of hope for Earth?"
    Then one of the seraphim rose,
Took a nuclear ember from the fire
And touched my lips to speak again,
To announce the word as long ago.
    And the Lord said to me,
"Return to Earth and echo her cry
Until humans know her pain.
Return to Earth and shout once more,
'Earth is full of God's presence
And God is suffering again.'"

An Oracle of Anguish

    Hear, O heavens and listen O Earth.
The ox knows its owner
And the sheep dog hears its master's voice,
But humanity does seem to know
To understand my agony.
Much of the country lies desolate
But humans do not feel the pain.
    Listen, O heavens above
And give ear, O planet Earth.
You were witnesses to my covenant
And can testify to my treaty.
I made a covenant with Earth
And all the creatures of Earth
Not to destroy with a flood
The fauna and flora of Earth.
I did not want to hear again
The dying cries of my creation.
    But listen now to their cries,
The deep groaning in the forests.
From the mighty cedars of Lebanon
To the majestic myrtles of Tasmania,
From the vast acres of the Amazon
To the dense jungles of Borneo,
Their voices rise to me,
Not in praise but in agony.

The lungs of these forests are ruptured,
Torn to pieces by chainsaws.
The voice of the tall timber is muffled
As it falls trembling to the ground.
    For now there is no rest on Earth,
No Sabbath for me to enjoy.
All I hear are cries of creation,
Caused by greedy human hands.
All I ask is a little peace.
Why can't they understand?

Song of the Vineyard

    Let me sing a song of love,
a song of my beloved vineyard
    I created my vineyard fertile,
A planet more vibrant than others.
Over millions of years, my breath
was the impulse that created life.
Beginning with tiny organisms,
I caused plant life to emerge,
Until vineyards were growing
and birds were enjoying the fruit.
    Over time I nurtured my vineyard,
Until spiders and snakes evolved.
Finally, from my deepest impulse,
A special Earth being was born,
An Earth being I named *adam,*
Made from the clay of *adamah.*
    And I commissioned this Earth being
To tend and preserve my vineyard,
To protect its heart and soul
And every Earth being that lives,
Each in its given habitat
Each with its own taste for wine.
    I even chose to fill my vineyard
With my presence, my *kabod.*
    But the Earth beings called *adam*
Had no great love for native vines.
They turned some vineyards into wastelands,
And fertile lands into salt pans.

They polluted some vineyards with toxins
And turned many an Eden into a desert.
I would like to drink red wine with you,
My beloved planet Earth,
With you and those I commissioned to keep you
A fertile vineyard filled with hope.
Instead of justice I found bloodshed;
Instead of righteousness, a cry!
I fear that if *adam* continues
To pollute my sacred vineyard,
The clouds may not form as once
And send their rain for my vines.

The Dream of YHWH

I have a dream that one day
There will be peace in the land.
    At the sacred centre of the land
The red rock will stand high,
And be seen from every vantage point,
As the symbol of peace on Earth.
    And people will come to that rock
To hear the truth imbedded there,
The words of the peacemaker,
The mediator of peace for all:
"Turn your swords into ploughshares
And your woomeras into wisdom sticks!
Turn your nuclear weapons
into gleaming grain silos!
Turn your long-range missiles
into long-term food storage!
Turn your massive defence budget
Into a war against poverty!"
    I have a dream for all nations
That they come to the centre,
To the navel of Earth itself,
To a table laden with welcome,
To a place of pure hospitality,
A meeting place of ancient peoples.

The Cry of Earth

I am the planet Earth,
The vineyard God has loved,
And filled with a sacred presence
The source of wonder and wisdom.
But instead of nurture from humans,
I have been turned into a factory,
Where the greedy create wealth
For their own selfish desires
And not for the good of the vineyard,
Not for the health of their planet home.
They join house to house
And add field to field for profit.
They join mansion to mansion
And one coal mine after another.
They join company with company
And leave refugees in their wake.
They join five star to five star
As slums increase in size.
They rise early in the morning
to kill unsuspecting species.
They drink late at night
Bathed in the waves of wealth
They do not regard the deeds of YHWH
Or see the work of God's hands.
The work of God's hands is fragile,
A fertile habitat made for humanity,
But the work of his hand can be turned
into a gruesome greenhouse age,
When all humans will cry aloud,
"We have been sent into exile!"
Know this well, while there is time:
Your exile is your own doing, not mine!

An Oracle on Sacrifice

Yesterday was ANZAC Day down under
When faithful Aussies and Kiwis
Remember the men and women
Who sacrificed their lives abroad

To keep their home land free.
    I dared to speak as a prophet
Many centuries ago in time,
Stating it very bold and clear
That God had no time for sacrifices
For burnt offerings of rams and bulls,
That God did not relish the taste
Of blood from lambs or goats.
The lifeblood belongs to God
and should not be spilled by killing.
    Yet now you come before me
With the sacrifice of human lives,
Young men and women killed
in the bloody battles of war.
And you ask me to bless the way
they fought, killed and died!
Why?

The Dream of Earth

    I also had a dream of hope,
A longing for the Messiah to come,
One whose spirit was in tune
With the mind of God in me,
One with the spirit of wisdom,
Linked with a scientific mind,
One with the spirit of truth,
Linked with the courage to act.
    He would not be deluded by appearances
Or influenced by public flattery,
But would decide in favour of the poor
To empower the weak and oppressed.
    He would also discern my condition,
A planet infested by human poisons,
A planet choking on greenhouse gases,
A planet whose climate is unbalanced.
And he would summon his people to act
To restore the balance of nature
In the sky, the air and the weather,
The surface and the soul of Earth.
    I dreamed of a day of peace,

When nature and humans were one,
Where aggression was set aside
And hospitality prevailed on Earth,
When the wolf would lie with the lamb,
The leopard lie down with the kid,
And a little child would lead them,
Through the most dangerous of places.
No one in that sacred centre,
Would harm, hurt or destroy,
But all would work for peace
And the healing of their planet home.
Then I, I would be filled again
With the knowledge of God within,
The wisdom that comes from below,
The impulse to search and know.
Some say the Messiah came,
Jesus, the Anointed One,
Acclaimed as the prince of peace
And filled with the spirit of God.
Millions of humans followed him
And trusted him with their lives.
But sad to say they turned away
From a dream of peace on Earth.
They longed for a place in heaven
And said "to hell with Earth."
So if the followers of Jesus, the Messiah,
Are not concerned with Earth as their own home,
And most of the minds of humanity
Are focused on prestige or wealth,
What hope do I have today,
Why should I dare to dream?
Perhaps, Isaiah, you might understand
And dare to proclaim once again:
"Holy, holy, holy,
 Earth is filled with the presence of God
A sacred site in the cosmos,
That no-one should pollute and profane.
Go, Isaiah, and preach once again
To bring me healing
And my children hope.
Shalom! Shalom! Shalom!
Earth is calling us home!

Part II

READING LITERARILY

DID THE SCHOLAR(S) GET IT RIGHT?*

Johnson Lim

Throughout the centuries, Gen 2:16–17, especially v. 17, has posed serious exegetical difficulties for many readers. While the command in v. 17 is clear, the consequence of disobeying the command is open to diverse interpretations. God had issued a stern warning to Adam that if he were to eat of the forbidden fruit, he would die that very day. However, not only did Adam *not* die—he even lived to a ripe old age of 930 years (Gen 5:5)!

Three fundamental questions arise as baffled readers grapple with the Rubik's cube intricacy in Gen 2:16–17. Linguistically, how do we translate the Hebrew phrase *kî bĕyôm ʾăkālĕkā mimmennû môt tāmût*?[1] Theologically, how do we explain the fact that God did not keep his word? Hermeneutically, should we allow our theological presuppositions to determine our interpretations?

A satisfactory solution to this exegetical conundrum should be accompanied by sound hermeneutics (see Lim 2006, 2002a, 2001). This means that all hermeneutical tracks must be in place for the textual train to reach its proper destination. The best textual train cannot reach its proper destination if the hermeneutical tracks are not properly laid (see Lim 2002b).

Several proposals have been given to resolve the exegetical enigma.[2] The first is to translate the Hebrew phrase *kî bĕyôm[3] ʾăkālĕkā mimmennû*

---

* It is my honour and privilege to contribute an article to this *Festschrift* honouring Professor Ed Conrad who was my *doctorvater* during my formative years at the University of Queensland. I have always been grateful for his guidance, supervision, and influence in my life. Readers will observe that the title of my article is similar to that of R. W. L. Moberly, "Did the Serpent Get It Right?" (1988). This is intentional because he is going to be my major conversational partner in this article. I am grateful to Andy Lie from Newcastle upon Tyne (UK) for reading critically an earlier draft and offering some helpful suggestions.

1. Note in the LXX the second person verbs in this verse are all in plural though Eve was not yet created, whereas in the MT they are singular.

2. Cf. Claus Westermann quoting Gunkel: "This threat is not fulfilled subsequently; they do not die immediately; this fact is not to be explained away, but

môt tāmût emphasizing death as a consequence of Adam and Eve's disobedience without specifying the exact time: "If you eat of its fruit you will surely die" (2:15–17 NLT).[4] A second is to translate the phrase "You shall surely die" (2:17) as "You shall become mortal." The Latin Vulgate is a good example of this: *"de ligno autem scientiae boni et mali ne comedas in quocumque enim die comederis ex eo morte morieris."* Interestingly, *Targum Pseudo-Jonathan* has the same idea, for it reads: "but of the tree *of which those who eat its fruit have the wisdom to distinguish* good and evil, you shall not eat, because on the day on which you eat [of it] you shall *incur the* death *penalty"* (2:17; Maher 1992a, 24).[5]

Among older commentators, Matthew Henry suggests: "Thou shall become mortal and capable of dying; the grant of immortality shall be recalled, and that defence shall depart from thee. Thou shalt become obnoxious to death, like a condemned malefactor that is dead in law" (1991, 9). Similarly, Adam Clarke says, "Thou shalt not only die spiritually, by losing the life of God, but from that moment thou shalt become mortal, and shall continue in a *dying state* till thou *die"* (1830, 44). Modern commentator Richard Freedman also takes the view that "what subsequently occurs [is a] divine act of mercy or relenting: they do not die immediately but are rendered mortal" (2001, 19).[6] In sum, Adam would become a "victim of death" (Alders 1981, 93) or "liable for death" rather than experience immediate death upon eating the forbidden fruit (Rosenberg 1993, 43). Hence, "the point of the whole narrative is apparently man's ultimate punishment rather than instantaneous death" (Speiser 1981, 17).[7]

A third option is the idea that God was joking with them! He did not mean what he said but was merely trying to frighten them to prevent them from eating the forbidden fruit. This is another interpretive

---

simply acknowledged" (1984, 225). Others like John Hartley (2000), Kenneth Matthews (1996), and Susan Brayford (2007) do not address the issue directly and leave out the discussion.

3. Note that the phrase *kî běyôm* can be translated as "when," "if," or "at that time." See Gen 2:4 and 5:1–2.

4. Bible translations which have opted for a general (non-intensifying) translation include the Living Bible, Revised Standard Version, and Moffat's translation.

5. Note *Targum Neofiti* to Genesis reads: "on the day that you shall eat you shall surely die" (Maher 1992b, 58). Also *Targum Onqelos* to Genesis has: "for on the day you eat from it you shall surely die" (Maher 1988, 44)

6. See also Plaut (1974, 21).

7. Speiser translates v. 17 as, "For the moment you eat of it, you shall be doomed to death" (1981, 15).

possibility. The fourth option is to take the text at face value—God lied. As John Gibson remarks, "On a plain reading of the text it is difficult to avoid the conclusion that at this point God is guilty of telling a lie. The man breaks the condition, but he is not instantly put to death as God threatened" (1981, 113). Hence, the outcome of the matter is a divine deceit. The fifth option is to read the verse as referring not to physical but spiritual death.[8] According to H. C. Leupold, "Dying is separation from God. That separation occurred the very moment man by his disobedience broke the bond of love" (1942, 124). Older commentators like Gray and Adams assert that the meaning of this verse is: "You will have the sentence of death which includes moral and spiritual death" (n.d., 18). Bruce Waltke and Cathi Fredricks remark, "Although the statement may refer to physical death, primarily in view is spiritual death, which entails loss of relationship with God and with one another" (2001, 87–88). Other variations include "being deprived of the possibility of rejuvenation by means of the 'tree of life,' as existed hitherto—in other words, inevitable expulsion from the garden" (Sarna 1989, 21) and "to be cut off from God" (Gowan 1988, 44).[9] A common rabbinic interpretation suggests that since "one day is like a thousand years to the Lord" (Ps 90:4; cf. 2 Pet 3:8), Adam and Eve died before the end of the first millennium![10] Let us examine each of the interpretive options and determine which one gives the best answer that fits the immediate context and wider canonical context.

The first option is a reasonable and brilliant explanation for the conundrum. It works with the presupposition that God cannot lie nor be inconsistent in his character. This option can be easily dismissed, however, because it seeks to "comment rather than translate" the text (Stigers 1976, 71). Exegetically, it is difficult—if not impossible—to arrive at such a conclusion based on the Hebrew syntax. Moreover, this claim lacks supporting textual or contextual evidence.

The second option makes good sense to explain the non-fulfillment of God's warning. However, are we justified to translate the Hebrew phrase *kî bĕyôm ʾăkālĕkā mimmennû môt tāmût* as mortality? This Hebrew phrase does not connote this idea at all. "Those who interpret 'condemned

---

8. Cf. John Calvin: "But it is asked what kind of death God means in this place. It appears to me that the definition of this death is to be sought from its opposite... For then was Adam consigned to death, and death began its reign in him" (1965, 127–28).

9. Cf. Job 7:21; Ps 88:5, 10–12; Isa 38:18–19.

10. Contra Charles John Ellicott "*In the day*...used, as in v. 4, for an indefinitely long period" (1959, 21).

to death' is an evasion of the text and its evidence" (Barr 1992, 10) and they seem to "rationalize a difficulty rather than to translate it" (Ferguson 2000, 37). Exegetically, one needs to take a big leap of faith to jump from "you shall die" to "you shall become mortal." Such an approach presupposes that man was created immortal but became mortal through disobedience. On the contrary, there is strong textual evidence to support that man is not mortal but would become immortal if he had taken the fruit from the tree of life. "Therefore, he must not be allowed to put out his hand to take fruit from the tree of life also, and thus eat of it and live forever...and he stationed the cherubim and the fiery revolving sword, to guard the way to the tree of life" (Gen 3:22–24).[11]

The third and fourth options have not been taken seriously by many scholars. The possibility that God was joking and lying would be unthinkable because of the character of God portrayed in the Scriptures (e.g. Num 23:19; 1 Sam 15:29; Titus 1:2; Heb 6:18).[12] Wayne Grudem drives home this point when he opines, "God always speaks truth when he speaks. He is 'the unlying God' (Titus 1:2, author's translation), the God for whom lying is impossible (Heb 6:18), the God whose every word is perfectly 'pure' (Ps 12:6), the one of whom it can be said, 'Every word of God proves true' (Prov 30:5)" (1994, 196).[13] Cassuto sums it up best when he says that it is inconceivable that "the Bible attributed to the Lord God an extravagant utterance that did not correspond to His true intention" (1961, 125). Similarly, Barr also contends that "there is no reason to attribute to him [God] any falsehood or lie in that story [Gen 2–3]" (2006, 21).[14]

11. Taken from the New American Bible. Cf. 1 Tim 6:16, where it is stated that only the deity has immortality. See also Dillman 1897, 138.

12. Ora Horn Prouser in his unpublished doctoral dissertation, "The Phenomenology of the Lie in Biblical Narrative" (1991), seeks to show that in biblical narratives, lying was not an immoral issue. God does not always speak the truth and those who lied need not be considered negative in their character. God is said to lie in Gen 18:13 and 1 Kgs 22:19–23, and encourages others to lie on other occasions (Exod 3:16–22; 1 Sam 16:2). He then goes on to say, "God never lies when he swears, but holds true to his oaths" (e.g. Gen 15:8–21; 24:7; Exod 13:11; Deut 6:10; Josh 21:41). See Chapter 5 on "Divine Deceit," especially p. 153. Unfortunately, the author deals only with Gen 3 and not 2:16–17. Scriptural verses that purportedly support the idea that God lied by proxy in sending prophets or lying spirits to deceive include 1 Kgs 22:23; 2 Chr 18:22; Jer 4:10; 20:7; Ezek 14:9; 2 Thess 2:11. This discussion is beyond the scope of the present study.

13. See also Geisler (2003, 356–69). Cf. Roberts (2002, 123–31).

14. In this article, Barr trenchantly rebuked Moberly for implying that he had called God a liar, which, he argues, he never thought or did. Moberly responded to Barr's article with "Did the Interpreters Get it Right? Genesis 2–3 Reconsidered"

The fifth option is a common and popular interpretation.[15] R. Moberly (1988) has most recently attempted to defend a metaphorical or spiritual reading of the text, although his focus is more on ch. 3. According to him:

> It is surely inconceivable that the Genesis writer could have allowed that in the situation of Genesis 3 the serpent could be right and God could be wrong… I suggest that there is only one avenue of interpretation open to us, namely that God's death sentence was indeed carried out, but in some other way than the obvious and straightforward way that his words initially implied God's death sentence. (1988, 13)

To shore up his proposal, he argues that the terms "death" and "life" suggest a metaphorical meaning referring to impoverished quality of life rather than to the termination of physical existence. He quotes Deut 30:15, 19; Prov 5:5f., 20–23, and 7:21–27 to reinforce his case (1988, 16). Taking his cue from those verses, he reasons that such a metaphorical sense can be applied to Gen 3 when it talks about "death." He also asserts that "since God's presence brings life (in normal circumstances), removal from his presence suggests a process of death." Disobedience to God naturally results in immediate retribution in the form of physical death but it does not always happen that way. The writer invites the reader to see that "death may be real in a qualitative sense in both the personal and public life of man" (1988, 18). Although he concedes that such an interpretation may have intrinsic weaknesses, he concludes that it offers "a coherent reading of the story as a whole, and is, as far as I can see, the only way of making sense of God's words and actions that is congruent with the rest of the Old Testament and with the story's own normative setting at the beginning of Genesis" (1988, 19).

Moberly's metaphorical reading of Gen 2:17 presents a number of serious problems, apart from his intertextual citations which do not bear the weight of his interpretation. Linguistically, the word "death" in the Old Testament is a reference to physical death.[16] In order to give credibility to the "spiritual death" interpretation, an exegete has to be lax with the biblical text by "spiritualizing" one or both of the phrases "in

(2008). It would have been interesting to read Barr's rejoinder. Unfortunately, he passed away on October 14, 2006 at the age of 82.

15. This is especially true of fundamentalist, conservative, and evangelical scholars. The fact that it is a common or popular interpretation does not *necessarily* prove that it is correct, but that it is a possibility.

16. Collins (2006, 161) concedes that the most common referent of the semantic range of the word "death" is physical death (e.g. Gen 5:5). He also asserts, however, that it can refer to "spiritual death." He gives two examples from Prov 12:28 and 23:13–14, which are not convincing. He fails to argue from the text and context.

the day" and "you shall surely die" to mean "you shall become mortal" and "you shall die spiritually" in the discourse between God and man.[17] As Gibson admits, "We may wriggle out of the difficulty in v. 17 by rendering it more freely than the Hebrew strictly permits" (1981, 113). John Walton drives home the point forcibly when he says:

> The theological logic that has been applied to this text in the past is that since Adam and Eve did not drop over dead on the first bite of the forbidden fruit or die shortly thereafter ("that day"), the warning from God *must* have referred to spiritual death. This is an excellent example of how exegetical shortsightedness can result in unwarranted theological conclusions. There is no reason to dispute the concept of spiritual death or to question that Adam and Eve's sin eventuated in that condition. It is a mistake, however, to deduce that the warning of 2:17 had spiritual death in mind because physical death did not occur right away. (2001, 175)

Not reading the text plainly, straightforwardly and literally, Moberly has hermeneutically violated an important protocol—a basic teaching that a text should be read literally unless there are textual markers to suggest otherwise.[18] In this case, there seems to be no textual warrant for a spiritual reading or for spiritualizing the text. Moberly's reading allows vacillation between "historical" and "metaphorical" reading which leads to the use of inconsistent hermeneutical methodology. The question then arises: Can a reader be allowed to do so arbitrarily? If so, on what grounds?

Intertextually, Moberly appeals to Deut 30:15, 19 and Prov 5:5–23; 7:22–27 to support his case. He claims that "death" and "life" suggest a quality of human life (e.g. "life" means good, God-related, and "death" means bad, accursed existence) and that this is well attested in the Old Testament (1988, 16–18). I do not see how the texts he has quoted corroborate his case. Even if he can prove that these verses are to be understood metaphorically, does it necessarily follow that this must be the way to read Gen 2:17?

Another line of argument used to support a metaphorical reading by Moberly and others is to study the phrase "you/he/they will surely die" in other passages such as Gen 3:4; 20:7; 26:11; 1 Sam 14:44; 22:16; 1 Kgs 2:37, 42; 2 Kgs 1:4, 6, 16; Jer 26:8; Ezek 3:18; 33:8, 14; and others.[19] In Moberly's view:

---

17.   Admittedly, by smuggling the New Testament texts (e.g. Pauline texts like Rom 5 and others) through the backdoor of the Old Testament, he may get away with a metaphorical or non-literal interpretation.

18.   See standard books on hermeneutics.

19.   For more scriptural references, see Gesenius 2006, 113 l–w.

The emphatic verbal form used ("You shall surely die"; *môt ṭāmût*) is similar to the standard idiom for the death penalty in a legal context, and the identical expression is used elsewhere in a variety of contexts, usually with the imminent demise of the addressee in view. God's words naturally mean an imminent termination of man's life if the prohibition is disobeyed. (1988, 4)[20]

However, Barr correctly and pointedly refutes Moberly's explanation with this argument:

None of these refers to a quality of life, better or worse. Moberly himself appeals to Hebrew usage, but is vastly contrary to his proposal. Of course the nouns "death" and "life" are found in religious and moral contexts that apply to the quality of human life. But this cannot be taken up and transferred to apply to God's words "you will surely die" spoken to Adam and Eve in Gen 2:1. That God, speaking to the primitive pair about the dangers from the tree, was saying to them "in the day you eat of it you will surely suffer a serious diminution of the quality of life" will not be taken seriously in the scholarly world. (2006, 12)

Moberly justifies his reading in his response to Barr by saying:

I am concerned with the logic of the narrative *as it impinges on the reader*, not as might relate to the characters within the story. Thus my judgment about the genre of the text is that it is more akin to a parable or one of Aesop's fables, whose purpose is to promote reflection and learning on the part of the reader/hearer, than it is to the kind of literature which one can find elsewhere in the Old Testament and with which we are familiar, *mutatis mutandis*, in the modern novel, which draws the reader into the imaginative world of the story and provokes reflection in relation to the characters' own thoughts and actions. (2008, 35 [original emphasis])[21]

A metaphorical reading of Gen 2:17 carries a few significant ramifications. First, it weakens the grammatical force of the prohibition, given the fact that the infinitive absolute before the finite verb expresses certainty and actuality.[22] Second, it suggests that God is an inept

---

20.   Parallel phrases may be insightful but should not take priority over any philological analysis of the text within its own context.

21.   In this article, he failed to give new evidence, or add anything substantial or decisive to buttress his reading except to clarify and justify his reading proposal, which remains unpersuasive to me and, I think, to Barr, too. To complicate matters, Moberly has muddied the exegetical waters by suggesting the genre of the narrative as akin to a parable or an Aesop's fable, which can be challenged on the internal and canonical logic of the narrative along with a chorus of objections from other scholars who hold different views.

22.   Grammatically speaking, *môt ṭāmût* is Qal infinitive absolute, and Qal imperfect 2 m.s. literally means, "dying you shall die." According to Gesenius, "The

communicator because he "fails to make his own intention plain" (Barr 2006, 15). This brings up a relevant question: Would the couple have understood God's communiqué literally or metaphorically? "Adam and Eve were bound to do, following the normal sense of usage in biblical culture," says Barr (2006, 15). Moberly sees "no reason to disagree with Barr's contention that their understanding of God's words should be within the normal constraints of mainstream classical Hebrew grammar and usage; if God said 'you will surely die' this would be taken to mean that termination of their existence would be imminent" (2008, 35). Third, if God does not say what he means and does not mean what he says, would that make God a liar ("at least close to one," to use Barr's phrase)? Barr further points out that "the liar uses words in a special or technical sense and thus deceives the victim, who understands them in their normal sense" (2006, 16). Such a theological position would be unthinkable and unacceptable to Moberly.

One final observation is that Moberly's reading is weakened further because he fails to mount a challenge or argue against Barr's view that "God changed his mind." But, more significantly, the interpretive option of "God changed his mind" gains more credibility and becomes more compelling when one realizes that, ironically, Moberly has written an article (1998) demonstrating successfully and arguing persuasively that God does change his mind![23] Barr's closing and fitting words are that Moberly "has to take more seriously one obvious common sense suggestion, namely that God changed his mind or, in the older language of the English Bible, 'repented'" (2006, 19).[24]

A plain and natural reading of the text suggests that the delay of the couple's punishment is due to the fact that God changed his mind[25] as suggested by earlier scholars.[26] "It is more reasonable to suppose that

---

infinitive absolute [is] used before the verb to strengthen the verbal idea, i.e. to emphasize in this way either the certainty (especially in the case of threats) or the forcibleness and completeness of an occurrence." See *Gesenius' Hebrew Grammar*, 113 l–n. Cf. "this Hebrew double verb construction's repetition is to add emphasis to 'you will die for sure, you will die on the day you eat it'" (Alter 1996, 9).

23. It is puzzling to me that he has not given any arguments to demolish the "God changed his mind" reading.

24. I part company with Barr on his interpretation of Gen 3. See Lim (2009).

25. For an introduction to a lexical study of the word "repent," see Parunak's excellent but out of date article (1975). See also Moberly (1998).

26. Textual evidence concerning God changing his mind abounds: Gen 6:6; Exod 32:14; Deut 32:36; 1 Sam 15:11, 35; 2 Sam 24:16; 1 Chr 21:15; Isa 38:1–5; Jer 15:6; 18:8; 26:3, 13, 19; 42:10; Amos 7:3, 6; and Jonah 3:10. On the other hand we have texts like Num 3:19; 1 Sam 15:29; Ezek 24:14; Mal 3:6; and Jas 1:17, which state

God in his mercy mitigates the severity of the penalty he had in the first instance ordained" (Bennett 1861, 99). Gunkel remarks, "It is an extraordinary example of divine mercy that he did not enforce the word" (1997, 10).[27] Skinner adds, "The simple explanation is that God, having regard to the circumstances of the temptation, changed his purpose and modified the penalty" (1930, 67).

To argue that the couple did die eventually is to miss the point of the text because that would be the logical consequence of their disobedience as seen in ch. 3. Moreover, Barr makes an insightful point when he says that "God's warning would only make sense had the punishment for disobedience been speedy.[28] Otherwise, no one would be deterred from doing evil if we were told that the consequence for disobedience would be a delayed punishment, that pay day would be some day, in the near future and perhaps a hundred years from now" (Barr 1992, 10).[29] Gordon Wenham adds, "The text is a straightforward warning that death will follow eating" (1987, 68). Only by straining, twisting, and massaging the text can one argue for a "spiritual death" interpretation. Moberly has offered a suggestive possibility that is less exegetically probable and

that God does not change his mind. This has led to the current theological debate between "open theism" and "classical theism." It is beyond the scope of this paper to deal with this topic.

27. Cf. "And one of the narrator's concerns may have been to show that God did not make good his terrible threat but had allowed grace to prevail" (von Rad 1972, 95).

28. The certainty and immediacy of death is emphasized in a few Bible translations; e.g., "for on the day that you eat from it, you will certainly die" (New English Bible); "The moment you eat from that tree, you're dead" (The Message), "if you do, you will die the same day" (Good News translation); "if you eat any fruit from that tree, you will die before the day is over" (Contemporary English Version); "for as soon as you eat of it, you shall die" (Tanakh). By and large, the English Bible translations have chosen to accentuate the verbal idea by making use of words such as "surely" or "certainly" as the best way to understand the Hebrew phrase *môt tāmût*.

29. Ironically, Barr argues that the punishment for disobedience is not "death" but "work"—the ground is put under a curse. "His death is not the punishment, but is only the mode on which the final stage of the punishment works out. He was going to die anyway, but *this* formulation of his death emphasized his failure to overcome the soil and his own belonging to it," the reason being the woman and the serpent's sentence of punishment does not mention death (1992, 9–10). I have three responses to make. First, this is an argument from silence. Second, lexical semantics teaches that the existence of a concept or referent is not limited to the presence of a certain vocabulary. Third, we are told that man would return to dust! Would that not be a picture of death?

satisfactory on syntactical and contextual grounds.[30] The verses he has quoted promise much but deliver little. Regrettably, his flawed reading imposes inordinate strain on the text and is lexically unsound and linguistically unjustified. He appears to have read more into the text than what is apparent. He makes a strong plea that a metaphorical reading offers a coherent reading of the biblical narrative and makes the best sense of God's words and actions consistent with the rest of the Old Testament. However, in my view, God changing his mind is a better interpretive option because it takes the text as it is and not as what it should be. This proposed reading observes Ockham's razor, which states, "entia non sunt multiplicanda praeter necessitatem (entities should not be multiplied beyond necessities)."

It is easy to suspect that Moberly's line of argument is forced because of his theological *tendenz* that if the serpent is right and God is wrong, then this implies God is a liar. Moberly is right to say that all reading is influenced and informed by one's pre-understanding or presupposition (2008, 37–40). However, that does not mean a reader should be given free rein. Though all reading is conditioned by the reader, is there no such thing as a valid or an invalid reading? As Jeanrond rightly asks, "Do we allow our pre-understanding to be challenged in the act of reading or do we impose it uncritically and violently on the text?" (1974, 6).

Hence, it is imperative in reading for a reader to scrutinize the text carefully and critically by observing textual constraints, and to practise "distanciation" which may be difficult but not impossible. Unfortunately, Moberly has failed to do that, hence distorting the meaning of the text. Instead of reading the text in its own right, he permits later texts to filter and determine its meaning. In other words, he leads the text instead of allowing the text to lead him. In the end, Moberly's exegetical train is running on the wrong track. Metaphorically speaking, he tries to have his exegetical cake and eat it but fails, because he undercuts his own solution.

In summary, a linguistic, hermeneutical, and theological reading, with serious consideration of various scholarly proposals and evaluation of contrary views, leads me to an ineluctable conclusion—that Gen 2:17, read plainly and straightforwardly, refers to "physical death" and to God's changing his mind. This plain, straightforward reading is in sync with the contour of the coordinates of the text and the logic of the narrative flow of the context. Such explanation offers an adequate, satisfactory,

---

30. It is good that as interpreters of the text, we are reminded to hear the text in its narrow context before bringing other texts from a broader context.

and reasonable exegetical explanation for the non-fulfillment of God's warning and the delayed punishment. The significant point to note is that God changed his mind not because of caprice[31] or pedagogical intention[32] but because of grace.[33]

31. For a contradistinction to the ancient Near Eastern gods, see Walton (2007).

32. Cf. "Nothing is said to indicate that God combined pedagogical intentions with this prohibition (in the sense of a 'moral' development of man). On the contrary, one destroys the essential part of the story with such rationalistic explanations" (von Rad 1972, 81).

33. For more details on the aspect of grace, see Lim (2002, 99–224).

THE ANOMALY OF INTERPRETATION

Roland Boer

I wish to explore a hunch: the anomaly is what ties all modes of literary interpretation to each other. By anomaly I mean the item that causes a problem, that causes a disturbance in the narrative or poetic scheme, that which does not compute and must therefore be explained and dealt with in one way or another. I would suggest that the anomaly functions as the trigger for every conceivable approach to texts. Indeed, it is as ubiquitous as texts themselves, as well as authors, readers, meanings and so on. Without the anomaly, interpretation would not exist. I make no apologies for such a universal statement, even though it emerges from a very particular and old passion of mine—the intersection between the work of Fredric Jameson and allegorical biblical interpretation. Since the rubbing together of these two is the moment at which the spark first arose, I will explore that intersection more fully before opening up my discussion to other methods. Although I restrict myself to the methods that have been and are used in biblical studies, it seems to me that my argument applies to the use of these methods more generally.

Anomalies

At the heart of the allegorical interpretation of the Bible—inaugurated by Origen in the third century C.E., cemented in place by Augustine and dominating until the arrival of modern historical critical methods in the seventeenth century—lies the anomaly, a feature of the text that then became the secret to interpretation. The allegorists seized upon one textual anomaly after another, which then became the keys that unlocked whole new vistas of interpretation and meaning. Now, that anomaly may have been a hitch in the story-line, a word out of place or perhaps a syntactical blip, but it was the crucial signal that a deeper meaning lay hidden. Jameson, I would suggest, follows a similar path in his interpretations: a master at looking awry and seeing a text or a problem from a whole new angle (which may well be a definition of allegory), what he seeks are traces or signals in the text of social and, above all, economic realities that the text conceals, mediates and to which it responds in various ways. For Jameson, such anomalies show up first and foremost in the form, rather than the content of a text.

Before going any further, let me offer an example or two, one from medieval biblical allegory and one from Jameson. A rather typical example is the story of Jonah and the whale—or rather the "big fish" as the Hebrew text has it. The anomaly in question is the following: "Jonah was in the belly of the fish three days and three nights" (Jonah 2:1; ET 1:17). Why three days and three nights? Why specify the time in this way? It is completely unnecessary for the story: Jonah flees God in a boat, a storm arises, the sailors appease God at Jonah's suggestion by tossing him into the sea, he is swallowed by a great fish, vomited up on the land, preaches doom and destruction on the city of Nineveh, which happens to repent from its sins in the last moment and is spared the promised destruction. Jonah sulks, since his glee at Nineveh's coming destruction has now been thwarted, so God teaches him a lesson with the plant that gives him shade from the sun and the worm that then eats the plant. In all of this, it is completely irrelevant how long he spent in the fish's stomach.

What to do with the three days and three nights? The allegorical interpreters took a hint from Matt 12:40: "For as Jonah was three days and three nights in the belly of the whale, so will the Son of man be three days and three nights in the heart of the earth." Given that the Gospel of Matthew places these words in the mouth of Jesus, then we have no better authority with which to understand the stomach of the fish, or the belly of the whale as Matthew puts it, as an allegory for Christ's burial in the tomb. Jesus, or rather, Matthew already stretches the connection with his "heart of the earth," but that becomes the springboard for the allegorical reading of Christ's descent into hell, as the Apostles' Creed would have it. And just as the fish spat Jonah out onto dry land after three days, so also Christ rose from the grave after "three" days (again, an allegorical stretch). This allegory, sanctioned by one no less than Christ himself, caught on so thoroughly that any representation of the fish and Jonah in medieval art and literature signalled Christ—it was none other than the "sign of Jonah" (Luke 11:29; Matt 12:39). Or rather, it gave license for an almost endless series of allegories, where every moment of Jonah's life becomes a signal of a comparable one in Jesus' life, where even the sailors (variously Apostles, Romans, Jews or Pontius Pilate), the sea (the water in which Pilate washes his hands), ship and storm become allegorically charged (see Sherwood 2000, 11–21). From here, Jonah and the great fish also became an allegory for the life of the individual believer, who was once dead in sin, but through Christ has a new life. Interpretation then moved onto the grand scheme of history, where Jonah's time of submarine transport (or at times the ship itself) became a sign of the collective of the faithful who, after the history of life on earth, enter into heaven at the close of that history. All of this was drawn from one anomaly.

I could invoke a whole range of other examples of medieval allegory, such as the interpretation of the escape of the Israelites from Egypt as allegories of the life of Christ who moves from death to life, of the individual believer who passes from sin to salvation and of the people of God who are on the path to heaven from this vale of tears. Or the spiritual and ecclesiological interpretations of the Song of Songs, as an allegory of Christ's love for Israel, or the Church or the individual believer, down to the breasts mentioned in Song 4:5 functioning as an allegory for the Old and New Testaments (Norris 2003, 165). But the example of Jonah will do for now. Let me reiterate my initial point, namely that the key lies in an anomaly that somehow demands further interpretation.

As far as Jameson is concerned, a good example of a comparable process is his interpretation of Rimbaud's poem, "The Ladies Who Look for Lice" ("Les Chercheuses de Poux"), especially the following stanza:

> He hears their lashes beat the still, sweet air;
> Their soft electric fingers never tire—
> Through his grey swoon, a crackling in his hair—
> Beneath their royal nails the little lice expire. (Jameson 1984, 74)

The anomaly here is the phrase "soft electric fingers," reinforced by lashes beating the still air and the crackling in his hair as the lice die. Jameson's question is: Why this mechanical, repetitive image of systematic killing? There is no overt or obvious reason for such an image. And his answer: "minute, electrical, deadly, blood-spilling in its very delicacy—I feel myself that it may not be too exaggerated to read here an expectation and a foreshadowing of that new thing, the modern fire-arm, the machine gun" (Jameson 1984, 75–76). The lice are mowed down by clacking fingernails as if by the machine guns. Yet this is only the first step, for what all this signals is a transformation of the body and its senses by the military technology of monopoly capitalism.

A few points are worth noting in this example. First, the anomaly of the machine gun image is in this poem a trace, figuration or representation of history, specifically of the history of capitalism. In the case of Rimbaud, he marks a transition from market or classical capitalism to monopoly capitalism. It is, in other words, an allegory of that shift within a mode of production. Further, such a figuration takes place through the body's senses, a recurring interest of Jameson. The senses register through their history of changes the social and economic context of human life. For Rimbaud in particular, this shows up in the new construction of an "adolescent" body—in the poem it is an adolescent boy who must undergo the delousing. Third, we find those traces in literature through what Jameson calls "sentence structure": the choice of syntax and words that is the fabric of sentences. Already Jameson's allegory has become rather complex: sentences and bodily senses act as connected allegories for the economic real of capitalism.

There is a multitude of such examples in Jameson's work, such as the sea in Joseph Conrad's novels, which acts as a limit to his work and is at the same time the manifestation of history (Jameson 1981, 241–42, 267, 269), or spatial representation (Jameson 2005, 296–313; 1991, 97–129; 1992), especially in architecture and film, or the breaks and discontinuities of genre within a work (Jameson 1981, 103–50; 2005, 254–66). But the point of contact with biblical allegory is the anomaly that sets interpretation on its way. Both Jameson and the biblical allegorists are interested in the items that do not compute in the text in question, a discomfort generated by the text, the odd detail of a narrative or poem, the breaks and ripples in form, stylistic clashes and apparently superfluous elements. These items do nothing as far as the world of the text is concerned; even more, they cannot be controlled by the dominant ideological and formal structure of the text. They signal an excess that chops up the text and bursts its boundaries.

Levels

All of what has gone before is really just the beginning. The more significant question is: What do they do with the anomaly? The biblical allegorists locked onto the anomaly and built a highly sophisticated method that placed the anomaly dead centre. And this is what Jameson draws from them, namely, a method that highlights the anomaly. Let me trace out how these methods were built up and systematized around the anomaly, for it seems to me that they provide a model for understanding how other methods work (to which I will turn in the final section of this essay).

If the medieval allegorists developed a four-fold approach in order to deal with the anomaly, Jameson has constructed a three-tiered approach that seeks to do much the same thing.[1] This is the well-known three-level

1. At this point, Jameson's take on allegory overlaps with his early notion of metacommentary, which he describes as "a reflexive operation proposed for staging

method—political, social and historical—that he lays out in the first chapter of *The Political Unconscious* (1981). It moves out to successively wider "semantic horizons," "phases" and "concentric frameworks" (Jameson 1981, 75–76). Indeed, this comprehensive effort at a method may be read as a detailed attempt to deal with the anomaly in interpretation. While the first, political level stays within the bounds of the text and its relation to immediate political events (the popular sense of "history"), the social level moves beyond the text to encounter other texts and indeed ideological positions, which turn out to be (not unexpectedly for a Marxist analysis) the complex expressions of class positions in conflict. Finally, the historical level moves even further to the vast sweeps of economic formations, or, more preferably, modes of production. Or, in Jameson's words,

> …such semantic enrichment and enlargement of the inert givens and materials of a particular text must take place within three concentric frameworks, which mark a widening out of the sense of the social ground of a text through the notions, first, of political history, in the narrow sense of punctual event and a chroniclelike sequence of happenings in time; then of society, in the now already less diachronic and time-bound sense of a constitutive tension and struggle between social classes; and, ultimately, of history now conceived in its vastest sense of the sequence of modes of production and the succession and destiny of the various human social formations, from prehistoric life to whatever far future history has in store for us. (Jameson 1981, 75)

Interpretation merges with nothing less than a theory of history itself. Coming straight out of the Hegelian Marxist tradition, with its dialectical leaps from one horizon to a yet wider horizon, as well as the mediation between the superstructure (text) and economics (mode of production) by means of class,[2] this method also owes a large debt to medieval allegory.

---

the struggle within an individual literary and cultural text of various interpretations that are themselves so many 'methods' or philosophies or ideological worldviews" (Jameson 1988, viii). Not a bad description of allegory. Compare his description of a dialectical reading, which comes close again: "we begin to glimpse the process of allegorical interpretation as a kind of scanning that, moving back and forth across the text, readjusts its terms in constant modification of a type quite different from our stereotypes of some static medieval or biblical decoding, and which one would be tempted (were it not also an old-fashioned word!) to characterize as dialectical" (Jameson 1991, 168).

2.	But note also that each level has a rather conventional structure of base and superstructure with its appropriate mediation. Thus, the political level moves from individual text to immediate politics via formal contradictions in the text and ideological antinomies; the social level moves from ideology to class via ideological

That tradition, as is well known, distinguished between four levels of interpretation, namely the literal (or historical), allegorical (or typological), moral (or tropological) and anagogic. These levels move through various phases, beginning with the surface meaning of the text, following its plot lines and so on. The second or allegorical phase makes a bridge between the Old and New Testaments, usually through the life of Christ, to whom all the stories and characters in the Old Testament are precursors or types—hence its alternative name, the typological. Indeed, the primary anomaly for allegory is precisely this relationship between "old" and "new"; or rather, the Hebrew Bible as a whole constituted a somewhat large anomaly for the early Christian writers. With this kind of initial motivation, it could hardly help making anomaly its over-riding concern. The moral level focuses on the life of the individual here in the present, pursuing what the text might mean for that life, mediated through the life of Christ. And then the anagogic moves out to the sweep of (Christian) history, especially the future, with the grand issues such as heaven and hell, predestination, the Last Judgement and the various prophecies that look forward to those moments.

There are one or two further things to say about this schema, but first let me quote a certain "Honorius of Autun" for a more contemporary statement of the method:

> Sacred Scripture is interpreted and understood in four ways: historically, allegorically, tropologically, anagogically. This is expressed by the table for the presentation of bread in the ark (Exod. 25:29ff.), which is supported by four feet. The ark represents the Church, in which service is rendered to Christ. The table is sacred Scripture, upon which bread is presented, that is, the food of souls. The four feet are the four kinds of meaning, that is to say: history when the thing referred to is narrated as it happened; allegory, when the thing referred to is expounded with reference to Christ and the Church; tropology, when it is applied to soul and spirit; anagogy, when it is understood of the celestial life. (Norris 2003, xix)

The main thing to notice about this conveniently schematic presentation by Honorius (who was known for his rather mechanical application of the method) is that it is justified on the basis of the Bible. Wherever four items turned up, such as the table of the bread of the Presence in the temple, or the four beasts of the throne in Ezek 1 and 10 or the four Gospels, they were read as scriptural warrant for the four levels of allegory. There is even a key text, Gal 4:22–24, that came to give license to

conflict; the historical level goes from the texts of a period to mode of production through signs of cultural change that leave their traces in the texts. For a fuller discussion, see my *Jameson and Jeroboam* (Boer 1996, 41–97).

the practice, coming from none other than the pen of Paul (or rather Tertius, his scribe): "For it is written that Abraham had two sons, one by a slave and one by a free woman. But the one from the slave was born according to the flesh, the one from the free woman through promise. Now this is an allegory (*allēgoroumena*): these women are two covenants." There is another meaning (the basic sense of "allegory"), suggests Paul, and that is the two covenants, one from Sinai and one from Christ—that primary anomaly of the "Old Testament" turns up again and again and again.

Further, although it is common to describe it as "medieval" allegory, the practice predates by a good few years the Middle Ages themselves. At the beginning stands Origen (184–254 C.E.), who, in response to the challenge of Marcion and the Gnostics who by and large rejected the Hebrew Bible (Marcion rather insightfully pointed out that the God of the Hebrew Bible was vacillating, ignorant and supported lascivious bandits like King David), suggesting the idea of a spiritual truth of the "Old Testament" that hinged on the figure of Christ. In other words, faced with the myriad anomalies of the "Old Testament," ones that Marcion and others all too gleefully exposed, Origen's approach was a direct response to that collection of anomalies. He did not, of course, conjure such an approach out of thin air, since Hellenistic writers were engaged in similar pursuits in relation to the Greek and Roman pantheons. Armed with his insight, Origen set to work, and although he asserted the importance of the literal level, he took to the spiritual sense with gusto. So much so that his spermatic spluttering pen (which may well have had something to do with those genitals he sliced off in an early moment of ascetic passion) produced far more commentaries on the Bible than the poor scribes who had to copy them afterwards could ever keep up with. They contented themselves with abridged versions, such as the *Commentary on Romans*.[3] For all the condemnations for heresy, along with the personal hatreds of his many enemies (he would have been an intolerable person to live or work with), it was to Origen that the later allegorists of the twelfth century and afterwards looked for their inspiration, including Dante's *Divine Comedy*.[4]

---

3.   The supposed rejection of allegory by the Antiochene theologians, Diodore and Theodore, who argued instead for "typology," is really nothing more than intellectual flexing. For the whole idea of "typology"—where various figures and events of the "Old Testament" such as Moses or David are types of Christ—breathes the same air as allegory.

4.   For an argument that seeks to link Jameson with Dante's allegorical approach, and then more broadly for a re-recognition of the deep connections between literary

It is all very well to assert that Jameson's method is analogous to allegorical interpretation, that they both have levels of interpretation that have been developed in an effort to systematise one's response to textual anomalies. But I much prefer a stronger connection, for it seems to me that Jameson's concern with the anomaly comes from these allegorical interpreters. Indeed, if we look more closely at the various levels of both Jameson and the medieval allegorists, then it becomes clear rather quickly that the first and last levels of both approaches bear more than a passing relationship to each other. Thus, the medieval literal level, which deals with the historical happenings and events mentioned in the text, comes close to Jameson's political level, which concerns the "punctual event and a chroniclelike sequence of happenings in time" (Jameson 1981, 75). As for the last level, while the medieval anagogic level focuses on the sweep of history from creation through to the new heaven on earth of the eschaton, Jameson's final, historical level deals with the complex interaction and sequence of modes of production, that is, "the succession and destiny of the various human social formations, from prehistoric life to whatever far future history has in store for us" (Jameson 1981, 76). It is precisely this ability to show how the individual text finds itself part of a much greater reality, namely the concrete totality of history, that Jameson finds so appealing about medieval allegory.

The connection is quite inescapable on the first and last levels of interpretation. However, it becomes a little rocky with the intervening levels. It is difficult to see, on the face of things, how the allegorical and moral levels of medieval interpretation, with their foci of Christ and then the life of the individual believer, relate to the resolute concern with social class and ideology in Jameson's second level. As might be expected, it is precisely here, at the moment when the schema cracks the text and opens it up to other elements of interpretation, that Jameson will invest much of his energy in reshaping the whole approach. I have explored the way Jameson does in fact transform the individual nature of the middle two levels in medieval allegory into his own social level in some detail elsewhere (Boer 1996, 30–42; 2005b) and I do not intend to go into those details here. Suffice to point out that Jameson fiddles with these intervening levels on more than one occasion. His main concern, it seems to me, is to render the vital allegorical level—on which the anomaly gains some interpretive traction—as a social rather than individual exercise: not so much Christ and the individual, but rather the social collective becomes in Jameson's method the allegorical key. And

criticism and biblical criticism, see Brown (2005a) and the responses to his essay (During 2005; Heschel 2005; Milich 2005; Brown 2005b).

the reason for such an interest in that middle level is that it mediates the connection between the anomalous and contradictory text and its historical location within modes of production.

All of these connections become quite concrete when Jameson engages directly with allegorical biblical interpretation, especially in his effort to turn the mediating levels of the allegorists into his important middle or social level: these are his engagements with Walter Benjamin and Northrop Frye.[5] In an early essay on Walter Benjamin (Jameson 1969; 1971, 60–83), Jameson offers a reading of Benjamin by means of the fourfold mode of medieval allegory. The catch is that Jameson inverts the second and third levels: over against the medieval order of literal, allegorical, moral and anagogical, Jameson cites them in that essay as the literal, moral, allegorical and anagogical. Once he has them in this order, he can recast them as the psychological, moral, aesthetic (religion of art) and historical levels. Now, I am less interested in the content (although history as the domain of the anagogic first appears here) than in his juggling of the middle levels. Jameson, it seems, is not comfortable with these two, seeking something else that will do the job far better. And this is especially so with that crucial allegorical level, the one that suggests there is far more to the text than meets the eye. Indeed, by switching the two levels he has in effect fused them into one, which then becomes the locus of allegorical activity.

This early search for a collective dimension to the crucial middle phases of medieval allegory gains another boost when he locks horns with Northrop Frye in *The Political Unconscious* (Jameson 1981, 28–33, 68–74; see also Xie 1996), now in the lead-up to outlining the three levels of his own method. Frye himself reinterprets the medieval levels, or "phases" as he prefers to call them, as follows (Frye 1957, 115–16):

---

5. The next few paragraphs summarize my argument in a couple of earlier publications (Boer 1996, 30–42; 2005a, 54–62). In his more recent *Archaeologies of the Future* (2005) Jameson also has a curious discussion of Ernst Bloch that begins suggestively to recast his Utopian program in terms of a tripartite allegorical structure of body, time and collectivity, only to close with the tantalizing but unexplained addition of a fourth level which then matches these levels up with the medieval schema; except that now we have the Utopian investment (literal), body (allegorical), temporality (moral) and collective (anagogic) (Jameson 2005, 4–9). It feels rather unfinished and highly suggestive: Is the body a form of secularized Christology? And is temporality a secularized eschatology? What about the collectivity and ecclesiology, and utopian investment and the Bible? Jameson might blanch at the suggested connections, but he does slip the four-level table in at the end without comment.

	Allegorical phases	*Medieval levels*
1.	literal and descriptive	literal
2.	formal	allegorical
3.	mythical	moral
4.	anagogic	anagogic

Jameson is after a distinctly social and collective focus in the middle realms of the allegorical approach. Now, as far as Jameson is concerned, what Frye has done is invert the third and fourth medieval levels: the third "mythical" phase becomes the focus of all that is collective and social—what is covered in the medieval schema by the last or anagogic level. For one who has always stressed the collective over against the overwhelming emphasis on the private individual of liberal ideology, Jameson rather likes this focus of Frye's work: if, as Frye argues, literature is a paler and later version of myth and ritual, then literature also must be understood as a "symbolic meditation on the destiny of community" (Jameson 1981, 70). What Jameson does not like is Frye's subsequent move, namely to make the final level a purely individual affair in which the whole issue of apocalyptic boils down to what happens to us as individuals. Here is Jameson: "The essentially historical interpretive system of the church fathers has here been recontained, and its political elements turned back into the merest figures for the Utopian realities of the individual subject" (Jameson 1981, 74). In light of this focus on the individual, Frye's fourth level turns out to be badly misnamed as the anagogic, for its concerns are really those of the third or moral medieval level.

At the same time, Frye's rearrangement does open up the possibility of inserting social and collective concerns into the mediating level of Jameson's own approach. If the essay on Benjamin suggested a search for something more adequate in the mediating level(s), and if Frye opens up the possibility that the social may indeed be found here, then it is the Marxist concern with social class that provides the content for this middle phase. At this point Jameson is quite a conventional Marxist, for in the relations between base (forces of production or economy, including nature, population and technology) and superstructure (the various elements of culture, ideology, law and politics), the mediation comes by means of the social, or "relations of production," which is none other than the organization of people by an economic system into classes. In other words, elements from culture, ideology or politics relate to the economic by means of the social, whose major concern is class conflict. Thus, while Jameson's first phase concerns the individual text and its relation to immediate political history, and if the final phase is that of history understood in terms of modes of production, then the allegorical middle phase is the social, and its prime interest is also the dynamic of class conflict.

What Jameson has done, then, is to transform the allegorical and moral levels of biblical allegory into his own social level of interpretation. In being so transformed, these mediating levels become the crucial mediation between the anomalies of the text and the contradictions of social formations (modes of production). At the point where the anomaly becomes systematized as a feature of interpretation, Jameson invests most of his energy to render it a collective rather than an individual moment. Not only is Jameson's method—a Marxist allegorical method— deeply enmeshed with biblical allegory, the deeper reason for that intimacy is the textual anomaly. Both medieval allegory and Jameson's own work may be read as efforts to deal directly and systematically with that question. In fact, they develop methods that put the anomaly squarely at the centre.

Interpretation

Is this the case with other methods of interpretation as well? Do these methods also have their *raison d'être* in the anomaly too? Here I can let myself speculate somewhat, offering a synoptic view of various methods. However, in order to anchor ourselves to the text, I show how each of these approaches deals with one text, namely Gen 1–3. Since I cannot hope to be exhaustive, let me give a representative example: traditional historical criticism and then feminist, Marxist, deconstructionist, psychoanalytic, postcolonial, ecological and reader-response readings.

So far I have argued that the biblical allegorists took their various anomalies in one direction, passing through the figure of Christ, into the inner life of the believer and then out into the realm of history and beyond. For all the violent rejection of allegory by its relatively recent usurper, biblical historical criticism, the underlying issue for that historical criticism still concerns the anomaly. Child of the Reformation and Enlightenment, with its claims to be "scientific" and "rational," historical criticism really boils down to an alternative response to the problems in the text. Let us see how that works out in Gen 1–3, a text on which historical criticism first cut its teeth (as every first-year Hebrew Bible student soon learns). Here, the initial anomaly was the differing names for God—Elohim in Gen 1:1–2:3 and then Yahweh Elohim in Gen 2:4– 3:24 (and then Yahweh in Gen 4)—which became in the hands of the French surgeon, Jean Astruc, the first hints for the famous documentary hypothesis. By the time it was fully formulated, especially by Well-hausen, we had the ordered and calendrical priestly source (P) for Gen 1:1–2:3, a more earthy Jahwist (J) source overlaid by the Elohist (E) in Gen 2:4–3:24 (and then a Jahwist source on its own in Gen 4)—in short, two creation stories in tension with one another. Of course, once you had sources (whether written or oral) you had to come up with a theory for their combination and editing, and so we find the full elaboration of a complex method called historical criticism with its various branches, especially source, form and redaction (tradition-historical) criticism, as well as a few contributors such as archaeology and the social sciences. An extraordinary amount of energy has been and continues to be devoted to this over-arching method, but my point is that it arose and was elaborated in response to the anomaly; or rather, in response to a whole collection of anomalies that focused on the inconsistencies, breaks, overlaps, contradictions, different ideologies and various styles of the Hebrew Bible. A comparable story might be told of the New Testament, especially with Q(uelle), proto-Matthew, proto-Luke and the relations between the various synoptic gospels.

For all its challenges to historical criticism, feminist biblical analysis too trades in the anomaly. The difference is that the anomaly shifts ground. Many feminists accepted and continued to accept historical criticism as a base method, but the problem now becomes one of the over-whelming patriarchal nature of both text and interpretation. This anomaly becomes acute if, like most biblical feminists, one is committed to church or synagogue and holds the Bible as a sacred text in some form or other. How does one appropriate a text that is so patriarchal, so deni-grating for women? At this point it is much easier to reject the Bible as authoritative and sacred, and to devote one's efforts to showing how and why such a book's authority and influence must be closed down. It is much more difficult to retrieve or detoxify the text. So the response to that anomaly has been to seek other anomalies in the text where the myriad patriarchal structures show up their inconsistencies, offering a wedge that may help break down the text's baleful legacy. In our example from Gen 1–3 various anomalies have turned up. Genesis 1:27 became a favourite for feminists seeking reform within church and synagogue: "So God created Adam in his own image, in the image of God he created him; male and female he created them." To be created in the image of God, went the argument, is to be created both male and female. Further, in a much debated argument from the late 1970s, Phyllis Trible (1978) tried to reclaim the text for feminists by focusing on another anomaly: in Gen 2 there is a predominance of the word "Adam" for the first human creation until the creation of woman from the Adam's side late in the chapter. Only here do we find a decisive shift from "Adam" to "*Ish*" (man) when "*Ishshah*" (woman) appears. Trible argued that before that moment in the narrative of the second creation story we find an undifferentiated human being, who becomes differentiated only with the creation and naming of woman. Much more has, of course, been written on Gen 1–2, but I have said enough to make my point: feminist analysis in its increasingly diverse forms is an effort to deal with anomalies. But note what has happened: the anomaly shifts ground depending on the assumptions of the method in question. If historical criticism concerns itself with the breaks and contradictions in the text, seeking to explain them by means of theories of sources, redaction, communities and scribal schools, then feminist analysis focuses on the inconsistencies and contradictions of the over-arching patriarchal nature of the texts and their interpreters.

Marxist critics have had their fair share of attempts to deal with Gen 1–3 as well. For example, Gale Yee (2003, 60–63; see also Simkins 2004) argues that Gen 2–3 exhibits a tension between two economic structures, a tension that points to a deeper economic one. Thus, in this text, especially the verse "Therefore a man leaves his father and mother and cleaves to his wife, and they become one flesh" (Gen 2:24), we find an agenda that favours the nuclear family. Yee reads this text (she accepts that it was produced by the Yahwist) as an explicit agenda by the new kingship under Solomon to break the social, cultural and economic allegiances to the older tribal structures and the *paterfamilias*. If one had primary loyalties to the clan, then the king would come a poor second. If the king was primary, then the clan allegiances would start to break down. In this light, nuclear families would be far more likely to support the king. Deeper down, however, lies a conflict of economic systems: if the clan embodied the "familial mode of production" in which "family household was the basic socioeconomic unit" (Yee 2003, 61), then the king sought to impose a tributary mode of production, in which tribute and loyalty were due to the king. By now my point is expected: the anomaly may have shifted, but an anomaly it still is. The difference is that the anomaly in the text—why a nuclear family?—becomes a signal of a tension at a social and economic level. While they might not agree on precisely how to read texts (I, for example, differ with Yee over Gen 2–3), Marxists do share the assumption that the various anomalies in the text, whether in terms of form, the patterns of language, or indeed the content of conflicting ideologies, point to contradictions and tensions in the underlying economic systems.

As for deconstruction,[6] for all the challenges that it may have provided to the coherence of texts and their interpretations, it too draws its inspiration from the anomaly. I would not be far off the mark by pointing out that without the anomaly, deconstruction would need to exit the stage, red-faced. It picks at the inconsistencies and incoherencies in texts, showing how the text begins to betray its various exclusions and blind spots upon closer analysis. In a good deconstructive reading, one is never sure whether it is an exposition of the text or a critical engagement, until the moment when everything turns on its head. Let me give two instances where deconstruction gains grip in Gen 1–3. The first is in the very first verse, which may read either as, "In the beginning God created the heavens and the earth," or, "When God began to create the heavens and the earth." I am, of course, not the first to point to the ambivalence in the Hebrew, but rather than take sides in what is really a theological debate (*creation ex nihilo* vs. some pre-existing substance), deconstruction focuses on the ambivalence itself. Why are both meanings possible? What is being admitted? What is excluded? One path to follow is to argue that what appears to be ambivalence in the Hebrew, an oscillation one way and then another, is in fact an effort to close off other possibilities. The text appears to be undecided over two possible meanings, but only two, thereby neatly excluding any other options and setting the boundaries for subsequent interpretations. However, what remains outside the text is a range of other options that the text will not entertain—primal conflict, the cosmic egg, self-generation, sexual procreation and so on. For a deconstructive reading, it is precisely this exclusion through ambivalence that becomes constitutive of the text itself. The second example comes from the story in Gen 2–3. I might focus on the inability to discern whether there are two trees or one in the garden: is there a tree of life and a tree of good and evil (Gen 2:9), or is it one tree in the midst of the garden from which they must not eat (2:17; 3:3)? But I prefer to draw attention to the anomaly of paradise itself that lies at the heart of the text. Why, in a world in which human beings may freely eat of any tree without work, where they stroll with God and chat in the evenings, is there a central flaw? Simply put, if one were to create paradise, why place within it the mechanism for its own demise? It really is the anomaly

---

6. Despite the disarming effort of those who practice deconstruction to follow the master and proclaim that it is not a method but simply a careful reading of a text, I take it as a method. For is not a method a collection of assumptions and strategies by which one reads and interprets? It would not be the first time the practitioners of one method proclaimed that they were interested only in the text and not in methods. One is tempted to respond: except for your own.

with any golden age, as David Jobling (1992a) has demonstrated so well. Rather than attempting to deal with this contradiction theologically (it would not be a golden age if human beings didn't have freewill), or in terms of narrative necessity (we would not have a story if they didn't get on with eating from the tree) or even existentially (it would be incredibly boring in such a paradise), a deconstructive approach points out that paradise could not exist without such a flaw.

A similar situation exists with psychoanalytic criticism, where the anomaly becomes the constitutive exception—that which is excluded is precisely what enables the story to exist in the first place. Thus, in Gen 1–3 we find different versions of this constitutive exception: the paradox of loss, where paradise becomes possible only at the moment of its loss (you don't know what you've got until it's gone); the afterthought of the creation of woman that actually makes her crucial to the whole system; the empty gesture where it seems as though the man and woman have a choice but do not; and the inherent transgression of eating the fruit that seems to be lamentable and undesirable but is built into the story itself (see further Boer 2006). Or in postcolonial and eco-criticism, the verse, "Be fruitful and multiply, and fill the earth and subdue it; and have dominion over the fish of the sea and over the birds of the air and over every living thing that moves upon the earth" (Gen 1:28), becomes highly problematic in the subsequent use of such a text to justify colonial expansion or the dominance of human beings within the total eco-sphere. Or, for queer criticism the anomaly lies in the apparent hetero-sexism (as much in its use as in the text itself) of the verse that says a man should leave his father and mother so that the couple may become one (Gen 2:24). Queer criticism may go on to point to the unstable gender and sexual identifications in the story, all the way from the amorphous "Adam" to the androgynous deity. And for reader-response criticism (Ed Conrad's great focus), it is the very concept of author-generated meaning that becomes the anomaly. Rather than excavating a text as a given, or assuming (an) author(s) responsible for the meaning of the text, reader-response criticism asks what might happen if we see meaning as something constituted by the reader. Indeed, all of these various approaches that I have surveyed produce their meanings through an active engagement by the reader with the text.

Conclusion

Rather than repeat my main argument (I have done so often enough already), I would like to offer three points in conclusion. To begin with, while each method exploits the anomaly for its own, the anomaly in question changes from one method to another. We saw this in my synoptic view of various approaches to Gen 1–3: the break between the two creation stories, the inconsistencies in the andro-centric nature of the text, the hints of socio-economic tensions, the way the text begins to become unstable on closer analysis, the constitutive exceptions on which the text bases itself and so on. Further, I cannot help wondering whether the methods in question create their own anomalies. Given certain basic assumptions (coherence, andro-centricism, incoherence etc.), the text will then exhibit anomalies in light of these assumptions. Finally, I find myself pondering whether it would be possible to imagine and perhaps construct a method that does not find its trigger in the anomaly. It would be a very different method from the ones to which we are accustomed.

EZRA'S "LOST MANUSCRIPTS": NARRATIVE CONTEXT AND RHETORICAL FUNCTION

Katherine M. Stott

Introduction

In a 1992 article published in *JSOT*, entitled "Heard but Not Seen: The Representation of 'Books' in the Old Testament," Ed Conrad wrote about the phenomenon of lost and found books in the Hebrew Bible. As a doctoral student working under Ed's supervision I was greatly intrigued by what he had to say on this topic and I have since then gone on to explore this subject in several of my own publications. One such publication, which also appeared in *JSOT*, focused on the relationship between the story of the book of the law in 2 Kgs 22–23 and comparable tales of lost and found books in classical literature. But there are other stories in the Hebrew Bible which also exhibit similarities to "book-find" reports from classical antiquity. One such story, upon which I would like to focus my contribution to this Festschrift in Ed's honour, appears in the book of Ezra and centres around two ordinances said to have been issued by King Cyrus in the first year of his reign. The first is the well-known edict (מכתב) of Cyrus (Ezra 1:2–4), permitting the Jews to return from Exile and to rebuild their temple in Jerusalem. The second is the Aramaic decree (דכרונה) of Cyrus (Ezra 6:2–5), said to have been found by King Darius in Ecbatana.

The opening six chapters of Ezra tell a story which is bracketed by these two references to ordinances issued by Cyrus. Having been granted official permission in the edict of Cyrus, the Jews exiled in Babylon begin to return to Judah and commence the rebuilding of the temple (Ezra 3:8–13). However, progress is soon thwarted by 'the people of the land' and eventually construction is brought to a complete halt in the reign of King Artaxerxes (Ezra 4). It is not until the reign of Darius that rebuilding resumes, although resistance still lurks. The Jews claim that they have the authority to rebuild the temple based on a decree of Cyrus, but various local officials are unconvinced. To resolve the matter, Darius is called upon to find the royal decree of which the Jews spoke (Ezra 5), and it is at this point that the Aramaic decree of Cyrus enters the story. A search is made for the document in the royal archives in Babylon, though it is actually found in Ecbatana, the Persian capital. As the Jews anticipated, the document permits the rebuilding of the temple and the restoration of its vessels. Thus, the opposition is put to rest once and for all, and eventually the temple is completed (Ezra 6).

In the past, there has been much debate about the two ordinances of Cyrus mentioned in this story, particularly concerning their relationship and their authenticity. For reasons which will be outlined further shortly, the most widely held view is to see the Aramaic document as an authentic decree, but the one in Hebrew as a literary invention. However, not everyone agrees. On one end of the spectrum, the authenticity of both ordinances has been defended by some. On the other end of the spectrum, it has recently been suggested that both could be literary inventions. In such a context, I propose to move the discussion in a somewhat different direction by considering not whether these documents were genuine or not but what purpose they serve in their narrative context. When the opening chapters of Ezra are read in conjunction with classical stories about lost and found books, it is possible to advance literary support for understanding these texts as performing a rhetorical function in the book, regardless of whether they are based on actual documentation or not.

Traditional Views

One of the major issues for commentators on the book of Ezra has been the question of whether the same royal edict lies at the base of the two ordinances presented in chs. 1 and 6 respectively. This possibility is suggested by the fact that both documents are said to have been issued by Cyrus in the first year of his reign. Furthermore, both texts concern the return of the Jews from exile and the building of the temple. However, there are differences between the two texts, a fact which challenges the hypothesis that the same royal edict lies at the base of both documents. Above all, one text (Ezra 1:2–4) is in Hebrew and the other (Ezra 6:2–5) is in Aramaic. Furthermore, the Aramaic document gives specifications for the building of the temple, which are absent in the Hebrew decree.

Various explanations have been advanced to explain these differences. Probably the most common view is to argue that the Aramaic document is the authentic decree and that the Hebrew document is a literary invention. This judgment is supported by the fact that Hebrew, unlike Aramaic, was not an official scribal language of the Persian Empire. Moreover, there are various other problems posed by the Hebrew edict, which raise doubts about its authenticity: (1) although there is evidence to suggest that Cyrus issued a decree allowing peoples exiled in Babylon to return to their native lands, many commentators consider it unlikely that Cyrus would have issued an edict on behalf of such a small nation as the Jews, and (2) the decree is coloured with biblical language, which seems out of place in an allegedly Persian document. For example, the document refers to Yahweh as "the God of heaven"—terminology which some regard as unlikely to have been used by a foreign king.

Although the differences between the two ordinances are most commonly explained in this way, not everyone agrees with this manner of resolving the discrepancies. E. Bickerman, for example, defends the authenticity of both documents. He explains the differences by suggesting that the documents represent "two independent records concerning the same case" (1976, 73). Recognizing that Hebrew, unlike Aramaic, was not an official scribal language of the Persian Empire, Bickerman maintains that the Hebrew text reflects an oral decree addressed to the Jews in their local language, while the Aramaic one represents the official Persian record of the ordinance (1976, 75). Bickerman also counters objections which challenge the authenticity of the Hebrew edict. For example, he defends the use of the terminology "the God of heaven" as a reference to Yahweh. According to Bickerman, "the Persian administration necessarily styled the deities of the subject peoples in agreement with phraseology used by the latter" (1976, 79). To support this argument he points to a number of instances in Persian texts where this seems to have occurred (see 1976, 79–80 for examples).

H. G. M. Williamson is another scholar who has defended the authenticity of the Hebrew edict in Ezra 1 (1987, 33–34). On the whole, Williamson endorses and builds upon the views of Bickerman. However, his explanation for the Jewish colouring of the Hebrew text differs slightly from that proposed by Bickermann. Unlike Bickerman, Williamson is prepared to admit that the record has probably "passed through Jewish hands" (1987, 34). Thus he sees terminology such as "the God of heaven" as an editorial addition.

More recently, Grabbe (1998) has re-advanced the more widely held position that Cyrus's Hebrew edict is not a genuine document. Moreover, and in contrast to the more standard view, he also doubts that the Aramaic document is authentic (a view which had earlier been asserted by Torrey 1970, 140–207). According to Grabbe, there are various problems with viewing the Aramaic document as genuine. First, he doubts the likelihood of Cyrus issuing such a "decree for the remote province of Judah." Second, he finds it hard to believe that Cyrus would "specify the particular dimensions of the building," especially given the fact that they are so strange. Third, Grabbe views the claim "that costs would be met by the temple treasury," as "Jewish propaganda pure and simple." Finally, he argues that the document uses language which he maintains post-dates the time it is alleged to have been written. According to Grabbe, all of these problems suggest that the Aramaic document in Ezra 6, like the Hebrew document in Ezra 1, "is either a Jewish invention or…has been edited by Jewish scribes" (Grabbe 1998, 131).

An Alternative Interpretation

It is not within my scope of interest to debate the authenticity of these documents. Instead what attracts my attention is the question of why these documents are mentioned in the story at all and what purpose they serve in their literary context. When the opening chapters of Ezra are read in conjunction with certain stories from Greece and Rome, it is possible to advance literary support for understanding these texts as performing a rhetorical function in the literature irrespective of whether or not they refer to actual documents.

As will be demonstrated in more detail shortly, there are many similarities between the opening chapters of Ezra and classical stories about lost and found books. Above all, if we can assume that the decree of Cyrus in Ezra 6 is in some way related to the edict referred to in the opening chapter, then it can be argued that the motif of loss and recovery, evident in the classical literature, appears also in the book of Ezra. Given the points of connection between the two ordinances issued by Cyrus in Ezra 1 and 6, I think it is reasonable to suppose that there is at least some sort of rhetorical connection between them. The edict in Ezra 6 recalls the former one in Ezra 1, even if they are not exactly the same. Both are issued by Cyrus and both are addressed to the Jews. Furthermore, both give specific authorization for the rebuilding of the temple in Jerusalem.

Assuming then that the two ordinances of Cyrus are connected, the opening six chapters of Ezra can be seen to tell a tale about an edict delivered by Cyrus that was forgotten and remembered. In the Hebrew edict Cyrus grants the Jews permission to rebuild their temple, but these plans are thwarted in subsequent years (see Ezra 4). The problems are only resolved, in the reign of Darius, when the Aramaic document is found in Ecbatana and confirms Cyrus's original authorization.[1] Strictly

---

1. Meyer believed that the discovery of the scroll at Ecbatana, and not in Babylon where it was expected to be found, was a detail "which no humans would have invented [was kein Mensch erfunden haben würde]" (1896, 47). However, as

speaking, the story in Ezra 1–6, unlike the following classical examples, may not be about a single document lost and found, since two separate documents may be envisaged. Nevertheless, the motifs of loss and recovery are still observable in the story, pertaining to the ordinance of Cyrus itself rather than the documents in which it is recorded. Indeed, there may be some rhetorical advantage to the way in which the motif of loss and recovery is expressed in the biblical text. By referring to two separate documents which both contain similar or perhaps complementary stipulations, the two are mutually corroborated, and hence invested with greater authority.

The Classical Texts

As noted before, there are many stories about lost and found documents in texts from the Hellenistic and Roman periods. Such stories are often understood by classical scholars as rhetorical ploys designed to bolster the credibility of the narrative in which they are mentioned and sometimes used to promote a particular ideological agenda.

An anonymously authored work from the time of Nero called *The Trojan War* is a good example of a text which incorporates a story about a lost and found book that serves the rhetorical purpose of enhancing its own authority. At the beginning of the story, the claim is made that the history of the Trojan War to be recounted is actually a translation of a Phoenician document written by a certain Dictys of Crete. This Dictys apparently went to the Trojan War, recorded a history of this campaign in Phoenician, and had the records buried with him in his tomb in Crete. Years later the texts were discovered by shepherds. Having passed through the hands of a number of authorities, they were ultimately presented to the Emperor Nero. When Nero received the texts, he had them translated into Greek by his Phoenician philologists and deposited them in the Greek library. We are thus led to believe that the account of the Trojan War that follows is based on this account by Dictys of Crete.

The history of Dictys is widely understood as a fictional rewriting of Homer's *Iliad*, and this story about its origins is generally regarded as a literary creation designed to bolster the credibility of the account. As Merkle points out, "in order to make his claim believable, the author felt it necessary to construct an elaborate *Beglaubigungsapparat*, that is, a collection of credentials," including this "complicated story of the

Torrey points out, "such bits of real life as this are just the business of any one who wishes to give his narrative touches of verisimilitude" (1970, 151).

discovery of the text" (1994, 185). It is designed to give the impression that this account is more reliable than that of Homer, because unlike Homer's version, it is based on an older and, in fact, eye-witness account (Frazer 1966, 7).

Another classical text which contains a similar story about lost and found documents is *The Wonders Beyond Thule*, by Antonius Diogenes.[2] Although a complete copy of this novel does not exist, it has been summarized in the *Bibliotheke* of Photius from the ninth century (for an English translation of this text, see Wilson 1994). According to Photius, the plot centres upon the travels of a man named Deinias, and also relates the adventures of his loving companion Derkyllis and her brother Mantias.

Towards the end of his life, Deinias travels to the island of Tyre where he relates his adventures to a man called Kymbas. After Deinias has recounted his tales, he calls upon Kymbas's companion Erasinides, who happens to be an "expert scribe," to record the tales on some tablets of cypress wood. He also asks Kymbas "to have two copies made, one for himself to keep, the other to be placed in his tomb when he died" (*Bibl.* 111a).

Corresponding rhetorically with this story about Deinias's tablets is a story of their recovery, related in a letter attached to the beginning of Diogenes' account. In this letter it is implied that the tales to be recounted are based on the documents of Deinias which were discovered on the island of Tyre, when the island was conquered by Alexander the Great and almost entirely destroyed by fire. After the fire, one of Alexander's soldiers discovered some surviving stone coffins, laying in the earth which he showed to the king and some others. While examining the tombs, they also found a small cypress box marked: "Stranger, whoever you may be, open this and learn something which will surprise you" (*Bibl.* 111b). In the box were the cypress tablets which had been deposited in Deinias's tomb according to his instructions.

As in the case of Dictys's *Trojan War*, the discovery of lost records is used here by the author as a literary device designed to establish the authenticity of his story.[3] Again the same motifs appear, such as the discovery of texts in a tomb and the presentation of the records to a king, in this case Alexander the Great. In fact, as Morgan points out, the author of this text went even further than most to achieve this purpose; "he did not simply present his text as an ancient narrative rediscovered and leave

---

2. It is not known when this work was written, though probably the second century C.E.

3. Bowersock (1994, 35–36); Morgan (1985, 481).

it at that" (1985, 482). In another prefatory letter attached to the beginning of the work he also claims to base his stories on "the testimony of earlier writers," and "at the beginning of each book he lists the authors who previously told such stories, so that his tall tales shall not appear devoid of foundation" (*Bibl.* 111a). As Morgan argues, the use of both strategies for assuring authenticity is redundant, and confirms the fictional nature of this work which Antonius Diogenes himself virtually admits anyway.[4] According to Morgan,

> ...the fact that he claims to be working from earlier sources, which he cites by name at the beginning of each book, is incompatible with the whole tendency of the archaeological apparatus. Either device by itself would have given the work verisimilitude, but together they cancel one another out. (Morgan 1985, 482)[5]

Having thus outlined two classical stories about lost and found books, the parallels to the Ezra story begin to emerge. Not only does the motif of loss and recovery appear in all these texts, but there are other similarities as well. For example, both the Hebrew and Aramaic decrees are said to have been issued by Cyrus and are therefore associated with a figure of great repute from the past like Dictys in *The Trojan War* and Deinias in *The Wonders Beyond Thule*. Furthermore, the discovery of the Aramaic scroll in Ezra 6 is authenticated and endorsed by a king. Thus, the role played by Darius is comparable to that which is performed by Nero in Dictys and Alexander the Great in Antonius Diogenes.

There is, however, one important difference between the classical stories and that which appears in Ezra. While the classical stories purport to be based on the lost and found documents to which they refer, the Ezra narrative does not claim or even implicitly imply that it is based on the lost and found ordinance of Cyrus. It is thus unlikely that the story in Ezra is designed to serve the same rhetorical function of bolstering narrative credibility as it does in the classical accounts. Rather an alternative explanation must be sought for what purpose it serves.

Pausanias's Description of Greece

As I have argued elsewhere (see, for example, Stott 2005, 106–30), there are a number of classical texts that use stories about lost and found books to promote an ideological agenda presented in the text. A good example

---

4. Antonius Diogenes says that "he invents things incredible and false" (*Bibl.* 111a).

5. In fact, according to Morgan this story may itself be a parody of other such works which utilize this strategy to bolster their credibility.

of such a story occurs in Book IV of Pausanias's *Description of Greece* which describes the history of conflict between the Messenians and the Spartans. Pivotal in this history is an account of a "secret thing" (τι ἀπόρρητος), which was buried and later rediscovered. Pausanias first mentions this secret thing in 4.20.4, just before the last stronghold of Messene is captured by the Spartans and the Messenians are forced into exile. According to the oracles, this thing, if kept, would ensure the recovery of Messene, if Messene were ever to be destroyed. If it were not kept, however, Messene would be overwhelmed and lost forever. Pausanias thus relates how the leader of the Messenians, Aristomenes, "knowing the oracles," buried it on the mountain Ithome in the hope of protecting this thing and hence Messene.

Hundreds of years later (in the year 369 B.C.E. to be precise), the Theban general Epaminondas conquered the Spartans, and allowed the Messenians to return to their land. It is at this juncture in his account that Pausanias describes the discovery of the "secret thing" buried on Mt Ithome. According to Pausanias, a certain Epiteles had a dream in which he was ordered by an "ancient man" by the name of Caucon to dig between a yew and myrtle on the mountain Ithome. The next day, Epiteles did as instructed in his vision, and in doing so, discovered an urn. Immediately, Epiteles took the urn to Epaminondas, told him about the dream, and asked him to remove the lid of the urn to see what was contained within. Inside, he discovered some very thin tin foil rolled "like a book" (ὥσπερ τὰ βιβλία) and on it were inscribed the mysteries of the Great Goddesses. This, Pausanias informs us, was the very thing deposited by Aristomenes, which would ensure the recovery of Messene, if it were ever conquered. The oracle, known to Aristomenes, was thus fulfilled and the discovery of the book preceded the return of the Messenians to their land and the reestablishment of Messene.

This story in Pausanias contains similar motifs to that of Dictys and Antonius Diogenes. All three of these stories are about documents that are buried and later discovered, having been lost to human knowledge for a very long period of time. Furthermore, all of the documents, once discovered, are presented and ultimately endorsed by a king or similarly supreme authority. Just as the documents discovered in the Dictys text and that of Antonius Diogenes are presented to Nero and Alexander the Great respectively, the "secret thing" of Aristomenes is presented to and validated by the Theban general Epaminondas.

The main difference between these stories is that the former purport to be based on the lost and found documents to which they refer, while that of Pausanias makes no such suggestion. Having said this, however, the story of the lost and found book in Pausanias can nevertheless be seen as serving a rhetorical purpose in its narrative context. As I have proposed elsewhere (see Stott 2005; 2008, 116–17), I believe this purpose has to do with legitimizing Messenian claims to the land. In my opinion, there is good reason to believe that this story, which Pausanias relates in the second century C.E., was originally created to represent Messenian interests sometime in the wake of 369 B.C.E., after Epaminondas conquered the Spartans and brought Messenian subjugation to an end.

In the wake of 369 B.C.E., there is evidence to suggest that the Spartans resisted Messenian independence. A good example of this occurs in the *Archidamus* of Isocrates, probably written in the year 366 B.C.E. As Pearson points out, "it is a political pamphlet in the form of a political speech, supposed to be delivered at Sparta by the Eurypontid king's son Archidamus." In the document, "the speaker rejects the plea of some of Sparta's allies to recognize the independence of Messenia as the price of peace with Thebes. Among other arguments Archidamus insists that the Spartans have a just claim to Messenia, which goes back almost to the Dorian invasion" (Pearson 1962, 404; see also pp. 405–7 and Oliva 1971, 196). In light of such evidence, I posit that the circumstances at this time appear to have been ripe for the creation of the story about the lost and found book of Aristomenes. By manufacturing a story about a book once possessed by their great hero Aristomenes, and recently rediscovered and endorsed by the Theban general Epaminondas, the Messenians could reinforce to the Spartans that the land was, in fact, rightfully theirs.

The possibility that the story of the lost and found book of Aristomenes was invented for such a purpose is also supported by the general scepticism which has long surrounded the historicity of Pausanias's history of Messene. Although it is accepted that Epaminondas did liberate the Messenians in 369 B.C.E., Pausanias's history is widely regarded as a largely invented account, created by the sources upon which Pausnanias depends, in the years following the foundation of Messene by Epaminondas. As L. R. Shero observes,

> It has long been fashionable to assume that most of what is told us by the ancient authors about early Messenian history…was invented in the period following the restoration of the Messenians in the fourth century BC, when the returning exiles, not having any considerable body of genuine national tradition, set out to supply the deficiency. (Shero 1938, 502; see also Pearson 1962, 397)[6]

---

6. For a more recent overview of the debate about the historicity of narratives about the Messenian past, see Alcock (1999, 333–41).

I therefore contend that, if it was possible for authors to create a past for Messene in the years after the establishment of this city, it was also possible for them to fabricate a story of lost and found documents justifying Messenian claims to the land.

While the story in Ezra bears general resemblance to classical stories about lost and found books, some particularly striking parallels appear in the story of the lost and found book of Aristomenes in Pausanias. In both Ezra and Pausanias, the story of a lost and found ordinance/book is intimately connected to a narrative about exile and return. While the two stories are not exactly the same, they share some important themes in common. Ezra tells the story of the lost and found ordinance of Cyrus in conjunction with the Jews' return from exile, the re-founding of Jerusalem, and the rebuilding of the temple. Likewise, Pausanias tells his story about the lost and found book of Aristomenes in conjunction with the Messenian return from exile and the re-founding of Messene (which incidentally also involves the rebuilding of temples). Another significant parallel between both stories is that the return is facilitated by an external power, who conquers the nation/city-state responsible for the original displacement of peoples. Just as Cyrus defeats the Babylonians and permits the Jews to return to their land, the Theban general Epaminondas conquers the Spartans, enabling the Messenians to return as well.

I advance that the story in Pausanias not only bears considerable resemblance to the story in Ezra, but also provides a clue for understanding its function, suggesting that an ideological agenda might be involved that has something to do with land claims. As argued above, the story in Pausanias may have been created to demonstrate that the Messenians had a legitimate claim to the land, in the face of Spartan resistance. A similar purpose may also have been served by the story in Ezra, which seems to represent the interests of certain persons laying claim to the land of Judah. It is tempting to postulate that the story may have been motivated by opposition to the temple in Jerusalem, since the story does its utmost to establish, in the face of such resistance, that legitimate authorization had been granted for the building. However, one must be careful about assuming that the "opponents" in Ezra bear any resemblance to groups which may have historically motivated the creation of this text. The adversaries in the story could also be part of the fiction, perhaps designed as a warning to virtual rather than real opponents.

Conclusion/Implications

I have myself in past publications suggested somewhat of a link between the literary/rhetorical functions that stories about lost and found books appear to serve in the Hebrew Bible and the possibility that these documents were fictional products created purely for their literary purpose. To be sure, this is indeed a real possibility as scholars such as Grabbe argue. Moreover, it is perhaps worth mentioning that the lost and found texts mentioned in the classical literature surveyed in this paper are generally regarded by modern interpreters as never having actually existed. By the same token, there is much to be gained in taking an approach to these stories that bypasses the question of whether they existed or not and takes a closer look at what role they serve in their literary context. I hope this paper has to some extent illustrated that value.

THE SIGNIFIER'S BODY:
POSTMODERN SEMIOTICS AND THE BIBLE*

George Aichele

[E]ven the names of things were not originally due to convention, but in the several tribes under the impulse of special feelings and special presentations of sense primitive man uttered special cries. The air thus emitted was molded by their individual feelings or sense-presentations, and differently according to the difference of the regions which the tribes inhabited. (Epicurus 2009)

The essence of words and images is put together by bodily motions, which in no wise involve the conception of thought. (Spinoza 1883, Part 2, Proposition 49)

It belongs to what we might call the linguistic revolution of the twentieth century that we have shifted from thinking of words in terms of concepts to thinking of concepts in terms of words. (Eagleton 1991, 193)

Postmodern semiotics begins with and always returns to "thinking of concepts in terms of words." The material body of the sign becomes for it crucial not only to the production of meaning, but also to its disruption. This materiality is the trace of non-identity or difference within any writing, which is veiled by the logocentric ideology that grounds the modernist understanding of text. The signified does not become uninteresting, but it loses the primary importance that it has for modern (classical) semiotics. In other words, postmodernism does not simply invert the modernist binarism of signifying body and signified meaning (soul, spirit). Instead the signified is regarded as a product, or even by-product, of semiotic mechanisms. The signified arises from the impact of external events or forces—that is, other bodies—on the signifier, and it is finally inseparable from this interplay of signifiers. Although modern semiotics remains valuable, it has of necessity become something richer and more

* Portions of this essay were originally presented to the Semiotics and Exegesis Section at the 2004 annual meeting of the Society of Biblical Literature. I thank Tom Craig and Maureen Connolly for inviting me to contribute to that program.

complex because of the postmodern transformations. In this essay I consider postmodern semiotics as a field for the reading of biblical texts, and a correlate rethinking of theology, in new and interesting ways.

Semiosis and Intertextuality

Postmodern semiotics has created two concepts that address the signifier's body in important ways. These concepts are "unlimited semiosis" and "intertextuality," and they are closely related to one another. Unlimited semiosis deconstructs the modernist binarisms of signifier and signified, word and thing, representation and reality, body and mind, flesh and spirit. This concept, which derives from C. S. Peirce, maintains that the symbol or linguistic sign[1] has three aspects, not two, which he called representamen, object, and interpretant. The signifier is a representamen or textual body, a physical thing. Yet this body denotes an object which is a concept or thought, a non-physical thing. To bridge this gap an intermediary or interpretant is required, but this connotative connection inevitably involves yet other symbols.

One consequence of this is that all three aspects of any symbol can themselves take the form of symbols, each composed of a representamen, object, and interpretant, and thus the meaning of every symbol is infinitely deferred, and infinitely variable. Every signified also signifies, and every signifier can be signified. This opens up a bottomless abyss of receding signs, and there is never any First Signifier or Final Signified, no end to connotative potential, and thus no absolute anchor to which a proper meaning could be attached. As Umberto Eco says, "signification…by means of continual shiftings which refer a sign back to another sign or string of signs, circumscribes cultural units in an asymptotic fashion, without ever allowing one to touch them directly, though making them accessible through other units" (1976, 71). Signification is always somewhat elusive and fluid, and connotation runs wild.

It is precisely because of unlimited semiosis that intertextuality is necessary, as the limit or control of semiosis. Otherwise meaning cannot be determined. Meaning is never "in" a text (representamen), to be dredged out by a careful reading; meaning is always formed between texts, as they are brought together in the understandings of actual readers. Each reader is a living repository of texts that she has read, a nexus in an intertextual network, and thus each reader is herself both product

---

1.   By far the most common type of word in any human language is the symbol. A very small number of words are indexes or icons. See further Eco (1976, 59–62) and Aichele (2001, 130–33).

and producer of intertextuality. As Roland Barthes says, "the Text…can be it[self] only in its difference (which does not mean its 'ind_viduality'); its *reading* is…woven entirely with quotations, references, echoes, cultural languages…antecedent or contemporary, which cut across it through and through in a vast stereophony" (1977, 159–60, emphasis added). In other words, texts do not mean by themselves, but always in relation to other texts.

Some biblical scholars restrict the word "intertextuality" to refer to the historical influence of one text on another, in the form of intentional citations or allusions. This limitation often appears to be an attempt on the part of theologically conservative scholars to neutralize the radical consequences of this concept even as they appropriate the terminology for their own purposes.[2] Julia Kristeva explicitly rejects such restrictions. According to her, "*inter-textuality* denotes this transposition of one (or several) sign system(s) into another…its 'place' of enunciation and its denoted 'object' are never single, complete, and identical to themselves, but always plural, shattered, capable of being tabulated" (1984, 59–60, her emphasis). For Kristeva, intertextuality is not a function of an author's intention, but rather a relation between the signifier and the reader. The reader is the point where an intertextual network comes to bear upon a text.

This concept implies that meaning is not built into texts, but rather it lies in spaces between textual bodies that are occupied by readers[3] and established by tensions between signifiers. Thus the limits of intertextuality are not confined to historical influence or authorial intention. Instead, the reader's ideology defines an intertext, a system of restraints that control semiosis, establishing a field in which acceptable readings can occur. In other words, ideology as intertext makes meaning possible.

On the macro level of language itself, ideology appears in what Michel Foucault calls "discursive formations," fundamental linguistic structures that are usually unconscious but which control the possibility or impossibility of saying any particular thing at some particular time and place (1972, 21–76). On the micro level of the actual utterance, ideology establishes the "proper" or "normal" meaning of those texts that are seen as crucial to the identity of specific groups of people. This may take the form of controls defining texts that are or are not to be read, or

2. This is but one aspect of a larger theological phenomenon, in which conservative scholars draw upon the terminology of postmodernism for purposes that are anything but postmodern.

3. The reader also has a body (which is also a text) but as reader, she is a field of concepts, a site of intertextuality.

the circumstances in which they may or should be read—that is, overt intertexts such as the "great books" of secular literature or the canon of the Bible. Insofar as the reader accepts such controls on semiosis, they may seem quite natural. Less explicit controls appear, as Barthes demonstrates, in numerous codes (not unlike Foucault's discursive formations) that govern the reading of a text, restricting and channelling the flow of connotations (1974, 11–21)—that is, the acceptable interpretants.

Intertextuality and unlimited semiosis are the two machines of significance, the break and flow of text and meaning.

> A machine may be defined as a *system of interruptions* or breaks... Far from being the opposite of continuity, the break or interruption conditions this continuity; it presupposes what it defines or cuts into as an ideal continuity. The machine produces an interruption of the flow only insofar as it is connected to another machine that supposedly produces this flow. And doubtless this second machine in turn is really an interruption or break, too... In a word, every machine functions as a break in the flow in relation to the machine to which it is connected, but at the same time is also a flow itself, or the production of a flow, in relation to the machine connected to it. (Deleuze and Guattari 1983, 36, their emphasis)[4]

The semiosis machine produces and disperses texts, and therefore it makes intertextuality possible. Conversely, the intertextuality machine limits and directs semiosis, elaborating but also confining the meaning of each text through its interplay with other texts. Unlimited semiosis then comes to a halt, and the result is the "reality effect," the ideological illusion of the "natural" (Barthes 1986, 127–48).

Both unlimited semiosis and intertextuality are relevant to Barthes's distinction between the readerly and the writerly text (1974, 4–6), which he also calls the "work" and the "text" (1977, 155–64). These two kinds of texts are better described as two relationships between readers and texts. Barthes's distinction concerns both the physical signifiers that make up a text and the intertextual and often ideological codes through which that text is read. The readerly text (or work) appears to be fully and naturally meaningful. It speaks for itself, and its meaning is "obvious" to the reader—that is, the text's semiosis is safely limited by the reader's ideology, and the intertextual machine works smoothly and invisibly.

In contrast, the writerly text is enigmatic and makes the reader conscious of her intertextual struggles to make the text meaningful. The writerly text, in Jacques Derrida's words, "produces the trace as a trace"

---

4. Although Deleuze and Guattari do not use either "unlimited semiosis" or "intertextuality," the relationship between these two concepts runs throughout their writings.

and "must interrupt the servile complicity of speech and meaning" (1978, 265, 266). Semiosis is out of control, and the text's meaning is undecidable. The opaque body of the signifier resists the workings of the intertextual machine. Nevertheless, some texts are more resistant than others, and some readers are more attuned to possible codes than are others. Hence "readerly" and "writerly" are relative judgments. Barthes's close reading of Balzac's novella, "Sarrasine," demonstrates that in even a very readerly text, semiosis may break free (1974, 211–17). The subversive flow of signification is never fully controlled by ideology.

Both unlimited semiosis and intertextuality imply that no meaning is intrinsic to any text. Instead, meaning must be attached to the text through some exterior process, the act of ideological violence which is reading. Every reading involves "eisegesis," hermeneutical decisions that curtail semiotic flows by selecting one potential intertext and rejecting others, thereby breaking the flow. Reading connects the semiotic machine that is the text to an intertextual machine that is the reader herself, and thus it limits the flow of semiosis by means of an intertextual "interruption," to use Gilles Deleuze and Félix Guattari's term. Reading plays endlessly with the text, and with its meaning. Meaning is always something that the reader brings to and imposes upon the text—that is, she always "reads into" the text.

This intertextual eisegesis is often disguised and called "exegesis," which is a prominent term in theology and biblical studies. The concept of exegesis is a product of logocentric modernism, for which meaning has been put into the text by its true "owner," the author (see Derrida 1981, 104). For the modernist ideology, the author provides the true interpretant that determines the text's meaning. The body of the text is of no value as such, but its inner "spirit," that of the author, must be respected. This meaning can be extracted by any careful reader through historical reconstruction of that author's intentions in writing the text. This author is an historical person, not the "implied author" who is an inevitable effect of reading the text—that is, of eisegesis. To interpret a text through exegetical reconstruction of its author's intentions severely limits the intertextual possibilities for meaning and effectively replaces the text with the story of "what the author meant." This story defines the "real" text, solving any problems of understanding and smoothing over any incoherencies in the actual physical text.

This modernist understanding of the privileged relation between a text and its author is still widespread in many areas of secular literary study. In relation to the Bible, where the text is regarded by Christian theology as the "word of God" and its historical author, although usually unknown, is nevertheless understood to be "inspired by God," the idea of exegesis becomes particularly potent. God becomes in effect the real author of the scriptures. In this context, the canon of the scriptures is understood to have a God-given unity and thus a coherent meaning that extends far beyond (and sometimes even quite contrary to) what the actual texts say. The canon is an overt intertext that juxtaposes its component texts to form a single signified, a "biblical theology," to be transmitted with authority to its readers. The faithful reader, who accepts the biblical canon as the correct intertext, has clear access to the divinely intended unity of its meaning.

In related but somewhat different versions of the concept of exegesis, the author is replaced by either the first readers or the intended readers of the text, who in relation to the Bible are usually thought to represent some form of Christianity or Judaism. "Canonical criticism" thus sometimes argues that the Bible can only be understood correctly as it is received by Christian (or Jewish) readers. Again exegesis functions to claim the Bible and its meaning as the special possession of those who have proper faith, and also to claim that this one intertext is better than any others and thereby to limit decisively the flow of semiosis. In either case, the search for the intended meaning of the texts derives from modernist logocentrism.

In contrast, for postmodern semiotics, eisegesis is inevitable, and exegesis is an illusion. Every reading of every text (even the most well-informed and "scientific") is profoundly influenced by the reader's ideology. Thus whether you read the Bible as a religious text or not, and whether you are yourself religious or not, ideological bias inevitably influences your understanding of it. What distinguishes postmodern ideologies from modernist ideologies is refusal of any Final Signified or one true meaning. Instead of seeking a definitive meaning, postmodern readings play with fragmentary, local, and always incomplete (even incoherent) truths—once again, with a strong preference for the signifier's body and correlated suspicion of every signified.

Implications and Possibilities

Biblical semiotics has long been willing to overlook the body of the signifier in favour of the signified content. That should be no surprise, for biblical scholars generally are far more interested in the soul or spirit of the text, it seems, than they are in its body. Immersed within what Derrida calls the "primordial non-presence" of writing (1973, 82), the raw materiality of the signifier is generally overlooked in the search for meaning. This gives weight to the claim that biblical studies remains deeply entwined with Christian theology.

Perhaps the willingness of scholars to ignore the physical aspect of the sign comes from acceptance of the logocentric Pauline notion that "the written code kills, but the Spirit gives life" (2 Cor 3:6). Once again a kind of Platonic dualism, between the physical, carved flesh of the written text and the spirit that "writes on your hearts," with a clear preference for the latter, underlies assumptions about what text is.[5] The signifier's body is ignored as worthless apart from the meaning it allegedly bears. Probably no biblical scholar would support this body/soul metaphor so crudely stated, but many continue to regard the Bible's signifiers as mere "vehicles" or channels through which an intellectual or spiritual signified is delivered.

Nevertheless, the code of the "semes" or signifiers is one of the five codes that Barthes uses throughout *S/Z*, and the importance of the material signifier surfaces often in the writings of Derrida, Eco, Deleuze, Kristeva, and other semioticians outside of biblical studies. As Barthes says in *Image–Music–Text*, "The Text…practises the infinite deferment of the signified, is dilatory; its field is that of the signifier and the signifier must not be conceived of as 'the first stage of meaning,' its material vestibule, but, in complete opposition to this, as its *deferred action*" (1977, 158, his emphasis). Indeed, although the canonical ideal of the Bible is that of a self-explanatory work, in many biblical texts meaning is continually deferred. The "field of the signifier" in biblical texts needs much more attention.

Semiotics and biblical text criticism have interests in common here. Text critical conjectures regarding the production and history of ancient manuscripts are surely relevant to the flow of semiosis in those texts. For example, the various endings of the Gospel of Mark that appear in different manuscripts effectively create at least three different "Marks," for different endings yield different stories. As distinct and contradictory "solutions" to Barthes's hermeneutical "enigma" (1974, 19), these multiple endings produce irreconcilable Marks, alternative textual bodies that signify in different ways the identity of Jesus and his relation to God, the way of the disciple and the paradox of repentance, and the parabolic secret of the kingdom of God. All three of these possible endings are included in most modern printed editions of Mark (although the choice between them is not always evident), but this then raises questions about the extent of the New Testament canon: which ending is the "proper" one?

5. See further Derrida (1981, 61–171).

Major variations in the text appear also in manuscripts of the Gospel of John, as well as other biblical books. Each of these differences between manuscript bodies inevitably signifies differently. No two of the biblical manuscripts are identical, and the differences range from very small disparities in spelling or word order to large variations in textual configuration. Many of these differences are apparently the consequences of simple copying errors or the inevitable fluidity of hand-written texts, but others probably result from attempts to "correct" the texts,[6] suggesting historical and theological factors at work in the efforts of ancient scribes. These differences of the signifier require semiotic study.

Ideological factors appear also in the explanations for these differences that are offered by modern biblical critics. The desire of some scholars to reconstruct original autographs, like the attempts of others to reconstruct the supposed Aramaic words of Jesus, strongly suggests a theological agenda: namely, to return to the author as *archē* and ultimately, the voice of God. However, identification of a "proper" physical text of any book written in a context in which the manuscript is the only form of writing is a highly questionable goal (see Gamble 1995, 83–87). Given the many differences between ancient manuscripts of biblical texts and what is known about ancient manuscript production, it is highly unlikely that the "original" text of any of them could ever be identified, or even that the concept is meaningful at all.

Another topic of interest to both text critics and semioticians is the appearance of repeated abbreviations of certain "holy names" (*nomina sacra*) such as "God" or "Jesus" in many Bible manuscripts. Does an abbreviated sign signify differently than the non-abbreviated sign would? What does the phenomenon of abbreviation itself signify? Yet another joint topic of interest is the significance of the codex. Biblical scholars have long recognized important semiotic and practical differences between scroll and codex, and at least some of the answers to the mystery of why early Christians adopted the codex to such a remarkable extent draw upon semiotic factors. In addition, if the Christian concept of the canon was made possible by the new technology of the codex, as it may well have been, then that should also be of interest to semioticians. "The Bible" as a unified signifying entity must be interrogated as a product of the technologies of writing.

Perhaps semiotics can also collaborate with text criticism in studies of other, more recent, technologies of writing. A modern printed edition of the Greek New Testament such as that of Nestle and Aland is quite different from any single manuscript. The selection of text to be included,

---

6. See further Ehrman (1993) and Gamble (1995).

as well as the form of the textual apparatus, also signifies. Elizabeth Eisenstein demonstrates that the printing of formerly hand-written texts that make up the Bible changes them in numerous ways (1979). Indeed, Eisenstein's book has quite a lot to say about the early printing of Bibles. These questions are not simply historical or even theological ones. They are also semiotic questions. The uniform text produced by the printing press signifies differently than ever-varying hand-written texts do. What semiotics and text criticism could offer one another is an interest in textual bodies as finely attuned to the differences between manuscript and printed (or digital) book as it is to the differences between manuscripts.

Scholars are just beginning to become aware of important semiotic differences between manuscript Bibles and printed ones, and we are even less conscious of semiotic differences between printed Bibles and electronic ones. Yet printed Bibles are already being replaced by digital Bibles. Again the body of the signifier is metamorphosing, and computers increasingly do our reading for us. Just as print Bibles signify differently than manuscript Bibles do, so digital Bibles also signify differently than print Bibles do. The signifier still has a body, but it is a very different body—surely just as different (although in different ways) as printed text is from manuscript. A computer file system or a Web page is not the same as a codex. Secular scholarship has already begun to address the question of the future of the book in a digital age.[7] Biblical scholars also need to start thinking seriously about this matter.

Once again I suspect that biblical scholars tend to fall back on logocentric assumptions that allow us to overlook the body of the signifier, and a question of semiotics coincides with a question of ideology. The luddite objections to reading digital text that one still frequently hears are not just reactions to the practical inconveniences of the current level of technology. They express deep fears about the fate of printed books and hence about the theological role of the Bible in human culture. Just as the print revolution correlated strongly with major changes in both the dissemination of the Bible and Christian theology, so it is very likely that the digital revolution will also result in deep changes in the ways that we access the Bible and in our thinking about it. The decline of the canon begins as an effect of print culture and accelerates in contemporary electronic culture (Aichele 2001, 38–60, 218–23).

Another area of biblical studies in which the signifier's body figures prominently is the question of translation. Although signifiers cannot ever be translated, strictly speaking, more attention needs to be given to

---

7. For example, Nunberg (1996).

how changes of signifier in translations necessarily transform the text's semiotic potential. Interlingual translation of texts is one important way in which semiosis unfolds, and secular semioticians have long been aware of the importance of translation and of its effects on both the "source" and "target" texts and on their respective meanings. Walter Benjamin, Roman Jakobson, George Steiner, Willard Quine, de Man, Derrida, and Eco have all published important statements on the possibilities and limitations of translation.

In contrast, not only histories of Bible translation (such as Norton 2000), but also studies of theoretical and practical aspects of Bible translation (such as Nida and Taber 1982), barely acknowledge that different theories of translation both correspond to different ideological positions and yield different translation results. For the "dynamic equivalence" approach to translation and its derivatives, which currently dominate the major Bible translation societies, only the conceptual, signified message relayed by the text needs to be translated—and it can be, without any loss ever of theologically crucial meaning. Once again, logocentrism prevails: a truth or meaning lies within or precedes the texts of the Bible, either implanted by an author's intentions or referring to an actual event. In contrast, the body of the signifier is a dispensable husk, a mere transport mechanism.

Only recently have biblical scholars begun to question the implications, both theological and linguistic, of the dynamic equivalence approach. The ideological aspects, not only of specific word choices, but of larger theoretical understandings of what translation is supposed to do or actually does, are very important. The practical possibilities and limitations of interlingual translations of texts of the Bible deserve further semiotic study. In addition, the interplay between semiosis and ideology in actual Bible translations, beginning with differences between Greek and Hebrew texts of the Jewish scriptures, but certainly not ignoring modern translations, also needs further detailed analysis.

Without the possibility of translation, many believers and other readers would have no Bible, and thus translation has been and still is an instrument of power. For example, the use of gender inclusive language in Bible translations is generally laudable, but since much language in the Bible is gender exclusive, that alteration may change the flow of semiosis. If this biases the target text in favour of one theological interpretation or against others, then the Bible is rewritten in our own image.

The masculine phrase "son of man" in Hebrew or Aramaic or Greek is frequently used in the Bible to connote a generic "human being" or "person," and this phrase is frequently translated with such gender neutral words in modern Bible translations, such as the NRSV. Despite this, translations of the New Testament Gospels, including the NRSV, often translate the Greek phrase *huios ton anthrōpon* as "son of man." Christians often believe that "son of man" is a special title that Jesus uses for himself alone and closely related to "son of God" and "Christ." Since each of the Gospels' Jesuses appears to be a male human being, the more literal but exclusive translation is allowed. These exceptions on the part of otherwise gender inclusive translations tend to reinforce this belief, and this results in texts that obscure the fact that each of the Gospels' Jesuses uses a phrase that appears many times in the Jewish scriptures to connote "human being."

All translations are biased by the translators' own eisegesis, but the best translations will be ones which do not conceal semiotic or ideological difficulties inherent in the source text. Readers deserve the right to judge the sexism and other oppressive language of the Bible's texts for themselves, and not to be protected from it. Furthermore, using translation to make the text say what we think it should have said or really means encourages the belief that the Bible is always right. It is another form of fundamentalism, and no different from the practice of conservative groups who continue to use gender exclusive translations precisely because they want to encourage sexism.

The Bible and Popular Culture

The tension between intertextual control and unlimited semiosis appears when the Bible as a canon is unable to control the reading of its constituent texts. As a canon, the Bible is a single signifier, but as a collection of books, it is made up of many diverse signifiers. Its component texts do not always cohere with and indeed often contradict one another. The power of the Christian canon to control the readings of these texts has weakened during the last several centuries as a result of cultural and technological changes, not least of which are the print revolution, the spread of literacy, and the rise of capitalism.[8]

These changes increase the tendency of readers to remove biblical stories from the canonical intertext, making more evident their writerliness and setting free a plurality of Moseses, Davids, Jesuses, and even Gods.[9] As readers have become more aware of the intricate relationships between the Bible and its various cultural environments, both past and

---

8. See further Aichele (2001, 38–60).

9. The strong relation between the biblical canon and monotheism is a theme of Miles (1996).

present, they have begun to explore the play between biblical texts and non-biblical texts in alternative, non-canonical intertextualities provided by secular culture, allowing new semiotic flows for the old books. Although semiotics has long played a substantial role in secular media and popular culture studies, it is only in recent years that biblical scholars have begun to give serious attention to films, novels, and other mass media, including television, music, video games, and comic books, especially when these productions are not explicitly "biblical" or "religious."

Many forms of intertextual play with the Bible are readily to be found among pop culture texts. In some cases, they simply reflect prevailing ideological positions and thus reinforce dominant theological understandings of the Bible. For example, Mel Gibson's popular movie, *The Passion of the Christ* (2004), draws upon venerable Hollywood traditions of sentimental "Jesus movies." Gibson's *Passion* plays fast and loose with biblical texts, freely harmonizing and rearranging and contradicting them, but always pandering to established beliefs and pious passions, much like a devotional tract or the rantings of a televangelist. For many of the movie's devout and functionally illiterate viewers, it has successfully rewritten the Bible.

However, other instances of cultural play offer radically different "translations" or contextualizations of biblical texts, provocative rewritings that also effectively remove the textual bodies from the canon of the scriptures. Alternative intertexts control the semiosis of the selected texts. These different intertexts and the semiotic processes that make them possible and effective play a large part in the de-canonization of the Bible. As the Bible increasingly fails to function as a canon in a secularized world, this pop cultural play with or on the texts of the Bible, even more than explicit Bible movies, replaces the "source text."

For example, in John Milius's movie, *Conan the Barbarian* (1982), the mighty adventurer, Conan of Cimmeria, is captured and tortured by his arch-enemy, Thulsa Doom, who charges Conan with stealing from "my house."[10] Thulsa Doom is the human form taken by the snake-god Set, and his house is a temple, from which Conan and his friends have indeed stolen jewels. Conan's punishment is to be crucified on the "tree of woe." Tied to a gnarled, surrealistic tree, Conan (played by a young Arnold Schwarzenegger) strikes cruciform body-building poses made of equal parts venerable European traditions of religious art and the "pulp magazine" fantasy art of Frank Frazetta.

---

10. All quotations are from the DVD version of the movie.

Conan dies, and on the second day he is raised from the dead, but not by any god. His companions, two other thieves and a wizard, restore him to life through magical incantations, including spells written on Conan's face and hands, and violent physical struggles against gods of the underworld who arrive to claim his spirit. Conan's friends raise him up to live again through their magic and their fierce warriors' determination that he not yet be dead forever. "All the gods, they cannot sever us," his friend Valeria says to the revived warrior. Valeria even offers to pay the "heavy toll" of his resurrection. Later, as she lies dying from one of Thulsa Doom's arrows, Valeria says, "I told [the wizard] I would pay the gods' toll." She gives her life as a ransom (compare Mark 10:45).

Although Robert E. Howard's *Conan* stories, on which Milius's movie is based, are rich in allusions to ancient mythology, afterlives of biblical texts are rare in them. However, a similar crucifixion scene appears in Howard's 1934 story, "A Witch Shall Be Born."[11] Conan is a thief and soldier of fortune, a wild, ignorant, and often brutal (and brutish) champion of the "sword and sorcery" sub-genre of literary fantasy, of which Howard's stories are among the best known. Conan is a barbarian from the outskirts of civilization, a marginalized person making his way in a world that neither admires nor understands him. The movie's narrator, one of Conan's companions, describes his story as "a tale of sorrow."

Yet despite its parody of the Gospels' stories of Temple scourging, passion, and resurrection, this movie's Conan is neither Christ nor Christ-figure. That would require something more—something that Gibson's movie also lacks. Conan does not announce the mystery of the kingdom of God, as Mark's Jesus does (4:11), but instead he lives by the "mystery of steel"—that is, the power of the sword. Conan's crucifixion comes not at the end of his life story but rather closer to its beginning, and the kingdom that he eventually wins for himself (and then loses again, in Howard's stories) is very much one of this world. Despite the fact that religion and magic play large parts in many of the Conan stories, Conan himself has little use for either. He worships the earth-god Crom, but he also despises him. What then does Conan's crucifixion story have to do with the Gospels' crucifixion stories?

If the meaning of a story is locked into its text at the moment of its formation and derives from the intention of an author, or even from its reproduction of some historical event, then the meanings of the Gospels' stories remain untouched by Conan's story. Likewise, if the Christian canon authoritatively directs the reading of its component texts, then

11. Republished in Howard (2003, 255–301). The crucifixion scene appears on pp. 266–72.

Conan's story is irrelevant to the Gospels, and vice versa. Conan's cruci-fixion is nothing more than an incidental episode, an allusion (perhaps blasphemous, at best humorous) designed to titillate the movie-going masses, and thus not unlike Gibson's movie. It is a product not so much of faith as of marketing and of what Benjamin called "the work of art in the age of mechanical reproduction" (1969, 217–51)—a process that begins with the printing of books such as the Bible. Conan's crucifixion is but one further development in a long trajectory of biblical afterlives, and a relatively minor one at that. It says something about the cinematic tastes of contemporary audiences, but it offers no insight into the Gospels' stories, or into the contemporary value of the canon.

However, if the meaning of a text is a product of eisegesis and the reader's ideology, then it is not some invisible substance safely tucked inside the text, to be uncovered by exegesis, and untouched by movies such as *Conan*. Instead meaning lies between textual bodies, in inter-textual configurations that are fluid and shifting. Meaning must be con-tinually re-negotiated by the reader, and it plays out differently from one reader to the next. The canon of the scriptures is then just one of many possible intertexts, no more important in the contemporary post-Christian world than any other. In that case, Conan's crucifixion scene opens up an intertextual nexus, a virtual hypertext link with both intra- and extra-canonical crucifixion scenes. Conan's friend Valeria becomes a female son of man, giving her life as a ransom for another. The Gospels' Jesuses have no friends like Conan's! Conan "fleshes out" another Jesus, sugges-tively filling narrative gaps in the Gospel accounts in new and perhaps unsettling ways.

Thus Conan's story not only reflects the Gospels' Jesus stories, but those Jesus stories also reflect Conan's story. The hermeneutical flow is "reversed," as Larry Kreitzer says (2002). Conan's crucifixion invites a reading of Jesus as a Conan-like hero in a non-biblical gospel that is a tale of sword and sorcery. The biblical Gospels all simulate narrative worlds in which magic is quite real, and each of their Jesuses has at least some association with violence and specifically the sword. In Matt 10:34, Jesus says "I have not come to bring peace, but a sword" (com-pare Luke 22:36–38),[12] and then a bit later, "[f]rom the days of John the Baptist until now the kingdom of heaven has suffered violence, and men of violence take it by force" (11:12; compare Luke 16:16). Is Matthew's Jesus such a "man of violence"? In Mark 14:47, one of Jesus' followers draws a sword and cuts off the ear of the high priest's slave (contrast Matt 26:51–52; Luke 22:49–51; John 18:10–11). Each of the biblical

---

12. All quotations from the Bible are from the RSV.

Gospels tells that the Romans release the murderous rebel Barabbas and crucify Jesus in his place, suggesting that the Romans perceive Jesus to be a violent and dangerous man.

Many of the words and deeds of the Gospels' Jesuses have violent overtones. Conan's rough behaviour also often gets him into trouble. He punches an obstreperous camel, knocking it out, but he never curses a fig tree for failing to feed him, even though "it was not the season for figs" (Mark 11:13). Indeed, the entire double scene of the cursing of the tree and cleansing of the Temple in Mark 11:12–21 reads like it could have been written by Howard. Mark's Jesus also offers some very Conan-like advice: "no one can enter a strong man's house and plunder his goods, unless he first binds the strong man; then indeed he may plunder his house" (3:27; compare Matt 12:29; Luke 11:21–22).

Perhaps the Gospels' Jesuses, or at least some of them, are also thieves and wanderers, not unlike Conan. When Mark's Jesus sits outside the Temple treasury with his followers, watching people make their donations (12:41–44; compare Luke 21:1–4), is he perhaps "casing the joint," preparing to "plunder" it? If so, then his words about the widow's mite take on a very different meaning! In Milius's movie, Conan's thievery gets him captured and then crucified. Similarly, each of the synoptic Gospels' Jesuses is arrested after his Temple break-in, as though he were a robber (Mark 14:48; Matt 26:55; Luke 22:52), and he is then crucified with two robbers (Mark 15:27; Matt 27:38; compare Luke 23:32).

Concrete Theology

To attend to the body of the scriptural signifier is to engage in what I have elsewhere called "concrete theology" (1985, 136–39). Like the "concrete poetry" and art of the Dada movement early in the twentieth century, concrete theology explores that which appears between (textual) bits and pieces, broken fragments, "found objects." It attends to the dispersed materiality of the signifier and to the flows and breaks of unlimited semiosis and intertextuality. This theology locates the signifier's body on a metaphysical border between sense and nonsense. That body is itself completely "literal" and senseless (Husserl's *hulē*), but it carries the potential for meaning, what Barthes calls "significance" (1977, 137).

Concrete theology does not return to the Dada movement, but it finds a model or ideal in that movement's fearless examination of the chaos that surrounds the human world and our struggles to find meaning. However, the biblical scholar as such is not a poet or artist, but rather a critic. Her job is not to create the signifier, but instead to recognize it, to

trace the flows of semiosis in the weave of texts, and to resist the decisive and violent sacrifice that logocentrism requires. Nevertheless, every
scholar is also a human being, and her language must be meaningful and
not sheer nonsense. She eventually decides on a meaning, and so the
sacrifice of the signifier's body is inevitable.

As Derrida famously says, "there will never be…any theology of the
Text" (1981, 258). Concrete theology must constantly question its own
possibility, seeking out what Jean-François Lyotard calls "the unpresent-
able in presentation itself" (1984, 81)—the signifier's body, the "that" of
the word itself. Therefore it is mystical in its way, but also radically
materialistic. It knows no Absolute or Final Signified; only "this" and
nothing else.

Part III

ENGAGED READINGS

"HEAR THEN THE PARABLE OF THE SEED": READING THE AGRARIAN PARABLES OF MATTHEW 13 ECOLOGICALLY

Elaine M. Wainwright

"Hear then the parable of the seed" may sound a discordant note for those who are familiar with the opening verse (Matt 13 18) of the Matthean Gospel's explanation of the parable of the seed that falls on different terrain (see Matt 13:4–9 for the parable and Matt 13:18–23 for its explanation). The invitation in 13:18—hear then the parable of the sower—likewise sounds a discordant note but within the Gospel text itself when it shifts the focus of the opening parable from seed, soil and yield to sower, from the more-than-human other to the human.[1] I became aware of this subtle shift as a result of turning an ecological reading lens on the Gospel of Matthew. In this study I will bring such a lens to a reading of selected parables from the Matthean Parable Discourse of Matt 13:1–52. In an opening section I will explore the type of reading that I am naming ecological, discussing its hermeneutical and methodological implications. Using the perspective and tools developed there, I will undertake an ecological reading of Matthew's agrarian parables that dominate the discourse.

It is a privilege to offer this study that gives attention to new hermeneutical and methodological perspectives to a festschrift in honour of Professor Ed Conrad. His scholarship and his mentoring of those of us

---

1. I use the phrase "more-than-human" to refer to all Earth-constituents (Earth designating the planet which is alive with interconnecting webs of life). I intend this phrase to include the human with and among all Earth-constituents. Used in the phrase "more-than-human other" it allows for distinguishing various categories when necessary. At times some human persons may be included in the more-than-human which is "other" than the dominant category of humans within systems of mastery and at other times the more-than-human "other" may refer to Earth-constituents whose life-form is other than human. I am grateful to Dr. Anne Elvey for conversations that have honed my use of this terminology and her reading of a draft of this paper.

who have journeyed from being his students to his colleagues have both been characterized by attentiveness to interpretive issues. As I tread new ground in this essay,[2] therefore, I express my gratitude to him for his support of my earliest forays into issues hermeneutical and to his collegial friendship across the years that have followed.

1. *Reading Ecologically*

Ecological issues over recent decades have been challenging the human community to a new consciousness of its place within interconnected ecosystems. Indeed, Mary Mellor claims that the basic tenet of ecology is "that all living organisms must been [*sic*] seen in relation to their natural environment," or that "[h]umanity must always be seen as embedded within local and global ecosystems" (1997, 1). A term that captures such embeddedness is *habitat*. Lorraine Code describes *habitat* as a "place to know" such that "social-political, cultural, and psychological elements figure alongside physical and (other) environmental contributors to the 'nature' of a habitat and its inhabitants at any historical moment" (2006, 37). She demonstrates that habitat is constituted by a complex set of relationships among all its more-than-human constituents, relationships that catch up these constituents in their materiality and sociality. Daniel Hillel, a Jewish environmental scientist, in *The Natural History of the Bible: An Environmental Exploration of the Hebrew Scriptures*, defines ecology as "the interrelationship between living communities and their habitats. Human ecology deals with the ways human societies are affected by, and, in turn, affect their physical and biological environments (including landscape, soil, water, natural fauna and flora, and climate)" (2006, 26). Like Code he sees habitat as constituent of the interrelationships that constitute ecology. Habitat will, therefore, function as a significant category of analysis in the approach I am developing.

As can be seen from the above, ecological consciousness requires a changed and changing perspective. It is not simply an adding of "nature" to already existing critical paradigms of interpretation such as feminist, queer or postcolonial. Rather, as Lorraine Code suggests, it is a new way of thinking, what she calls *ecological thinking*. For her, such thinking constitutes a "new social imaginary" which she describes as the "often-implicit but nonetheless effective systems of images, meanings, metaphors, and interlocking explanations-expectations within which people,

---

2. Research for this essay is part of a larger project—an ecological reading of the Gospel of Matthew that will be one volume in the Earth Bible Commentary Series.

in specific time periods and geographical-cultural climates, enact their knowledge and subjectivities and craft their self-understandings" (Code 2006, 29). Ecological thinking is, indeed, a new hermeneutic, one that is characterized by the multidimensionality and interconnectedness of ecology itself. At its core is a repositioning of human thinkers, knowers and actors as Earth-beings in complex interrelationships with all other Earth-beings or Earth-constituents and, some would add, with the sacred or transcendent (Haught 2006, 22).[3] Its "newness," however, draws attention to another or other operative social imaginaries, one of which is that of mastery which has constituted millennia of at least Western culture but other cultures of Earth also (see Plumwood 1993).

Ecological reading is one of the processes and procedures within ecological thinking. Given, however, the pervasiveness of the already instituted imaginary of mastery with its various manifestations of oppression, a *hermeneutic of suspicion* will be necessary. Such a perspective is well known within feminist epistemology (Haraway 1991) and biblical studies (Schüssler Fiorenza 1992, 2001). It will be a significant practice not only within a shift toward a new social imaginary but in the reading of the biblical text ecologically (see Habel 2008, 1–8). Pervasive anthropocentrism and a domination and/or erasure of women, the colonized and the more-than-human other have characterized the ideology of/in author, text and reader from the genesis of the biblical text through its long history of interpretation to the present. It is essential, therefore, that a suspicion attentive to these interlocking processes of erasure and mastery characterizes every phase of the ecological reading process.[4] This, however, will not dominate the reading but will be in dialogue with attention to habitat as key to an ecological perspective that will enable new or reconfigured reading/s to emerge.

---

3. Haught recognizes and argues for what he calls "religion's bold claims that there is *more* than nature," and he goes on to suggest that "a good name for this *more* is mystery" (2006, 22; emphasis is that of the author).

4. Suspicion as a key to ecological reading has characterized the most extensive and systematic project in ecological reading of the biblical text, namely the Earth Bible project co-ordinated by Norman Habel who led the Earth Bible Team from Adelaide, South Australia, in its development of 6 key ecojustice principles to guide contributors to what emerged as a 5-volume *Earth Bible* (see http://ehlt.flinders. edu.au/theology/institute/earthbible/ [accessed 25 February, 2009]). He also established in 2004 the current Ecological Hermeneutics Consultation within the Society of Biblical Literature, editing with Peter Trudinger a volume of papers from that Consultation in which he re-emphasized the principle of suspicion together with that of retrieval and identification. He has most recently initiated the Earth Bible Commentary Series to be published by Sheffield Phoenix for which he is Chief Editor.

Methodologically, my ecological reading is attentive to the various textures of text such as developed by Vernon Robbins: inner texture, intertexture, social and cultural texture, ideological texture and sacred texture (Robbins 1996). I wish, however, to give more attention to the permeability of author/text/reader and their worlds than the social constructionist approach of Robbins makes possible. While attention to habitat will characterize my reading of the various textures, I have changed what he calls the social and cultural texture of the text to the *ecological* texture. This is the result of a recognition that the ecological fabric or habitat (which includes the social and cultural but contextualizes it in a more-than-human world) is not only encoded in the text but is present in the very materiality of the text—the papyrus, vellum or paper and web of ecological processes which constitute it—and all those elements of habitat and their interconnectedness of the first century to which the text linked and links its past and present readers even if these have been erased or backgrounded. Timothy Morton says that "all texts coordinate relationships between inside and outside" (Morton 2007, 79), suggesting that it may be necessary to shift the relationship between foreground and background in order to pay attention to the complex web of relationships in a text that I am calling "habitat." This may be particularly so in relation to an ecological reading given that the emphasis of the biblical text, or perhaps more particularly our reading of that text, has been on the human or the human/divine nexus almost to the exclusion of habitat. There are already literary, historical, socio-cultural and archaeological studies and processes that will assist in the reading of the ecological texture. I will extend these studies to the interrelated aspects of habitat and ecosystems of the first century that have not been given attention in the knowing of place in the Matthean story, together with understandings of cosmology, of geography and of the interrelationship that constitutes Earth and its hi/story. Contemporary critical theories in relation to place/space, time and materiality will also be drawn into an ecological reading to highlight aspects of the text's ecological texture.

The process that can best hold together the various types of studies of the text named above for reading the ecological texture of the text I call *inter-con/textuality* (Liew 1999).[5] I use this term in order to highlight the reciprocity of text and "context" in an ecological reading as this has

---

5. Since developing this approach, I have learnt that Tat-siong Benny Liew has already used the terminology "intercontextuality." My use differs significantly from his in that his focus is on texts being interpreted in contexts in which power relationships are always operative, especially when those contexts are characterized by a history of colonialism. While power is a key analytic category in ecological reading also, inter-con/textuality is used very differently in my approach.

already been discussed above, the interweave into this reciprocity of those multiple aspects of habitat already highlighted and the shift in consciousness necessary to hear those aspects of Earth encoded in the text that have been silenced by previous readings so that they are almost forgotten by readers or to hear the erasures which the text evokes. From such a hermeneutical and methodological position, an ecological reading of Matt 13 can begin.

2. Reading Matthew 13 Ecologically

That same day Jesus went out of the house and sat beside the sea.[2] Such great crowds gathered around him that he got into a boat and sat there, while the whole crowd stood on the beach.[3] And he told them many things in parables. (Matt 13:1–3)

These opening verses of Matt 13 can very easily be overlooked as readers turn attention to what is considered the important material in this chapter, namely Jesus' teaching in parables. The verses are, however, rich in detail when reading ecologically. The reader is provided with temporal location (on that same day), with physical location (out of the house, by the sea and in a boat) and social location and interdependence (great crowds gather around Jesus on the beach). Code emphasizes that "temporal, physical, social location and interdependence are integral to the possibility of being, knowing and doing" (2006, 69) within ecological thinking and they are woven into the fabric of Matt 13:1–3.

The first aspect of this ecological texture that the reader of Matt 13:1–9 encounters is the temporal: on that day or on that same day/*en tē hēmera ekeinē*. This particular identification of time is not typical of the Matthean narrative (the only other occurrence of this phrase is 22:23) but time indicators characterize the entire movement of the narrative (e.g. 2:1, 7, 16; 3:1, 13; 4:1, 11). This day has been shaped by the sociality already connected with it, namely significant controversy with the Pharisees (12:14–15, 24–45) on the one hand and Jesus' proclaiming a new fictive kinship or household on the other (12:48–50), presumably from within a house (see 13:1 with its reference to leaving the house). Temporality functions interconnectedly with spatiality and social interaction, each of which are complexly interwoven into the opening verses of this narrative creating what Jon May and Nigel Thrift call TimeSpace to capture the multiple and heterogeneous experience of social time and the inseparability of time and space and sociality in this experience (May and Thrift 2001, 3–6). The human actor, Jesus, moves from the constructed space of "the house" to the edge of the sea and into a boat on the sea. A large crowd of people gathers around him on the seashore.

As May and Thrift point to the heterogeneity of TimeSpace, Sarah Whatmore offers insights into what she calls hybrid geographies and which I would expand to hybridity of habitat. She says of geographies understood as hybrid that they "implode the object/subject binary that underlies the modern antinomy between nature and society and... recognize the agency of 'non-human' actants—acknowledging their presence in the social fabric and exploring ways of making it register in the vocabularies of social [and I would add literary] analysis" (1999, 27). Her notion of hybridity as it applies to habitat will enable readers of this biblical text to likewise "recognize the agency of 'non-human' actants"— an important aspect of the Parable Discourse.

Jesus comes out of the house, the material and located space of human habitation but also that space in which human kinship structures are conceived and enacted. In the Matthean narrative, house is also the place outside which Jesus' own kin were located in 12:46, thereby disrupting the established understanding of the space called "house." Jesus sits, a gesture that Carter notes designates teaching but also the "authoritative exercise of a king's reign" (2000, 282). But such a human action is not separate from but intimately connected to location: by the sea. The seashore links land and sea but also draws into the narrative intertextually the primordial separation of land and sea (Gen 1:9–10), evoking for contemporary readers the long story of Earth's emergence. The sea's edge is, therefore, a marginal space. Here it is associated with the new fictive kinship of 12:46–50 evoked by the reference to "that same day." This multidimensional TimeSpace is peopled by a large crowd (13:2) from whom Jesus separates himself by getting into a boat. The boat, the sea and the seashore function to create meaning—they give authority or power, relational authority and power, to Jesus in that they both separate him from and yet relate him to the crowd on the marginal strip/the beach. The materiality or spatiality of houses, boats and sea/shores intertwine and interact with that of human bodies, Jesus and the crowds in a sociality that is complex and multidimensional.

This is the hybrid habitat in which and from which Jesus speaks to the crowds in parables, parables that each draw on the human/habitat nexus in which he and his listeners are embedded. Indeed, Jesus the parabler draws Earth and its ecological processes into the pithy narratives that are the parables imaging what is at the heart of his preaching, the *basileia* of the heavens/sky.[6] John Haught has suggested that the evolution of the

---

6. I do not translate *basileia*, the Greek word generally translated as kingdom or empire, as it would have been understood in the first-century Roman context in order to break into the imagery of mastery and domination that the words "kingdom" and

cosmos is the most "fundamental mode of the unfolding of the divine mystery" (2004, 236; see also Berry 1999, 170)[7] and it is Earth and its processes as part of that cosmos which Jesus parables or stories, allowing traces of this divine mystery to unfold in and through them.

2.1. *Matthew 13:3b–9*

This parable is rich in inter-con/textuality, rich in the hybridity of habitat that we have already been exploring. The words given to Jesus by the Matthean redactor in 13:18, "you then hear the parable of the sower," have functioned to draw attention to the sower in the parable of 13:4–8. The text of the parable, is, however, much more multi-dimensional.

Exploring the ecological texture of the text, we note first that the sower may be imagined as slave or tenant farmer on one of the large Herodian or Roman estates which were becoming more numerous in the growing entrepreneurial or latifundial processes in first-century Galilee; or she or he may have been a self-sufficient small farmer, member of a farming family (see Freyne 1994, 105–10 and Fiensy 1991, 75–117). Each would have been interconnected with their social fabric in different ways but would have shared the understanding of the seasons with their rhythms of time for planting and for harvesting, recognizing *timetables and rhythms* and *social discipline* as two of the features of TimeSpace in its multidimensionality that May and Thrift have highlighted (May and Thrift 2001, 3–4). The sower is engaged in a task, that of sowing seed, the seed not being specified but implied in the verb *speirein*. It is likely to be wheat or barley evoking the two most common agricultural products of Galilee in the first century seen throughout the region in areas like the Bet Netofa Valley just north of Nazareth and Sepphoris or the Gennesareth plain on the north-west corner of the Sea of Galilee. Such would have been well known to Jesus and his followers (Hanson and Oakman 1998, 104) or to Galilean readers of the Gospel in the same way that seed and its sowing in the Syrian countryside would have been known to Syrian-based Matthean communities.[8]

"empire" evoke in (a) present context/s. I also want to hold together two possible translations of *ouranos*, a word that carries connotations of divinity and divinity's location in the heavens as well as evocations of the sky and the cosmos in which Earth participates.

7. Berry takes this further when he says that "[w]e need to experience the sequence of evolutionary transformations as moments of grace."

8. Segal (1991, 26–27) proposes that the early inception and reception of the Matthean Gospel took place in "a rather loosely confederated group of congregations, united by missionaries" across "an arc of settlement that included both the

The clear patterning of the Greek draws readers into the process and the outcome of the sowing:

> ...*en tō speirein auton ha men epesen* (as he sowed, some seeds fell...)
> *kai* (and)... (v. 4)
> *alla de epesen epi*...(others fell upon...)
> *kai* (and)... (3 times—vv. 5, 7, 8)

The seed seems to be being cast as ancient agricultural writings confirm (Xenophon, *Oeconomicus* 17.7; Varro, *On Agriculture* 1.29.2). This links the sower intimately to the process of planting with the goal of growing grain to feed one's family, one's animals and to have seed for the next year's planting. The pressure on farmers or tenants to produce abundant harvests so as to develop exports for the Empire also lurks within the world that the parable creates. The parable draws the reader into the ecosystem or ecocycle of sower and seed. Birds take up the seeds on the pathway so that they are fed. Weeds take up their groundspace so that there is insufficient space for the sower's seed in some places. The sun with the wind and the rain, elements that are not named, perhaps constituting a "re-mark" (a foregrounding of what is backgrounded; Morton 2007, 54), enable the seed to grow but if the root is not deep enough, some plants will wither under the sun and others will be choked out by plants which are not useful in the agricultural cycle. The seed that falls on the soil prepared for it produces richly. This ecological process functions metaphorically within the parable which captures indeed a network of actants in this hybrid habitat—from sower, to seed, to bird, sun, earth/soil, weeds and thorns.

Stephanie Nelson, in the foreword to her study of Hesiod's and Virgil's poems on farming, says that "because farming is inescapably a part of human life...it may provide a clue to what is most basically human, and so a clue to our place within the cosmos" (1998, v). Jesus the parabler and his audience would have known intimately the agricultural system of their first-century Galilee and the Matthean author and readers that of Galilee/Syria and it is this which Jesus uses to evoke meaning beyond the parable itself (Wilder 1974, 136–37, 141). In his first parable by the sea he invites listeners/readers into the parabolic process through knowledge/experience in the same way that Xenophon can say that "anyone who does not know what the soil is capable of producing... would not know what he ought to plant or to sow" (*Oeconomicus* 16.3).

Galilee...and Pella...arched into Syria through Antioch and Edessa," with Galilee and Antioch being two fixed points. It is this position that I hold to in relation to the initial context of reception of the Gospel.

Listeners would have known, as did Cato (*On Agriculture* 5.1, 34.2, 35.1) and Varro (*On Agriculture* 1.4–9), the importance of the soil and its various types for particular crops. They too would have known the prolific nature of grain given the right conditions as well as the desired proliferation in the face of the Roman taxation on a small farmer's grain or soil. Varro (*On Agriculture* 1.44.2) notes the variety in yields: tenfold in one district, fifteen in another, even a hundred to one near Gadara in Syria while Pliny (*Natural History* 18.21.94–95) proclaims that nothing is more prolific than wheat, giving yields of 150, 360 and 400. Given, however, that Pliny's figures in particular are in the context of impressing the emperor, such figures may be exaggerated. Indeed Moldenke and Moldenke in their study of plants in the Bible suggest that a yield of about 20-fold can be expected of a crop of wheat in the Levant but that good soil and certain strains might produce "60 or even 100 grains each" (2002, 233). The three ears of grain springing from one stalk on the coins of Agrippa I (Madden 1967, 104–5) like the seeds of the parable, symbolize the fertility of the land. In the former, however, abundance is attributed to the reign of Agrippa. In the latter, the parabler Jesus does not make an attribution at this point but given his proclamation of the *basileia* of the heavens/sky that will follow in a number of parables, there may be an evocation of divine presence (Matt 1:23) even in Jesus' lack of explicit attribution. Life processes in agrarian Palestine/Syria in the context of the Roman Empire are drawn into the parable and invite reflection.

This first parable is not introduced by the phrase the reader will come to expect as the story moves on: the *basileia* of the heavens/sky is like… Rather, Jesus simply presents the complexly woven world of the more-than-human in which multiple actants are intertwined. Two different cosmologies are implicitly in tension within the parable and the network of associations it creates. First there is that of the emperor and his representatives, whether a Herodian king in Galilee (Agrippa) or landowners supporting the imperial system, who are claimed as the source of abundance. On the other hand, the parable evokes a more complex system of interwoven elements that intersect in the process of sowing seed. The surprise is that there is an ecology that can produce abundance. It is, however, hybrid, consisting of multiple actants including hints of divine presence. Jesus simply invites reflection on or attentiveness to the richness of habitat and what such attentiveness will allow readers/listeners to hear: let those who have ears, let them hear.

2.2. *Matthew 13:10–17*

Matthew 13:10–17 is a tantalizing text breaking into the rich imagery of
Jesus' proclamation. First, it appears to be entirely anthropocentric and
second, it constructs a hierarchical wedge between two human groups,
the crowds and the disciples. These aspects cause tensions in the ecological texture of the text. The disciples break into the hybridity of habitat
noted at the beginning of the Parable Discourse. They are said to separate
themselves from the crowd by their speech ("Why do you speak to *them*
in parables?") even though it is almost impossible for the reader to
imagine how they might have physically separated themselves from the
crowd standing on the beach so that they are able to converse with Jesus
who is "in the boat." Not just the social fabric woven into the ecological
texture but the heterogeneity of habitat is shattered (13:2). The remainder
of the exchange continues the construction of hierarchal dualisms: to you
it has been given/to them not (v. 11); the one who has/the one who has
not (v. 12); those who seeing, do not see and hearing do not hear/blessed
those who see and hear (vv. 13–16).

Intertextually, it is difficult to understand the negative implications of
speaking in parables which the words of the disciples construct since
parables are the medium of the wise scribe of Sir 39:2–3, and in Wis
6:22 wisdom is equated with the revealing of *mysteria*. These are not set
over against one another in the Wisdom literature as they are in this
segment of the Gospel, the only time that the word *mysterion* occurs in
the entire Gospel (see Matt 13:11). Indeed, what will emerge as the
Parable Discourse unfolds is that both crowds and disciples receive the
parables in which Jesus does unfold understandings of the *basileia* that
he preaches not just to the disciples but to all those listening. The
Matthean ecological reader will, therefore, be attentive to this segment of
the text and the challenge which Jesus' teaching in parables presents to
the social imaginary of mastery encoded in it.

2.3. *Matthew 13:18–23*

The rich Earth imagery and evocative tenor of Jesus' parable of the seed
and the soil is tempered by the continuation of the anthropocentrism of
the previous verses in the call to hear the *parable of the sower* (13:18–23)
in the language of the Matthean community of interpretation and story-
telling. The imagery and tenor are interpreted in a one-to-one correspondence with a human response to the "word of the kingdom" (13:19), the
only occurrence of this phrase in the Matthean Gospel. The parable
evokes the *basileia* in hybrid more-than-human processes, the interpretation renders it in terms of ethical response. One opens up to ever richer
possibilities of imagery through its grounding in habitat, the other is an

application to human behaviour, couched in androcentric language that seems devoid of habitat. Both the evocative and the ethical are significant elements of Jesus' preaching of the *basileia*. An ecological reading will, on the one hand, call attention to the multi-dimensionality of the imagery and its relationship to habitat as well as the implications of such for determining ecological ethics. On the other hand, such a reading alerts readers to the univocality of the allegorical interpretation and its grounding in human behaviour only, reminding them that the word of the *basileia* spoken in ecological imagery invites an ecological response that will, in its turn, be multidimensional and born out of attentiveness to Earth.

2.4. *Matthew 13:24–30*

Matthew 13:24 introduces readers to phraseology that will become familiar as the Gospel continues to unfold: *hōmoiōthē hē basileia tōn ouranōn* ("the kingdom of heaven/sky may be compared to"). There are aspects of this *basileia* of the heavens or the sky that can only be understood by way of metaphor and image like a finger pointing at the moon, to borrow a metaphor from a Zen sutra (see Kapleau 1966, 167, 174). As with the initial parable, the ecological texture of this parable is constituted by habitat. It evokes TimeSpace where humans and human activity of sowing, seed in all its potential for life and the production of many seeds in the cycle of sowing and harvesting, and the soil which receives it as well as weeds and their impact within the agricultural cycle all actively intersect in the ecological texture of the text.

This parable draws readers once again into the world of seed, sower, soil and yield that characterizes this Parable Discourse (12 of the 16 verses in Matthew in which some form of *speirein*/to sow occurs are in Matt 13—vv. 3, 4, 18, 19, 20, 22, 23 [×2], 27, 31, 37, 39). Also *anthrōpos*, except when qualified as an *oikodespotēs*/householder in 13:52, seems to function as a generic indicator of the human actor/s not only in this parable but in the discourse as a whole (13:24, 25, 28, 31, 44, 45), although the *anthrōpos* of v. 24 is named as *oikodespotēs* in v. 27. The parable which begins in generic terms of a sower sowing good seed in a field evoking the processes discussed above moves into imagery of the larger estate on which an *oikodespotēs* has not workers but *douloi* or slaves. The narrative and metaphoric world created by this parable is quite complex and is often overlooked by biblical scholars who move immediately to the allegorical interpretation of the parable in vv. 37–43 and allow it to obscure the hearing of the parable itself and its wealth of imagery (see McIvor 1995).

While in the initial parable of Matt 13, the various places of reception of the seed which determined the different yields could be seen as part of the natural ecosystem, in this parable, there is direct human intervention into the process of sowing, germination and growing to harvest and it is a negative intervention. The human subject sows good seed (*kalon sperma*) in the field, evoking the agricultural process of the initial parable. What the *basileia* of the heavens or sky is compared to is the growing of good seed which is interrupted by an enemy coming while all are sleeping and sowing *zizania* (weeds) among the grain (*siton*). There is an ambivalence, however, around *echthros*/enemy at this point in the narrative. Listeners have been instructed to love their enemies (5:43–44) and that the enemy is of one's own household (10:36). Might the enemy of this parable be a slave of the household or a local brigand seeking to bring about social transformation in the face of the development of Roman landed estates?[9] Tension or rupture is introduced into the parable but its source is left obscure.

The *zizania*/weeds, a *hapax legomenon* in both the LXX and the New Testament, occurs only in this parable and its allegorical explanation (13:25, 26, 27, 29, 30, 36, 38, 40) and is rare in ancient Greek (Moldenke and Moldenke 2002, 134). It seems to be equated in *Geoponica* 2, 43 with a particular type of weed, namely *aira* (BDAG, 429), which, as Theophrastus says, "comes from degenerate wheat and barley." He goes on to say that it "loves chiefly to appear among wheat" and in this same paragraph muses that "in the case of nearly every crop there is a plant which grows up with it and mingles with it, whether this is due to the soil which is a reasonable explanation, or to some other cause" (Theophrastus, *Enquiry into Plants* 8.8.3). While the grain and the *zizania*/weeds might grow naturally together, in the parable, however, there is a very explicit intervention—it is an enemy who has scattered the *zizania* among the good seed. And since they grow well together, it is not surprising that the presence of the weeds does not become visible until the grain appears. The rhythm of the season and human agricultural practices, two dimensions of time, intersect with the life-cycle of the grain and it is this which evokes the *basileia* of the heavens/sky and into which a counter movement is introduced whose processes are very similar, indeed hardly distinguishable until the final phrase of coming to fruition or seed.

9. I am grateful to Professor Sean Freyne for this insight and for his critical reading of this article.

It is at this point in the narrative that the reader learns that the *anthrōpos* of the parable is an *oikodespotēs*/householder with slaves. It seems, however, that the householder and not the slaves was responsible for the planting of the good seed. (Varro, *On Agriculture* 1.17.2 says that "freemen…till the ground themselves as many poor people do with the help of their families") and the vigilance of the *douloi*/slaves on behalf of the householder suggests that they work together with him for the good of the whole *oikos*. What we see in this parable is the Roman practice of using slaves and masters as literary figures in *exempla* or example stories, a practice taken over by early Christians (Harrill 2006, 3), especially, as one might expect, in the parables. This practice participates in the maintenance of the social imaginary of mastery that Harrill says was "widely diffuse in the ancient Mediterranean, which supported what the Romans called *auctoritas*" (2006, 2). The ecological reader will read against the grain of this aspect of the text, noting, however, the shared participation of householder and slaves in the desired outcome of the crop for the household, each exercising particular power within the complex web of power as discussed by Pomeroy in relation to the work of Xenophon (1994, 65–67).[10]

The surprising or confronting aspect in the parable, especially to the Gospel's first-century hearers, would have been the instruction given by the householder to the *douloi*, namely to leave both the grain and the *zizania* to grow to the harvest (v. 30). Xenophon says that "if weeds spring up with the grain and choke it by robbing it of its nourishment," then it is "reasonable…to send in men to hoe the soil" (*Oeconomicus* 17.15), while for Varro (*On Agriculture* 1.30), "crops should be weeded, that is, the grass cleared from the crops" and he links this agricultural practice with time: "between the vernal equinox and the rising of the Pleiades."[11] The householder of the parable also interacts with time but the advice given to the slaves is to *aphete*/leave the weeds and the grain to grow to fruition together. This householder does not seem to be concerned about the weeds robbing the grain of nourishment as was

---

10.   Varro also notes that "foremen [who may themselves be slaves] are to be made more zealous by rewards, and care must be taken that they have a bit of property of their own" (*On Agriculture* 1.17.5).

11.   Moldenke and Moldenke (2002, 134) suggest that "poorer people do not clean it out of their grainfields, lest in so doing they accidentally pull up and thus lose a single grain plant" but they do not give documentation to support this claim at least in antiquity. If this was so, the parable's imagery moves between the larger landowner and the poorer subsistence farmers and if the latter is evoked, then the parable's imagery draws on a justice motif characteristic of the Matthean Gospel.

Xenophon. Rather the focus is on the *kairō tou therismou*/the time of the harvest. This is to be the time of separation, this is the culminating point of the parable which images the *basileia* of the heavens/sky.[12]

Kairos can carry with it connotations of a period characterized as crisis time (BDAG, 497). In the parable, however, it seems to designate one moment in the agricultural process when both weed and grain come to fruition and so it is time for the harvest. Echoes of the *crisis* may, however, function faintly in the text, especially given that the only other reference to *therismos*/harvest is in Matt 9:37–38 where the metaphoric aspect seems to be strong. Also the related imagery of the *siton*/grain being gathered into the *apothēkē*/barn while the weeds (or the chaff) are burnt has been used metaphorically to describe the role of John the Baptist (3:17). This parable invites attentiveness to TimeSpace and the sociality associated with it in ecological processes if one is to understand the *basileia* of the heavens/sky. The parabolic turn ruptures hearers'/readers' expectations and invites them into a new TimeSpace/sociality nexus—it entails a waiting, a waiting on the *kairos* or the time, not of human making, but the time that is shown to be the time of fruition and the time of separation, the time that Earth and its processes will manifest. The challenge is to be able to distinguish what is grain and what is weed and to know the point at which such distinguishing can happen—this is invitation into *mysterion* which is associated with the divine whose presence in Earth's processes has been made visible in a particular way in Jesus (Matt 1:23). This presence reveals itself in and through Earth in which TimeSpace and sociality of the more-than-human intertwine. I will not treat here the explanation of this parable given to the disciples when they move into the house (Matt 1:36–43) as it, like the explanation of the seeds and yields, has a univocality to it that limits the multidimensionality of imagery in the parable itself.

2.5. *Matthew 13:31–34*

Matthew 13:31–34 continues the unfolding of the Parable Discourse, drawing on the visible, the material available to Jesus' listeners both experientially as well as imaginatively or parabolically. Inter-con/textually, it is the processes of the material that are highlighted by Jesus

---

12. The imagery of this parable for an ecological reader can evoke the contemporary ecological approaches to weed management which are often complex and attentive to ecosystems in which "life form," "growth form" and "lifespan" have a place and in which "multiple ecological interactions" have their place (see Håkansson 2003 and Liebman, Mohler and Staver 2001).

as parabolic and thus constituting the ecological texture of the text of Matt 13:31–34. The focus of the first parable in this small segment is the mustard seed that is sown in a field, continuing the agrarian imagery of previous parables. What Jesus highlights as parabolic at least for first-century Galilean or Syrian audiences is that this tiniest of seeds known to them, grown as a herb for its oil as well as being beneficial for health (Pliny, *Natural History* 19, 54, 170), exceeds their expectations. Moldenke and Moldenke (2002, 61) note that it may well have been the smallest seed planted and cultivated in first-century Palestine and Syria, while Michael Zohary (1982, 93) says that "it is conspicuous in the vegetation around the Sea of Galilee and farther north." This smallest of seeds grows up to become a shrub or almost a small tree, from between three to four feet up to ten to fifteen feet (Moldenke and Moldenke 2002, 59). As such it can become a home for birds that feast on its seeds. The parabolic imagery is extended, however, to the birds making their dwelling place or their nests there. The surprising interconnectedness of the ecosystem becomes a source for Jesus' challenge to the readers'/hearers' imagination in relation to the *basileia* of the heavens/sky. Even the smallest deserves attention because of the potential within it—a significant parabolic challenge within an ecological reading.

This symbolism continues into the next parable, linked as it is by the phrase *allēn parabolēn* (another parable). Imagery shifts from the field in which tiny mustard seeds were planted to the daily activity of the leavening of flour carried out by the women of a household or households, women who may have been householders themselves, wives or daughters of householders, or slaves. The activity of leavening would have been visible and known to all members of the household (and hence the audience) as it was carried out in workrooms that may or may not have been gendered spaces (Meyers 2003, 44–69), or in courtyards which may have belonged to one household or been shared. Hybridity of habitat constitutes the ecological texture of this text as readers imagine the leaven, the small amount of fermented dough that permeates what is approximately a bushel or thirty-four kilos of flour, enough to feed a hundred people according to Warren Carter (2000, 291). Again the contrast between small and large characterizes the parable, but in this instance it is the permeation of the leaven through such a large amount of flour that startles listeners' imagination, the parable ending with the statement: the whole was leavened! Intertextually, this fermentation process contrasts with the starkness of unleavened bread that was a reminder of the people's slavery in Egypt (Exod 13:3; cf. Exod 12:15, 19; 13:7; Deut 16:3). The *basileia* of the heavens/sky that Jesus images in terms of habitat of which leaven is one small element points to freedom from such slavery. An ecological reading will seek to understand what the leaven is that is needed today to permeate human consciousness and ecological ethics so that the freedom of the entire more-than-human community might be imagined.

3. *Conclusion*

Jesus, the parabler of the *basileia* of the heavens/sky, engages his audience of both crowds and disciples with aspects of Earth and its processes, of human and habitat that were familiar to them in their everyday lives. These constitute the ecological texture of the Matthean Parable Discourse in Matt 13 and they engaged Gospel hearers/readers of first-century Galilee/Syria with their world and reflection on it in a way that opens up potential for imagining divine presence intimately related to the unfolding of Earth and to the mystery of the *basileia* of the heavens/sky toward which the parables point.

In undertaking an ecological reading of some of the key agrarian parables of Matt 13, I have demonstrated how attentiveness not just to the human, which is the more common approach to interpreting biblical texts, but a recognition of habitat in all its hybridity of Earth constituents and processes in the ecological texture of the text enables the parables to be heard more evocatively. Inter-con/textuality enabled me to re-member the world in/of the text in all its materiality—not just as a construct of an author but with a consciousness of the porous borders between text and world and yet also not collapsing the distinction between text and world. Rather than being reduced to univocal meanings related to human behaviour, the parables are able to function in ways that draw readers/hearers into greater attentiveness to Earth's processes. There is an invitation to wait on Earth's processes, attentive to the time when particular actions need to be taken. There is a challenge to attend to the smallest of beings if one is to know and understand the *basileia* of the heavens/sky within an ecological consciousness that ecological reading points to; and there is a recognition of the power of the small in changing the large. It is only having attended to the process of the parable and Earth's processes into which it draws listeners that they may be able to envisage the ecological ethics which the parables might call forth. These, however, will be multidimensional since Earth's processes are multidimensional or hybrid involving multiple actants in the more-than-human community and not able to be reduced to univocality.

Parable functions evocatively in the Gospel text and it also functions evocatively in a contemporary ecological reading of this text. It opens into *mysterion*, leaving open, in words borrowed from Kate Rigby, "the incalculable possibility of divine visitation" (Rigby 2004, 431) or in Matthean terms whispers of divine presence with us/with Earth (Matt 1:23). This is not a presence that separates from Earth but indeed is embedded in it as human is embedded in habitat in ways that perhaps only poetry and parable can make present.

GETTING TO KNOW YOU:
REFORMATION MARRIAGE IDEOLOGIES
AND CONTEMPORARY DEBATES ON SAME-SEX MARRIAGE

Michael Carden

It was Ed Conrad who encouraged me into the study of biblical reception and the history of biblical interpretation. It was also Ed who encouraged me to take up the study of the reception history of Sodom and Gomorrah. So it's appropriate that in this volume, dedicated to my friend, colleague and teacher, my contribution makes a return to Sodom and Gomorrah. It is also appropriate that my essay will initially explore the hetero-normative dynamics of Calvin's commentary on Gen 19. On a couple of occasions, Ed found that ideas he thought new, including his own reading of the anonymous messenger guiding Zechariah in the book of the Twelve as the prophet Haggai, had been discussed and condemned by Calvin five centuries ago.

In the seminal *Homosexuality and the Western Christian Tradition* (1955), Derrick Sherwin Bailey argued that when, in Gen 19:5, the Sodomites demand Lot bring out his guests so they might "know" them, the Sodomites were not actually declaring a sexual intent but were instead wanting to check the guests' bona fides. Bailey argued that the homophobic interpretation of Sodom was based on a misinterpretation of the word "know" as conveying a sexual intent on the part of the Sodom-ites. His opponents argued that this interpretation was naïve, flying in the face of a weighty tradition that understands "know" as signifying sexual interest by the Sodomites in Lot's guests. However, in Christian tradi-tion, Bailey's interpretation of "know" is not a novel one. John Calvin also broke with tradition to argue that the Sodomites were saying that they wanted to check the credentials of Lot's guests. Unlike Bailey, who wanted to break down the homophobic interpretation of the Sodom story, Calvin argues that the Sodomites make this claim to mask their true erotic intentions and thus trick Lot into handing over his guests. Thus, unlike modern anti-homophobic interpreters, Calvin's reading is designed to demonstrate how dangerous same-sex desire can be. His novel approach underscores what I term a theology of the closet that is part and parcel of a broader ideology of marriage as a guarantee of heteronormativity and a bulwark against sodomy. That this ideology is very much part of the Reformation project will be demonstrated by a brief segue into the work of Calvin's contemporary, Heinrich Bullinger. I will then examine how this ideology is developed in an execution sermon by Samuel Danforth from American New England, which draws on this theology of the closet as well as the specific linkages of Sodom, the bestial and the homoerotic that Bullinger makes. This theology of the closet, with all its contradictions, continues to serve as a structuring social ideology (especially in the Anglosphere), as I will show in a final brief overview of contemporary debates concerning homosexuality and same-sex marriage.

"How Great is the Corruption of Our Nature"

In Calvin's view, everything happens through the will of God and the scriptures exist to instruct believers in this fact:

> Thus it becomes the faithful to be employed in reflecting in the histories of all times, that they may always form the judgement from the Scripture, of the various destructions which, privately and publicly, have befallen the ungodly. (Calvin 1984, 480)

Genesis 19 is one such exemplary destruction. Sodom, itself, is a "horrible example of stupor" where the people's "sense of good and evil being extinguished" meant that they "wallow like cattle in every kind of filth" (Calvin 1984, 484). Importantly, Calvin observes, "this disease too much prevails in all ages, and is at present too common," and so "it is important to mark this circumstance" (484). Calvin is not specific about "this disease" but he does foreshadow that "in the next chapter, (Moses) explains the most filthy crime which reigned in Sodom" (491). However, he continues, citing Ezekiel, that "luxury from the fulness of bread" led to pride and cruelty on the part of the Sodomites which resulted in them being "given up to a reprobate mind" and "driven headlong into brutal lusts" (491). That Abraham is forewarned in Gen 18 of Sodom's fate through a direct encounter with the deity signals the singular importance of the events of Gen 19. The story of Sodom serves as a lesson of

> …how tyrannically Satan proceeds when the dominion of sin is established. And certainly, seeing the propensity of men to sin, and the facility for sinning are so great, it is not surprising that one should be corrupted by another, till the contagion reached every individual. For nothing is more dangerous than to live where the public licence of crime prevails. (Calvin 1984, 490–91)

Using these metaphors of illness, Calvin establishes Gen 19 as an ideo-story on which to ground his own theo-political vision of the ideal society. The particular role of this story is to give ideological justification for whatever social prophylaxis is necessary to establish and maintain this ideal society. Genocide serves to reinforce a theology of the closet to underpin a heteronormative order. Lot and his family, on the other hand, will serve as models for the believer, especially those half-hearted in their faith and willing to make compromises with an ungodly order.

This approach is evident from Calvin's discussion on the opening events of Gen 19, in which the angels encounter Lot sitting at the gates of Sodom. Calvin refuses to speculate on Lot's reasons for being there. He acknowledges that many (Christian) interpreters have argued that Lot waited every day at the gates to welcome strangers, but points out that there is no indication in the text that such is the case. Alternative explanations, for example that he was waiting for his shepherds, are just as likely. Nonetheless, Calvin states that Lot's commitment to the practice of hospitality can be assumed from the opening verses but that one need not read a zealous commitment on Lot's part. However, there is more at play here than simple hospitality in Calvin's reading of Lot. Lot urges the angels to stay with him not "merely for the sake of supplying them with a supper, but for the purpose of defending them from the force and injury of the citizens" (Calvin 1984, 496). Thus Calvin highlights a looming sense of menace in his reading of the exchange between Lot and the angels. He says,

> ...the angels act, as if it were safe to sleep on the highway; and thus conceal their knowledge of the abandoned wickedness of the whole people. For if the gates of cities are shut, to prevent the incursions of wild beasts and of enemies; how wrong and absurd it is that they who are within should be more exposed to still more grievous dangers. Therefore the angels thus speak, in order to make the wickedness of the people appear the greater. (496)

A city with its walls and gates is meant to be a place of refuge. Surely a person could assume it would be safe to sleep in the streets. By pressuring the angels, Lot shows that he is not only hospitable but also "careful...of his guests" and is concerned "lest they should suffer any dishonour or injury" (496). For Calvin, the biblical narrative implies that there is violence, at least, rife in the city. Thus, the exchange between Lot and the angels helps to set up a narrative tension for the reader.

This suspense is resolved by the siege of Lot's house where "in a single crime, Moses sets before our eyes a lively picture of Sodom" (496). Overwhelmed by lust, the Sodomites surrender to ferocity and barbarism, readily conspiring "to perpetrate the most abominable crime"

(496). Same-sex desire is taken by Calvin as a sign that the Sodomites have surrendered any humanity—"they rush together like brute animals" (496)—but it is also a culmination of their wickedness. They are not "contaminated with one vice only, but are given up to all audacity" (496). Indeed, taking his cue from Rom 1, Calvin suggests that same-sex desire is itself a punishment from the deity for their impiety. The Sodomites forgot their creator and gave themselves over to material excess. Consequently they are punished with same-sex desire, which signifies how much they have perverted "the order of nature…so that confused chaos is the result" (497). To illustrate this chaos, Calvin uses metaphors that dissolve differences of species and age. The Sodomites "rush together like brute animals" (496), showing that they were "completely destitute…of all remaining shame; for neither did any gravity restrain the old, nor any modesty, suitable to their age, restrain the young" (497). Same-sex desire represents the collapse of all boundaries and authority, marking a society as ready for obliteration.

That same-sex desire is the culminating point of a process of corruption and rebellion is further highlighted by Calvin's surprising interpretation of the word "know" in the Sodomites' demand. Unlike his predecessors, Calvin refuses to read the word "know" as having a clearly sexual meaning, even though he recognizes that it is used in this sense elsewhere in the biblical text. In Gen 19, he argues it has a different meaning, "as if the men had said, We wish to know whom thou bringest, as guests, into our city" (Calvin 1984, 498). In other words, the Sodomites demand that Lot bring out his guests in order to have their credentials checked. While Calvin appears to anticipate the pro-gay interpretation pioneered by Bailey (1955), Calvin's purpose is very different. Bailey and other pro-gay interpretations today argue that the Sodomites are challenging Lot's right to bring strangers into the city and are questioning the right of the angels to be in their midst. Calvin argues, instead, that the men of Sodom "would have spoken, in coarser language, of such an act" and, thus, they use the word "know" to disguise their real sexual intentions (Calvin 1984, 498). They are attempting to trick Lot into handing over his guests.

Calvin's argument is designed to show just how abominable and dangerous same-sex desire really is, and furthermore provides a base for a theology of the closet. Fundamental to his argument is this question: If Lot was regularly entertaining guests, was his house being regularly besieged and was he regularly offering his daughters to these mobs? Surely not, otherwise Lot would have warned the strangers to leave the city and not take them under his roof to face the full onslaught of Sodomite assault. Calvin suggests, therefore, that what happened this night is a new development or an ultimate excess on the part of the Sodomites. Lot had a general idea of the evil of his neighbours but, "he had, nevertheless, no suspicion of what really happened, that they would make an assault upon his house; this, indeed, seems to have been quite a new thing" (Calvin 1984, 498). Their attempt at subterfuge does not fool Lot. Indeed, by the assault on Lot's house the Sodomites have outed themselves and thereby marked themselves as beyond redemption and fit for destruction. This outing is their ultimate punishment. Behind it is the design of the deity, making public what was hidden:

> So the wicked, after they have long exulted in their iniquity, at length, by furiously rushing onward, accelerate their destruction in a moment. God therefore designed, in calling the men of Sodom to judgement, to exhibit, the extreme act of their wicked life; and he impelled them, by the spirit of deep infatuation, to a crime, the atrocity of which would not suffer the destruction of the place to be any longer deferred. (498)

Shameless and thoroughly corrupt, the Sodomites break down their closet doors and declare themselves outside Lot's house. Unless thoroughly suppressed, same-sex desire will eventually overcome any sense of shame and manifest for all the world to see. I noted above that Calvin sees same-sex desire itself as a form of punishment. By surrendering to it the Sodomites "render themselves altogether hateful and detestable to God and to men" (499). Calvin further warns his audience,

> …if this severe vengeance of God so fell upon the men of Sodom, that they became blind with rage, and prostituted themselves to all kinds of crime, certainly we shall scarcely be more mildly treated, whose iniquity is the less excusable, because the truth of God has been more clearly revealed to us. (497)

Calvin offers his audience a nightmare scenario if they fail to adhere rigorously to the godly life. Unlike the Sodomites, they have had the revelation of the Christ event. This fact means that if they don't strive to keep themselves faithful to their salvation, then their fate will be just as bad, if not worse, than the Sodomites.

I would argue that from this point Lot emerges in Calvin's commentary as a negative example, someone who does not trust enough in his Lord. From now on, all of Lot's choices have an ill result meriting Calvin's rebuke. In particular, by offering his daughters to the mob, Lot shows that, despite his faith, he has not developed an appropriate spirit of trust, instead allowing his mind to be "carried hither and thither by hastily catching at wicked counsels" (Calvin 1984, 497). While Lot was brave and committed to the virtue of hospitality in going out to face the mob, by offering them his daughters he falls down by not trusting sufficiently in the deity. Such weakness on Lot's part demonstrates the power of the ungodly society to weaken and corrupt the faithful, thus reinforcing the imperative for believers either to separate themselves from such a wicked order or to suppress it. A godly society is a school for godly living as is the reverse.

Indeed, it is possible to read the remainder of Calvin's commentary on Gen 19 as charting the fall and redemption of Lot. Lot suffers in Sodom's ruin yet his suffering is not innocent but deserved, resulting from his insufficient application to cultivate the godly life. In this pessimistic vision, Lot represents the good man who is too entangled in a corrupt world but who is nevertheless marked for salvation. This salvation can only come about through the chastening interventions of the deity. Calvin's reading of Lot's fall makes a strong contrast to the portrait of Lot in Luther's commentary on Gen 19. For Luther, Lot is an exemplary figure and model for believers and only once does he ever rebuke Lot. Lot and his household demonstrate for Luther how the innocent can suffer grievously when evil is allowed to reign unchecked. Lot, his wife and his daughters are tragic victims in an apocalyptic scenario of melodramatic intensity. For Calvin, however, there are no innocent victims. Lot, his wife and his daughters, all suffer in Sodom's ruin, yet their suffering is not innocent but deserved and results from their insufficient application to cultivate the godly life. By their inconstancy, they have made themselves prey to the corrupting influence of Sodom: "although while dwelling in Sodom, (Lot's) heart was continually vexed; it was scarcely possible that he should avoid contracting some defilement from a sink of wickedness so profound" (Calvin 1984, 508). Such an influence will surely need a very stern medicine to counter-act it. If Lot is redeemed in the end, it is only because what befalls him from now on is a very stern medicine indeed.

While Lot's fall could be said to have started once he opted to live in Sodom, in Calvin's reading it only becomes apparent on offering his daughters to the mob. It is only from this event that Calvin becomes more and more critical of Lot and, again in contrast to Luther, offers no extenuating comments for what becomes of his family. Instead, they serve as examples of how the potential for salvation can be squandered when not taken seriously by believers. Lot will reveal that "indolence of the flesh" by which "we slowly and coldly set ourselves to escape the judgement of God, unless…deeply stirred by the dread of it" (Calvin 1984, 503). Lot's tardiness and prevarication in fleeing the city are likewise counted against him. Calvin sees both as a sign of Lot's sloth and doubt about what lies ahead. Lot allows a "multiplicity of cares and fears" (506) to distract him from acting in prompt obedience to the deity.

His attachment to his comfort and possessions is a means by which Lot allows "satan (to) interpose many delays" (506). Such attachment and indolence can be understood as the soil in which Satan sows the seeds of *luxuria*. Lot and Sodom form a continuum of *luxuria*, from its beginning to its culminating climactic endpoint. Lot's attachment and prevarication betrays a germinating attachment to the ways of Sodom. That he is virtually dragged from the city by the angels demonstrates "the mercy of God" (507) who pardons Lot for this prevarication. However, Lot sins again by refusing to flee to the hills and asking to be allowed shelter in Zoar. By so doing, Lot "rests not upon the word of God, he slides and almost falls away" (510). This cupidity on Lot's part will result in his punishment when he subsequently suddenly changes his mind. Calvin disagrees with others who regard Lot's appeal to take shelter in Zoar as an example of pure prayer pleasing to the deity. Instead Lot "indulges himself in opposition to the word" (509), but his prayer is granted because "it is no new thing for the Lord sometimes to grant, as an indulgence, what he, nevertheless, does not approve" (511). The flight from Sodom reveals Lot's "immoderate carnal affection" by which "he is held entangled by those very delights which he ought to have shunned" (509).

Not only Lot, but also his wife is thus entangled, in her case fatally. Indeed, bearing in mind that Lot is head of a household, if he is compromised so too are those whose direction is his responsibility. As women, Lot's wife and daughters require male authority to keep them on the godly path. If Lot the patriarch is distracted from that path, then it is no surprise that they are too. This same pattern can be seen in Luther's commentary, though for Luther "women are weak by nature" (Luther 1961, 298) and need the constant guidance and leadership of men, their husbands and fathers. So if Lot is distracted, even more so will be his wife and daughters. The difference in Calvin's approach is that he does not allow the women any innocence on their part for their bad choices due to Lot's and their own resulting distraction. Thus, Calvin offers several possible motives for Lot's wife to turn back and for her subsequent fate. Perhaps she turned back to "have more certain evidence before her eyes" or out of "pity to the perishing people" (Calvin 1984, 514). Pity is not a concept prominent in Calvin's commentary, and so, unsurprisingly, he concludes that it was the former option, incredulity on her part, that caused her to look back. Citing Luke 17:32, Calvin infers that "she was moved by some evil desire…and…did not cheerfully leave Sodom" (514). Thus her looking back also represents a form of rebellion, demonstrating that, through attachment to things of this world, *luxuria* results in the rejection of the divine ordinance. She represents those discontented with divine favour, who "glided into unholy desires" and "fix their eyes on some other object than the proposed prize of their high calling" (515). Lot's wife is further along the continuum of *luxuria* than her husband and, no doubt, Calvin would agree with Luther's evaluation of female weakness as the reason. So, even though she is not innocent, her fate shows the terrible consequences that occur when the head of the patriarchal household is distracted from his godly role through inordinate attachment to the worldly ways of Sodom. However, despite her death, Calvin is confident "that God...spared her soul because he often chastises his own people in the flesh, that their soul may be saved from eternal destruction" (515). Thus, both Lot and his wife can stand for those believers who do not completely adhere to the word and allow themselves to be complacent in the face of an ungodly society. They can expect punishment in this world as a way of ensuring their salvation in the next. If evil befalls the faithful, then they must re-examine themselves to ascertain how they have compromised and strayed from the path of righteousness.

The cup of Lot's suffering is not filled by the death of his wife. As I noted above, Calvin believes Lot was subsequently punished for refusing to flee to the hills, wanting instead to take shelter in Zoar. Calvin does not elaborate on this suggestion. However, I believe that this apparent oversight is due to the fact that the English translation of his commentary omits the rape of Lot by his daughters. No reason is given for this omission—it is simply "deemed necessary" (Calvin 1984, 518 n. 1). Nevertheless, there are many clues in later commentaries of the era that, unlike Luther and many other commentators before him, Calvin condemns the daughters for what they do to their father. One clue emerges when Calvin wonders what became of Lot's servants. Calvin is not greatly exercised about them, probably because, as will be seen below, he finds servants undesirable for his idealized household. So, Calvin merely observes during his discussion of Lot's flight from Sodom that, despite references to Lot's many servants earlier in Genesis, no mention is made of them here. He concludes that it

> ...is, nevertheless, probable that some servants went forth with him, to carry provisions and some portion of furniture. For, whence did his daughters obtain in the desert mountain, the wine which they gave their father, unless some things, which Moses does not mention, had been conveyed by asses, or camels, or wagons? (Calvin 1984, 504)

In other words, while the biblical text only speaks of Lot, his wife and their daughters, Calvin understands that they were accompanied by some servants carrying basic provisions. If such be the case, then Lot and his daughters could not have been alone later in the cave. Consequently, the daughters could not have assumed that they and their father were the only survivors and, thus, the only hope of the continuation of the human race. Certainly, Calvin's implication was detected by Andrew Willett who summarily discounts it as "not so probable" (1633, 182). Willett further informs us that Calvin declares the daughters to have committed a very great offence "against the law of nature" (183). And Abraham Wright goes as far as to say that by their action "Lot's daughters will prove Sodomites" (1662, 30). What greater horror than to flee from that which is monstrous only to discover that you have brought some of that same monstrous reality with you. Wright declares that Lot would surely have wished he had escaped alone from Sodom. In other words, he suggests that Lot would have preferred his daughters were incinerated in Sodom, such being most definitely a cruel fate. For further confirmation that this reading would accord with Calvin, then, one need only turn to Wright's near contemporary, John Trapp, who cites Calvin frequently in his own commentary. Trapp says of Lot's flight to Zoar, "so he should have done at first; and so he had obeyed God, saved his wife, and prevented that sin of incest with his daughters" (Trapp 1649, 149). By his prevaricating and failure to obey the divine commands, indeed by questioning the divine commands, Lot is shown not to have the mettle to be a proper patriarchal head of the heterosexual household. Consequently, he is not able to constrain the secret sodomitic desires of his wife and daughters and so, not only his wife dies but, his daughters suffer a fate worse than death.

I want to return my discussion to Calvin's commentary with some thoughts on genocide. I will preface them with Abraham Wright's concluding comments on the rape of Lot:

> …yet even this unnatural Bed was blessed with encrease, and one of our Saviours worthy Ancestors sprung after from this line. Gods Election is not tyed to our means; neither are blessings or Curses ever traduced. The chaste Bed of holy Parents hath often bred a Monstrous Generation; and contrarily God hath sometimes raised an holy Seed from the Drunken Bed of Incest or Fornication. Thus will God magnifie the freedom of his own choice, and let us know that we are not born but made good. (1662, 30)

There is nothing inherently good in human beings, and the deity will sometimes elect those from the most corrupt lineage, as was the case with Ruth of Moab. Furthermore, the godliest parents can more often raise up the most reprobate sinners because it is the choice and subsequent tutelage of the deity that makes saints of humans and nothing else. The godly society is no guarantee of godly people. Wright's thinking summarizes themes in Calvin's commentary quite explicitly, and I will now return to Calvin's text, where such thinking serves to justify the logic of genocide as the ultimate sanction for maintaining the godly society.

Like many commentators before him, Calvin raises the question of the infants of Sodom and considers whether it is just that they should perish with their parents. Unlike Luther, he provides a more coherent though unpalatable justification while warning that humans, as contingent beings of limited understanding, are not really qualified to question divine justice. His basic point is that "the human race is in the hand of God, so that he may devote whom he will to destruction, and may follow whom he will with his mercy" (Calvin 1984, 513). As noted earlier, the deity's mercy is not above destroying the saved along with the damned as part of a pedagogy of salvation. However, Calvin's point is that deity can and will destroy whomever it will. Humans should not apply their standards to the deity. However, he further argues that "the whole of that seed was accursed and execrable, so that God could not justly have spared, even the least" (513). Calvin regards the whole human race as corrupt and worthy of damnation. Why it would have been especially unjust for the deity to spare even the least of the Sodomites is not clear. Perhaps it is that, by having surrendered themselves to same-sex desire, the entire people have crossed a line from which there results only one possibility—mass extermination, not only for themselves but also for their children, who have themselves become somehow contaminated.

Calvin's vision is a profoundly pessimistic one. Lot's fate illustrates Calvin's point that in a corrupt and corrupting world, the deity intervenes to destroy the wicked and redeem the good. While to the outside observer it would appear that everyone is destroyed, the believer can have confidence that the apocalyptic but temporal fires that fall upon themselves and their ungodly compatriots will save them, the godly, from the eternal fires of damnation into which the ungodly are cast. But such pessimism serves as a strong motivator for making sure the godly order is maintained.

I said before that Gen 19 serves as an ideo-story on which Calvin can ground his own theo-political vision of the ideal society. As the archetypal anti-society, Sodom's shadow becomes the point of contrast by which to throw into relief the godly society. This godly society is founded on, grounded in, the patriarchal heterosexual household and family and so the story of Sodom provides the basis for a theology of heterosexuality in which marriage is mandated for all. Like the society for which it is a cornerstone, heterosexuality is hierarchical and misogynist.

The man is the head of the household and governs it by right of being male. The woman is subordinate to her husband but shares with him, or, more correctly, assists him in the governance of the household. Hers is the interior, domestic space—she is within the household as, at Mamre, Sarah was found within the tent. However, this subordinate status of women means that the only true relationship of equals is that between men of the same social status. These homosocial bondings are fraught with homosexual panic. I have argued elsewhere (Carden 2003) that Luther employs homosexual panic as a tool to prevent cross-class relationships and to maintain the class hierarchy that is primally modelled in the patriarchal household—the patriarch rules wife, children and servants. Calvin, on the other hand, takes homosexual panic to its logical result and invents the nuclear family. He exhorts his followers to be "well content to have few servants, or even to be entirely without them" (Calvin 1984, 370). Servants are undesirable members of a household because, even though off-limits for genuine homosocial relationships, by being under the same roof (homo)sexual possibilities might still arise. The godly society is heteronormative, grounded in a regime of the closet that derives its power from the threat of omnicide and, worse, eternal damnation because in the end there can be no guarantee of who is counted as among the godly or the ungodly.

A Vision of Continence

Calvin is mapping through commentary the outlines of what his fellow Reformer, Heinrich Bullinger, terms the continent society. In Bullinger's *Decades*, a collection of his sermons, we can see the same use of Sodom as an anti-type of the godly society and Sodom's fate likewise serves as a warning of what happens if the godly allow any leeway to the ungodly. Indeed, Sodom and Gomorrah are representative of the church of the wicked, headed by Satan, which parallels and is locked in struggle with the church of the godly, headed by Christ. Bullinger terms this congregation "Babylon, …a synagogue, …a stew of the devil, the kingdom of the antichrist," which contains "all such as are wicked…the heathen, Turks, Jews, heretics, schismatics…all such as are professed enemies to Christian religion" (Bullinger 1968, 5:11). Additionally Lot is a model for believers of the "present delivery of the saints" (Bullinger 1968, 3:95). Like Noah before him in the Deluge, Lot and his family "were by the mighty hand of God delivered from…the horrible fire that fell upon Sodom" (95).

Bullinger clearly associates Sodom with complete sexual transgression and depravity, but, in his sermon on sexual sins, he is at times uncertain as to what represents ultimate depravity, homoeroticism or bestiality. Citing the proscriptions against both in Lev 18 and 20, he declares,

> We have also a very severe, but yet a most just punishment laid by God himself upon the pates of the detestable Sodomites: for with fire and stinking brimstone sent down from heaven he consumed those filthy men to dust and ashes; which ashes he washed away with the waves of the Dead Sea, because he would not have so much as the very cinders to remain of so wicked men. Moreover, their whole cities and fruitfu fields were burnt with fire. For it was not requisite that any one jot of the substance of those most wicked men should remain undestroyed. (Bullinger 1968, 1/2:418)

In this most extreme genocidal fantasy, the Sodomites are utterly obliterated because of sexual transgression, not even their ashes are allowed to remain. However, this passage reminds us that the impulse to genocide contains within itself its own contradiction. It is essential that something remain of the Sodomites, if only a "reproachful memory" (418), because the threat of genocide is a fundamental requisite for policing desire.

Employing Leviticus to develop his argument, Bullinger's condemnation of homoeroticism has followed a similar treatment of incest, similarly illustrated with Levitical proscriptions. These three sins—incest, bestiality, male–male sex—are covered together in the relevant proscriptions in Lev 18 and 20. Thus, by condemning homoeroticism and bestiality together, Bullinger employs a Levitical taxonomy (this association of bestiality with homoeroticism as sins of Sodom, if that is Bullinger's intent, would be a rare instance in the reception history of Gen 19).

Bullinger opened his sermon extolling the virtue and worthiness of marriage for all Christians. He then progressed through various categories of sexual sins, including the sin of rape, which featured a rare Christian reference to the outrage at Gibeah, the parallel story to Gen 19 that concludes Judges (and which will also appear in Danforth's text, as discussed below). The sins of incest, "sodomy" and bestiality are the final categories to be discussed and Bullinger appears to follow a model of leaving the worst to last, dealing with what he considers to be the most abhorrent sins as briefly as possible.

With these final three—incest, "sodomy" and bestiality—as if to highlight their abomination, Bullinger relies on images of cosmic retribution whereas for the other sexual sins he only cites examples of war, civil war and individual retaliatory murders to underscore their seriousness. It is this cosmic scale of punishment that brings me back to Bullinger's attempt to link bestiality with Sodom and the homoerotic, his ultimate forms of sexual transgression. Bullinger cites Leviticus to prove that the land itself vomited out the Canaanites because of their incest. In contrast to this passive image, the story of Sodom is one of direct divine intervention and retribution. There is no such graphic biblical narrative that can be associated with bestiality and so I read Bullinger as using Levitical authority to apply the spectacle of Sodom's destruction to bestiality as well as to its by now traditional referent, same-sex desire. My interpretation is confirmed when, on the following page, Bullinger gives a summary of his discussion of sexual sins. It is almost as if he wants to clarify his intent when earlier he cited Sodom. He declares, "he most heinously of all...in meddling with beasts committeth filthy sodomy" (Bullinger 1968, 1/2:419). Ironically, before declaring bestiality "most heinous," Bullinger omits homoeroticism ("sodomy") from his final listing. In his earlier discussion he has specifically and separately identified each. Bestiality might be most heinous but in declaring it to be "filthy sodomy" the homoerotic has been rendered ultimately unspeakable. The irony lies in the fact that Bullinger relies on the force of this utter unspeakability of the homoerotic to render bestiality abject and abominable. In trying to equate bestiality and homoeroticism, he still declares the homoerotic the most heinous of all.

To conclude his sermon, Bullinger then maps out features of continence, the regime by which sexual sin is suppressed and sexual virtue maintained. Continence is not just for single people but for the married as well. It is in fact the regime by which married life is maintained, preventing society from collapsing into the chaos of Sodom. Immediately after describing Sodom's fate, Bullinger declares that "all things else are forbidden, that do incite or allure us to unlawful lusts" (Bullinger 1968, 1/2:418). These lusts are not only provoked by gluttony, drunkenness and rich living but also by the "hearing or reading of dishonest ditties and bawdy ballads; or by looking on and beholding wanton dances, unseemly sights, ribald talk and filthy examples" (419). He then continues outlining continent practice not only in speech and food and drink, but also in clothing and building design (422)! Thus Bullinger builds a regime of prescription sustained by the spectacle of genocide.

A Youth Grown Old in Wickedness

I come from Australia, which began as an enterprise of creating a British penal Sodom in Eden. The United States, however, began (in part) as an attempt at building a new Jerusalem. It was in that seventeenth-century New England Jerusalem that Samuel Danforth preached a sermon on Sodom and her sins, to mark the execution of a certain young man, Benjamin Goad. While the sermon is both appalling and abhorrent, it clearly draws on the Reformation theology of the closet and graphically illustrates the lethal and contradictory threads of Sodom and homophobia in which Benjamin Goad lost his life.

The sermon appals because Danforth is determined to counter any feelings of sympathy his audience might harbour for this young man. He does so by painting a terrifying portrait of apocalyptic menace. Drawing on the story of Sodom, he attempts to demonstrate how this menace has become so manifest in the body and person of Goad that it requires his death. However, I am immediately struck by a problem with this sermon because it is not clear that Goad can be classified as a denizen of Sodom. He is guilty of bestiality, not sex with men. Danforth's sermon is an exercise of stretching the boundaries of Sodom, strongly reminiscent of Bullinger, so as to make Goad an object of loathing and panic.

Danforth begins declaring the Sodomites to be "extremely wicked, prodigiously unclean, monstrously profuse in all manner of lechery, obscenity and lasciviousness" (1994, 2). He then cites Jude 7, that the Sodomites were guilty of "fornication and going after strange flesh" (KJV). Under the former he lists masturbation together with all manner of heterosexual sin, including incest. Under the latter he lists sodomy, "filthiness between parties of the same sex... Males with Males... Females with Females" (4), and bestiality "or Buggery" (5). Of sodomy he says that it was so common among the Sodomites that it is named after them to "their perpetual infamy" (4). It is a sin against which "no indignation is sufficient" (4). It is the sin for which Sodom is destroyed. But Danforth wants to use this trace of sodomy and its fiery punishment to abject the bestial. He does so by painting all sexual sins, including masturbation, as a rebellion against and a threat to the godly heterosexual order grounded in marriage.

Important for Danforth's argument is the mechanism of the closet. Goad might be a youth but "he has grown old in wickedness" (9). Rebellious and disobedient to his parents, he had long practiced masturbation and "often attempted Buggery with several Beasts" before "God gave

him over to it" (9). Goad had for several months been having sex with
animals secretly. Eventually, in his arrogant wickedness he committed
"this horrid Villainy in the sight of the Sun, and in the open field, even at
Noon-day, proclaiming his sin like Sodom" (9). It is almost as if God has
led Goad to break down these closet walls so that he might be offered up
in sacrifice on the altar of heterosexual marriage.

Goad's fate is a warning to any who are "not afraid to go on impeni-
tently in the same sins" (13) that they, too, will be outed from their
closets. It is a warning especially to all the youth of the Colony. Danforth
says, "God is willing to prevent the ruine of our lewd and vicious youth,
therefore hath he set before them this awfull Example for their Admoni-
tion" (15). Being completely in control God has outed Goad to remind
the community that

> (i)f we ransack our own hearts, and search and try our wayes, we shall finde
> such sins with us, as may justly provoke Divine Wrath and Vengeance…
> The gross and flagitious practises of the worst of men, are but Comments
> upon our Nature… The holiest man hath as vile and filthy a Nature, as the
> Sodomites, or the men of Gibeah. (11)

Here Sodom serves as an apocalyptic sign of divine wrath. In the parallel
story of Gibeah (Judg 19–21) there is no such divine intervention over
similar circumstances, however the tribes of Israel declare war on the
perpetrators, a war that spirals into a genocidal civil war against the tribe
of Benjamin. Consequently Danforth cites Gibeah as authorization for a
community to take action themselves. The sermon concludes with a
detailed list of strict measures that the community should follow. These
rules of personal and communal, particularly household, behaviour are
as strict as any monastic regimen. Unlike monastic rules, Danforth's goal
is to ensure strict adherence to the order of patriarchal heterosexual
marriage (again echoing Bullinger's rule of continence for maintaining
the godly society). In this apocalyptic portrait of sexual excess, however,
the fear of the homoerotic appears to have lost its moorings. It lurks
behind every act of masturbation,[1] every moment of heterosexual desire.
By casting the nets of Sodom to draw in every sexual sin, Danforth
paradoxically reveals the homosexual panic, which is the genesis of this
rigid heterosexual order. The more rigidly this order is enforced, the
more deeply it is stamped with homoerotic potential. As Danforth himself has said, everyone is at heart a sodomite, every heterosexual is at
heart a homosexual.

---

1.   Danforth's greatest anxiety seems to be aroused by thoughts of masturbation.

Sodom's Second Coming?

I would suggest that current US Christian conservative and fundamentalist discourse against lesbian, gay, bisexual and transgender (LGBT) people is grounded in Calvin's and Danforth's apocalyptic logic. The Christian Right sees our struggle for liberation as our being outed by God for our presumed destruction. Sodom and Gomorrah serve as the archetypal warning of a society marked by and consequently destroyed because of same-sex desire. In this Christian discourse, same-sex desire is a marker of a deeper disorder which can only find its ultimate expression in that which is most abominable, loathsome and rejecting of the divinely ordained order of things. Therefore openly expressing and surrendering to same-sex desire outs a person and a society as being completely beyond redemption and thus fit for destruction.

The current debates concerning same-sex marriage are a good example of this logic. In the scheme of things, the notion of same-sex marriage is something very bourgeois and tame. Indeed, same-sex marriage can be understood as a heteronormatizing appropriation of the homoerotic by late capitalist society in analogous ways to Nancy Fraser's account (2009) of capitalist appropriation of much of the women's movement and second wave feminism.

Yet fundamentalist rhetoric invests the push for same-sex marriage with a dire eschatological quality that would otherwise be belied by its sheer conformity to both the traditional valuing of marriage, in Christian and other societies, and current capitalist ideologies of consumption and the household as a site of capitalist citizenship. Thus, F. Lagard Smith sees the push to same-sex marriage as "dismantling the nuclear family" (1993, 191), the nuclear family being identified with the "traditional family" (192). The struggle for same-sex marriage strives to "press for the legitimacy of (the homosexual) lifestyle—fully subsidized by the rest of society" (203). Through adoption of same-sex marriage "our own sense of family (is) hijacked for an unworthy cause…sinful behaviour (that) is neither hallowed nor worthy" (209). The entire LGBT struggle for justice is portrayed by Smith as an eschatological "call to arms":

> Gay rights is not just another political issue. Nor is it just another moral issue. Gay Rights presents us with the ultimate issue of our time: Whether or not God will ever again be honoured in our nation. (245)

Any compromise means opening up the gates of Sodom and, once that happens, the believers' assurance of their own salvation is put in doubt. This apocalyptic logic requires either complete separation from godless society or a godly, fascist uniformity.

. Charles Colson attempts a more measured argument not reliant on apocalyptic panic but which reveals an explicit theology of compulsory heterosexuality, nonetheless. According to Colson, the whole debate represents a clash between two worldviews, which he identifies as the Complementary model and the Choice model. Of the latter, he says,

> This world-view assumes that the universe is malleable and that individuals create their own truths, their own values. Sexuality has no intrinsic purpose, it is merely an opportunity for pleasure, intimacy, and reproduction. Family structure is as pliable as Play-Doh, and virtually any form is acceptable. Here the right to marry is no more than the right of individuals to participate in state-defined benefits. (1996, n.p.)

In contrast, the Complementary model assumes

> that the universe was created with an objective moral order, that the two sexes are part of that order, that marriage is the fundamental social institution by which we unite our lives in family and kinship relationships. This model is virtually universal in traditional societies; it underlies the marriage laws in all 50 states; and it is compatible with Christianity. In legal terms, the right to marry means the state's recognition of a prior moral order. (1996, n.p.)

However, this Complementary model is really nothing more than the Reformation model of the godly society underpinned by the heterosexual patriarchal household. Colson identifies this model with a primordial and heterosexual moral order of the universe. In an imperialistic move, Colson claims an ancient cross-cultural lineage for this compulsory heterosexual moral order as the only universal form of establishing kinship relations. And yet even in Christian history, this is not true. As Alan Bray points out concerning family and kinship in medieval Christendom,

> The difficulty for the modern viewer lies in that modern society recognizes only one such "voluntary" kinship, in marriage: in the past others have subsisted alongside it, and their aggregate effect was that (in England at least until well into the seventeenth century) an individual lived in effect in a potential plurality of families... But the cumulative effect of such a multiplicity of forms of "voluntary" kinship was to embed the family within a wider and encompassing network of *friendship.* (2000, 27)

My own position is that these other and older forms of voluntary kinship likely suit same-sex relationships (and probably most opposite-sex relationships too) much better than marriage does and that their restoration is a much better liberationist goal than simply a liberal and bourgeois marriage equality. Ironically, in terms of Colson's argument, most of the proponents of his so-called Choice model take as their template his so-called Complementary model of marriage and household.

Colson, himself, subscribes to a compulsory marriage model that emerged from the Reformation and was adopted by capitalist society as its preferred form of affinity/kinship. No doubt there are economic imperatives supporting the capitalist preference for the Reformation marriage model (and it took twentieth-century consumer capitalism to make the Calvinist nuclear family the societal standard). Perhaps this model provides a happy medium between the atomism of the Market and the dangerous linkages of solidarity through friendship that run so much against competitive free market principles. Furthermore, this marriage model has given the modern capitalist state considerable opportunity for regulation of sexuality and affinity. This regulatory quality of the marriage model is highlighted by Focus on the Family, a fierce opponent of anything queer, which declares that marriage is not just about procreation but also "encourages sexual regulation, a characteristic that historically has been the most important factor in creating and preserving healthy and productive cultures" (Focus on the Family 1999). And ironically this is the same argument made by many proponents of same-sex marriage. Scott Bidstrup argues,

> A benefit to heterosexual society of gay marriage is the fact that the commitment of a marriage means the participants are discouraged from promiscuous sex. This has the advantage of slowing the spread of sexually transmitted diseases, which know no sexual orientation and are equal opportunity destroyers. (Bidstrup 2000)

So in one sense, then, the struggle for same-sex marriage (especially if it is to be the only form of relationship recognition provided by the state) can be seen as advancing the Reformation agenda of marriage for all. But rather than a compulsory heterosexual model, it represents a shift to a compulsorily heteronormative model, bringing queer folks as much within the orbit of societal regulation as straight folks. Nevertheless, for the Religious Right, as Danforth proclaimed, everyone is at heart a sodomite, and therefore marriage becomes the only guarantee of heterosexuality, of a godly sexuality. Same-sex marriage paradoxically undermines that guarantee while at the same time advancing the Reformation tyranny of marriage impelled by it.

A Woman is Being Beaten and Maybe She Likes It? Approaching Song of Songs 5:2–7

Julie Kelso

(for Ed Conrad, a gentle man)

> I slept, but my heart was awake. Hark! My beloved is knocking. "Open to me, my sister, my love, my dove, my perfect one; for my head is wet with dew, my locks with the drops of the night." I had put off my garment, how could I put it on? I had bathed my feet, how could I soil them? My beloved put his hand to the latch, and my heart was thrilled within me. I arose to open to my beloved, and my hands dripped with myrrh, my fingers with liquid myrrh, upon the handles of the bolt. I opened to my beloved but my beloved had turned and gone. My soul failed me when he spoke. I sought him, but found him not; I called him, but he gave no answer. The watchmen found me as they went about in the city; they beat me, they wounded me, they took away my mantle, those watchmen of the walls. (Song 5:2–7, RSV)

Introduction

In the Song of Songs, the beating of the woman by the watchmen in 5:7 is generally understood to be either part of a dream or waking fantasy by the woman. Briefly, having risen to open the door to her beloved, she is stunned to find that he has left. She goes out searching for him, but the watchmen instead find, beat, bruise and strip her (Song 5:2–7). This is a problematic moment in the text, especially for those who wish the Song to be understood as an egalitarian model of love between the sexes. However, according to Virginia Burrus and Stephen Moore's (2003) recent work on the Song, developed especially in light of Roland Boer's own pornographic x-egesis, the "beating" scene might just subvert the oppressive reduction of woman to passive sexual partner, even victim, expressing instead woman's desire for masochistic enjoyment.

Burrus and Moore do pay particular care to the obvious question of abuse. They insist, though, that the text is ambiguous:

...the line between the female masochist and the battered woman may
continue to blur troublingly—as though it were actually impossible to
distinguish in the end between a woman whose rapist claims "she asks for
it" and a woman who quite literally asks for it, in the "contractual"
context of s/m eroticism. (Burrus and Moore 2003, 48–49)

Ultimately, they insist that this ambiguity in Song 5:2–7—the difficulty
of distinguishing "the pain-filled pleasure of a bottom and the pleasure-
less pain of a battered woman"—is essential to maintain. The queer,
often pornographic elements (possibilities?) of the text, drawn out
implicitly in the writings of medieval allegorists and most explicitly in
the work of Boer on the Song, destabilize the gender binary that thwarts
women's sexuality and subjectivity under the regime of heterosexuality,
i.e. *heteronormativity*.

In this study I want to focus closely on this particular queer-
pornographic reading of the beating scene. I shall first give a detailed
description of Burrus and Moore's essay, followed by what I think is an
important criticism of the idea that a woman's desire for (contractually
agreed-upon) pain is subversive. This criticism of such a position is that
"woman" is precluded from the place of subject in the formation of
contract and thus cannot actually agree to anything unless she assumes a
masculine subjective stance. Here, I engage with the work of the feminist
philosopher Carole Pateman. I want to suggest that feminism does *not*
ultimately profit from a queering of erotics, or specifically from understanding female masochistic fantasies to be subversive, as Burrus and
Moore suggest. Instead, drawing upon the work of Luce Irigaray, I argue
that we need to take seriously the idea that sexual difference has only an
"unthought" status in Western cultures, and that a feminist reading of the
Song needs to think this through. However, I can only paint some broad
brushstrokes here and hope that future feminist work might take up the
few suggestions I make as a conclusion.

The Myth of (Egalitarian) Hetero-Sex

In their essay "Unsafe Sex: Feminism, Pornography and the Song of
Songs," Virginia Burrus and Stephen Moore challenge what has come to
be the conventional feminist reading of the Song: that it is a proto-
feminist text that provides us with a lusty woman's heterosexual desire
for her man and that the song offers us a picture of egalitarian relations
between the sexes. In other words, the last few decades of feminist reading of the Song have cast it as a rare example of egalitarian love and lust
between the sexes. Unlike all other biblical texts, the Song succeeds in

giving us a desirous woman's voice, as well as a man's—voices that are somehow audible as non-patriarchal; the Song gives us desire for hetero-sex without the necessary encumbrances of marriage and/or procreation, i.e. what defines heterosexuality under patriarchy. This feminist picture of the song is one of uninhibited hetero-sex outside of marriage. In Burrus and Moore's words, the song is "reconstrued...as a paeon to unmarried love and lust, with no wedding veil in sight and no apparent intent to procreate" (p. 26). For example, according to Phyllis Trible, "there is no male dominance, no female subordination, and no stereo-typing of either sex" in the Song (Trible 1978, 161), only harmony and a mutually respectful sexuality:

> Born to mutuality and harmony, a man and a woman live in a garden where nature and history unite to celebrate the one flesh of sexuality. Naked without shame or fear...this couple treat each other with tenderness and respect. Neither escaping nor exploiting sex, they embrace and enjoy it. Their love is truly bone of bone and flesh of flesh, and this image of God male and female is indeed very good... Testifying to the goodness of creation, then, eroticism becomes worship in the context of grace. (Trible 1978, 161)

Similarly, Alicia Ostriker finds the Song to be an outstanding example of the "non-patriarchal" love between the sexes, stating that "the Song is, in effect, the quintessence of the non-patriarchal... It includes no representation of hierarchy or rule, no relationship of dominance and submission, and (almost) no violence" (Ostriker 2000, 43). The problem is that there *is* violence in the Song, and it is violence inflicted upon a woman by a group of men (5:7). Stating that there is "almost" no vio-lence, with "almost" parenthesized, alerts us to the grave problem that this verse presents for feminists who would otherwise rightly leap upon this verse as evidence of patriarchal violence against women, were it in a different text.

For Burrus and Moore, while feminist scholars who critically read the Song clearly are problematizing the heteronormative assumptions about hetero-love and hetero-sex (that it take place in matrimony and that it have the *telos* of procreation), they don't go far enough. Indeed, the work of Trible, Ostriker and others (notably the contributors to the two vol-umes of the *Feminist Companion to the Song of Songs*) ends up casting heterosexuality as a transhistorical, transcultural and ultimately norma-tive human expression of love, especially *eros*. However, Burrus and Moore contend this stance is problematic given that, since the 1990s and the emergence of queer theory, heterosexuality, like homosexuality, needs to be understood as a nineteenth-century construct (cf. Halperin

1990 and Katz 1995). And in the broader spheres of feminist theory and practice, heterosexuality has come to be reducible to the eroticization of gender *in*equality, to the point that from the 1970s, feminism, at least in its Anglo-American forms, has almost washed its hands of heterosexuality, arguing for lesbian and queer practices as perhaps the only viable options for feminist sexual practice. So, how are we to understand this desire, in feminist biblical studies, for the Song to be "the model expression of an erotics of gender *equality*" (p. 30)? Burrus and Moore claim that this desire within feminist biblical studies is characteristic of a more general feminist desire for an "attempted redemption, if not outright reinvention, of heterosexual sex" (p. 30). Thus, these readings contain both a scathing critique of heterosexuality as eroticized gender inequality, as it is understood, and a wishful and wilful reinvention of an ideal: heterosexuality as egalitarian. At this point, they rather cursorily refer to the work of Luce Irigaray (and I'm going to return to this brief reference to Irigaray's work later). Characterizing this feminist biblical desire in light of broader trends in feminist thinking ultimately leads to a certain revelation. While this desire for egalitarian hetero-sex may be enunciable, in reality things are quite different, as Carole Fontaine reveals (for them):

> Introducing the second *Feminist Companion to the Song of Songs*, Carole Fontaine, in between noting how feminist biblical scholars have "appropriated this book as peculiarly their own" and asserting that "it would be hard to find a feminist scholar who does not share, cross-culturally and cross-every other way, some of our collective delight in reading this book," urges that we "allow ourselves the pleasures of reading as women on a topic that revels in sexuality (*however dismal the realities may be*)." (Burrus and Moore 2003, 30; quoted material is from Fontaine 2000, 13, 15; emphasis in final quote added by Burrus and Moore)

Here we encounter the problem feminists inevitably face, according to Burrus and Moore, when it comes to reinventing or reimagining heterosexuality as egalitarian: the theory is not consistent with the reality; or rather, the *fantasy* is not consistent with the reality. Following their citing of Leo Bersani's famous statement about the big secret concerning sexuality ("that most people don't like it") they make what would at first seem like a curious turn to pornography. They state: "And, stereotypically, feminists are among those who like it least. Now, pornography epitomizes the kind of sex that most people, feminist or not, claim to like least of all" (Burrus and Moore 2003, 30).

Ultimately, however, this shift to the domain of pornography is warranted. Burrus and Moore turn to the question of pornography and its presence in the Song because it is a presence enabled by the literal readings of unadorned and unencumbered sensuality provided for us by feminist interpretations of the Song, though at the same time largely ignored by feminists. They note that only male scholars such as Michael Goulder (1986) and David Clines (1995) have perceived and critically condemned (in the case of Clines) the pornographic sensibilities of the Song. As they point out, Cheryl Exum rightly claimed that feminists need to be more critical of the Song, like their male counterparts, while at the same time continuing "to insist on their right to appropriate it positively, even through 'misreading'" (Burrus and Moore 2003, 32; Exum 2000, 26). That no-one is prepared to align pornography with a feminist agenda is ultimately what Burrus and Moore want to challenge and rectify.

Pornography and the Problematic Spectre of Liberalism

While feminist readings of the Song do celebrate the sexual longings of a man and a woman outside of marriage, Burrus and Moore find that the rejection of pornographic reading is in fact a repression of the pornographic, a repression that sustains a problematic valorization of heterosexuality, as invented in the nineteenth century, that works according to the marital ideal of "true love," or the spiritualization of the carnal, one that normalizes procreative sex as "sexual instinct." They state:

> We are suggesting that feminist interpretation of the Song of Songs has successfully disrupted, but by no means cleanly "liberated" itself from, the modern ideology of heteronormativity, with its distinctive inflection of the ideal as "true love" as "an intense spiritual feeling powerful enough to justify marriage, reproduction, and an otherwise unhallowed sensuality." (Burrus and Moore 2003, 33–34)

As Burrus and Moore point out, only one contemporary scholar has been brave enough both to take the literal reading of the Song as highly sexual to its inevitable pornographic conclusion *and* to argue that the pornographic reading has a subversive potential. For those not familiar with this aspect of Boer's work, here is an example of his pornographic reading of Song 2:8–17 (as provided by Burrus and Moore):

> Beth Rabbim and Leb Bannon make their appearance here. (*I haven't heard of them, but both of them have kinky reputations.*) It begins with a long tongue darting over Beth's very ample breasts, "leaping over the mountains, bounding over the hills" (2:8). As the camera pans out, somewhat shakily, the large pink nose and muzzle of a "gazelle" (2:9) come into view. Beth has her eyes closed and groans, enjoying the rough tongue

of the animal. But now a "young stag" (2:9) walks over, sniffs Beth's mons venus, pondering her interwoven pubes: "Look, there he stands behind our wall, gazing in at the windows, looking in at the lattice" (2:9). (*Oh my God, I think, he's not going to fuck her, is he?*) (Boer 1999, 66)

This type of reading (intentionally humorous, I suspect) is obviously meant brazenly to demystify things, notably the sacred character of the Bible in general but also the sacred character of the Song's hetero-sex and hetero-love, as feminist readers have insisted for some time. Burrus and Moore claim that Boer's various x-egetical readings of the Song reveal what has yet to be properly noticed about the text (though one of the Church Fathers, Gregory of Nyssa, gestures towards this possibility): that it is sado-masochistic in structure and this structure provides us with what Karmen Mackendrick (1999) calls "counterpleasures." Boer's hyper-pornographic reading presents us with a breathless and seemingly endless series of sex acts between humans (male–female, male–male, female–female, orgies, etc) and humans and animals, to the point that each act in itself seems to exist in anticipation of the next, and the next, and so on. It is through this ultra-excessive and pointless sex-scapade that Boer is able to

> thereby escape the repressive regime of heteronormative sexuality—of which pornography is a notable, but by no means necessarily subversive, byproduct… In other words, by taking the pornographic reading to the point of "failure," Boer begins to succeed at productive perversity: ceasing merely to react, his commentary begins effectively to resist the Censor and the near-ubiquitous ideological apparatus that is ever at the latter's disposal. (Burrus and Moore 2003, 38–39)

However, this delaying and frustrating refusal of satisfaction is precisely the logic of masochistic pleasure. In a response to Burrus and Moore, Boer (forthcoming) rightly challenges their common use of s/m as the model of "counterpleasures," when their argument is clearly dependant on the logic of masochism only. This partnering of sadism and masochism, as Boer points out, is a common error. The sadist is the one who loves to inflict pain upon an unwilling victim, while the masochist is the one who derives pleasure from the pain of failed satisfaction: "Crucial to the masochistic structure, with its bottom and top (who cannot be a sadist) is the contract to which both parties are held, and the norm is for the *bottom to seek a top for such a contract*" (Boer, forthcoming).

Now, sadism is of concern when it comes to the beating scene in 5:6–7. Or rather, it is the concern of Cheryl Exum and Fiona Black in their readings of the scene, readings that also want to challenge the overly awed and hetero-idealized, now-traditional feminist responses to the

Song (Black and Exum 1998). The beating scene is clearly problematic if the Song is to be understood as an egalitarian model of heterosexual desire and love. It reads:

> I opened to my beloved but my beloved had turned and gone. My soul failed me when he spoke. I sought him, but found him not; I called him, but he gave no answer. The watchmen found me as they went about in the city; they beat me, they wounded me, they took away my mantle, those watchmen of the walls.

Earlier, in 5:2, we are told that the woman slept, but that "her heart was awake." According to Exum and Black, because the text doesn't explicitly state that she is dreaming, it is possible to interpret the beating scene as a woman's fantasy. But, they ask, is this really what a woman would fantasize about, or is it more likely that it is, "like the entire biblical Song—a male fantasy representing what a male author might like to think a woman dreams about?" (Black and Exum 1998, 339–40). What Exum and Black, along with Clines and others who insist on the patriarchal logic of the text, cannot entertain is the possibility that a woman is fantasizing about masochistic pleasure, "a specific woman's insistent desire to suffer physical pain at the hands of a man (or another woman)" (Burrus and Moore 2003, 44). All of this, they acknowledge, depends upon a wilful act of misreading, and so naturally they return at this point to Boer's take on the scene. After some initial fisting from Frank, the s/m scene becomes heightened, Boer tells us, with 5:6–7:

> ...as she "opened to [her] beloved" he "turned and was gone." (*OK, I was mentally leafing through my Lacan, finding the place on the insatiability of desire*). The hand, the man and the schlong are gone, and her searching and calling yields no results (5:6); instead, "the sentinels found" her, tied her up, "beat" her and "wounded" her, leaving her without her "mantle" (5:7). The s/m of fisting has given way to that of bondage, beating and pain. (*Is this coerced domination or the desired and pleasurable dynamics of power? It is hard to tell.*) But Sue seems to get off on this, for, as she tells the sexy "daughters of Jerusalem," "I am faint with love" (5:8). (Boer 1999, 69)

Overall, what Boer succeeds at doing via his overtly pornographic reading, according to Burrus and Moore, is to subvert the heteronormative economies of desire which are teleologically lack-based. The queer contribution made by the Song, as Boer reads it, is to frustrate entirely such an economy because the desire here is precisely "not to 'get' anything or anywhere, in fact, but rather to continue to *want*, ever more intensely, ever more insistently, and hence ever more pleasurably" (Burrus and Moore 2003, 45). Specifically, Boer dares to entertain the possibility of masochistic desire, while noting the difficulty we have in ascertaining whether this is coerced domination or the pleasure of masochistic eros.

Now, the turn to pornography is not without its problems, as decades of feminist debates concerning it will, and still do, testify. Ultimately, the issue concerns the question of censorship. Here is what Burrus and Moore have to say:

> But what of pornography? In relation to heterosexuality, pornography can be said to constitute a double sign. On the one hand, it is the sign of what is *excluded* by heterosexuality (*epitomised by heteronormativity, with its teleologies of matrimony and/or monogamy* [emphasis added]). On the other hand, it is a sign for what is just barely *included* in heterosexuality— "an unhallowed sensuality." If pornography is a particular and extreme instance of the incitement to sexual discourse, liberating what is only constituted in the first place by repression, *resistance* to pornographic readings will undeniably remain crucial to feminist strategy. Paradoxically, however, outright *censorship* of the pornographic may also prove problematic for feminist interpretations. This is especially the case for any feminism that seeks not to "reinvent" heterosexuality but rather to subvert or evade it—for example, by retrieving the eroticism of an ancient text, such as the Song of Songs, that predates both (modern) "sexuality" and (an equally modern) "pornography," that is other than heterosexual, yet also not homosexual, thereby eluding the hamfisted clutches of those dualistic categories altogether. Such is the interest motivating the current essay. (Burrus and Moore 2003, 34)

Burrus and Moore, while not *exactly* fence-sitters ("Ceasing to react either with or against pornography"), are careful to situate themselves initially, and sporadically, in both camps for strategic reasons, though by the end of the essay it is clear that they side with the anti-censorship camp. They do address the obvious counter-argument that women who fantasize about being beaten have internalized their position as passive non-agents in an oppressive hetero-sexual erotic economy, thus existing as both the victims and perpetrators of patriarchy. They insist, though, that the text is ambiguous:

> …the line between the female masochist and the battered woman may continue to blur troublingly—as though it were actually impossible to distinguish in the end between a woman whose rapist claims "she asks for it" and a woman who quite literally asks for it, in the "contractual" context of s/m eroticism. (Burrus and Moore 2003, 48–49)

Burrus and Moore insist on the transgressive mimicry at work in queer erotic fantasy, a mimicry that doesn't simply resemble and reinscribe dominant ideologies concerning sexuality, but rather dissembles and reassembles reality. In short, they argue that fantasy must be recognized as potentially subversive of oppressive and hegemonic ideologies like patriarchal hetero-normativity:

> Women who take pleasure in fantasies of erotic violence, whether such women be casual consumers of bodice-ripping romances or serious practitioners of sado-masochistic sex, have consistently concerned and scandalized liberal feminism…Yet the power of fantasy not only to affect but even to constitute reality should not be underestimated. By taking female fantasies of erotic violence seriously, we may come less to fear their potential for passively shoring up an oppressive sexual *status quo* than to acknowledge their capacity to subvert it actively from within. The patriarchal sexual order is, arguably, already disrupted when a woman constructs herself as an actively desiring subject, even if—*perhaps especially if*—what she desires is a good beating. (Burrus and Moore 2003, 48)

Ultimately, their argument is that both readings of the beating scene (the critical feminist argument that it is an instance of pleasure-less beating, of the eroticization of sexual inequality; and the queer argument that it is an instance of pleasurable masochistic desire) are together both valid and indispensable for feminists: "An adequately theorized feminist erotics may require that we both continue to denounce, and dare to celebrate, the beating of the woman in the Song; that we let genders oscillate and eroticisms queer; that we both remain within, and subversively exceed, the normative enclosure of modern 'sexuality'" (Burrus and Moore 2003, 49). To allow that both readings are valid and to insist "that we both continue to denounce, and dare to celebrate, the beating of the Song" has a dizzying and subversive effect on "the normative enclosure of modern 'sexuality.'"

I think two questions need to be asked in response to this idea that a queerified erotic or pornographic reading of the Song can reveal for us something of the subversive nature of the poem, and more generally that feminism needs queer theory to move beyond the perils of heteronormativity/heterosexism. First, I want to question the subversive potential of the idea that a woman might desire erotic pain. And second, I want to question the idea that subjective fluidity and multiplicity is the best response to heterosexism.

Erotic Pain and Contract

At the heart of this debate is the suggestion that we perhaps need to take female fantasies of erotic violence seriously, even though they have, as Burrus and Moore point out, concerned and scandalized liberal feminism.

The liberal feminists Burrus and Moore presumably are referring to are those theoreticians on the anti-pornography side of the so-called sex wars of the 1980s. Within those now well-known debates, critics of pornography gained the label of "sex-negative" feminists (thus, Burrus and Moore's comment about the stereotypical feminists' disliking for sex). Of course, not all liberal feminists are anti-pornography, advocating the censorship of it. Actually, we need to ask what kind of liberal feminism Burrus and Moore mean here (and it is the position they ascribe to Exum and Black), because it seems to me that the spectre of liberalism certainly haunts their own thinking. Most notably, they seem to be against the idea of censorship, consistent with one of the darling ideas of classical liberalism. One of the fundamental tenets of liberalism, at least in its classical/contractarian form, is the right of all adult individuals to produce and consume whatever cultural products they choose so long as this does not impinge upon someone else's freedom or bring harm to others. For example, John Milton, in his *Areopagitica* (1644), famously defends the principle of free speech for all against the imposition of censorship (well, except for some Catholics), importantly claiming that even "wrong ideas" are necessary and should be allowed to "grapple" with Truth.

In other words (despite the Christian moralism inherent in Milton), I think that the turn to queer theory, pornography and the valorization of contractual masochistic arrangements as a means of escaping the tyranny of heteronormativity needs to be addressed in light of the liberalism that actually underwrites it. The type of feminism they allude to is broadly known as egalitarian liberal feminism, as opposed, say, to classical or contractarian liberal feminism (though this is still quite reductive). Under classical liberalism, censorship is never justified because individuals by right have the freedom to watch, read, write, do whatever they want, especially with their bodies; the individual is said to hold sexual property rights over his or her own body. The State must offer minimal, if any, intervention into the lives of its citizens, understood as autonomous individuals. For egalitarian liberal feminists, the State is a necessary ally. Both positions are problematic, not only because of the overt and universalized individualism of liberalism, but also because of the mind–body dualism that haunts it (who or what is this "I" that holds property rights over "her" body?). Moreover, and as such, there is a real problem concerning the issues of freedom, choice and free choice.

In *The Sexual Contract* (1988), the political philosopher Carole Pateman challenges the liberal terms that have become givens: "freedom," "autonomy" and "choice," arguing that our use of these terms forgets that what underwrites them is the exclusion of women. Pateman's

study is of the classic texts of Western liberalism, specifically in the
tradition that has come to be known as contractarianism. Generally,
according to this tradition, morality is not innate, not something belonging to our status as God's children. Morality comes about through this
agreement that rational individuals make so as to live in civil society, to
protect themselves and their rights from the others who naturally threaten
them (because of their inherent self-centredness and greed, according
to Hobbes). Crucial to this is the idea that we hold rights over our own
bodies: the rights to do as we please with what is our own (this is
Lockean, in principle). While the classical contract theorists have many
differences, what Pateman demonstrates is that our contemporary understanding of the individual and his rights and civil freedom stems from a
consistent principle at work in classical contract theory: woman is never
party to that contract that institutes society. As such, theoretically woman
as woman is never party to any contract within that society created by
contract. If a woman wishes to enter into contract, she must assume a
masculine subjective position.

Addressing the criticism against feminists like Andrea Dworkin who
object to sado-masochism, while also, incidentally, being anti-censorship
(criticism that generally plummets to the level of dismissal based on
accusations of moralism and/or a failure to acknowledge the parodic or
transgressive mimeticism at work in s/m practices), Pateman states:
"...sado-masochism is less a rebellious or revolutionary fantasy than a
dramatic exhibition of the logic of contract and of the full implications of
the sexuality of the patriarchal masculine 'individual'" (Pateman 1988,
186). In other words, s/m practices are, as such, the inevitable outcome
of the social contract, a theory that purports to acknowledge the non-
gendered identities of the "individual," but on close inspection simply
eradicates women from the picture. Referring to the ideal of gender
neutrality and gender fluidity that belongs to contract, as opposed to what
she calls "status" (following Sir Henry Maine; paternal rights over sub-
ordinates, including women), she writes:

> The final victory of contract over status is not the end of patriarchy, but
> the consolidation of the modern form. The story of sexual contract tells
> how contract is the medium through which patriarchal right is created and
> upheld... When contract and the individual hold full sway under the flag
> of civil freedom, women are left with no alternative but to (try to) become
> replicas of men. In the victory of contract, the patriarchal construction of
> sexual difference as mastery and subjection remains intact but repressed.
> Only if the construction is intact can the "individual" have meaning and
> offer the promise of freedom to both men and women so that they know
> to what they must aspire. Only if the construction is repressed can women
> have such an aspiration. Heterosexual relations do not inevitably take the

form of mastery and subjection, but free relations are impossible within the patriarchal opposition between contract and status, masculinity and femininity. The feminist dream is continuously subverted by entanglement with contract. (Pateman 1988, 187–88)

Thus, the so-called subversive potentials of non-heteronormative models of sexual practice and pleasure are caught up in the web of contract and, as such, subvert only the feminist dream of social and political existence for women. In less harsh terms, I would say that in light of all this, a queerified pornographic reading of the Song definitely unsettles heterosexism but, following Pateman, I do not think it can subvert it; such a reading disconcerts, to be sure, but it does not subvert heterosexism.

In a recent article concerned with challenging the legal legitimacy of heterosexism in any form, Drucilla Cornell suggests that, paradoxically, the basis of heterosexism is in fact a *lack* of heterosexuality:

Rigid gender stereotypes so evident in heterosexist consciousness wipe out the *heteros*, or otherness, of our singularity. I argue that it is precisely this singularity, and the love for what has been lost, that helped foster the nostalgia that led to the reinvestment in heterosexism seen so strongly today. (Cornell 2007, 230)

Cornell's argument is that the power of heterosexism cannot be undermined without an alternative ethic of love, one that enables the *heteros* of our *singularity*. While Cornell explores this alternative ethic through Derrida's metaphor of lovance, I want to conclude this essay by turning to the work of Luce Irigaray, in particular her polemical idea that sexual difference, and thereby heterosexuality, is yet to exist in recorded or symbolic history.

Radical Heterosexuality:
The Love that Cannot *(Yet) Speak Its Name?*

Burrus and Moore's preference for a feminism "that seeks not to 'reinvent' heterosexuality but rather to subvert or evade it" and their earlier, casual mention of Irigaray as a reinventer of heterosexuality warrants further comment. Anyone familiar with Irigaray's work will know that such a casting of her thinking is now incredibly problematic. Irigaray seems rather consistent throughout her writings: the only sexuality of which we can speak is monosexuality, that is, an understanding of sexuality, sexuate identity, subjectivity understood after Freud and especially Lacan as utterly dependent upon the body and its cultural inscriptions (including sexuality) as only theorizable from one position—the masculine position.

In *An Ethics of Sexual Difference*, Irigaray (1993), evoking Heidegger, states that each age has but one issue to "think through." For Irigaray, this one issue of our time is sexual difference, a project with far reaching implications for other major issues of our time (ecological, economic, political and social). Her argument is that all past and current discourses on sexuality, be they caught up in a pseudo-dualistic understanding of subjectivity and/or identity (man and woman, male and female, hetero-sexual and homosexual) or be they post-structurally multiple and fluid positions, consistently elide the feminine subject and expropriate and colonize women. What we may call dualistic thinking is in fact, accord-ing to Irigaray, not actually a demonstration of the two, but merely the one, a monological framework within which the feminine does and can not actually exist in its own right; the feminine is "This Sex Which is Not One." And when it comes to subjective, polymorphic multiplicity, Irigaray, like Pateman, justifiably has her doubts:

> ...do women rediscover their pleasure in this "economy" of the multiple? When I ask what may be happening on the women's side, I am certainly not seeking to wipe out multiplicity, since women's pleasure does not occur without that. But isn't a multiplicity that does not entail a rearticu-lation of the difference between the sexes bound to block or take away something of women's pleasure? In other words, is the feminine capable, at present, of attaining this desire, which is *neutral* precisely from the viewpoint of sexual difference? Except by miming masculine desire once again. And doesn't the "desiring machine" still partly take the place of woman or the feminine? Isn't it a sort of metaphor for her/it, that men can use? Especially in terms of their relation to the technocratic? (Irigaray 1985, 140–41)

On the one hand Irigaray recognizes multiplicity as crucial to an ade-quate theorization of women's sexuality. And yet, on the other hand, as Margaret Whitford (1991) explains, the celebration of (the philosophers') multiplicity for Irigaray "merely confirms the sexual indifference of our culture, in which women's difference is not *represented* in the symbolic" (Whitford 1991, 84). Heterosexuality, by definition a sexuality charac-terized by a love between (for Irigaray) two different, sexuated subjects who remain distinct and un-appropriable, cannot exist within the frame-works of monological and/or polymorphic thought. Indeed, for Irigaray, Western thinking can be characterized by its failure to think "the two." Somewhat counter-intuitively, she argues that while we have been able to think "the one" and "the multiple," as yet "the two" eludes us. Or rather, the history of Western thinking is a history of the (unconscious?) refusal to think "the two" of sexual difference. As Penelope Deutscher (2002) puts it, Irigaray claims that:

the thinking of sexual difference has been repeatedly avoided, or ignored, or foreclosed, or reduced into a thinking of the same. One constant of Irigaray's work is the view that western culture has been engaged in the constant process of actively not thinking sexual difference. On that basis, while there is not and has not been sexual difference, there is the trace of a possible sexual difference in that active and repeated cultural action of "not that." The need to think sexual difference in terms of the simultaneous "there is not" and "there might be" precludes Irigaray from posing a simple question, "Is there sexual difference?" Rather than introducing it in such terms, she presents sexual difference as a foreclosed conceptual possibility that has not yet been recognized as culturally significant. (Deutscher 2002, 108)

Thus, it is not a matter of *re*inventing heterosexuality as it is of actually inventing, or rather *thinking*, it in the first place. According to Irigaray, the conditions necessary for sexual difference, and thus for the possibility of heterosexual love, are yet to exist. All of Irigaray's work about sexuality to date is, I think, best read in light of this point. Irigaray is not trying to reinvent heterosexuality, but rather to push the possibilities of its coming into being further along, arguing that its appearance in our culture (and only this) will subvert patriarchal heterosexism. For Irigaray, the unthought status of sexual difference in our cultures has had and continues to have grave effects for men and women, though in different ways. If we think through sexual difference, understood as recognition of two irreducibly distinct sexuated subjects, man and woman, we will effect a change for the better in our world:

> Sexual difference would constitute the horizon of worlds more fecund than any known to date—at least in the West—and without reducing fecundity to the reproduction of bodies and flesh. For loving partners this would be a fecundity of birth and regeneration, but also the production of a new age of thought, art, poetry, and language: the creation of a new poetics. (Irigaray 1993, 5)

It is evident that, for Irigaray, the monologic of hom(m)o-sexuality not only has dire effects on the lives of women especially, but also men, though less so. Furthermore, the culture of death that reigns under Western hom(m)o-sexual patriarchies also has catastrophic effects on nature. Thus, our task is one of great exigency.

I want to suggest that this "thinking through" needs to be understood as utopic (in Louis Marin's sense of the term; Marin 1984), as an engagement that does not seek to resolve or synthesize the contradiction that is sexual difference (where two potential models of desire and subjectivity might be in harmonious embrace, without negativity in any sense of the term). Rather (and this is crucial), it is to be understood as both an impossible and a necessary philosophical and political endeavour; as an urgent "meditation on the impossible, on the unrealizable in its own right," as Fredric Jameson (2005) famously defines utopian thinking. Importantly for Irigaray, such a "thinking through" the impossibility of sexual difference involves an encounter with the texts of our heritage, from classical Greek mythology, philosophy, science, literature and religious texts—those texts we hold sacred in various ways. According to Irigaray, the Song of Songs might be a potentially rewarding text with respect to developing our thinking about sexual difference. She suggests, however, that this productive contribution to our thinking about sexual difference is only possible "if one knows how to read" the Song (Irigaray 1993, 115). And as Deutscher explains, it is important to realize that our cultures and texts can and need to be analysed "as expressing symptoms of their malaise of an absence of sexual difference" (Deutscher 2002, 109).

Rather than leaping into a celebration of a queerified pornographic reading (including introducing a queer God, as Burrus and Moore do), might we not be better advised to analyse the means by which woman's subjectivity continues to be overridden and indeed elided by the logic of contract that seems to underwrite the theoretical edifice of such a wilful act of misreading? Thus, I want to ask: What if we read the Song of Songs as a utopic text with sexual difference—a genuine heterosexuality—as its *impossible* horizon, what it struggles and fails to announce? Might this not be a possible way to read all of those frustrating slippages of gender and subjectivity at crucial moments in the text—as symptoms of the failure of "the two"? And might it not also be a productive way to read the grotesque descriptions of the lovers' bodies—as symptoms of the impotence of language to construct an ethics of corporeal, sexuated subjective difference?[1] Might not the beating of the woman, even if one desired by her, also be evidence of the "malaise of an absence of sexual difference" in some way? As such, if we return to the Song with these questions in hand, it may be that the Song of Songs can be read as a sacred text that reveals a masculine desire for a sexual "other," one not defined/definable by him, and thus impossible to imagine, despite his poetic attempt. My primary hypothesis, what I can only gesture towards here, is that the desire we might "hear" in the Song is a desire for (what I am calling) "radical heterosexuality": a call for an (impossible) recognition of irreducible sexuated difference as erotic possibility. In other

---

1. For a detailed and important discussion of the grotesque and the Song of Songs, see Black (2009).

words, the Song of Songs may be read as seeking (and importantly fail-ing) to represent an erotics outside the logic of mono-sexuality. It may seek (and fail) to represent a love that *cannot* (yet) speak its name. When we come to realize just how sexual difference (and thus heterosexuality) has failed to be thought—specifically in this text recognized as one of the great amatory discourses of our tradition—and turn our attention to the *maladies* of this failure, then, *and only then*, might we begin to subvert the tyranny that is patriarachal heterosexism.

FIRST PEOPLE, MINORITY READING:
READING JONAH, FROM OCEANIA

Jione Havea

> It galls us that Western researchers and intellectuals can assume to know all that it is possible to know of us, on the basis of their brief encounters with some of us. It appals us that the West can desire, extract and claim ownership of our ways of knowing, our imagery, the things we create and produce, and then simultaneously reject the people who created and developed those ideas and seek to deny them further opportunities to be creators of their own culture and own nations. (Smith 1999, 1)

"First People" is one of the terms of identity that researchers and theologians use in referring to the Aborigines, the indigenous people, of Australia (Budden 2009, 5–6). It echoes the label "First Nations" used in reference to Native Americans in Canada and the USA. Both phrases, however, fail to do justice to the complexity of the indigenous groups (Smith 1999, 6–7). First People is a convenient way of referring to diverse indigenous groups as if they are homogenous, and it reflexively permits one not to learn their names in their native languages. It is much easier for an English speaker to talk about Aborigines and First People instead of learning to say and speak about, for instance, Bitjara, Darug, Ngalia, and so forth. In referring to First People, in general, one risks losing sight of the particularity of each group. So the terms of identity are also markers for the loss of identity.

"First People" has temporal ingredients, recognizing their existence in Australia prior to the arrival of Europeans with the First Fleet, who disembarked with the idea that Australia was *terra nullius* ("land belonging to no one") and they refused to honor the presence and agency of Aborigines (Brett 2009, 8–12). Then the "Second People" include the people who came on the First Fleet and the rest of us later migrants— FOBS ("Fresh-off-the-boats," referring to Asians and Pacific Islanders), Boat People (refugees) and so forth. "First People" is therefore loaded, but it does not anchor the people in the land as *Tāngata whenua* ("people of the land") does for Maoris in Aotearoa–New Zealand (*tangata 'i fonua* in my native Tongan tongue). The Maori people (*tāngata*), who celebrate being a part of the Polynesian migration to the islands of Oceania (see DeLoughrey 2007, 161–95), connect themselves to the land (*whenua*). *Tāngata whenua* is not about who arrived or who was established first, but about being rooted (in the *whenua*, the land), so it has spatial markers and points of contact.

As a Polynesian, I (maybe uncritically) connect First People with *Tāngata whenua* mainly because my mind needs to be rooted in some space and context. I can imagine and speculate, with ease, and I can do so wildly, but I also need to be anchored. Whether that makes me a materialist is not important to me, but I must add that in terms of *Tāngata whenua*, root (*whenua*, "land") is inseparable from people (*tāngata*).[1] This is the case also in the story of Jonah, which opens by rooting the people of interest in Nineveh, "that great city" whose "wickedness" has come up to YHWH (1:1–2). The focus of the story of Jonah falls on non-Israelites (cf. Timmer 2009, 12–15). The people of the land are city dwellers, and their conduct intertwines with the fate of the city. There is no separation, as if the place is independent of its inhabitants, or vice versa. The perceived lot of one intertwines with the expected fate of the other. They rise, grow, shrivel, prevail and/or fall together.

In privileging the interests and people of Nineveh I bounce back Ben Zvi's invitation for "double reading" of the "double ending" of the book in Jonah 4:11 (as assertion and as rhetorical question). "Since the question of whether YHWH destroys, or does not destroy, Nineveh is central to the plot of the book, this double ending is tantamount to a double reading of the prophetic book, one in which Nineveh is destroyed and another in which it is not" (Ben Zvi 2009a, 13). I do not seek certainty with regards to YHWH's attitude toward Nineveh, but I invite imagining of how YHWH's message to and desire for Nineveh might be perceived by the *Tāngata whenua* of Nineveh.

I come to the story as a Polynesian, reading on behalf of Nineveh and its people, mindful at the same time of the critique by Linda Tuhiwai Smith cited above. I do not pretend to represent or speak on behalf of Nineveh and the Ninevites. Rather, I read in solidarity with them and I am aware that the reading I offer might be seen as another "superfluous exegetical toy" (Guillaume 2009, 9). So be it. The story of Jonah, to borrow Timmer's words, is "a mass of nonsensical contradictions" (Timmer 2009, 12; cf. Gaines 2003, 3).

---

1. Unfortunately, the word *tāngata* (in many of the Polynesian languages) also means "man."

Minority Biblical Criticism

> The primary defining context for those who live in Australia is invasion.
> Invasion is about land and country, social location, power, place in the
> world, and meaning. (Budden 2009, 17)

Biblical criticism is a field in which many interests and powers exercise
and jostle, establish and empower, draw lines and exclude, resist and
subvert, reconsider and repress, and more. One of the more recent moves
is toward minority biblical criticism, as put forth in *They Were All
Together in One Place? Toward Minority Biblical Criticism* (Bailey,
Liew and Segovia 2009).[2] The editors acknowledge that the word
"minority" (which they understand as having less to do with number and
more to do with power) is problematic and so they explain in the Preface:

> We employ the term with reference to "minoritization" or the process of
> unequal valorization of population groups, yielding dominant and minority
> formations and relations, within the context, and through the apparatus, of
> a nation or state as a result of migration, whether voluntary or coerced. We
> are, therefore, using "minority" simultaneously to signify (on) this demean-
> ing practice and to challenge, contest, or change the term's meaning, even
> when we are no longer putting the term in quotation marks. (Bailey *et al.*
> 2009, ix)

The contributors to *They Were All Together in One Place?* write out of
the realities of three minority racial groups in the USA: African-Ameri-
can, Asian-American, and Latino/Latina-American. They come together
in the book, as an alliance, to address such matters as race, color, place,
gender, area, sexuality, language, migration, symbols, and how those are
(mis)understood and/or (mis)used in different realms and in biblical
texts. When it comes to the processes of minoritization in the lives of
migrants and their communities, the double-edged sword of race and
color make very deep cuts. This is true in the USA as well as in Australia, and in many other countries, where foreigners (who are minority in
terms of number and power) do not feel quite at home. And the darker
the skin color of the foreigner is, the less welcomed s/he is in the new
land (diaspora). Minority biblical criticism is, in the first place, attentive
to processes of minoritization that are based on race and color.

   That is easier said than done, especially with regard to the Hebrew
Bible and its pro-Israelite fever. When Israel is the minority, or the
minoritized subject, as during the Assyrian occupation and the Babylonian exile, the Hebrew Bible draws readers to identify and sympathize

---

   2.   See the book reviews by Jonathan Draper and Gerald O. West of South Africa
in *Review of Biblical Literature* (http://www.bookreviews.org).

with Israel. But when Israel has power and becomes the force that minoritizes others, on the basis of race and color, the Hebrew Bible lulls the reader toward celebrating the God-given victories of Israel. How does a minority biblical critic come to terms with instances where God and Israel are behind the processes of minoritization, or when God endorses and allows imperial powers to prevail? From where will justice come, when God is awry? For whom?

The minority biblical critic cannot be colorblind, even if God and the biblical narrator are. Moreover, the minority biblical critic must pay close attention to identities and behaviors that are determined or ignored along racial lines, bearing in mind the mantra-like naming of Canaanites, Hittites, Amorites, Perizzites, Hivites, and so forth, since the first arrival of Abram in Canaan. Note how the list grows from just the Canaanites in Gen 12:5–6. Racial lines are drawn too boldly in the Hebrew Bible to be ignored.

Like blocks in a setup of dominoes, color and race stand and fall with other blocks (e.g. age, gender, class, sexuality, etc.). But the Bible is more complicated than a structure of dominoes, because color and race have several manifestations that emerge at different points in the biblical account. Not all non-Israelites are wicked. For instance, Rahab the Canaanite and Cyrus the Persian break the expected mould. Conversely, not all Israelites are favorable characters, whether dark or fair-skin. King David of Judah is far from being a model man, father, husband, or leader.

A minority biblical critic is interested in both how race and color play out, or are suppressed, in the unfolding of the biblical account, taking note of who gets promoted, tolerated, drowned, rescued, ignored and/or forgotten in the process. When non-Israelites and darker-skin characters are uprooted or pushed down, a minority biblical critic would rise and resist. On the other hand, if a non-Israelite and darker-skin figure shines, a minority biblical critic would cheer and celebrate. Minority biblical criticism is therefore committed and biased.

So what's new, or what's up, with minority biblical criticism? As the saying goes, minority biblical criticism, as constructed in *They Were All Together in One Place?*, sings tunes that other choirs already sing, in harmony with the voices of feminists, LGBT critics, liberation critics, ideological critics, cultural critics, and more. What is special, though, is the opportunity to associate, to join a coalition, an alliance, in community, in solidarity, and that is welcoming to me, and I imagine the same feeling for other islanders, migrants, outsiders, and strangers. Heads up from me, therefore, and legs up as well, insofar as minority biblical criticism is about gathering, rather than setting apart, which greases the wheels of minoritization.

Given that the majority of readers of the story of Jonah would sympathize with the cause and people of Israel, Nineveh would be the city of minoritized subjects. Herewith is one of the points of tension in the present study, for the minoritized subjects with whom I identify are beneficiaries of a colonizing empire in the ancient world (cf. Timmer 2009). I therefore suspect that in the eyes of many critics, I am selling my soul to the empire and I am opting for subjects with whom I should not identify. Such is the lot of minority biblical criticism.

That the biblical text favors Israel but disfavors Nineveh does not mean that readers should do the same. Readers might opt, like Jonah, to be thrown overboard (from the text). Such is the joy of minority biblical criticism.

Nineveh

[Nineveh to Judah] I'm a city. I don't set policies. The monarchy does. The male monarchy does. When the king is successful in war, he lavishes adornments on me… When he fails, I am burned and pillaged; I sit in the dust and mourn my children who die because of military policy. You care about your people too—women and children and men, most of whom probably care most about having enough to eat and a way to keep warm at night. We haven't chosen these battles. They have been foisted on us. Others make decisions and we bear the consequences. (Davies 2004, 93)

Nineveh is declared to be a great city in Jonah 1:2 and 3:2, but the narrative is not clear about its size. This ambiguity has to do with Jonah 3:3b, which may be read as saying that it would take someone three days to walk the length of Nineveh; that it would take someone three days to have a proper visit of all the vicinities of the city; that it would take Jonah three days to reach the city from the place where the big fish spit him out; and so forth (see Halton 2008). Nineveh is so great that no one really knows how great it is.

Nineveh is not an Israelite city, and it is said to be wicked (1:2), but what exactly made it wicked and the extent to which it was wicked are not revealed. Was Nineveh wicked because it was a great city? Great because it was a wicked city? Wicked because it was a non-Israelite city? Was it said to be great in order to intensify its wickedness (that is, its wickedness was as great as its size)? Since the narrative is not clear about its size, one can surmise that the wickedness of the city is as ambiguous as its size.

Juxtaposing Y HWH 's first (1:2) and second (3:2) demand for Jonah to go to Nineveh reveals a shift in the reason given for why Jonah should go:

Go at once to Nineveh, that great city, and cry out *against* it; for their wickedness has come up before me. (Jonah 1:2, NRSV)

Get up, go to Nineveh, that great city, and proclaim *to* it the message that I tell you. (Jonah 3:2, NRSV)

At first, YHWH demands that Jonah should go *at once* (so NJPS) because Nineveh was wicked (1:2). The second time around (3:2), Nineveh is not presented as wicked at all. The reason given in the second text is that YHWH has a message to be delivered *to* Nineveh, but this message is not *against* Nineveh as in the first text (cf. 1:2). The shift in the tone of the demand and in the characterization of Nineveh suggests that something is also shifting in the will of YHWH. YHWH has moved. And the way that the people of Nineveh responded to Jonah's message—they believed YHWH, fasted and put on sackcloth, and their king was moved to do likewise (3:5–10)—gives the impression that Nineveh was not as wicked as YHWH first declared.

If one reads Jonah together with Nahum, in which Nineveh is perceived as a whore (Nah 3:4–7) who is to be violated, plundered and annihilated (see Davies 2004, 91–95), one senses Jonah shifting the attitude towards Nineveh. Nahum announces the destruction of Nineveh; Jonah on the other hand presents a repentant God: "God saw what they did, how they were turning back from their bad ways. And God renounced the punishment planned to bring upon them [Nineveh], and did not carry it out" (3:10). The turning of Nineveh initiated the turning of YHWH, the change in Nineveh's way comforted and relented YHWH. Would a wicked city have that kind of effect on YHWH? It looks like that Nineveh was not as wicked as YHWH initially announced, and so I wonder if it was deemed to be wicked mainly because it was a non-Israelite city. The narrator does not entertain this kind of speculation.

Another side to the identification of Nineveh as a "great city" invites further pondering, from the standpoint of minority biblical criticism, and this has to do with the fact that most cities, ancient and modern, are multiracial and multilingual. The bigger the city, the more diverse are the languages, the citizens and their ways. Such a cradle for diversity would be appalling for any authority that seeks to centralize and monopolize, whether in terms of politics, culture and/or religion.

There are two places in the story of Jonah that point readers to the matters of race, language and cultural diversity. The first is the encounter with sailors in the ship going from Joppa to Tarshish (1:3–16), crossing between two locations, languages and cultures. The sailors were from people who were different from Jonah's (cf. 1:8), so they must have spoken different languages, and they worshipped different gods from

Jonah's. And the second instance has to do with the people of Nineveh, who also had different languages, cultures and gods. The story involves a Hebrew who understands the language that YHWH speaks, but so did the big fish (2:11), interacting with sailors and Ninevites who speak other languages. At the underside of the story are narrative clues and strands that point readers to a plot which interweaves multiple tongues. Readers would therefore expect the story, and the characters in the story, to be multilingual.

The Jonah narrator however does not take the significance of multi-lingualism (and of multiculturalism) seriously. But minority biblical critics do (cf. Garcia-Treto 2009, 67–70) and several questions invite consideration. In the book of Jonah, who spoke whose language? Did Jonah speak the languages of the sailors and the Ninevites? Or did the sailors, who would have served other Hebrews, and the Ninevites, who were city folks, and would have encountered people from other cultures and tongues, understand and speak Hebrew? The narrator does not explain, and is thus not as sensitive as the narrator of Daniel, for whom it was important to point out a shift from Hebrew to Aramaic in his narra-tive (Dan 2:4). The narrator of the Jonah story operates like someone from a dominant language group, who expects others to learn and under-stand his language.

In ignoring the language differences between Jonah and the other characters in the story, the narrator downplays the potential for being "lost in translation." This is especially critical given that the story circles around YHWH demanding Jonah to deliver a message against/to a non-Hebrew speaking people. This issue is important also for ones from outside of dominant language groups, who constantly have to live in the world of translations. The narrator expects everyone in the story-world, as well as his readers, to understand and interact in Hebrew. In my read-ing, the narrator's disregard for different tongues, given that he wrote in Hebrew, adds up to a power move on his part.

From the standpoint of *Tāngata whenua*, the favoring of a language that is not one of the local ones can be seen as an attempt to strangle and suffocate the native and local languages. In Oceania, at present, for instance, many indigenous communities have lost their native languages and this is particularly haunting because of the inter-connection between language and identity. The Jonah narrator's disregard for the local lan-guages of Nineveh is therefore insensitive and disrespectful, and wicked.

Loss of language quickens loss of identity. But this does not mean that language and identity can remain unaltered, forever. They too, like cultures, change and transform. But when the loss of language and identity is forced upon the people, because of a push for synchronicity, disregard and/or negligence, the loss is more acute. And communities that are in diaspora are more vulnerable to the loss of language and identity than those that remain in their birthplace and native homes.

In the eyes of the Jonah narrator, Nineveh lost its privilege to have a different language and identity. For in the end, the people of Nineveh renounced their (evil) ways and became god-fearers. Nineveh became a city of the Hebrew God. Nineveh was spared, and YHWH was spared from bringing punishment upon its people (3:10). Doesn't this mean that Nineveh was not (or, no longer) wicked? On what grounds, according to whose judgment, may one say that Nineveh is or is not wicked?

Notwithstanding, at the end of the story, Nineveh is still a rejected subject. Jonah raves to YHWH for renouncing the punishment planned for Nineveh, and he was so angry that he asked YHWH to take his life (4:3). His anger boiled up again when God sent a worm to attack the plant that gave him comfort from the sun, and again he wished that he was dead (4:8). The story then ends with a verse (4:10) that, Ben Zvi suggests, invites a double reading: to consider that YHWH cares for Nineveh, and to assert that YHWH wants to destroy Nineveh. In both cases, however, Nineveh is still uncaringly portrayed as "that great city, in which there are more than a hundred and twenty thousand persons *who do not yet know their right hand from their left*, and many beasts as well" (4:10b, my italics). YHWH may have relented and spared the city of Nineveh (3:10), but YHWH still thinks that the people of Nineveh are stupid. They are, so to speak, like beasts.

I attribute the disrespect that the narrator and YHWH have toward Nineveh to ethnic and racial biases. They both favor Israel, and they could not free themselves from those idiosyncrasies. And so, in this double reading, Nineveh was spared, physically, but condemned, in perception.

Jonah

[The Big Fish to Jonah] I am the big fish who saved your life once. The one who sustained you till you could come back to the world of human beings. I have to admit that I did not do that because I liked you. (Davies 2004, 89)

There is something troublesome with Jonah not wanting to go to Nineveh. He explains later, with the benefit of hindsight, that it had to do with YHWH being "a compassionate and gracious God, slow to anger, abounding in kindness, renouncing punishment" (4:2). Jonah justifies his refusal to go by appealing to YHWH, from whose service, the narrator explains, he fled (1:3). Jonah points to YHWH, but I want to point toward

Nineveh. What was it about Nineveh that Jonah did not want its people to also experience YHWH's kindness?

One of the most insulting things that anyone can do to the *Tāngata whenua* is to say or show that s/he does not want to come to the *whenua* (land). The *whenua* is home, and it is the point of connection of the people to their ancestors and genealogies (*whakapapa*), customs, practices and stories (*talanoa*). These, together, locate and therefore root the *Tāngata whenua*. In this regard, anyone who does not want to visit the *whenua* (land, home) refuses to embrace the roots of the *Tāngata whenua*. From the standpoint of *Tāngata whenua*, therefore, Jonah's flight away from Nineveh is insulting.

In fleeing to Tarshish, Jonah did not want to gift Nineveh the opportunity to experience YHWH as a repentant God who is both irate and vicious as well as compassionate and gracious. Jonah did not want Nineveh to receive God's forgiveness and blessing, to celebrate the renouncing of the punishment planned against them, and to know what it is like to be forgiven by one's enemies (cf. Gaines 2003, 12). Such attitudes are not encouraged by the *Tāngata whenua* of Oceania, who rejoice in receiving visitors not just because of the gifts and blessings that they might bring, but also because of the opportunity to be hospitable.

The reception that the people of Nineveh gave Jonah suggests a culture of hospitality. In the very first day when Jonah started preaching, and even though there were still 39 days to go before the projected overthrow was to take place (3:4), the people of Nineveh believed God, proclaimed a fast, and great and small alike put on sackcloth (3:5). Nineveh did not tarry. They acted right away. Jonah came with words of destruction, and the people of Nineveh received him with open minds. Most preachers, and so colonizers, fantasize about this kind of outcome, where their audience accepts their message without any questions. Whether the outcome was real or fantasy is beside the point for this part of my reading. I am intrigued that the people of Nineveh welcomed and accepted Jonah, a stranger with a strange message, which reflects a culture of hospitality similar to that of the people of Oceania. (But this does not mean that I would welcome Jonah.)

When Jonah arrived preaching in a non-local language, he entered the city with a foreign tongue. He comes like a missionary, announcing destruction on the local people. His language, his message and his smelly body would have been offensive to the people of Nineveh. Yet, they embraced his message. They accepted him even though there is no mention of him approaching the elders and minders of the city to seek their permission so that he could address the people. Every *Tāngata whenua* knows that there are protocols when one comes to a foreign land, that there are certain rituals that need to be performed, and respects that need to be recognized, before one could give a public talk. Jonah did not perform any of those before he started preaching. In the eyes of *Tāngata whenua*, therefore, Jonah *was* disrespectful to the ways and customs of Nineveh.

Moreover, in the eyes of *Tāngata whenua*, again, Jonah was disrespectful toward YHWH also. First, by fleeing without informing YHWH that he will not perform the demanded task. He just got up and left, with no apology given, as if there was no relationship between him and YHWH. Second, by not wanting YHWH to be compassionate and gracious toward Nineveh. He did not want YHWH to have a change of heart and mind, to be repentant and complex. And third, by wishing that he was dead instead of engaging YHWH in conversation. A sore loser, Jonah was.

Oceania

Lin Onus, an Australian Aboriginal artist, commented:

> On the sixth day God created the earth, on the seventh day he rested, and on the eighth day he stuffed it up for Aboriginal people. (cited in Brett 2009, 7)

This essay looked at Jonah through the lens of *Tāngata whenua*, from Oceania. The upshot is a crosscultural reading that resists the drive of the biblical account, in favor of Nineveh. Resistant readings are necessary, for God and others have "stuffed it up" for Nineveh, for Aborigines, for First Peoples, for people of the land, and of the Seas. My reading, one might argue, is disrespectful of Jonah. I constructed my reading in solidarity with Nineveh, whose lot reflects the experience of many communities in Oceania with foreign missionaries and colonizers. Because our communities fought and resisted the Christian mission and the Western expansion, I hesitate to accept that Nineveh wholeheartedly accepted Jonah, on day one. As such, I will continue to be disrespectful of Jonah, as a prophetic character and as a book.

I was drawn to the story of Jonah because it has a fish story,[3] and now have come to realize how smart the fish was: it spit out what it did not want. Wouldn't it have been *wicked* had the fish spit Jonah out onto a land far away from Nineveh!

---

3. There are other Oceanic elements in the story that this reading fail to address: sailors, boat, fish, prayer, plant, worm, and so forth. I leave those for another occasion.

BIBLICAL JUSTICE:
RECOMPENSE, REVENGE AND RESTORATION

Paul Morris

חסד־ואמת נפגשו צדק ושלום נשקו

Mercy and truth are met together; righteousness and peace have kissed.
(Ps 85:11)

Restorative Justice

צדק צדק תרדף

Justice, justice you will pursue. (Deut 16:20)

In his writings on the prophets of Israel, Ed Conrad advocates readings of our inherited and "alien" texts that challenge the implicit assumptions of the changing fashions of biblical scholarship and the ways in which the ancient is rendered contemporary (Conrad 1991, 1999, 2003). The theological assumptions of implied audiences are often powerful determinants of how these meanings may be generated, and he cautions us wisely against premature biblical theologies. The present essay raises significant issues of how the Bible is being read, interpreted and applied in the contemporary world and underlines the importance of the link between academic biblical research and present interpretative communities. The prophets were intensely concerned, as were biblical authors more generally, with justice/righteousness. In the present study I intend to explore one current notion of justice, restorative or transformative justice, and, in particular, the discourse that supports it on biblical grounds. Further, I will explore the implicit elements in definitions of this sort of justice and how they relate to particular historical, theological positions. My focus is not on the mass of arguments and evidence for the efficacy or otherwise of restorative justice but rather on the ways in which the

Bible is utilized in support and the frameworks for these understandings. I will conclude by reflecting on the demand made by Christian proponents of restorative justice that we urgently need to reconsider the relationships and responsibilities of citizens, their communities and the state, and that the Bible has an absolutely central role to play in this.

Restorative justice appears as an unprecedented success story from its invention, reconception or rediscovery in the 1970s, via its support by voluntary groups, scholarly and justice system advocates, activists and enthusiasts, to its uptake by governments and authorities across the world to give what has oft been termed "the restorative revolution" or the "paradigm shift in criminal justice" (Gavrielides 2007, 14–15). The first recorded usage is by Albert Eglash, who, starting from the "crisis" in criminal justices systems, distinguishes three responses: the two existing models, the "retributive" and the "redistributive," which focus on criminal acts and deny the victim(s) participation; and the "restorative," where the emphasis is on repairing the relationship between offender and victim, and second the harm done to the victim (Eglash 1977). He effectively named a number of existing trends and widely held views about the perceived failures of the criminal justice system. For example, the first victim offender reconciliation programmes began in Canada (1974) and the US (1977) arising out of Mennonite communities, alongside a number of other developments that directly involved communities, including the later incorporation and recognition of indigenous justice practices, such as sentencing circles. Many of these involved Christian institutions and personnel.

Since 1977 the literature has expanded exponentially among criminologists, legal theorists, policy makers, moral philosophers, theologians and other authorities on restorative justice. This literature, while largely ostensibly secular, has a number of foundational figures with explicit religious agendas and/or viewpoints. For example, criminologist Herman Bianchi argued for a rejection of the Western civilization's dominant system of "justice as retribution" in favour of "justice as reconciliation," which he called "Tsedaka justice," referring to the Hebrew conceptual cluster around righteousness and justice (Bianchi 1973, see also Bianchi 1995). A most significant figure both as a leading proponent of restorative justice and as a teacher of a generation of Christian and other followers is the Mennonite social thinker, Howard Zehr. The author of the foundational text, *Changing Lenses: A New Focus for Crime and Justice* (Zehr 1990), and a number of other studies including *The Little Book of Restorative Justice* (Zehr 2002), he established the first victim–offender reconciliation programme in the United States. He understands crime as a "wound in human relationship" that creates the obligation to restore and repair (Zehr 1990, 181) and insists that while retributive justice focuses on violation of law, restorative justice stresses the violation of people and relationships (Zehr 1990, 199). We will return to consider Zehr further below. Daniel van Ness, addressing the resources and sources for developing restorative justice, argued that the needs and rights of victims are central to what he refers to as "biblical justice" and that this entails the restoration of the community by resolving the harm done by offender to victim (van Ness 1986).

Australia and New Zealand have played a most significant role in the creation of programmes of restorative justice within existing justice systems. John Braithwaite's notion of "re-integrative shaming" (Braithwaite 1989) led to the RISE (Re-Integrative Shaming Experiment) project at the Centre for Restorative Justice, at the Australian National University. Braithwaite and his colleagues sought to replace negative "stigmatizing shame" with admission of guilt and a shame, or social disapproval that would promote re-entering communities. Re-integrative ceremonies were developed along these lines. His work was also the basis of the trial project at Wagga Wagga, New South Wales, and this model, albeit controversial even in Australia, was "exported" to England and the US. Religious and theological concepts have also played a role in the literature, so, for example, the discussion of the sometimes ambiguous role of forgiveness in shaming in restorative conferencing (Johnstone 1999). Since the late 1980s in New Zealand restorative practices have been applied to all juvenile criminal cases, and some cases involving Maori offenders (Children, Young Persons and their Families Act 1989). Cunneen posits that the involvement of hapu (sub-tribe), iwi (tribal) and whanau (extended families) draws on Maori traditions (Cunneen 1997). Sentencing judges have been directed to consider restorative processes (Victims of Offences Act 1987; Criminal Justice Act 1985; Sentencing Act 2002; and Parole Act 2002). There has also been considerable interest in these New Zealand initiatives and their application in the US (Schmid 2001). Gibbs raises an interesting question in relation to restorative justice and indigenous peoples when it is the State who is the offender (Gibbs 2009).

Restorative justice continues to grow as alternative to, in parallel with, and integrated within criminal justice systems around the world. As a notion it has been continually debated as to its legitimate limits and extents (Daly 2000). For example, Zehr and Mika contend that many schemes labelled restorative justice are in reality repackaged retributive and punitive programmes (Zehr and Mika 1998, 47–49). Restorative justice has been distinguished from, and conflated with, community justice, transformative criminal justice, and mediation (McCold 2004). There are ongoing issues of coercion and mediation freely entered into when criminal trials, prosecution and imprisonment can be avoided by agreement on the part of offenders (Alexander 2006). The literature has highlighted a lack of widely agreed principles and the gaps between practice and theory, with the lawyers and legal academics arguing for theoretical priority and those involved with practice understanding the theorists to be running behind and distanced from grass roots innovations and initiatives. More recently, restorative justice has been extended to mediation practices in employment, race relations, bullying in schools, and in sexual and physical abuse cases (Muyebe 2009) and hate crimes. Following the Truth and Reconciliation Commission in South Africa (van der Spuy 2007), restorative justice is increasingly linked to post-trauma international peacemaking contexts, including Chile, Rwanda, the Solomon Islands, and Sierra Leone.

Defining restorative justice is problematic as its usage is broad, and can range from aspects of tribal, aboriginal and indigenous justice systems, via victim–offender mediation schemes involving community and family in juvenile cases, and prison reform, to the internationally brokered efforts at peacemaking (Crawford and Newburn 2003; Hoyle and Young 2002; Wilcox 2004). Usage is not always consistent and sometimes deliberately so and there is a growing technical literature on these very concerns. Besides the increasing take up and reports of successes, what sustains reflection on restorative justice is the basic dichotomy, albeit one that is regularly challenged as being in danger of being too absolute, between the focus being on punishment versus the attempted restoration of relationships. In practice, restorative justice schemes operate with sectors of the offender population alongside the mainstream justice system in Canada, New Zealand, and Australia, in some European countries and across the Pacific Island nations

In New Zealand there have been mixed results from an evaluation pilot in four district courts, with many mediation conferences not actually taking place at all, although when they do they can reduce the number of cases taken to trial. Some 98% of the New Zealand public, however, in the 1999 referendum voted for tougher criminal sentences and currently Parliament is considering a "three strikes" bill. Restorative justice practices are now integrated alongside new prison building programmes, although it is important to recognize that restorative justice schemes are very much minor in a punitive system deeply committed to incarceration, humiliation, social and psychological alienation. There are parallel patterns in Canada, the US, and in England and Wales.

The Bible, Christians and Restorative Justice

עשה משפט יתום ואלמנה ואהב גר לתת לו לחם ושמלה
ואהבתם את הגר כי גרים הייתם בארץ מצרים

He supports the cause of the orphan and widow, and loves the stranger,
by giving him food and clothing. Therefore you should love the stranger,
for you were strangers in the land of Egypt. (Deut 10:18–19)

There are Christian churches and groups involved across the justice spectrum—from evangelical judicial populism calling for sterner sentences and advocacy of the death penalty on the grounds that these are demanded by "biblical justice," to those committed to penal reform on the same grounds. Here I want to look specifically at the role of Christians in restorative justice. Major denominations have formally supported programmes of restorative justice. In the US, the Presbyterian Church (USA), the Methodist Church, the Catholic Bishops of America, and The Baptist Peace Fellowship have all endorsed such programmes. One recent Canadian study reports that the majority of volunteers working in restorative justice programmes are Christian (Souza 2004, 64). In addition to religious support for programmes from religious NGOs, churches, Christian organizations, and individuals who publicly identify as Christian, there is some evidence that there is take-up by offenders who have "found Jesus," often in prison, and that successful mediation is aided by a sharing of religious viewpoint by offender and victim (Jehle and Miller 2006). Restorative training courses and programmes of study are often located within religious institutions or under the rubric of the study of religion, for example, the Centre for Justice and Peacemaking at Eastern Mennonite University; the Restorative Justice Program in the School of Religion at Queen's University, Canada; and the programme at the Boston Theological Institute. Some restorative programmes, such as faith-based prison initiatives, are largely administered, funded and supported by churches and Christian groups (Burnside 2005). There are also studies of the spiritual processes held to be at work in restorative justice (Bender and Armour 2007; Pranis 2004; Hadley 2001).

I want to focus on the ways in which biblical support is harnessed to undergird and promote restorative justice. This is done in the main by biblical theologies of justice, that is, selective biblical verses and passages as interpreted through particular Christian traditions and sub-divisions and presented as normative and authoritative Christian teachings. Materials are carefully selected to support specific positions, often as calls to action or in order to foster particular values and promote certain virtues. In the growing number of popular Christian theologies of biblical justice, we find the Old Testament accounts of justice starkly contrasted with the New; so, for example, N. T. Wright argues that while justice features prominently in the Old Testament it is only with Jesus that justice is "reordered in the world" and the "the process of redemption begun" (Wright 2006, 99). Christian supporters of restorative justice all make reference to the foundational biblical idea of "shalom" as the basis of the just community envisaged by the Old Testament Covenant, arguing that this refers not exclusively to an ancient Jewish community or any Jewish community but the Church or the proto-Christian community. Further, these writers all understand this to be only the foundation for the development of a full model of restorative justice arising out of Jesus' rejection of the concept of retribution (Matt 5). This fundamental distinction between the retributive and restorative models of justice is the very foundation of the "new" justice. In the Christian literature, the retributive model is associated with the Old Testament *lex talionis*, "an eye for an eye" (עַיִן תַּחַת עַיִן, Lev 24:19–21; Exod 21:22–25; Deut 19:21). Even when this is read more positively, for example, as setting a limit on retaliation, it is contrasted with the later teachings of Jesus' rejection of "an eye for an eye" (Matt 5:38–42). So, for example, Zehr emphasizes the central role that Jesus plays in his deliberations on restorative justice, He contrasts an "eye for an eye" with Jesus' injunction to love your enemies and links these with an unfolding revelatory theology of justice with the progression from the Genesis' law of Lemach, via an eye for an eye, to fulfilment only in Christ's universal love (Zehr and Toews 2004). Zehr is typical of much of this writing. Often Old Testament ethics are formally "affirmed" but only as mediated and completed by New Testament teachings.

This idea of a gradual moral unfolding of revelation entails a particular reading of the Old Testament. Even when the Old Testament is actually read, it is read wholly through the lens of the New. So, for example, in Waldemar Janzen's Mennonite study of Old Testament biblical ethics there are more references to Jesus than to almost anything else in the index. He describes Abraham as quite "unlike the rest of the Old Testament," as "Christlike" and as "a preview of the New Testament ideal…before this full fruition in the life and message of Jesus" (Janzen 1994, 10). There is no Old Testament ethic, at least not an independent one, Old Testament "institutions and rituals" are "superseded" by Christ (194), leaving only a partial and disembodied ethic awaiting completion in Jesus by means of a series of ethical stages from communal, via Torah, to Jesus' ethic of love. Sometimes, Christianity is itself held to be responsible for the retributive model of justice, with Christians over-emphasizing the "angry and vengeful God." So, for example, Herman Bianchi counsels Christians, particularly Evangelicals, to reject these

Old Testament dimensions in favour of the true Christian teachings of love and peacemaking (Bianchi 1994). Their theologies of justice are cavalier with Old Testament texts and either read it as a staged moral drama fulfilled in Jesus or as a set of principles and positions that can be reordered in the New Testament to give the framework of a Christian biblical justice. Over and over again the same texts are cited and repeated in article after article, book after book, church declaration after declaration. So, for example, advocates of restorative justice repeatedly cite John 8:7, 11, and Luke 22:34, while the prison reformers refer to Luke 4:18 and Matt 25:39.

To take a Catholic example, Father Jim Consedine, an advocate of restorative justice, particularly in prisons in New Zealand, defines his task as bringing "Christ's message to crime, law and order" for "only Christians infused with the Spirit of Christ will be able to see Christ in the prisoner. It is the Christ in us that will see the Christ in them." He rejects "an eye for an eye" in favour of Jesus' emphasis on "forgiveness and reconciliation" and sees this innovation as the "heart of the New Testament understanding of justice" (Consedine 2005).

This is indeed a strange hermeneutic: the Old Testament is selectively read in the light of the New, highlighting the New Testament materials found in the Old, and then elements that are held to be reaffirmed and confirmed are selectively emphasized alongside the rejection of the rituals and institutions of the Old that were part of the moral context, effectively leaving the New. Pauline texts play a significant role in this re-reading of the Old Testament. Paul's central notion of "justification" is, of course, associated with justice and understood to be both a reaffirmation of Jesus' ethics and a rejection of the Old Testament practices and patterns of just behaviour.

There are other issues that need not detain us here. In perusing Christian literature in support of restorative justice there is very little if any mention of the real risks and dangers involved. The risks include reported frequent restorative meetings where emotional outbursts lead to humiliation, scolding and stigmatization, and of course longitudinal benefits are hard to analyse, never mind quantify. Declan Roche talks of the "almost blind faith in restorative justice" (Roche 2003, 19). Pavlich sees the State appropriating mediation to expand its control and power over the lives of individuals and contends that restorative justice fosters victimhood while failing to address the social factors that underlie much crime (Pavlich 2005). In summary, there is not a great deal of supportive material for contemporary programmes of restorative justice in the Bible, and biblical support is by broad sweeping and selective reordering of biblical sources. The Bible can just as easily support other current models of justice. It is reminiscent of eco-theologies, equally selective and modern, but drawing on a number of earlier frameworks of reference in the interests of contemporary relevancy and motivation for action.

Supersessionism

> We are the true spiritual Israel, and the descendants of Judah, Jacob, Isaac.

> The Scriptures are...not yours, but ours. (Justin Martyr, *Dialogue with Trypho* 11:5, 29.2)

The third of my themes is that of supersessionism, sometimes referred to as replacement theology. Although my focus will be on the historical Christian theological supersessionism of its Jewish antecedents and its modernist legacies, supersession, literally "sitting over" or "sitting on," can be phenomenologically discerned as a pattern of progressive, contested legitimacy across the annals of the history of religions: from Islam's supersessionism of Judaism and Christianity, Baha'i supersessionism of Islam, Mormon supersessionism of other Christianities, as well as parallels from across the religious traditions of Asia and elsewhere. In each case ideological or theological supersessionism impacts on the superseded religious community, most usually in negative ways.

"Supersessionism" was first used by William Paley to designate the Christian triumphalism of the advent of Christ over Jewish Law (Paley 1790, 167). It was utilized by a number of authors later in a similar fashion in relation to the "Church" and the Jews or Jewish Law and as a translation of the German "aufgehoben" in works such as F C. Baur's *Paul: The Apostle of Jesus Christ*. Since the 1970s and the systematic post-Shoah reflections on Christianity and antisemitism, the term has been used in a much more negative fashion to indicate the theological underpinnings of the history of Christian anti-Judaism (Isaac 1971, 294; Baum 1974). Since that time, although supersessionism has been taken up in the churches (Presbyterian Church in Canada 2009, Edelman 2004), by biblical scholars (Klawans 2006) and theologians (Vlach 2010), as yet there is no systematic study of the phenomenon, in relation to Jews and Christians, or more generally. This discussion is part of a wider debate about historical Christian self-understanding reflected in the uneasy, fraught and problematic relationship with the Jewish people and the Jewish law with the parameters being set by the declaration of Marcion as the first heresy at one end and the frequent but changing charges of "Judaizing" at the other.

Supersessionism, therefore, is a relatively new notion read back into Christian history, and while the basic idea appears straightforward enough—the claim that God's promises had been transferred from the Jews to the new Church, that Christ replaced the Law, and that Christian self-understanding entails the rejection of Jewish claims and legitimacy—the details often raise concerns about when, where and by whom. The growing awareness of the plural histories of the early churches and the complicated histories of the first five centuries of the relationships between Jewish and Christian communities should lead us to considerable caution about the reading of scriptural and later texts as clearly expressing a particular form of supersessionism. In Christian history there have been a number of discernibly different forms of supersessionism, some emphasizing the Church replacement of the former "people of God," while others have seen Jesus Christ as the replacement for the Jewish people. Supersessionism continues to be qualified in the literature. So, for example, the Jewish scholar, David Novak, considers the claim that the new covenant is a fulfilling addition, or that it replaces the Old, both to be supersessionist. The former he refers to as "soft supersessionism" and the latter as "hard supersessionism," that is, "The old covenant is dead. The Jews by their sins, most prominently by their rejection of Jesus as Messiah, have forfeited any covenantal status" (Novak 2004, 66). R. Kendall Soulen offers three forms of supersessionism: economic (Jews are no longer part of divine plan); punitive (Jews are rejected by God because they rejected Christ); and structural (the true religion and relationship is between God and humankind and not only with the Jews). This latter view he understands to date from Duns Scotus and to be widely held, and, while all three are supersessionist and to be resisted, the third is less evidently dangerous (Soulen 1996). To date, the most complete typology of supersessionism comes from Donaldson Terence, who lists five types with various sub-categories that allow him to identify the different models in the New Testament and in Christian history, giving considerable scope for further discussion and refinement (Donaldson 2009).

Relationship
Binary Opposites
—Israel opposite of true people of God (e.g. Marcion)
—Israel polar opposite from beginning; there have always been Jewish "saints" alongside the spiritually blind majority

Discontinuity and Supersession
—Israel failed, sinned and was rejected; replaced by Church
—Israel's necessary preparatory role for the coming of Christ; now past

Continuity, Redefinition and Reconstitution
—Israel superseded by Christ who is the only continuity with the past
—Israel as superseded totally by Jewish remnant plus Gentiles
—Israel as superseded with Gentiles now added to Jewish core

Solidarity and Mission
—Jewish Christ believers as remnant or agents for Jewish conversion

Co-existence in Anticipation of the Final Redemption
—"All Israel will be saved" (Rom 11) continuity
—Israel and Church relate to God through parallel covenants
—Jewish Christ believers as remnant or agents for Jewish conversion

These three examples, and there are others too, disaggregate super-sessionism so that there are more or less acceptable versions of the relationship clearly distinguished from their unacceptable supersessionist cousins—that is, they all offer an apologetic account of supersessionism without the necessity of the radical rethink mooted in the 1970s of a new Christology (Ruether 1974), of reconsiderations of two parallel and ongoing covenants (van Buren 1995), or more sophisticated and inclusive versions of Christian universalism.

What I am interested in here, however, is the crude theological version of the Christian theological suppression of its Jewish heritage, with its roots in what became the New Testament of the growing demarcation of the transition from "fleshy Israel" to "spiritual Israel" (Gal 5:16–18; Rom 7:5–6; 8:2; 1 Cor 15:44–49), from the now "false Israel" to the now, new "true Israel," from "the Jews" to the new ecclesia. The new "churches," divine promises now transferred to them and their futures assured, are opposed to poor old Israel, who are left only with past and future condemnations for rejection, rebellion, and being stiff-necked. As it relates to justice, it posits a Jesus who departs from his Jewish context embodying the climax of a simple progressive morality from *lex talionis* (Old Dispensation) to the Christian, universal restorative ethic (New Dispensation); from justice to mercy from Law to love; and from body to spirit. This model is alive and well and all too readily found in con-temporary Christian literature and scholarship on restorative justice, often most evident where Matt 5:17 is quoted but, of course, repudiating the people of Israel and their ways and fulfilling them anew. All of Donaldson's types of supersessionism can readily be found in the restorative justice literature, particularly types 2 and 3.

I do not intend to develop it here, as it is less evident in the biblical support for restorative justice, but there is a recent and discrete body of scholarship on St. Paul and supersessionism, often based on how Rom 11 is interpreted and understood. For example, Lloyd Gaston's *Paul and*

Torah (Gaston 1991) seeks to develop a non-supersessionist account of the relationship between the Church and the Jewish people. The Epistle to the Hebrews has been interpreted in a dual supersessionist movement by Jewish and Christian communities (Eisenbaum 2005).

The supersessionist hermeneutic highlights the radical nature of the new and the contrast with the old while incorporating elements of the old within the new schemas. The new messiah comes to be seen as a departure from the Jewish society of his time, in terms of authority, legality, prophecy, spiritual powers, and as the embodiment of this supposedly new model of justice and reconciliation. Rhetorically, the new temporal fulcrum for humanity has been established and a new era, an epoch of salvation and redemption begun. There are other contemporary forms of theological supersessionism. For example, the papal document, *Dominus Iesus* has been understood by many commentators to have retreated from the attempts at non-supersessionism in Vatican II, *Nostre Aetate*, and returned to an explicit supersessionist position (Edelman 2004).

There is a modern version of supersessionism which I refer to as "secular supersessionism." It takes the foundational replacement theology of the present to the past but replicates it in a seemingly secular guise. Some interpretations of Hegel's "sublation" would fall into this category. A more obvious example is the French *philosophes* and their negativity towards Jews and Judaism, not on theological supersessionist grounds, but on the secular supersessionist grounds that the Jews have "done their dash" and are no longer relevant to the march of a universal, progressive history. Many of the dominant discourses of modernity are supersessionist in this way. Jaspers, Bellah and Toynbee, for example, all promote a secular supersessionism where the coming of the universal delegitimizes Jews and Judaism as "fossils" or "ethnic" or stuck in the wrong axial age (Morris 2006; Gregersen 2006).

Secular supersessionism impacts on liberal forms of Christianity and on biblical scholarship. The former is well illustrated by the Jesus Seminar and its portrayal of Jesus as a Wisdom figure—yet not just another wisdom figure, but the very exemplar of Old Testament wisdom. In Lloyd Geering's recent study of Ecclesiastes, he concludes that poor old, Old Testament, Ecclesiastes "found no answers," but merely needed Jesus' "kingdom of God" for "completion" (Geering 2010, 210).

Secular supersessionism also clearly operates in the writings of secular proponents of restorative justice where they have inherited the progressive and pejorative version of the distinction between retributive and restorative justice. The reference, however, is no longer to Christianity and its historical supersession of Judaism but rather with the need to supersede the modern punitive criminal justice system. Here the super-session is implicit and contrasts modernity with almost anything else—true restorative justice as opposed to modernist Christianity, the Judeo-Christian tradition, all tribal and indigenous cultures, and even all religious traditions, as by Fresno, California (Fresno, VORP 1982, 4).

We need a short theological detour before the conclusion. Is super-sessionism inevitable? Is it simply an expression of the Christian truth that Christ came to complete or fulfil Judaism and did so by invalidating any independent Jewish alternative outside of them converting now or later to Christianity or suffering damnation in this world and the next? If Christian universalism entails salvation only through Christ, then surely Judaism is superseded? This raises difficult questions—perhaps too diffi-cult—and as the 1980s ended so did the earnest attempts at tackling these issues. Supersessionism demands an answer to the theological issue of what constitutes the uniqueness of Jesus Christ and how this might be conceived of in non-supersessionist ways. This is a version of what we might call the "Vermes dilemma," that is, since the beginnings of the recovery of the Jesus of "first-century" Galilee and Judea, dated from George Foot Moore in the 1920s; as we more fully acknowledge the Jewish context, the nature of Jesus' distinction becomes more difficult to conceive and establish. The discussions around the world in a number of churches can be followed as they struggle with this. For example, the Presbyterian Church in Canada has recently issued its report on super-sessionism, a report that began with an enquiry in 2003 as to whether Jews should be the targets of missionary activities. They acknowledge the necessity of recognizing the distinctiveness of Christianity and determine a numbers of options for undertaking this without falling back into forms of supersessionism (PCIB 2009).

Conclusions

ויגל כמים משפט וצדקה כנחל איתן

> But let judgment run down as waters, and righteousness as a mighty stream. (Amos 5:24)

What has been argued is that Christian biblical theologies of justice supporting a particular modern practice, restorative justice, are almost all supersessionist and reaffirm an older prejudicial way of understanding the relationship between the Old and New Testaments and the Jewish people and their traditions and the Christian Church. Should super-sessionism really be an issue in relation to restorative justice? Does this really matter? Given that the prison population has doubled in three decades in New Zealand and recidivism rates are very high and almost any intervention will have some positive impact, does it matter if the Christian support for restorative programmes is misguided or a recent reconstruction, albeit one that replicates an older Christian prejudice? If one person is "saved" or restored, is it not worth it? Is it not written "And whoever saves a life, it is considered as if he saved an entire world" (*m. Sanh.* 4:5; *b. Sanh.* 37a)? Recently, my house was robbed and a number of irreplaceable family items were stolen, the police saw little prospect of the items being returned and suggested that they were probably quickly fenced at a fraction of their value most likely to feed a drug habit. They did, however, warn us that they might return for other stuff. I half-relished the prospect of their return as I clutched my cricket bat, angry at the thoughtless arrogance of their smashing their way into my home. However, I had no desire to meet them. Without genuine and sustained reference to the economics, psychology and politics of the situation, restorative justice offers little but the growing evidence that those involved, particularly offenders, feel better afterwards. The talk of community involvement in our atomized, capitalistic society is much more problematic than much of the well-meaning Christian literature on restorative justice suggests. The failed promise of much restorative justice is the shallowness of its grasp of our economic and political contexts.

What has supersessionism got to do with this? Supersessionism, by detaching Old Testament ideas so readily and selectively from their textual and social contexts and restructuring within supposedly new and often contrasting paradigms, evacuates them of much of their meaning. A recent example is Jonathan Klawans' study of sacrifice and temple in ancient Judaism. His argument is that the scholarly imposition of a supersessionist, progressive frame on these topics—of the prejudicing of ritual over inwardness—has distorted our understanding of them and led us to misread totally the biblical texts and to misinterpret their contextual significance. What is true of sacrifice and the temple is equally true of biblical notions of justice, in fact of almost every element of Old Testament theological exegesis. The supersessionist accounts of biblical justice remove the social dimensions of kith and kin, tribe and clan, locality and history, truth and traditions from discrete discussions of justice. The community is always an already existing fact and is to be made righteous or holy; but when there is no community per se there are only actors and agents forging links between individuals and often contingent groups. Restorative justice advocates are right that crime is a collective responsibility—but it is not any collective, but an actual community linked by memory, familial ties and experience. When Jesus talks of the "good Samaritan," it is not any Samaritan but a person concretely encountered within the context of a lived and experienced community. There is an extensive rabbinic literature on the *ger toshav*, the resident alien. Rather than understand Jesus to be superseding Jewish "ethnic" identity in favour of a Christian universalism, we might more accurately read this as the need to extend community to all those who live among us. This is a much more modest claim, but one that accords with the literature of the time and refuses to depart from a concrete communal context.

What is wrong with supersessionism is that it distorts and prematurely theologizes the specifics of the different models of Old Testament justice so that the richness cannot be recovered, so that instead of guiding situations within and between communities we seek and get a formula to be applied in a radically different context in a deracinated, de-territorialized and de-contextualized fashion where assumptions about community can be problematic. The dynamic nature of life, with its rituals and practices, as depicted in the Old Testament is filled with crisis situations—political, economic and spiritual—and has much to offer those reflecting on contemporary life. Dorothee Sölle wrote about suffering and loss that only after acknowledging the irreparability of loss, the impossibility of vengeance and finally being freed of the burden of finding meaning in what had taken place, only then did the will to live take over and the healing begin (Sölle 1975).

Ed Conrad's warnings about premature biblical theology are most apposite here as we retrieve meaning from our ancient texts by critically distancing them from our theologies, and by developing readings in this creative gap that in turn impact upon our theologies, as we struggle with concerns shared, such as justice, across time and concrete and implied communities.

A WEB OF FASCINATION:
MARXISM AND THE BIBLE

Roland Boer

What I propose to do here is explore a fascination of mine, namely the relationship between Marxism and the Bible.[1] In fact, my own enthralment is but a product of their mutual fascination with each other. For Marxists cannot quite seem to put the Bible behind them, and biblical scholars often have a distinct affinity for Marxism. So what I offer is a synopsis of the history of that relationship in order to dispel some ignorance, offer some critical assessment of the current situation and ponder what the future might hold.

I have organized my discussions in three sections, although there are myriad overlaps between them: I begin with various uses Marxists have made and continue to make of the Bible, the underlying motive being the search for political insights and models. From there I consider the contributions various Marxist studies have made or in fact have the potential to make to biblical studies (and there is some work that needs to be done here). Finally, I track, somewhat critically, the uses biblical critics have made of Marxist methods in dealing both with ancient literary texts and the political and economic context of those texts.

Back to the Classics

It is worth beginning with what is in fact a commonplace, namely that Marx and Engels knew their Bibles rather well. Apart from Engels' early Christian commitment that he relinquished with much anguish (Marx and Engels 1975, 2:121–22, 155–58, 189–264, 313–51), I content myself with one instance, before passing on to Marx's strongest (potential)

---

1. In doing so, I draw inspiration from Ed Conrad's own enthusiasm for new approaches to the Bible.

contribution to biblical studies. If you dare to venture past the well-known first chapter on Feuerbach in the early sections of *The German Ideology* (Marx and Engels 1976, 5:19–581), the section that staked out the first somewhat rough outlines for historical materialism, and move into the endless tight pages on Bauer and Stirner, then you will notice that the very structure of the critique owes itself to the Bible. Dubbed "Saint Bruno" and "Saint Max," Marx and Engels pepper their critique with biblical quotes and wheel out one biblical theme after another to argue that both Bauer and Stirner offer a barely concealed theology in their reading of Hegel. But perhaps my favourite section is that third chapter on Max Stirner, organized in terms of the books of the Bible. Thus, we find the first section entitled "The Old Testament: Man" and the second "The New Testament: Ego." Both have a discussion of the "economy" of the testaments. While Genesis is favoured in the first section, the Gospel of John the Divine becomes the preferred focus of the second, and the whole closes with "Solomon's Song of Songs or the Unique." Not averse to some delightful satire, Marx and Engels pull apart Bauer's spiritualist appropriation of Hegel, but they do so by invoking the Bible in depth. And this was not the last time the Bible appears in their work, for any patient reading of *Capital* (Marx and Engels 1975, vol. 35), for instance, will uncover one allusion after another to biblical motifs.

Paradoxically, however, the most important contribution to biblical studies comes precisely in a discussion that does not acknowledge the Bible, except in passing, and that is the controversial section on the Asiatic mode of production in the *Grundrisse* (1973). Here Marx outlines the various features of perhaps the most contested and controversial mode of production: the production of wealth through tribute, an overarching bureaucracy based in the imperial centre, a static political and economic structure, the *corvée* or periodic labour in the service of the state by citizens, and a centripetal focus on that infamous "oriental despot." Here is Marx: "A part of their surplus labor belongs to the higher community, which exists ultimately as a *person*, and this surplus labor takes on the form of tribute etc., as well as of common labor for the exaltation of the unity, partly of the despot, partly of the imagined clan-being, the god" (Marx 1973, 473 [emphasis in original]). Marx's major concern was to analyse British colonial rule in India, but later he ceased to mention the Asiatic mode of production, particularly because he was less enthusiastic about the ability of British colonialism to break the stagnation they saw in Indian economies (see Ghosh 1984, 39–53).

For some parts of biblical studies, this section of the *Grundrisse* has become a crucial text, and I want to flag that issue here, for it will return later in this essay. Barely reconstructed as the "tributary" mode of production, its basic features in biblical studies are as follows. The basic means of production involved the various techniques associated with widespread hand-tooled agriculture and domesticated animals. Any new developments in technology were directed towards agriculture—improved quality of implement metal, or irrigation, and so on. The relations of production involved a multitude of small landholders who paid tribute to various layers of a significant bureaucracy, at a local, "national" and imperial level. At the top of the bureaucracy is the imperial centre— Babylon, Egypt, Asshur, etc.—where the tribute is lavished upon a standing army (used to ensure the regular payment of tribute and to increase the empire), buildings of imperial government and religion, and the relatively large number of officials required to keep the system running. Politically, the concentration and reorganization of power necessary for the formation of a state followed remarkably similar patterns: the gradual differentiation of wealth and power and their concentration in certain individuals, usually called chieftains, and then the elevation of such chieftains into kings of various types as the state became more complex and established. Based on constant conflict and efforts to overcome one's neighbours, the states of the ancient Near East did not, for instance, operate by means of oligarchies or citizen assemblies (as in Greece) or a senate (as in Rome). And this pattern also applied to the smaller states such as Moab, Ammon, Phoenicia and Judah, which merely struggled to replicate the patterns of the larger imperial states. Culturally and ideologically, religion or the sacred was the central language for expressing political, philosophical, juridical and political control (except that it is a little anachronistic to put it this way). The production of space in the Asiatic mode of production depended upon the layering of tribute payments enforced upon the peasants: there were very few centres of bureaucracy (i.e. the ancient "city") towards which all tribute was directed, followed by the subservience of even these spaces to a larger centre, of which the smaller centres seem like various points on the spokes of a wheel. Spatial practice was then focused upon the flow towards and away from the centres, and this movement was inextricably tied up with the religious centralization in the places of power and their status as the destination of tribute. Domestic space was then ordered in terms of the need to maintain such a system, while the family unit was a much larger entity, focused on ensuring that enough was produced to survive and pay tribute. This familial situation necessitated having as many children as possible with the presence of multiple generations, all co-existing in basic four-roomed dwellings (including cohabitation with animals), resulting in a life-span that did not get one much past the early thirties.

The catch with all of this is that the first full-length Marxist study of the Bible—Karl Kautsky's *Foundations of Christianity*—studiously avoids the Asiatic mode of production in his discussion of ancient Israel, which had fallen somewhat out of favour by the time he wrote in 1908. Its absence is all the more marked when we note that he is quite comfortable with the Ancient or slave-based mode of production in speaking of the Hellenistic context of the early Christian community. Yet, this extraordinary and unfortunately neglected text offers a thorough history of the Bible in its political and economic context, with a sweep that ends with the early Christian Church. Kautsky is probably most remembered for his claim that the early Christian community, beginning with Jesus and then reflected in the Acts of the Apostles (2:42–45; 4:32–35), was a communist one. And he was not the only one to do so, for at the same moment Rosa Luxemburg in her *Socialism and the Churches* (1970) takes a similar line. Although neither one cites the other, one can assume some cross-over between them, given that they were long-time associates, if not occasionally friends. Luxemburg uses the same verses from the Acts of the Apostles, but, unlike Kautsky, traces the gradual dissolution of the theme in a brief sketch of the history of the Church. Although the idea was kept alive by some of the early Church leaders, such as John Chrysostom, her polemic is directed at the current state of the Church, its enmeshment with the state and its thoroughly conservative politics and the way it has betrayed its origins. The deeper problem, however, is that with the communism of goods we have merely the communal ownership of products. In the end, such an approach is unsustainable since it does not address the issue of production itself.

Both studies pay a re-reading, although Kautsky's is more thorough. Some of the issues he raises—such as the economic patterns of agriculture, labour, land, latifundialization and the internal tensions and contradictions of the economic systems—are very much current issues (even if they have in part been reinvented). Not only does he make use of all of the major ancient sources, such as Josephus, Pliny and Tertullian, but he refers to some of the great biblical scholars of the time— Wellhausen and von Harnack stand out, names that are still important in biblical studies. At times he has a tendency to rely on biblical sources to reconstruct his history, but in that respect he is not different from other scholars at the turn of the nineteenth century. And his motivation? "Whatever one's position may be with respect to Christianity, it certainly must be recognized as one of the most titanic phenomena in all human

history… Anything that helps us to understand this colossal phenomenon, including the study of its origin, is of great and immediate practical
significance, even though it takes us back thousands of years" (Kautsky
2007, 1).

Western Marxism

Already the trajectories begin to run in a number of directions, but rather
than follow them all at once I will keep my focus on Marxist encounters
with the Bible, looping back later to pick up some of the other issues,
particularly that of modes of production. The great link from the earlier
phase of Marxist work on the Bible must be Ernst Bloch: indeed, if we
substitute "Bible" for "Christianity" in the quotation from Kautsky a few
lines above, then it would give voice to Bloch's underlying motivation
for finding it one of the great sources of inspiration for his own work.
Although I should stretch this motivation a little further: for Bloch the
Bible formed the worldview of so many people—workers and peasants—
who were at the centre of the communist project in Eastern Europe.
Rather than discard the Bible, he argued that communism needed to
understand its revolutionary drive.

Along with Walter Benjamin and Theodor Adorno, Bloch may be
numbered among those Western Marxists who reflected at some length
on the Bible, in contrast to Althusser, Lefebvre, Gramsci and Lukács
who concerned themselves with theology and ecclesiology (see further
Boer 2007). But these engagements take some distinctly different tracks
from those of Marx, Engels and Kautsky. For Bloch, Benjamin and
Adorno are concerned more with the issues of myth and its discernment,
as well as Adorno's crucial category of theological suspicion. On one
side, my concern is with the function of the Bible in the frame of their
work as a whole. Thus, the over-riding drive for Bloch and Benjamin is
to use the Bible as a resource, however complex their engagements might
be, for rethinking certain problems within Marxism, of which the underlying one would have to be the search for a way to break out of capitalism. Adorno's encounter is a little more ambiguous than this, drawing
deeply on the Bible while developing a critique that is of relevance for
biblical studies itself.

But let me stay with Bloch, who, along with Kautsky, is one of the
few Marxists to have written a book on the Bible, the little-read *Atheism
in Christianity* (1972). Here he undertakes a distinctly Marxist introduction to the Bible suffused with his own distinct agenda, namely to
discern the thread of subversion within the Bible. He identifies a logic

there of rebellion against overlords and oppression, marked most strongly by the drive to overturn the God of the oppressors. And that logic leads eventually to a protest atheism that enables the emergence of the human once God has faded from the scene—hence the "atheism" within Christianity. As part of this agenda, Bloch focuses on myth, which I find one of the most promising elements of his work. For Bloch, myth is neither a pure false consciousness that needs to be unmasked, nor a positive force without qualification. All myths, like ideologies, no matter how repressive, have an emancipatory-utopian dimension about them that cannot be separated so easily from deception and illusion. Thus, in the very process of manipulation and domination, myth also has a moment of utopian residue, an element that opens up other possibilities at the very point of failure. Bloch is particularly interested in biblical myth, for the subversive elements in the myths that interest him are enabled by the repressive ideologies that show through again and again.

Thus, Bloch asked of myths: Do they speak of transformation and liberation? Do they have cunning heroes who win through a ruse? But this requires some distinction within the broad category of myth, between the despotism and domination of myth proper and those that, like later fairy-tales, subvert such domination. The story of Prometheus in Greek mythology, or the serpent in Paradise in the Bible, give voice to this "fairy-tale" element in myth. Bloch would much prefer to keep both the conformist and non-comformist elements of myth rather than no myth at all, since the banishment of myth discards the "joyful message," the "deepest utopian theme" (1998, 300) of mythology along with all that is oppressive. He is, of course, trying to run myth through dialectics—"destroying and saving the myth in a single dialectical process" (1972, 37). At his best, Bloch's discernment of myth is an extraordinary approach, for it enables us to interpret the myths of the Bible as neither completely reprehensible nor utterly beneficial. That is to say, it is precisely through and because of the myths of dominance and despotism that those of cunning and non-conformism can be there too.

In contrast to Bloch, Benjamin's interaction with theology is a critical field worn down with many crossings, but as for the Bible there is far less commentary. Here I need to make a distinction well known in biblical studies but less so outside: against the annoying assumption that biblical studies is a subset of theology, a position reiterated ad nauseam mostly by theologians but even by those who should know better such as Paul Ricoeur (2000), biblical studies is a distinct discipline that is really a subset of literary criticism rather than theology.

At the heart of Benjamin's intriguing and idiosyncratic appropriation of the Bible lies his failed effort to use the Bible in order to develop a way to break out of the mythic hell of capitalism. He does so by drawing on the final or anagogic level of the old allegorical mode of biblical interpretation, with its vast schema that runs from creation to eschaton. Thus, in the extraordinarily influential last chapter of *The Origin of German Tragic Drama* (1998) Benjamin offers a deep reworking of the fourfold medieval allegorical schema—literal, allegorical, moral and anagogic—to argue that in the Baroque mourning plays we find the marks of a fundamentally Christian mode of exegesis that is possible only with the Fall. For in a fallen world only ruins and traces remain of the pre-lapsarian world; allegory then becomes the means of a failed deciphering of salvation in those ruins. If in the *Trauerspiel* book Benjamin sets his sights on simultaneously describing and developing a theory of allegory, then in *The Arcades Project* (1999) he would come to use the method itself in all its fragmentary and broken form—hence the curious status of the work as a vast collection of quotations and commentary.

Let me focus on the anagogic level of allegory—that curious and sophisticated mode that characterized more than a millennium of interpretation—and pick up first his earlier concern with the point of origin, particularly the first chapters of Genesis. Thus, in "On Language as Such and the Language of Man" he juxtaposes Gen 1–3 and 10 (the story of Babel) to argue for pure language. This is none other than the language of the name—the first language is Adam's naming of the animals in Gen 2—in which man communicates with God in and not through language (Benjamin 1996, 65). Such a language, however, remains lost, having fallen into the "prattle" (*Geschwätz*), the over-riding concern with bourgeois communication, that Benjamin reads into and out of the confusion of languages in the Babel story. And it is this pure language, primordial and harmonious, for which translation strives in its push towards the eschatological moment in which pure language will be restored (1996, 253–63).

Already the juxtaposition of creation and eschaton is manifest, but he will shift his focus decidedly towards the latter in *The Arcades Project* (*Passagenarbeit*). Here this "inveterate adversary of myth" (Wohlfarth 1997, 67) focuses his energy on various ways of thinking through the break from the mythic hell and dream-work of capitalism, represented in its most advanced and decayed form in the Paris of the nineteenth century.[2] He does so by means of the dialectical image, the caesura of the

---

2. As a general introduction to *The Arcades Project*, nothing surpasses that by Tiedemann (1991).

explosion out of history, waking from a dream. Yet the mark of his failure in this project lies in the very language he uses. For he resorts, as has been well noted in feminist criticism of Benjamin, to sexual language, particularly in terms of women and maternal functions. But this language is precisely that of the biblical myths of creation and eschaton. Even when he does not explicitly invoke the Bible in his writing, the mark of the Bible's presence in his texts is where they overflow with the language of sexuality, the gendered text, women as mythical other and the incessant repetition of birthing metaphors. In other words, at the point where he seeks a way to think through the breach in the myth of capitalism he reverts to biblical myths, especially those of Genesis and the eschaton, a reversion marked by the language of giving birth.

However, in this failure, in this reversion to myth in the effort to rupture myth itself, Benjamin unwittingly provides a way of rethinking the category of myth in both politics and biblical studies. In his very use of myth it seems to me that Benjamin begins to imagine the possibility of the future not by taking terms from our present and projecting them into the future, but by working in reverse: the terms and concepts of a communist future, however degraded and partial they might be in our present perception and use of them, provide the way to think about that future itself. In other words, the very eschatology of the biblical myths themselves suggests that myth is one crucial way in which we might reach across the divide between a capitalist present and a communist future to draw terms from that future itself, however imperfect they might be. The problem, of course, is that if the future is as radically distinct—however gradual or sudden a transition might be—as Marxists like to think, then the very ways of thinking and arguing will also be qualitatively different. Here lies the reason for the unwitting insight of Benjamin's focus on myth: the inescapably mythic nature of the material with which Benjamin works—the narratives of creation and the messiah—suggest that the language of myth, with all its promises and dangers, provides one way of imagining a very different future.

Elsewhere I have argued that both Bloch and Benjamin are linchpins for a reconsideration of political myth for the Left, carrying on Georges Sorel's unfinished project. But any such project will require a decent dose of Adorno's theological suspicion. Along with his famous ban on images, these two items form the basis of his engagement with the Bible. The two are, of course, closely related, for the *Bilderverbot*—the ban on images drawn from the second commandment in Exod 20/Deut 5—has at its heart the criticism of idolatry that becomes crucial for Adorno's critique of secularized theology. The important texts here are the formidable but enticing *Kierkegaard: Construction of the Aesthetic* (1989),

The Jargon of Authenticity (1973) and the much more widely read *Dialectic of Enlightenment* (co-authored with Max Horkheimer, 2002).

Adorno would call on the ban on images, in its full dialectical glory, time and again in various areas of his work, from music criticism through aesthetics to reflections on utopia. In that famous passage from *Dialectic of Enlightenment*, Adorno and Horkheimer stress that the ban destroys myth and conciliates magic in the idea of God: "The Jewish religion... places all hope in the *prohibition on invoking falsity as God, the finite as the infinite, the lie as truth*" (2002, 17 [emphasis in original]). Already we can see the implications for utopia and philosophy with their focus on the dialectic of rejecting falsity, finitude, lies and indeed belief itself that comes in the way of salvation. But what I want to do here is peddle backwards for a moment to the second commandment itself in order to clarify the logic of idolatry that lies behind Adorno's appropriation.

Here we find a prohibition on making (*ʿsh*) any hewn or cut image (*pesel*). Just to ensure that the ban is comprehensive, the commandment specifies that the image should not be in the form (*temunah*) of anything in the heavens, on earth or in the seas beneath the earth. More importantly, however, it follows the first commandment, "you shall not have other gods before my face" (Exod 20:3; my translation): neither gods in the first nor their images in the second commandment, not even an image of the Hebrew god Yahweh. In the slippage between god and image we find the bite of the polemic against idolatry, for the catch is that once we disconnect the image from its referent (god), *the image itself becomes a "god," an idol in place of god.* I want to focus on two uses by Adorno of this logic, namely the critique of the personality cult and theological suspicion itself.

As for the former, the dialectic of christology, simply put, enables the personality cult: only through the logic of the God-human, that is Christ, does it become possible to raise another human being to divine status. In other words, precisely because God becomes a human being in Jesus Christ (if we push the divinity far enough we end up with the very human Christ and vice versa) can a human being become god—not just Christ, but any human being. Not merely a critique of the theological underpinnings of a consistent problem for the Left, this argument also becomes part of the larger agenda of theological suspicion. And that suspicion emerges with great force in the demolition job on Kierkegaard. "All I leave is a memory" might have been Adorno's slogan, for time and again he pounds Kierkegaard's effort to construct a philosophical system based on theology. That system rattles to pieces on either the irresolvable paradoxes that fail to become dialectical or the historical conditions of Kierkegaard's work. In a different vein, theological suspicion also appears in the criticism of secularized theology in *The Jargon of Authenticity*. Here, in his attacks on both liberal theology and philosophy that is a barely concealed secularized theology, Adorno argues that the danger lies in the smuggled structures of authority that come with the terms now emptied of their theological content. In short, such moves risk the idolatry identified in the ban on images.

Alongside the reassessments of myth that come from Bloch and Benjamin, it seems to me that Adorno's theological suspicion is crucial for biblical studies and Marxist thought. For the latter the danger of secularized theology remains, as we will see. For the former, Adorno reminds us that the Bible and theology are the most uneasy of associates. for the fractious and disparate texts of the Bible were gathered and colonized under protest by church and synagogue. Any biblical inter-pretation, in fact, needs to operate with a perpetual theological suspicion to prevent the text dissolving into theology.

Neo-Paulinism, or, After Western Marxism?

Beneath the diversity of the tracks I have followed until now, from Kautsky's argument for early Christian communism to Adorno's ban on images, there are two discernable patterns. The first seeks to understand the Bible in distinctly Marxist terms. The Bible then becomes something of a case study, not least because of its status as sacred scripture within church and synagogue. And the second engages in the more ambiguous task of locating possible political insights, of generating, if you will, thoroughly secularized motifs for political struggle. Although the two run closely together in Bloch's work, the second agenda lies at the centre of those who come after the close of Western Marxism with Adorno. And yet, Adorno's warning about the danger of secularized theology hangs over this new work, which may be called, following Alberto Moreiras, neo-Paulinism (2004).

What do we find in this new moment, characterized as it is by a curious vibrancy of Marxism whose paradoxical mark seems to be a widespread sense of crisis and downturn? A situation marked simultaneously by a focus on a particular section of the Bible—the letters of Paul and the New Testament more generally—and by a notable caesura from the earlier deliberations of Western Marxism on the Bible. Agamben is, of course, the exception here, but such a lack of connection becomes all the more curious in light of the similarity of the underlying drive that I identified in the preceding paragraph: namely the search for viable political models from the Bible.

Thus, with the closing down of believable and viable models for revolutionary politics, especially the figure of Lenin, Alain Badiou and Slavoj Žižek look to St. Paul (or rather, Paul, since we really need to dispense with the "Saint") in the New Testament. Paul is in this case Jesus' Lenin, the one who codified and brought to fruition the revolutionary implications of the charismatic founder. What Badiou (2003) attempts to do with Paul is materialize or laicize his central doctrine of grace, and that grace is none other than the unverifiable fable of Christ's resurrection. As grace, this assertion is necessarily a fable, one that is outside all of the canons of cause and effect. But Badiou is actually interested not in the resurrection itself but Paul's experience and naming of the event, a process he identifies as the Truth-Event. For in naming this event, Paul establishes a militant group characterized by fidelity to the event, love and a confident hope. Paul is then the militant *par excellence*, one who writes occasional pieces (epistles) while on the run, constantly organizing, making up policy on the run and thereby bringing into being a vast movement. In terms of Badiou's own philosophy of being and event, Paul's fundamental philosophical achievement is to found a notion of the universal by means of a contingent and specific moment, a universal that is thereby democratized and made available for any human being (Badiou's background in mathematics comes to the fore here, especially the breakthrough of Godel and Cohen and the possibility of multiple complete sets of universals [see Hallward 2003, 323–48]). Or, to put it in more political terms, Paul enables a constitution of the political subject whose basis is not the inclusion of an individual within a political process, but rather the constitution of the subject as an exception (i.e. by means of grace).

Now, despite Badiou's neglect of the earlier heavy political import of Paul's texts, especially the explosive epistle to the Romans in the context of the Reformation, or even the neo-orthodoxy of Karl Barth, I must admit to being quite taken with Badiou's reading of Paul, especially the necessary fable at the heart of any political movement, which may in many respects be seen as carrying on Sorel's call for an underlying political myth on the Left. I am much less enamoured with the efforts of Slavoj Žižek and Terry Eagleton. Although Žižek, following Badiou's cue, eventually works his way to a materialist grace at the close of the final book of his "Christian" trilogy, he finds that he must leave his beloved Jacques Lacan by the side of the road, however reluctantly and temporarily. What I find in these three books—*The Fragile Absolute* (2000), *On Belief* (2001) and *The Puppet and the Dwarf* (2003)—along with his earlier engagement with both Badiou and Paul in *The Ticklish Subject* (1999) is that Žižek works his way through Paul in order to become a political writer. That is, his explicitly Leninist position can only emerge through the New Testament: Lenin's absolute freedom is indeed the political expression of grace. The problem is that Žižek lumps such a reading of grace in with Christian love and ethics: love, especially that espoused in the famous passage of 1 Cor 13, becomes one with grace in a fashion that is thoroughly alien to Paul. If anything, as Badiou points out, love follows as a response to grace. And when Žižek throws ethics into the mix, we have a Roman Catholic notion of grace that is far from the irruption that Badiou emphasizes as the key to Paul's position. To be fair to Žižek, he does move beyond this to a starker and more political notion of grace in the closing pages of *On Belief* and *The Puppet and the Dwarf*, but in the latter book he calls upon a messianism reminiscent of Benjamin that then becomes subject to the criticism of redeemer figures (or the personality cult) I drew earlier from Adorno's theological suspicion.

Although I find some of these moves problematic for reasons at which I can only point, I must admit to finding Žižek's work thoroughly intriguing. It is just that, on Paul, Badiou is a better read. As is well known, Eagleton too is a pleasure to read, but the recent return to his theological roots in the Catholic Left of the 1960s and early 1970s has all the problems associated with an emphasis on both Christology and ethics. Although these reflections are scattered over a number of recent works, especially *The Gatekeeper* (2001), *Figures of Dissent* (2003a) and *After Theory* (2003c), the most sustained moments may be found in *Reason, Faith and Revolution* (2009a), *Trouble With Strangers* (2009b), *On Evil* (2010) and the final chapter of the book on tragedy, *Sweet Violence* (2003b). In a chapter that is a lightly revised version, more than three decades later, of the final chapter of his last theological book, *The Body as Language* (1970), Eagleton finds that the great value of the story of Christ's death is that he becomes the scapegoat or scandal. He locates echoes in other literature from ancient Greece through to contemporary fiction, but the key lies in the political model of identity with the outcast and rejected—for Eagleton the majority of today's global population—and then their overcoming of oppression that is modelled on the resurrection. While Eagleton no longer believes in such doctrines, he finds much political value in the paradigm itself as well as Christ's teaching: Jesus Christ becomes the well-known political messiah with a revolutionary ethics. It matters less that this is not particularly new. But what is more problematic, especially in light of Adorno's criticism of the personality cult, is that Eagleton returns squarely to a redeemer figure, in this case perhaps the central redeemer figure in Western culture.

I am tempted to invoke the analogy of the Gospels in the New Testament to the relations between Badiou, Žižek, Eagleton and Agamben: if the first three are the synoptics, connected to each other in complex patterns of dependence and independence, then Giorgio Agamben is St. John, a voice separate from Matthew, Mark and Luke, yet one that covers very similar territory. A new wave of critical work has begun to follow the English translation of *Il tempo che resta* (2005 [Italian 2000]; see also Agamben 2004). In contrast to the others, Agamben engages directly with the earlier moments of Western Marxist appropriations of the Bible, specifically Benjamin's notion of the messianic, which he interprets in two senses, one in terms of time and the other in terms of act. As for the question of time, he argues that messianic time is a suspended moment (*kairos*) between an instant of chronological time and its fulfilment. This moment in between is the "time that remains" until the end of the current political order. As far as the messianic act is concerned, Agamben argues that it deactivates the law in order to pump up its potentiality so that it may be fulfilled—a little like a footballer who is rested in the middle of the game so that he may come on in the last minutes.

There are two problems with Agamben's argument, it seems to me, and they concern his understanding of the term "messianic" and his focus on the law. First, as a paradigm of the political, Agamben sets the messianic up as a distinct category, and yet for all his efforts he cannot avoid its christological associations. The most telling moment is when he translates the Greek *Iesous Christos* as "Jesus Messiah." Second, Agamben's resolute focus on the law—so much so that Paul becomes a thinker of the law and the messianic deals mainly with the law—means that he has little room for grace. On this matter he couldn't be further from Badiou: in the great divide of Paul's thought, one sides with law and the other with grace. I must admit to preferring the political possibilities of Badiou's materialist grace, especially the unexpected political moment that breaks into the current order, than Agamben's concern with a fulfilled messianic law.

Agamben's other great concern has more mileage. I refer here to his emphasis on the remnant rather than Badiou's universal. For Agamben, Paul uniquely carries through a series of distinctions that when layered over one another begin to break down and cut across conventional distinctions. Thus, when we look at the way Paul operates, juxtaposing wisdom and foolishness, spirit and letter, law and grace, Jew and Greek, male and female, slave and free, then we end up with the remnant, a division of existing divisions, those left over after all of the distinctions have done their work. Except of course that the remnant is crucial in some Hebrew Bible texts, especially among the prophets. They are the few who, through no merit of their own, remain after all of the destruction has done its work and thereby come to represent the whole. Not so much the revolutionary vanguard as that bewildered leftover, the remnant comprises the least worthy of any group which then becomes the locus of unexpected possibilities.

Although I have concerned myself in this section with the search for viable political models in the pages of the New Testament, preferring Badiou's focus on the rupture of a materialized grace or Agamben's concern with the remnant, there is also a distinct contribution they can make to biblical scholarship itself. And that is quite specifically the radically political nature of Paul's texts that runs against the overly benign and liberal readings of Paul by New Testament scholars as the great and somewhat comfortable institutionalizer. All of which should really come as no surprise, since Paul's texts have been at the centre of political debate before—the Reformation and the fundamental political reorganization of Europe is but the most telling example.

Marxism and the Ancient World

I want now to shift my focus, albeit gradually, away from the use that sundry Marxists have made of the Bible for political insights and possibilities and consider the contributions that Marxism has made to biblical studies (both potential and actual). I begin with some sporadic studies of the ancient world, specifically those of G. E. M. de Ste. Croix and Perry Anderson's *Passages from Antiquity to Feudalism* (1974). If Ste. Croix's book, *Class Struggle in the Ancient Greek World* (1981), has been largely forgotten in Marxist debate and neglected in Classics, then Anderson's book is more well known. Ste. Croix sought to apply orthodox Marxist categories such as class and class conflict to ancient Greece. His work cries out for incorporation into current discussions, even if its conclusions need some concretization of abstract Marxist categories. For the problem that he shows up is the danger of applying categories abstracted in the analysis of capitalism to a non-capitalist system. Unfortunately biblical criticism carries on this tendency, merely shifting terminology slightly while holding onto the basic terms of class and so on. I will return to this question later, but let me shift to Anderson's study.

His concern is with another staple of Marxist analysis, namely the tension between and transition from one mode of production to another, from the Ancient or slave-based mode of production to feudalism. Given the differences between the two, Anderson tracks the way feudalism arises over time from the intersections between Roman slavery and

Germanic tribal structures in which the Roman *servus* becomes the feudal serf and the rest of the feudal hierarchy arises. Yet these relations of production are but part of a more fundamental shift in the mode of production in which the extraction of surplus value moves from the vital role of the ubiquitous slaves (only slaves in fact "worked") to that of the serfs, indentured to the lord but no longer "owned" by him. A major element of Anderson's analysis is to show how the specificity of European feudalism led to capitalism, while the very different history of the East (his comparison) did not. The problem with Anderson's analysis is that we do in fact have two test cases: while China did not move from feudalism to capitalism for specific reasons (it closed down at the crucial moment where, from a position of great wealth and influence, it may well have surpassed Europe), Japan did in fact move onto capitalism from a feudal structure.

Apart from the pressing need for more Marxist analysis of the ancient world, I want also to ask what the interest might be for biblical studies. Ste. Croix's work is directly relevant for New Testament studies, embedded as the New Testament is in the intersection between the Hellenistic world and the ancient Near East. But so also is Anderson's text, particularly his considerations of what is still called in many circles the Ancient or slave-based mode of production, for this is the dominant mode under which the New Testament came together.[3]

Here Come the Russians

This somewhat sporadic work on the ancient world by Western Marxists now needs, belatedly, to come into contact with a long and lively tradition of critical reflection in Soviet-era Russia. Much of this work has been unavailable since it remained untranslated, but it was also dismissed in the context of the Cold War (see especially Dunn 1981). Here the debates, based on the ever-new archaeological data from the ancient Near East, turned over the relations between the Asiatic, Ancient and feudal modes of production as the best descriptors of political economy in Greece and the ancient Near East. Some, such as D'iakonov, whose work has been translated, argued for a long time that the economic system of the ancient Near East was in fact a form or mode of feudalism, the same mode of production found in China (see D'iakonov 1969, 1987). In the later years of his life he felt that feudalism was inadequate

---

3. The studies of slavery in the New Testament tend to make use of comparative data from slavery in the United States. See, for example, Callahan (1998) and Harrill (2006).

and argued for two phases, Early Antiquity and Imperial Antiquity, with their big economies based on the labour of indentured labour, or what he calls "helots," the formation of states and then empires (the economic structures of which ensured a mutual give and take of resources), and the shifts in technology from copper to brass implements and weapons (D'iakonov 1999, 21–55). He defined his position over against two others, one that wanted to see the presence of slavery in the ancient Near East on par with that of the Ancient or slave-based mode of production of Greece and Rome (so Dandamaev 1984), and the other that wished to maintain the concept of an Asiatic mode of production. As Dunn argues, despite all the battering it received, the Asiatic mode of production has an uncanny knack of returning. And one of its proponents, although for polemical purposes, was Karl Wittfogel (1963), who argued for the viability of the Asiatic mode of production in terms of the need for and organization of irrigation. Wittfogel saw a conspiracy theory in Stalin's rejection (something that Dunn stresses hardly affected the debates), arguing that communism itself was the epitome of "oriental despotism" (an argument that rendered his approach palatable in the Cold War West).

All of this becomes immediately relevant to biblical studies, which has been undergoing something of its own modes of production controversy. To date I can list the familial or domestic mode of production (with thanks to Sahlins), the tributary mode of production and the clientalistic mode of production that have been postulated and remain very much alive in biblical studies. This is a crucial debate, not least because of the opposition to other positions that merely see a nascent capitalism as the context in which the Bible arose, but before I can get to that debate I need to make a brief detour through three other engagements with Marxism by biblical critics.

Liberation, Political and Materialist Exegesis

Of the three, the liberation and political theologies that emerged from the 1960s were initially of a more theological nature (which I always insist is a distinct discipline that perpetually seeks to colonize biblical studies). I will, however, begin with the small contribution from neither England (political theology) nor Latin America (liberation theology), but continental Europe. Fernando Belo's *A Materialist Reading of the Gospel of Mark* (1981) has always been something of a maverick in biblical scholarship.[4] Bringing together semiotics, structuralism and Marxism,

---

4. See the summary in Clevenot (1985).

Belo's great model is Roland Barthes's *S/Z*, a reading of Balzac that broke it down into a whole series of codes (hermeneutic, cultural, proairetic, semic, referential and symbolic). This is a distinctly literary reading—rather than the preferred sociological emphasis of most biblical critics working with Marxism—with a political bent: in the context of class conflict in first-century B.C.E. Palestine, Jesus becomes a political operator who challenges not so much the religious leaders of his time, but the Roman Imperial order on behalf of the powerless. Mark's passion narrative, with its focus on the death of Jesus, becomes a distinctly political account that registers the marks of empire on Jesus' body. And his resurrection asserts that this was one realm the Romans did not control, a mark of insurrection and source of hope for current subversion. While Belo's text is often cited, his inability to develop his insights in further work has left it resembling an inaccessible island, or perhaps a work well before its time, within New Testament scholarship.

Belo's book appeared in 1981, emerging from work in the 1970s, but if we push back a decade then we find that the movement and journal *Slant* was causing a stir in the Roman Catholic Church of a sixties England and liberation theology taking shape in both Americas. While Gustavo Gutiérrez's classic *The Theology of Liberation* was published in 1969, James Cone's *A Black Theology of Liberation* appeared in 1970 in North America and independently from the movements in Latin America. Leonardo and Clodovis Boff (1987) and Juan Luis Segundo (1985) followed Gutiérrez in what became an extremely well-known movement within and outside the various Churches, although most were Roman Catholic. While their arguments focused on giving distinctly economic and political tints to key Christian doctrines such as sin, grace, the incarnation, salvation and redemption, a significant number of biblical critics, such as Jorge Pixley (1987), Jose Miranda (1974, 1982), J. Severino Croatto (1981), and Elsa Tamez (1982) concerned themselves with the Bible.

In the work of these scholars, coming from a context of liberation and anti-colonial struggles throughout Latin America—Castro in Cuba, Allende in Chile, the Sandinistas in Nicaragua to name but a few—and the involvement of certain elements of the Roman Catholic Church with the peasants engaged in the struggles themselves, we find the same themes as those that emerged both in the circle around *Slant*, including the early texts of Terry Eagleton that I mentioned a little earlier, and the moves toward black liberation theology in North America, of which Cone's book was the key text. The scandal of the liberation theologians, as with *Slant* and Cone, was the conjunction of Marxism and theology.

And the result was an emphasis on God's preferential option for the poor, read in texts of both the Hebrew Bible and New Testament, the distinctly political elements of the Kingdom or Rule of God, the political and revolutionary dimensions of the Jesus movement, a revolutionary ethics and a critical engagement with major currents of Western thought. Although there is a good deal of systematic theology, especially in the work of Gutiérrez, Segundo and Cone, liberation theologians rely heavily on the Bible. The two foci of liberation theology have been and remain the narrative of the Exodus in the Hebrew Bible and the figure of Jesus Christ in the New Testament.

Yet, despite the hype, liberation theologians have always held Marxism at a distance, using its methods for analysing capitalism, the social, political and economic dimensions of oppression and exploitation. But they have maintained an ontological reserve, arguing that without some form of divine transcendence one cannot avoid fetishizing what is human. So, the only perspective that avoids idolatry, the raising of human beings or the products of human hands into the status of gods, is ontological transcendence itself. And this includes Marxism, the proletariat or indeed the leader of the movement. The significance of the political and liberation theologians is similar to that of Badiou and Agamben, namely that it is not so much a matter of "add Marxism and stir"; rather, this work showed and continues to show the inescapably *political* nature of these texts.

Marxist Biblical Critics in the New World Order

Of all these disparate trends—materialist, political and liberation exegesis, along with the Russians and occasional Marxists interested in the ancient world—liberation theology has been the most influential for those who work within the discipline of biblical criticism. This is particularly true for Itumeleng Mosala, Gerald West, Norman Gottwald and Richard Horsley. Mosala (1989), explicitly acknowledging the role of his approach in the struggle against apartheid in South Africa (he now holds a senior post in the ministry of education), seeks to apply Marxist categories of class and ideology to the traditional determination of sources in the books of Micah and Luke. In doing so he seeks to uncover the way questions of class, gender and race overlay each other in such sources. Some work has been done more explicitly with Marxist literary criticism and biblical texts, especially David Jobling (1991, 1992a, 1992b, 1998), Mark Sneed (2004) and my own work (1996, 1997, 2003, 2007). Whereas Jobling seeks to connect feminism, psychoanalysis and deconstruction for some of the most astute readings of the Hebrew Bible I have encountered, and Mark Sneed has offered a metacommentary of Qoheleth (Ecclesiastes) in light of Fredric Jameson's texts, my work has focused on the contributions of Marxist philosophers and literary critics from Adorno to Žižek.

However, what I will do for the remainder of this essay is draw nigh unto the other area where Marxism has become part of the fabric of biblical studies, namely in the social sciences. Here we find Norman Gottwald (1985, 1992, 1999), Gale Yee (2003), Ron Simkins (1999, 2004) and Mark Sneed (2004). In particular, my interest is in what might be called a biblical modes of production controversy, although it is less a heated debate than a warm encounter between friends. Here I link up again with my earlier discussions concerning mode of production, especially among the Russians, G. E. M. de Ste. Croix and Perry Anderson.

The narrative begins with Norman Gottwald's monumental *The Tribes of Yahweh*, first published in 1979: here he redefines the Asiatic mode of production as "tributary," arguing that at the turn of the first millennium B.C.E. emergent Israel overthrew the dominant "tributary" mode of production of the ruling Canaanites and established in the Judean hills a "communitarian" mode of production which he designates as more egalitarian and more cooperative than that from which it emerged. The monarchy subsequently saw a return to the "tributary" mode under pressure of the surrounding dominance of this mode. For Gottwald, the "communitarian" mode is the key, rising and falling from the moment of emergent "Israel" to the early Christian and Jewish practices of communal cooperation rather than domination over against both the residual "tributary" mode and newer slave-based mode of the Hellenistic world.

While a pioneering work in biblical studies, Gottwald also began a trend that is very much part of contemporary discussions. Not only did he retool the Asiatic mode of production as "tributary," but the "communitarian" mode is also a reworking of primitive communism, with some bits and pieces from tribal society and neolithic agriculture thrown in. Subsequently Carol Myers, in her *Discovering Eve* (1988), relied heavily on Gottwald but brought in Marshall Sahlins' notion (1968, 1972) of the familial or domestic mode of production in order to reshape Gottwald's communitarian mode. Myers was, however, working outside any Marxist framework (there is no mention of class conflict or ideology in her text), and yet the domestic mode of production has now been adopted by a range of biblical scholars, including David Jobling, Gale Yee and Ronald Simkins. I have argued elsewhere that such an argument may be traced back to the work of Engels, Lewis Henry Morgan, and J. J. Bachofen's troubled argument for a prior moment of matriarchy (Boer 2005c). But

Simkins has gone a step further, criticizing the Asiatic mode of production in light of Hindess and Hirst (1975) in order to outline a new theory of mode of production in monarchic Israel. For Hindess and Hirst, tribute is but another name for tax, and every mode of production has some form of tax: in other words, there is nothing unique about this mode of appropriating goods or surplus. Further, the absence of class, apart from the distinction between peasants and state functionaries, does not provide the mechanisms for the formation of the state, which requires divisions between various groups in society that are usually theorized in terms of class. The final criticism Simkins levels at the Asiatic mode of production in relation to ancient Israel is the issue of private property, since in the traditional terms of the Asiatic mode of production all ownership was in the hands of the state. Yet the notion of private property, particularly in terms of ancestral rights, appears in the Hebrew Bible, although this should be understood as proprietorship rather than the possession of things, private property in terms of rights which were divided between the state and individual peasants.

In light of these difficulties, Simkins proposes a different taxonomy for monarchic Israel, distinguishing between what has now become the commonplace (in biblical studies) domestic mode of production and a patron–client, or clientalistic, mode of production as the prime mode by which surplus was acquired, used and distributed, and by which social relations operated. This basic dyadic relation accounts, argues Simkins, not only for economic exchange but also the ideologies of reciprocity and societal structures (elite and peasants, king and people, Yahweh and the state) as well as unequal social relations in which the client relied on the patron for access to the means of production.

These arguments in biblical studies are torn in two directions (apart from the tendency to assume positions based on earlier scholarship): on the one hand, there is a clear desire to avoid applying various categories from Marxism in the fashion of a template, an effort to be sensitive to the peculiarities of the ancient Near East and the biblical text. On the other hand, we seem to be falling foul of a variation on the modes of production controversy that bedevilled Marxist economics in the 1970s and 1980s (see Foster-Carter 1978; Feiner 1986). For a time, the appearance of yet another vagary led to the suggestion of more and more modes of production until the term itself became meaningless. What is needed, it seems to me, is not only a revisiting of the Soviet debates, but also an intersection with other current forms of Marxist economic theory, such as the over-accumulation theories of Mandel and Wallerstein, but above all the Regulation School. But that is another task.

Conclusion

I am very much aware of the breaks and interruptions between various efforts to bring Marxism and the Bible into contact with each other. However, I want to draw three brief conclusions from this synopsis of the interaction between the two. First, over against the widespread refusal of religion among what we might call the secular Left, the Bible has been and remains a distinct source of inspiration for liberating and revolutionary movements, from Thomas Müntzer at least until present-day liberation theology (Hugo Chavez counts liberation theology among his greatest influences). We might picture it as a vast reservoir of utopian and liberating images and metaphors, often embodied in myths, that the Left ignores at its peril. Second, the catch with such uses of the Bible is that all too often they are surrounded by religious belief, matters of the gods and so forth. Such a position on the Bible is by no means necessary (and would have to be one of the strangest assumptions). At this point, it seems to me that Adorno's theological suspicion is a powerful tool. For what it enables is an engagement with the Bible while negating the historical tendency to reify its characters, especially the gods. Third, biblical critics that make use of Marxist methods often carry on their tasks in isolation from the wider community of Marxist scholars and activists. This situation has led to selective uses of Marxist ideas and methods, along with large areas of neglect such as Marxist literary theory. It also means that biblical critics simply do not notice when Marxists do in fact engage with the Bible, as with the recent spate of work by Badiou and Agamben. Ideally, what I would like to see is far more cross-fertilization between Marxist biblical scholars and other scholars on the Left.

DYING TO BRING HEAVEN DOWN TO EARTH: THE MOTHER OF MELCHIZEDEK AND MIRACULOUS, MESSIANIC MOTHERS IN THE BIBLE*

Michael Carden

The figure of Melchizedek has only a brief walk-on part in Genesis and yet he becomes an important figure in the Hebrew Bible, the New Testament and extra-biblically. In Ps 110, he is the archetype of a royal priesthood, attributed there to the Davidic kings. This psalm is of great importance to the New Testament and is quoted in Matt 22:4; Mark 12:36; Luke 20:42–43; Acts 2:34; Heb 1:13; 5:6; 6:20; 7:11, 17, 21; 10:13. Hebrews compares Jesus to Melchizedek, the latter prefiguring the former who is now the perpetual heavenly high priest. At Qumran, Melchizedek is portrayed as a heavenly being and savior figure who will appear at the imminent end of the age. The heavenly Melchizedek is a figure in some later Christian and Gnostic texts, where he is the Light Bearer, bringing the waters of baptism and even being equated to the Holy Spirit.

In some of these later texts, as a heavenly being, Melchizedek is without mother or father. On the other hand, many Rabbinic texts equate him with Shem (to subordinate him to Abraham), making his mother the wife of Noah. To counter later "Melchizidekian" Christian and Gnostic groups, some Christians adapted Jewish stories of Abraham, to shape tales of Melchizedek's birth and upbringing in a pagan family and his subsequent rejection of paganism for the One God, with a parallel intent to subordinate him to Abraham and, consequently, to Jesus (Robinson 1987). However, there is one text, *2 (Slavonic) Enoch*, in which there is a

* Thanks to my colleague, Julie Kelso, who read the penultimate draft of this essay and provided feedback enabling me to fine-tune some of my points. In this essay, I go for a walk with Luce Irigaray and end up at Sodom and Gomorrah. That's where I started with Ed Conrad and this shows just how many interconnected threads and themes can be traced from that story, as he suspected when he pointed me to this path.

remarkable account of the conception, birth and infancy of Melchizedek, not shaped by such agendas. Most striking is that Melchizedek is here conceived miraculously/asexually and born under miraculously macabre circumstances following the death of his mother. Indeed, the account explicitly links themes of miraculous motherhood with sexual transgression and its cost. Accused of immorality by her husband, Melchizedek's mother drops dead. He is subsequently born from her corpse.

In this essay, I will reflect upon the ways patterns of sexual transgression and the repression/appropriation of the maternal body are interwoven with the themes of miraculous (messianic) motherhood in *2 Enoch* and Genesis. Melchizedek's biblical debut in Genesis is framed by accounts of mothers whose pregnancies are miraculous (Sarah) and/or disreputable (Lot's daughters). Through her miraculous motherhood, Sarah becomes a new Eve, the progenetrix of Israel, a divinely chosen people, from whom will come the Davidic priest-kings of the order of Melchizedek. It could also be said of Lot's daughters that, by the incestuous rape of their father, they likewise initiate the Davidic line of the Messiah. The mother of Melchizedek resembles these women in that hers is a miraculous but clearly disreputable pregnancy by which she too becomes progenetrix to a priestly lineage culminating in a messianic figure.

A Mother Usurped—The Mother of Melchizedek in 2 Enoch

The date and provenance of *2 Enoch* are unknown. It is only preserved in Old Slavonic manuscripts (the oldest dating from the fourteenth century), of which only "a few…have the text in any degree of completeness," most of them supplying "only brief extracts…usually with drastic abbreviation or extensive reorganization" (Andersen 1983, 92). The text exists in both short and long recensions, not all of which include the Melchizedek story, although there is no evidence that it ever existed separately. Horton (1976, 81) regarded it as very late and did not include it in his study of ancient Melchizedekian traditions. However there now seems to be a scholarly consensus that would date *2 Enoch*, including the Melchizedek story, to the first century C.E. (Collins 1998, 243), probably prior to the destruction of the Temple in 70 (Böttrich 2001, 451). *2 Enoch* is structured in three parts: Enoch's ascent into the heavens and transformation into a heavenly being, his return to earth and instruction of his sons, the establishment of the cult under Methuselah. The Melchizedek story concludes the third part and is concerned with establishing the continuity of this antediluvian cult/priesthood perhaps to legitimate a "non-Levitical priesthood by making it predate the flood" (Bow 2000, 37).

The story concerns Sopanim/Sothonim,[1] who is wife to Nir, brother of Noah and priest in succession to Lamech and Methuselah. She is described as "sterile and never having given birth to a child by Nir" (*2 En.* [J] 71:1). Nevertheless, despite her sterility, she conceives miraculously, and in her old age, even though "Nir the priest had not slept with her, nor had he touched her, from the day the Lord had appointed him to conduct the liturgy" (*2 En.* [J] 71:2). Ashamed and embarrassed, she hides herself through most of her pregnancy. As the time of delivery drew near, "Nir remembered his wife and called her to his house" (*2 En.* [J] 71:4). She comes to him and, seeing her pregnant, he accuses her of adultery, telling her to "depart from me…so that I might not defile my hand on account of you" (*2 En.* [J] 71:6). She protests her innocence given her old age, saying, "I do not understand how my menopause and the barrenness of my womb have been reversed" (*2 En.* [J] 71:4).[2] Nir rejects her pleas and tells her to "(d)epart from me, or else I might assault you and commit a sin in front of the Lord" (*2 En.* [J] 71:8). Sopanim then falls at his feet and dies. Distressed, Nir goes to his brother for help. Noah consoles him that no one else knows of Sopanim's pregnancy and that her death was not from his hand. Together they resolve to bury her secretly, at which point the text says, "And a child came out from the dead Sopanim…he sat on the bed at her side" (*2 En.* [J] 71:18). This is no ordinary child. He has the physical development of a three-year-old; he speaks, blessing the Lord; he is clothed and wears "the badge of priesthood…on his chest, …glorious in appearance" (*2 En.* [J] 71:19). Returning for Sopanim's corpse, the brothers are first terrified by what they see but then declare "God is renewing the priesthood from blood related to us" (*2 En.* [J] 71:19). They name the child, dress it in priestly robes and feed it holy bread. Sopanim will now be buried publicly, "they washed her, and they clothed her in exceptionally bright garments, and they built a shrine for her" (*2 En.* [J] 71:22). Some time after the birth, Nir is told by the Lord that Melchizedek will be taken to the Paradise of Eden before the Flood where "he will be priest to all holy priests, head of the priests of the future," from whom will finally come "a great archpriest, the Word and Power of God" (*2 En.* [J] 71:29, 34). Nir blesses the Lord, saying,

---

1. Orlov (2000, 25–26) gives a number of possible meanings for both her name and her husband's derived from possible Hebrew originals. Sothonim could mean "end of afflictions/sorrows" or alternatively "hidden." Nir could mean "light/luminary," as befits his priestly status, or "clearing/breaking down the earth," making him a harbinger of the coming Deluge.

2. In the short recension she says, "I do not know how the indecency of my womb has conceived" (*2 En.* [A] 71:7).

> Blessed be the Lord, the God of my fathers, who has told me how he has
> made a great priest in my day, in the womb of Sapanim [*sic*], my wife.
>
> I had no child in this tribe who might become the great priest, but this is
> my son and your servant and you are the great God (*2 En.* [J] 71:30–31)

When Melchizedek is with Nir forty days, the Lord sends the archangel
Michael (Gabriel in the short recension) to fetch the child to Paradise/
Eden. In the long recension, Nir then dies and the story closes with Noah
being commissioned to build the ark.

While the story "proves that the idea of a supernatural conception was
not at all so strange in Early Jewish thinking" (Böttrich 2001, 462), the
circumstances of this pregnancy and birthing are morbidly bizarre and
disturbing. For Sopanim, her pregnancy is not a blessing but a curse that
brings about her death. The child in her womb is a cuckoo, his implanta-
tion being without her assent, without even the opportunity for her
assent. She experiences no Annunciation; no angels will speak with her.
Her womb has been usurped; she is nothing but a function, "a container
for the child" (Irigaray 1993, 41). And no angel will speak for her, either,
so she must hide in shame and fear. She knows that this "mysterious
conception leads, first of all, to the repudiation of the woman in the first
place" (Irigaray 1991, 164). At long last, when close to term, her time of
hiding is ended by her husband's summons. On seeing her, he reacts with
violent denunciation. His main concern is that he does not strike her and
sin against his Lord, the same Lord who has cuckolded him. In the face
of his threats and accusations, she protests her honor and integrity.
Finally she drops dead at his feet. Is death her only recourse to repudiate
the being within her, to refuse to give it birth? By her death, she both
denies consent to and explicitly reveals the inexorable process of the
"appropriation of woman's body by the father or his substitutes"
(Irigaray 1985, 189) that underpins the patriarchal social and metaphysical order. Explicitly revealing because her death cannot prevent it. The
child is born anyway, a monstrous prodigy that strikes Nir and Noah with
awe. But the death of she who was the vehicle for this heavenly being to
come to earth, necessitates their taking on the "maternal–female role"
(Irigaray 1991, 161). They wash him, clothe him, feed him and name
him. Only then is there an Annunciation—to Nir, who receives a vision
of the Lord telling him of the child's destiny. In Nir's hymn of praise—
his Magnificat?—he completes the appropriation of the maternal by
naming this child his son, by virtue of his ownership of the womb of
Sopanim, "my wife." Nir's assertion of paternal right, is consistent with
the patriarchal ideology of monogenesis whereby the male sows the seed
and the female (womb) is the field in which the seed is transformed and

from which it is then brought forth (Delaney 1991, 30–36). No other (earthly) male has violated Nir's womb/field, so by (patriarchal) rights, this child born of Sopanim is established in Nir's house as *his* son. "One kinship line submits to the other" (Irigaray 1991, 144).

Yet, ironically, by taking on the maternal–female role Nir is setting himself up for an appropriation, mimicking that which Sopanim endured. In the symbolic order, the world, the flesh, the material, is said to *represent* the realm of the feminine, while the divine, the heavenly, the spiritual *belongs* to the realm of the masculine (Conway 2003, 168). Nir himself will die and the Melchizedek child be taken up into the heavenly realm of the Father to be installed in the Paradise of Eden (womb?).

Eden Restored? Sarah's Motherhood and the Return of the Repressed

According to Beverly Bow (2000, 35), of "the five barren women in the Hebrew Bible, Sopanim most resembles Sarah." This resemblance is appropriate because the figure of Melchizedek first appears biblically in Genesis as a figure who blesses and receives tithes from Abraham, Sarah's husband. Melchizedek walks into (and out of) a saga of new beginnings involving miraculous motherhood, sexual transgression and the appropriation/repression of the maternal body. These elements are brought to bear around the question of progeny, ostensibly for Abraham, but in reality for Sarah. Like Sopanim, Sarah is both sterile and old. In the course of the saga, Abraham will have a son by Hagar and then six sons by Keturah. Therefore, Isaac will always be first and foremost Sarah's son, not Abraham's. Furthermore, Sarah is the one exception to Bow's assertion concerning those five barren women that "both biblical and postbiblical texts make plain that the woman's husband fathers her child" (2000, 35). Indeed, she is a sign that the "virgin-mother... is more ancient and more recent than the Father and the son" (Irigaray 1991, 171). Sarah's miraculous motherhood is an evocation of that primal maternal potency of Eden, that self-fecundating potent Earth (Gen 2:6) from whom is drawn the primal Adam.

Like Sopanim, too, Sarah's miraculous motherhood is marked out by sexual transgression. Not once but twice, her husband–brother passes her off to foreign potentates as his sister. On both occasions, the deity intervenes to protect Sarah from the attentions of strange men. By so doing, Sarah is marked as under divine protection. One of the problems of miraculous motherhood, made all too horribly plain in Sopanim's story, is that to an outside observer there is no difference between miraculous motherhood and illegitimate motherhood—ominously Sarah conceives and gives birth to Isaac following her encounter with Abimelech of Gerar. It is perhaps because of this dangerous proximity, that the narrative cannot let go of the sister–wife pattern but will play it again with Rebekah. But the pattern is changed in Rebekah's case as if to highlight Sarah's experiences as unique to her alone. Rebekah experiences no risk, she is not taken into Abimelech's household, no one else attempts to take her either. There is no divine intervention at all and her true status is only uncovered after the pair have been in Gerar "a long time" (Gen 26:8), after which Abimelech, looking out of the window, spots Isaac fondling Rebekah. The final difference, Rebekah is already a mother of twins.

Unlike Sopanim's story, Sarah's conception of Isaac is related in the text and in it the divine role is described in very concrete terms. The deity visits Sarah (Gen 21:1)—in the Hebrew the word used, *paqad*, can be translated as "visited" or "attended to/dealt with." In Rabbinic tradition, the word is read as "remembered," in line with other accounts of miraculous conceptions in the Hebrew scriptures (Gen 30:22; 1 Sam 1:19). However, the use of *paqad* here singles out Sarah from those other accounts where it is not employed. The deity visits Sarah and "did for Sarah as he had promised"—the Hebrew behind this doing can also have the meanings of "make" or "effect." Rabbinic exegesis has understood the following verse relating that Sarah conceives and then bears a son (Gen 21:2) as paralleling this one. Thus, her conception is to be read beside her being visited by the deity while Isaac's birth is what was done or effected for her through this visitation. Also remarkable about the Genesis account is the minimal role Abraham plays here. This absence is also found in both *Jubilees* and the *Zohar*. According to *Jubilees*, Isaac's conception is an event that involves only Sarah and the deity: "And in the middle of the sixth month the Lord visited Sarah and did unto her as He had spoken and she conceived. And she bare a son in the third month" (16:12–13). Similarly, in the *Zohar*, it is said, "Besides visiting Sarah, God also did something to her in the region on high" (1:115a). While Genesis then says that Abraham names and circumcises Isaac, it is actually Sarah, not Abraham, who speaks in vv. 6–7, using wordplays on laughter, the basis of Isaac's name.

Laughter is the response to both Annunciations—to Abraham and then to Sarah[3]—of Isaac's conception and birth. Sarah's laughter is the sign that she is listening, "(r)eceptive to the whole of the world" and responsive to "the breath of the spirit" that "overcomes walls dividing property"

---

3. Sopanim is denied an Annunciation, but one is granted post-natally to the pseudo-father (mother), Nir.

(Irigaray 1991, 180). Her Annunciation, in Gen 18, begins with Sarah securely out of sight, sequestered in Abraham's tent. Initially, the deity appears to accept this fact and proceeds as if this is another Annunciation to Abraham. However, the focus is clearly on Sarah alone. Abraham is told that when the deity returns Sarah shall have a son (not that Abraham will have a son borne to him). It is Sarah and Sarah alone who counts here. As the account progresses, Abraham's control over Sarah is broken down. On hearing the promise that she will have a child, Sarah laughs. The deity questions her reaction but does so by addressing Abraham, responding to Sarah via Abraham. Sarah then answers the deity directly and, in answer, the deity directly addresses her. What begins as an interaction between the deity and Abraham ends as an unmediated interaction between the deity and Sarah.

As noted above, both *Jubilees* and the much later *Zohar* infer Sarah's miraculous, virgin motherhood, but these themes can be found in other Jewish, Rabbinic and Christian texts. Philo of Alexandria specifically states in *Posterity and Flight of Cain* that, through her barrenness, Sarah has been changed into a virgin (*Post.* 134). Such restored virginity demonstrates for Philo that the deity will only converse with the soul when it has transcended its effeminate appetites and become like Sarah, "ranked once more as a pure virgin" (*Cherubim* 50). Most suggestively in relation to the conception of Isaac, Philo says of Sarah's laughter that it represents "a new act…sown by God in the whole soul for the birth of joy and great gladness, which…is called 'laughter'…'Isaac'" (*Quest. Gen.* 4.17, see also *Abraham* 206)—the allegory works because it fits the story's paradigm. In later Rabbinic tradition the birth of Isaac is accompanied by many prodigies—barren women conceive, women everywhere spontaneously and copiously lactate, the sick are healed and the blind and deaf regain sight and hearing. However, the greatest prodigies are associated with Sarah and Isaac themselves. Sarah gives birth without the pain of childbirth with which Eve was cursed.[4] She, too, lactates prodigiously and many children are brought to her to be nursed and are thereby blessed with righteousness. But the prodigy concerning Isaac relates directly to whether or not Abraham is his father, a matter of considerable anxiety in Rabbinic texts. As if to allay such anxieties, Jewish tradition says that Isaac's face was changed miraculously to be the exact copy of the elderly face of Abraham.

Sarah's miraculous "virgin" motherhood could, likewise, stand behind the reference to her in Heb 11:11. As Pieter van der Horst points out, this

---

4. Sarah's miraculous motherhood, therefore, becomes the restoration of the primal Eden, as befits this new beginning effected by the deity.

verse, which has greatly exercised many translators and commentators, literally seems "to say Sarah that received power to emit semen" (1996, 113). Drawing on a survey of ancient theories of embryology and reproduction, both Rabbinic and Gentile (1996, 117–33), he argues that the passage should be translated literally, that Sarah, through faith, received power to emit seed. In particular, he reads Heb 11:11 from the perspective of the duogenetic embryologies of both the Greek Hippocratic and later Rabbinic traditions that allowed for a two-seed model of reproduction, by which both the male and female emitted semen. He notes that in the Talmud the sex of the child was determined by whose semen was emitted first—if the mother, then the child is male, whereas, if the father, then a daughter is conceived (*b. Nid.* 31a, cited van der Horst 1996, 131–32). However, Heb 11:11 can just as easily be read the same way from a monogenetic standpoint, in which case, then, Sarah's faith gave her the power to emit semen and from that semen alone Isaac was conceived. From the monogenetic perspective, this Sarah clearly instantiates the self-fecundating Edenic earth in Gen 2:6.[5]

From the perspective of this miraculous motherhood, the Binding of Isaac is seen in a different light. As Bronner points out, the question has been regularly asked why was "Sarah…not consulted by her husband at the pivotal moment of Abraham's great test" (Bronner 2004, 7). According to Bronner, Jewish tradition has suggested that "Sarah's maternal love would overpower her religious responsibility" (2004, 7). Phyllis Trible declares that "patriarchy has denied Sarah her story, the opportunity for freedom and blessing" (Trible 1992, cited Bronner 2004, 8) because "Sarah more rightly should have been tested…as Isaac is truly her only son" (Bronner 2004, 8). But it is precisely because of this fact that Sarah is excluded. The Binding is the means by which Isaac is transformed from Sarah's son into Abraham's son, through the exercise of the patriarchal power of life and death[6] over the products of the Father's womb-fields, a power that is justified/valorized by being portrayed as a test of faith, as faithful submission to divine fiat. The logic of transformation/usurpation accounts for Rabbinic traditions in which Isaac

---

5. But is this the maternal "as imagined…within a male Imaginary universe" (Kelso 2003, 88)? Has Sarah become male, foreshadowing Jesus' promise to female disciples in *Thomas* 114:2–3? For Philo, Sarah's menopause/barrenness represents the control of the "female" aspects of the soul—"irrational…akin to bestial passions, fear, sorrow, pleasure and desire"—which "clearly belongs to minds full of Law" (*Quest. Gen.* 4.15). Such minds "resemble the male sex and overcome passions and rise above sense-pleasure and desire" (*Quest. Gen.* 4.15). Again, does the allegory work because it fits the paradigm?

6. Imitating the life-giving maternal wombpower of Male imagination?

barely survives Abraham's attempted sacrifice. By one account, when the knife of sacrifice miraculously dissolves under the tears of the angels, Abraham attempts to slay Isaac using his thumbnail. Whether with blade or thumbnail, another tradition says that Abraham still cuts Isaac, with the boy losing a considerable amount of blood. Other traditions speak of Isaac's soul leaving his body temporarily and another says that Isaac was actually killed and burnt on the altar but was miraculously reconstituted and restored to life. Avivah Zornberg goes as far as saying that the sole reality of Isaac's life is the dread fact of "his ashes…piled on the altar" (Zornberg 1995, 128). Reduced to ashes and reconstituted/offered on the altar, Isaac at last becomes Abraham's son.

The logic of this transformation/usurpation/appropriation requires that Sarah's death immediately follows the binding of Isaac, a narrative connection long recognized in Rabbinic traditions.[7] In various accounts, it is her horror at what Abraham has done that causes her death. Indeed, Abraham deliberately keeps his plans and actions hidden from Sarah. Sammael/Satan, in an effort to thwart Abraham's plans, exposes everything to her. By one account he comes to her and tells her that Isaac has been sacrificed and burnt upon the altar. According to Zornberg, he "paints for her the horror and pathos of an old, demented father actually killing a helplessly crying child" (1995, 124). Sarah begins to cry and wail and, giving three sobs and then three wails, she dies. In another account, Satan appears to her in the form of Isaac and relates to her what has happened. Sarah dies in horror, her only response being: "What has your father done to you?" (Zornberg 1995, 25). In a variant of this account, Isaac himself stands before Sarah and tells her everything. She dies in horror at the reality of what has transpired. Her death, like Sopanim's, is a protest, a "no!" to what happens.

When Daughters Speak—Clearing the Way?

When first we meet them, Lot's daughters are hidden inside the Father's domain, at the entrance to which stands the father confronting a rampaging mob, who demand access to his guests. In response Lot offers his daughters to this mob, perhaps as hostages to assure the good conduct of his guests, but more likely to be raped in place of his guests. By so doing, Lot demonstrates his own adherence to the ideologies of Sodom (Jewish traditions say that he had been appointed chief justice of Sodom). The threatened rape of his (male) guests is an attempt to feminize them, thus

---

7. It is only after her death that the text can confidently declare that Abraham begot Isaac (Gen 25:19).

declaring them to be not real men. It derives from the misogynistic order of penetration by which men rule over women but under which a man's masculinity/privilege can be taken away through being subjected to penetration himself. Lot's offer of his daughters in place of his guests is an attempt to protect the masculinity/privilege of his guests, which marks his own status as patriarch/host. The women have no rights, no voice, no self-determination in this misogynist order. They are property to be transacted among men (fathers), bargaining chips in intra-male conflicts.

However, the guests are angels, agents of a higher Power (Father?). They intervene and initiate a series of events leading to the overturning, destruction of Sodom's oppressive misogynist order. By this process, the daughters are transformed, no longer hidden, silent and powerless—they emerge to speak and act, to exercise agency, a rare event in the Hebrew Scriptures.[8] Having fled with their father to the hills, and believing there are no men left upon the earth, they resolve to get him drunk so that they can have sex with him, without his knowledge or consent, to secure progeny. So, the image of rape returns but this time there is a reversal, a poetic justice perhaps. The daughters, who were offered up for rape by their father, are now in control of events. Lot is rendered powerless and silent; thoroughly intoxicated and subject to his daughters, his authority is stripped from him. As powerless women, subject to abuse, they have risen up and asserted their own power. Both daughters conceive sons, making them foremothers to two nations, Moab and Ammon.

Ilona Rashkow chooses to read this story as an account of a father committing incest with his daughters. It appears to be "the prototype of parent–child incest…more directly related to actual clinical incest than the Oedipus story" (1998, 104). Rashkow's position is common to many feminist commentators (Jackson 2002, 41–43) and reads this story as the Father's version of events designed to cover up the truth. However this reading denies these women their agency and silences their voices. While I think Jackson claims too much in calling the author of this narrative one of the "first feminist theologians," I think the story can work to suggest "a new reality" and offers the prospect of a "transformed world" (2002, 46). Indeed, the messianic implications of these women exercising agency have long been recognized by both Jewish and Christian commentators. From the elder daughter comes Moab and from Moab will come Ruth the foremother of David. From the younger daughter, as foremother of the Ammonites, will come Naamah, the wife of Solomon and mother of Rehoboam. Both Ruth and Naamah are in the line of the

---

8. Compare the outrage at Gibeah in Judg 19–21, which concludes with a series of pack rapes of women who remain silent and without agency.

Messiah, who for Christians is Jesus of Nazareth. Thus it could be said that by raping their father, these women initiate the lineage of kings, the line of the Messiah. They can act this way because the deity's intervention has destroyed the interlocking systems of power and privilege under which they were subjected in Sodom. In the *Zohar*, by placing the wine in the cave for the women to get their father drunk, it is even said that the deity was an accomplice here (*Zohar* 1:110b–11a).[9]

However, it is not just the destruction of the system that enables these women to act—they act following the destruction of their mother, turned into a pillar of salt, forever looking back on ruined Sodom. Does the messianic trajectory require the death of the mother—Lot's wife, Sopanim, even Sarah? Are the daughters of Lot in reality "dutiful daughters…women who knew their sacred duty" (Walker 1998, 11) for preserving their father's line? Does not the death of Lot's wife confirm "the mother–daughter tie must be severed so that woman can enter into desire for the man–father, to take the place of the mother while never having a relationship with her…*ensuring the repetition of the social order*" (Kelso 2003, 106–7, italics in original)?[10]

Conclusion—All the Weary Mothers

Is that all there is then—these stories of miraculous/messianic mothers can do no more than illustrate/expose the Father's inexorable Law of repression/usurpation of the maternal body? Are these women merely projected male wombs acting in accordance with and in order to sustain the "hom(m)o-sexual" logic of the Male symbolic order (Irigaray 1985, 171)? Clearly that is self-evident in Sopanim's story. She is snared in the webs of patriarchal authority and left with no alternative to conceive and die, her death requiring that the Melchizedek child becomes responsible for its own birth. I say "its" because the Melchizedek child is truly monstrous, born with the power of speech yet unable to communicate with Nir, Noah or the reader. Oblivious to all around it, and taken up to

---

9.   Rabbinic commentators, never shy to defame Lot, have awarded him a limited responsibility, but without taking away the agency of the daughters. Thus Lot woke up on the first night while the elder daughter was raping him and not only did not try to stop her but did not let on that he knew what was happening and then feigned drunkenness the following night so as to have sex with the younger. But at no time were the women aware of the complicity of their father and neither was he responsible for their original decision to act as they do.

10.   And doesn't Sopanim's death affirm her honor, her adherence to the values of the patriarchal order?

heaven, it foreshadows those monsters whose birth brings death to their human hosts in the Alien films.

Nevertheless, I concur with Margaret Barker's observation that the stories in Genesis served as "*the means by which profound issues were addressed in a culture which had storytellers rather than philosophers*" (http://orthodoxeurope.org/print/11/1/8.aspx, her emphasis). Genesis is not a monologous text but contains tensions, excesses by which the stories "speak against themselves...(unconsciously) affirming" what they consciously deny (Walker 1998, 28). And not just Genesis but perhaps all the texts of the biblical world function this way, even in the man's world of *2 Enoch*.[11] These tensions preclude monologous readings, and may require each reading be multivalent. One obvious tension, especially in that man's world of *2 Enoch*, is the very motif of miraculous motherhood, a motif that necessitates sexual transgression (who is the father of this child?). That it is not necessary is evidenced by the parallel stories of Noah's birth in *1 Enoch* and the *Genesis Apocryphon*, in which, despite being a remarkable and prodigious child, Noah's conception and birth are purely mortal. Does miraculous motherhood evoke Eden, whose restoration is promised in the Melchizedek account, and whose aura signifies that Isaac represents a new start (the outbreak of laughter)? Eden is the time before the contemporary order by which woman's "desire shall be for your husband and he shall rule over you" (Gen 3:18). This time-before-patriarchy is further suggested by the weakening of the Father–husband's control over the body of the Daughter–wife, as is glimpsed in YHWH's annunciation to Sarah, and whose fear of which arouses violent impulses in Nir. With the daughters of Lot, the father's control is swept away completely. While it can be said they act in obedience to a patriarchal logic, the way they act is in breach of so many other patriarchal taboos. Could the patriarchal order withstand such transgressive obedience by all its daughters?

Lot's daughters act both because Sodom is destroyed and their mother has perished in that destruction. Genesis simply reports her death but gives no reasons as to why she looks back. Unsurprisingly, this absence has generated mostly misogynist and defamatory speculation on the part of Jewish, Christian and Muslim commentators. Nevertheless, someone glimpsed in her death an alternative possibility that complements the transgressively messianic acts of her daughters. According to a minority trajectory in Judaism, she looks back out of compassion; she looks back for her other married daughters in Sodom to see if they follow behind. In

---

11. Sopanim is the only female character in *2 Enoch* and disrupts its hom(m)o-sexual logic by her mere presence.

other words, the death of Lot's wife is the unintended consequence of an extraordinary moment of mother–daughter solidarity. Even though it results in her death, this solidarity predicates the collaboration of her unmarried daughters who speak and act together, generating an appropriate moment of messianic potentiality—appropriate because "the moment the mother–daughter relationship is symbolized and valued, a social order that relies upon the exchange of women and the exploitation of their bodies begins to collapse" (Kelso 2003, 108).

I confess that the daughters of Lot have long been biblical favorites of mine, and that I like the way they have confounded generations of commentators into grudging admiration. Their audacity and lack of concern for bourgeois moral tenets means that they can never be just dutiful daughters of patriarchy (let alone disempowered incest victims). I am also glad that some Rabbinic traditions have afforded Lot's wife the opportunity to shake loose from her immobility (a stocks in which she has long been subjected to misogynistic pillory) and allow her to express a very human solidarity. As a son, too, I am glad that Sarah is not implicated in the Akedah—that nightmare travesty of homicidal faith—that she might have protested it even at the cost of her life. Her laughter is a moment of creative potency, by which she crosses thresholds to inaugurate new possibilities (which she can nonetheless betray through her treatment of Hagar). These women could be read as mere marionettes in a patriarchal shadowplay, but their characters in the text and subsequent traditions exceed, and thus revealingly destabilize, the strictures of the male symbolic. Even Sopanim, who is not allowed to be more than a womb of heaven and dutiful wife, whose only option is death, is not completely confined by the stricture of the text. Her son is a monster and her husband is callous, craven in his vainglorious piety; yet she, in her terror and confusion, strikes a chord of humanity, capturing the reader's sympathy, while at the same time exposing (the falsehood of) the story's patriarchal dynamics.

BIBLIOGRAPHY

Ackroyd, Peter R. 1982. Isaiah 36–39: Structure and Function. Pages 3–21 in *Von Kanaan bis Kerala: Festschrift für J. P. M. van der Ploeg*. Edited by W. C. Delsman et al. Neukirchen–Vluyn: Neukirchener Verlag.

———. 1978. Isaiah I–XII: Presentation of a Prophet. Pages 16–48 in *Congress Volume: Göttingen, 1977*. VTSup 29. Leiden: Brill.

Adorno, Theodor. 1989. *Kierkegaard: Construction of the Aesthetic*. Translated by R. Hullot-Kentor. Theory and History of Literature 61. Minneapolis: University of Minnesota Press.

———. 1973. *The Jargon of Authenticity*. Translated by Knut Tarnowski and Frederic Will. Evanston, Ill.: Northwestern University Press.

Adorno, Theodor, and Max Horkheimer. 2002. *Dialectic of Enlightenment: Philosophical Fragments*. Translated by J. Cumming. New York: Continuum.

Agamben, Giorgio. 2005. *The Time That Remains: A Commentary on the Letter to the Romans*. Stanford: Stanford University Press.

———. 2004. "I am sure that you are more pessimistic than I am…": An Interview with Giorgio Agamben. *Rethinking Marxism* 16:115–24.

Aichele, George. 2001. *The Control of Biblical Meaning: Canon as Semiotic Mechanism*. Harrisburg: Trinity Press International.

———. 1985. *The Limits of Story*. Chico: Scholars Press/Fortress. Updated version online: http://home.comcast.net/~gcaichele/writings/limits.pdf.

Aitken, K. T. 1993. Hearing and Seeing: Metamorphoses of a Motif in Isaiah 1 39. Pages 12–41 in *Among the Prophets: Language, Image and Structure in the Prophetic Writings*. Edited by Philip R. Davies and David J. A. Clines. JSOTSup 144. Sheffield: JSOT.

Ajzenstat, Oona. 2001. *Driven Back to the Text: The Premodern Sources of Levinas's Postmodernism*. Pittsburgh: Duquesne University Press.

Alcock, S. E. 1999. The Pseudo-History of Messenia Unplugged. *Transactions of the American Philological Association* 129:333–41.

Alders, G. Ch. 1981. *Genesis*, vol. 1. Grand Rapids: Zondervan.

Alexander, R. 2006. Restorative Justice: Misunderstood and Misapplied. *Journal of Policy Practice* 5:67–81.

Alter, Robert. 1996. *Genesis: Translation and Commentary*. New York: W. W. Norton.

Andersen, F. I. 1983. 2 (Slavonic Apocalypse of) Enoch. Pages 1:92–100 in Charlesworth 1983.

Anderson, Perry. 1974. *Passages from Antiquity to Feudalism*. London: New Left.

Bäckersten, Olof. 2008. *Isaiah's Political Message: An Appraisal of his Alleged Social Critique*. Tübingen: Mohr Siebeck.

Badiou, Alain. 2003. *Saint Paul: The Foundation of Universalism*. Translated by R. Brassier. Stanford: Stanford University Press.

Bailey, Derrick Sherwin. 1955. *Homosexuality and the Western Christian Tradition*. London: Longmans, Green & Co.

Bailey, Randall C., Tat-siong Benny Liew and Fernando F. Segovia, eds. 2009. *They Were All Together in One Place? Toward Minority Biblical Criticism*. Atlanta: SBL. Leiden: Brill.

Baltzer, Klaus. 2001. *Deutero-Isaiah: A Commentary on Isaiah 40–55*. Translated by Margaret Kohl. Hermeneia. Minneapolis: Augsburg Fortress.

Barker, Margaret. N.d. Paradise Lost. Cited 21 October 2004. No pages. Online: http://orthodoxeurope.org/print/11/1/8.aspx.

Barr, James. 2006. Is God a Liar? (Genesis 2–3)—and Related Matters. *Journal of Theological Studies* 57:1–22.

———. 1992. *The Garden of Eden and the Hope of Immortality*. Minneapolis: Fortress.

Barthel, Jörg. 1997. *Prophetenwort und Geschichte: Die Jesajaüberlieferung in Jes 6–8 und 28–31*. Forschungen zum Alten Testament 19. Tübingen: Mohr Siebeck.

Barthes, Roland. 1986. *The Rustle of Language*. Translated by Richard Howard. Berkeley: University of California Press.

———. 1977. *Image—Music—Text*. Translated by Stephen Heath. New York: Hill & Wang.

———. 1974. *S/Z*. Translated by Richard Miller. New York: Hill & Wang.

Baum, G. 1974. Introduction. Pages 1–22 in Ruether 1974.

Baur, F. C. 1876. *Paul: The Apostle of Jesus Christ*. London: Williams & Norgate.

Begg, Christopher T., and Paul Spilsbury. 2005. *Flavius Josephus: Translation and Commentary*, vol. 5. Judean Antiquities 8–10. Leiden: Brill.

Belo, Fernando. 1981. *A Materialist Reading of the Gospel of Mark*. Translated by M. J. O'Connell. Maryknoll, N.Y.: Orbis.

Bender, K., and M. Armour. 2007. The Spiritual Components of Restorative Justice. *Victims & Offenders* 2, no. 3: 251–67.

Benjamin, Walter. 1999. *The Arcades Project*. Translated by Howard Eiland and Kevin McLaughlin. Cambridge, Mass.: Belknap.

———. 1998. *The Origin of German Tragic Drama*. Translated by J. Osborne. London: Verso.

———. 1996. *Selected Writings*. Vol. 1, *1912–1926*. Translated by Marcus J. Bullock and Michael W. Jennings. Cambridge, Mass.: Belknap.

———. 1969. *Illuminations*. Translated by Harry Zohn. New York: Schocken.

Bennett, W. H. 1861. *Genesis*. The Century Bible. Edinburgh: T.C. & E. C. Jack.

Ben Zvi, Ehud. 2009b. Is The Twelve Hypothesis Likely from an Ancient Reader's Perspective? Pages 41–96 in *Two Sides of a Coin: Juxtaposing Views on Interpreting the Book of the Twelve/The Twelve Prophetic Books*. Edited by James D. Nogalski and Ehud Ben Zvi. Piscataway, N.J.: Gorgias.

———. 2009a. Jonah 4:11 and the Metaprophetic Character of the Book of Jonah. *Journal of Hebrew Scriptures* 9, no. 5:2–13.

———. 2003. *Signs of Jonah: Reading and Rereading in Ancient Yehud*. JSOTSup 367. Sheffield: Sheffield Academic.

———. 1996. *A Historical-Critical Study of Obadiah*. BZAW 204. Berlin: de Gruyter.

Bercovitch, Sacvan, series ed. 1994. *Execution Sermons*. Library of American Puritan Writings 5. New York: AMS.

Berry, Thomas. 1999. *The Great Work: Our Way into the Future*. New York: Three Rivers.

Bersani, L. 1988. Is the Rectum a Grave? Pages 197–222 in *Aids: Cultural Analysis, Cultural Activism*. Edited by D. Crimp. Cambridge, Mass.: MIT.

Beuken, Willem A. M. 2003. *Jesaja 1–12*. Translated by Ulrich Berges. Herders Theologischer Kommentar zum Alten Testament. Freiburg: Herder.

———. 1991. Isaiah Chapters LXV–LXVI: Trito-Isaiah and the Closure of the Book of Isaiah. Pages 204–21 in *Congress Volume: Leuven, 1989*. Edited by J. A. Emerton. VTSup 43. Leiden: Brill.

Berges, Ulrich. 2008. *Jesaja 40–48*. HThKAT. Freiburg: Herder.

Bianchi, H. 1995. *Biblical Vision of Justice*. Elkhart, Ind.: Mennonite Central Committee.

———. 1994. *Towards a New System of Crime Control*. Bloomington, Ind.: Indiana University Press.

———. 1973. Tsedaka Justice. *Review for Philosophy and Theology* 3:306–17.

Bickerman, E. 1976. The Edict of Cyrus in Ezra 1. Pages 72–108 in *Studies in Jewish and Christian History*, Part 1. 3 Parts. AGAJU 9. Leiden: Brill.

Bidstrup, Scott. 2000. *Gay Marriage: The Arguments and the Motives: A Personal Essay in Hypertext*. No pages. Cited 28 September 2003. Online http://www.bidstrup.com/marriage.htm.

Black, F., and J. C. Exum. 1998. Semiotics in Stained Glass: Edward Burne-Jones's Song of Songs. Pages 315–42 in *Biblical Studies/Cultural Studies: The Third Sheffield Colloquium*. Edited by J. C. Exum and S. D. Moore. Gender, Culture, Theory 7. Sheffield: Sheffield Academic.

Black, Fiona. 2009. *The Artifice of Love: Grotesque Bodies and the Song of Songs*. London: T&T Clark International.

Blanchot, Maurice. 2003. Prophetic Speech. Pages 79–85 in *The Book to Come*. Translated by Charlotte Mandel. Stanford: Stanford University Press.

Bledstein, Adrien Janis. 1993. Is Judges a Woman's Satire of Men who Play God? Pages 34–54 in *A Feminist Companion to Judges*. Edited by Athalya Brenner. Sheffield: Sheffield Academic.

Blenkinsopp, Joseph. 2006. *Opening the Sealed Book: Interpretations of the Book of Isaiah in Late Antiquity*. Grand Rapids: Eerdmans.

———. 2000. *Isaiah 1–39*. AB 19A. New York: Doubleday.

Bloch, Ernst. 1998. *Literary Essays*. Translated by Andrew Joron et al. Stanford: Stanford University Press.

———. 1972. *Atheism in Christianity: The Religion of the Exodus and the Kingdom*. Translated by J. T. Swann. New York: Herder & Herder.

Blum, Erhard. 1996–97. Jesajas prophetisches Testament: Beobachtungen zu Jes 1–11, Part 1. *ZAW* 108:547–68. Part 2. *ZAW* 109:12–29.

Boer, R. Forthcoming. *Fleshly Readings*. London: Routledge.

———. 2007. *Criticism of Heaven: On Marxism and Theology*. Leiden: Brill.

———. 2006. The Fantasy of Genesis 1–3. *Biblical Interpretation* 14:309–31.

———. 2005c. Women First? On the Legacy of Primitive Communism. *JSOT* 30: 3–28.

———. 2005b. A Level Playingfield? Metacommentary and Marxism. Pages 51–70 in *On Jameson: From Postmodernism to Globalism*. Edited by C. Irr and I. Buchanan. Albany: State University of New York Press.

———. 2005a. Terry Eagleton and the Vicissitudes of Christology. *Cultural Logic* 8. No pages. Online: http://eserver.org/clogic/2005/boer.html.

———. 2003. *Marxist Criticism of the Bible*. London: Continuum.

————. 1999. Night Sprinkle(s): Pornography and the Song of Songs. Pages 53–70 in *Knockin' on Heaven's Door: The Bible and Popular Culture*. Biblical Limits. New York: Routledge.

————. 1997. *Novel Histories: The Fiction of Biblical Criticism*. Sheffield: Sheffield Academic.

————. 1996. *Jameson and Jeroboam*. Atlanta: Scholars Press.

Boer, Roland, and Edgar Conrad, eds. 2003. *Redirected Travel: Alternative Journeys and Places in Biblical Studies*. JSOTSup 382. London: T&T Clark International.

Boff, Leonardo, and Clodovis Boff. 1987. *Introducing Liberation Theology*. Tunbridge Wells, Kent: Burns & Oates.

Böttrich, Christfried, 2001. The Melchizedek Story of *2 (Slavonic) Enoch*: A Reaction to A. Orlov. *Journal for the Study of Judaism in the Persian, Hellenistic and Roman Period* 32:445–70.

Bow, Beverly A. 2000. Melchizedek's Birth Narrative in 2 Enoch 68–73: Christian Correlations. Pages 33–41 in *For a Later Generation: The Transformation of Tradition in Israel, Early Judaism and Early Christianity*. Edited by R. Argall, Beverly Bow, and R. A. Werline. Harrisburg, Pa.: Trinity.

Bowersock, G. W. 1994. *Fiction as History: Nero to Julian*. Berkeley: University of California Press.

Boyarin, Daniel. 1993. *Carnal Israel: Reading Sex in Talmudic Culture*. Berkeley: University of California Press.

Braithwaite, J. 2003. Does Restorative Justice Work? Pages 320–52 in Johnstone 2003.

————. 1989. *Crime, Shame and Reintegration*. Cambridge: Cambridge University Press.

Bray, Alan. 2000. Friendship, the Family and Liturgy: A Rite for Blessing Friendship in Traditional Christianity. *Theology and Sexuality* 13:15–33.

Brayford, Susan. 2007. *Genesis*. SCS. Leiden: Brill.

Brenner, Athalya. 2005. *I Am… Biblical Women Tell Their Own Tales*. Minneapolis: Fortress.

Brenner, A., and C. Fontaine, eds. *The Song of Songs*. A Feminist Companion to the Bible 6 (second series). Sheffield: Sheffield Academic.

Brett, Mark G. 2009. *Decolonizing God: The Bible in the Tides of Empire*. Sheffield: Phoenix.

Bronner, Leila Leah. 2004. *Stories of Biblical Mothers: Maternal Power in the Hebrew Bible*. Dallas: University Press of America.

Brown, Bill. 2005b. Reply: The Future of Illusions. *PMLA: Publications of the Modern Language Association of America* 120:883–85.

————. 2005a. The Dark Wood of Postmodernity (Space, Faith, Allegory). *PMLA: Publications of the Modern Language Association of America* 120:734–50.

Brown, Cheryl Anne. 1992. *No Longer Silent: First Century Jewish Portraits of Biblical Women*. Louisville, Ky.: Westminster John Knox.

Broyles, Craig C., and Craig A. Evans, eds. 1997. *Writing and Reading the Scroll of Isaiah: Studies of an Interpretive Tradition*. Leiden: Brill.

Brueggemann, Walter. 1991. Editor's Foreword. Pages vii–ix in *Reading Isaiah*. By Edgar W. Conrad. OBT 27. Minneapolis: Fortress.

Brunner, Emil. 1943. *The Divine–Human Encounter*. Philadelphia Westminster.

Budden, Chris. 2009. *Following Christ in Invaded Space: Doing Theology on Aboriginal Land*. Eugene, Ore.: Pickwick.

Bullinger, Heinrich. 1968. *The Decades of Henry Bullinger*. Translated by H. I. [*sic*]. Edited for the Parker Society by Thomas Harding. Cambridge: Cambridge University Press, 1849–52. Repr. New York: Johnson.

Buren, P. van. 1995. *A Theology of the Jewish–Christian Reality*. Lanham, Md.: University Press of America.

Burnside, J. 2005. *My Brother's Keeper: Faith-based Units in Prisons*. Abingdon: Willan.

Burrus, V., and S. Moore. 2003. Unsafe Sex: Feminism, Pornography, and the Song of Songs. *Biblical Interpretation* 11:24–52.

Callahan, Allen Dwight, Richard A. Horsley, and Abraham Smith, eds. 1998. *Slavery in Text and Interpretation*. Atlanta: SBL.

Calvin, John. 1984. *Commentary on the First Book of Moses Called Genesis, Commentaries*, vol. 1. Translated by J. King. Grand Rapids: Baker Book House. Originally published for the Calvin Translation Society, 1847–.

———. 1965. *Genesis*. Translated by John King. Edinburgh: Banner of Truth Trust.

Camp, Claudia V. 1987. Female Voice, Written Word: Women and Authority in Hebrew Scripture. Pages 97–113 in *Embodied Love: Sensuality and Relationship as Feminist Values*. Edited by Paula M. Cooey et al. San Francisco: Harper & Row.

Carden, Michael. 2003. It's Lonely at the Top: Patriarchal Models, Homophobic Vilification and the Heterosexual Household in Luther's Commentaries. Pages 185–200 in Boer and Conrad 2003.

Carr, David M. 2005. *Writing on the Tablet of the Heart: Origins of Scripture and Literature*. Oxford: Oxford University Press.

———. 1996. Reading Isaiah from Beginning (Isaiah 1) to End (Isaiah 65–66): Multiple Modern Possibilities. Pages 188–218 in Melugin and Sweeney 1996.

Carroll, Robert P. 1997. Blindsight and the Vision Thing: Blindsight and Vision in the Book of Isaiah. Pages 79–93 in Broyles and Evans 1997.

———. 1986. *Jeremiah: A Commentary*. Old Testament Library. Philadelphia: Westminster.

Carter, Warren. 2000. *Matthew and the Margins: A Socio-Political and Religious Reading*. JSOTSup 204. Sheffield: Sheffield Academic.

Cassuto, Umberto. 1961. *A Commentary on the Book of Genesis: From Adam to Noah, 1–VI:8*. Jerusalem: Magnes.

Cato, Marcus Porcius. 1999. *On Agriculture*. Translated by William Davis Hooper. LCL 283. Cambridge, Mass.: Harvard University Press.

Charlesworth, J. H., ed. 1983–1985. *The Old Testament Pseudepigrapha*. 2 vols. Garden City: Doubleday.

Childs, Brevard S. 2001. *Isaiah*. OTL. Louisville, Ky.: Westminster John Knox.

———. 1979. *Introduction to the Old Testament as Scripture*. Philadelphia: Westminster. London: SCM.

Cixous, Hélène. 1993. *Three Steps on the Ladder of Writing*. Translated by Sarah Cornell and Susan Sellars. New York: Columbia University Press.

Clarke, Adam. 1830. *The Old Testament: Genesis to Deuteronomy*. Nashville: Abingdon.

Clement of Alexandria. *The Stromata*, or *Miscellanies Book*. Cited 2 February 2007. No Pages. Online: www.earlychristianwritings.com/clement.html.

Clements, Ronald E. 2007. The Meaning of תורה in Isaiah 1–39. Pages 59–72 in *Reading the Law: Studies in Honour of Gordon J. Wenham*. Edited by J. G. McConville and Karl Möller. London: T&T Clark International.

———. 2002. Isaiah: A Book Without an Ending. *JSOT* 26:109–26.

———. 2000. The Prophet as Author: The Case of the Isaiah Memoir. Pages 89–101 in *Writings and Speech in Israelite and Ancient Near Eastern Prophecy*. Edited by Ehud Ben Zvi and Michael H. Floyd. Atlanta: SBL.

———. 1996. *Old Testament Prophecy: From Oracles to Canon*. Louisville, Ky.: Westminster John Knox.

———. 1985. Beyond Tradition-History: Deutero-Isaianic Development of First Isaiah's Themes. *JSOT* 31:95–113.

———. 1982. The Unity of the Book of Isaiah. *Interpretation* 36:117–29.

———. 1980. *Isaiah 1–39*. New Century Bible Commentary. Grand Rapids: Eerdmans. London: Marshall, Morgan & Scott.

Clevenot, Michel. 1985. *Materialist Approaches to the Bible*. Translated by W. J. Nottingham. Maryknoll, N.Y.: Orbis.

Clines, D. J. A. 1995. Why is There a Song of Songs and What Does It Do to You If You Read It? Pages 94–121 in *Interested Parties: The Ideology of Writers and Readers of the Hebrew Bible*. Edited by D. J. A. Clines. Gender, Culture, Theory 1. Sheffield: Sheffield Academic.

Code, Lorraine. 2006. *Ecological Thinking: The Politics of Epistemic Location*. Studies in Feminist Theology. Oxford: Oxford University Press.

Collins, C. John. 2006. *Genesis 1–4*. New Jersey: P. & R.

Collins, John J. 2004. *Introduction to the Hebrew Bible*. Minneapolis: Fortress.

———. 1998. *The Apocalyptic Imagination: An Introduction to Jewish Apocalyptic Literature*. Grand Rapids: Eerdmans.

Colson, Charles. 1996. Why Not Gay Marriage? *Christianity Today*. No pages. Cited 28 January 2002. Online: http://www.christianitytoday.com/ct/6tc/6tc104.html.

Cone, James. 1970. *A Black Theology of Liberation*. Maryknoll, N.Y.: Orbis.

Conrad, Edgar W. 2003. *Reading the Latter Prophets*. Edinburgh: T. & T. Clark.

———. 2000. Messengers in Isaiah and the Twelve: Implications for Reading Prophetic Books. *JSOT* 91:83–97.

———. 1999. *Zechariah*. Sheffield: Sheffield Academic.

———. 1996. Prophet, Redactor and Audience: Reforming the Notion of Isaiah's Formation. Pages 306–26 in Melugin and Sweeney 1996.

———. 1992. Heard But Not Seen: The Representation of Books in the Old Testament. *JSOT* 54:45–59.

———. 1991. *Reading Isaiah*. Minneapolis: Fortress.

Consedine, J. 2005. *Restorative Justice: The Christian Option*. No pages. Cited 1 October 2010. Online: http://www.stalbans.org.nz/teachings/guests/consedin.htm.

———. 2003. The Maori Restorative Tradition. Pages 152–57 in Johnstone 2003.

———. 1995. *Restorative Justice: Healing the Effects of Crime*. Wellington: Ploughshares.

Conway, Colleen. 2003. "Behold the Man!" Masculine Christology and the Fourth Gospel. Pages 163–80 in *New Testament Masculinities*. Edited by Janice Capel Anderson and Stephen Moore. Atlanta: SBL.

Cornell, D. 2007. The Shadow of Heterosexuality. *Hypatia* 22, no. 1 (Winter):229–42.

Coyle, J. Kevin. 1978. The Fathers and Women's Ordination. *Église et Théologie* 9:51–101.

Crawford, Adam, and Tim Newburn. 2003. *Youth Offending and Restorative Justice: Implementing Reform in Youth Justice*. Cullompton, Devon: Willan.

Croatto, J. Severino. 1981. *Exodus: A Hermeneutics of Liberation.* Translated by S. Attanasio. Maryknoll, N.Y.: Orbis.

Cunneen, C. 1997. Community Conferencing and the Fiction of Indigenous Control. *The Australian and New Zealand Journal of Criminology* 30:292.

Daly, K. 2003. Restorative Justice: The Real Story. Pages 363–81 in Johnstone 2003.

———. 2000. Revisiting the Relationship Between Retributive and Restorative Justice. Pages 35–54 in Strang and Braithwaite 2000.

Dandamaev, M. 1984. *Slavery in Babylonia: From Nabopolassar to Alexander the Great (626–331 BC).* DeKalb: North Illinois University Press.

Danforth, Samuel. 1994. The Cry of Sodom. Pages 1–25 Bercovitch, eds., *Execution Sermons.*

Darr, Katheryn Pfisterer. 1994. *Isaiah's Vision and the Family of God.* Louisville, Ky.: Westminster John Knox.

Davies, Philip R. 2007. *The Origins of Biblical Israel.* London: T&T Clark International.

———. 2006. Amos, Man and Book. Pages 113–31 in *Israel's Prophets and Israel's Past: Essays on the Relationship of Prophetic Texts and Israelite History in Honor of John H. Hayes.* Edited by Brad E. Kelle and Megan Bishop Moore. London: T&T Clark International.

———. 2004. *Yours Faithfully: Virtual Letters from the Bible.* London: Equinox.

Delaney, Carol. 1991. *The Seed and the Soil: Gender and Cosmology in Turkish Village Society.* Oxford: University of California Press.

Deleuze, Gilles, and Félix Guattari. 1983. *Anti-Oedipus.* Translated by Robert Hurley, Mark Seem, and Helen R. Lane. Minneapolis: University of Minnesota Press.

DeLoughrey, Elizabeth M. 2007. *Routes and Roots: Navigating Caribbean and Pacific Island Literature.* Honolulu: University of Hawaii Press.

Derrida, Jacques. 1981. *Dissemination.* Translated by Barbara Johnson. Chicago: University of Chicago Press.

———. 1978. *Writing and Difference.* Translated by Alan Bass. Chicago: University of Chicago Press.

———. 1973. *Speech and Phenomena.* Translated by David B. Allison. Evanston, Ill.: Northwestern University Press.

De Santis, Solange. 2000. Bishops Focus on Schools Crisis: Lutherans, PWRDF, liturgy also discussed. *Anglican Journal (Canada)* December. Cited 16 August 2005. No pages. Online: www.anglicanjournal.com/126/10/canada)#.html.

Deutscher, P. 2002. *A Politics of Impossible Difference: The Later Works of Luce Irigaray.* Ithaca: Cornell University Press.

D'iakonov, I. M. 1999. *The Paths of History.* Cambridge: Cmabridge University Press.

——— ed. 1987. *Ancient Mesopotamia: Socio-Economic History: A Collection of Studies by Soviet Scholars.* Moscow: Nauka.

———. 1969. Slave-Labor vs. Non-Slave Labor: The Problem of Definition. Pages 1–3 in *Labor in the Ancient Near East.* Edited by M. Powell. New Haven: American Oriental Society.

Dillman, August. 1897. *Genesis Critically and Exegetically Expounded,* vol. 1. Translated by W. B. Stevenson. Edinburgh: T. & T. Clark.

Donaldson, T. 2009. Supersessionism in Early Christianity. *Canadian Society of Biblical Studies* 69:1–27.

Douglas, Jane Dempsey. 2003. Luther on the Image of God in Women. Pages 72–79 in *Feminism & Theology.* Edited by Janet Martin Soskice and Diana Lipton. Oxford Readings in Feminism. Oxford: Oxford University Press.

Dunn, Stephen. 1981. *The Fall and Rise of the Asiatic Mode of Production*. London: Routledge & Kegan Paul.

During, Simon. 2005. Toward the Postsecular. *PMLA: Publications of the Modern Language Association of America* 120:876–77.

Eagleton, Terry. 2010. *On Evil*. New Haven: Yale University Press.

———. 2009b. *Trouble With Strangers: A Study of Ethics*. Oxford: Wiley-Blackwell.

———. 2009a. *Reason, Faith, and Revolution: Reflections on the God Debate*. New Haven: Yale University Press.

———. 2003c. *After Theory*. New York: Basic.

———. 2003b. *Sweet Violence: The Idea of the Tragic*. Oxford: Blackwell.

———. 2003a. *Figures of Dissent: Critical Essays on Fish, Spivak, Zizek and Others*. London: Verso.

———. 2001. *The Gatekeeper: A Memoir*. London: Penguin.

———. 1991. *Ideology*. London: Verso.

———. 1970. *The Body as Language: Outline of a "New Left" Theology*. London: Sheed & Ward.

Eco, Umberto. 1976. *A Theory of Semiotics*. Bloomington: Indiana University Press.

Edelman, Diana. 1994. Huldah the Prophet: Of Yahweh or Asherah? Pages 231–50 in *A Feminist Companion to Samuel and Kings*. Edited by Athalya Brenner. Sheffield: Sheffield Academic.

Edelman, S. 2004. Supersession Rears Its Ugly Head in the Church's *Dominus Iesus*: A Contextual Analysis. *Shofar* 22, no. 2:4–11.

Eglash, A. 1977. Beyond Restitution: Creative Restitution. Pages 90–101 in *Restitution in Criminal Justice*. Edited by J. Hudson. Minnesota Department of Corrections.

Ehrman, Bart D. 1993. *The Orthodox Corruption of Scripture*. Oxford: Oxford University Press.

Eisenbaum, P. 2005. Hebrews, Supersessionism and Jewish–Christian Relations. SBL Hebrews Consultation.

Eisenstein, Elizabeth L. 1979. *The Printing Press as an Agent of Change*. 2 vols. Cambridge: Cambridge University Press.

Ellicott, Charles John. 1959. *Ellicott's Commentary on the Whole Bible*. Grand Rapids: Zondervan.

Epicurus. 2009. Letter to Herodotus. Cited 4 August 2009. No pages. Online: http://www.epicurus.net/en/herodotus.html.

Eusebius, 1989. *The History of the Church*. Translated by G. A. Williamson. Rev. ed. London: Penguin.

Evans, Craig A. 1989. *To See and Not Perceive: Isaiah 6.9–10 in Early Jewish and Christian Interpretation*. JSOTSup 64. Sheffield: JSOT.

Exum, J. Cheryl. 2000. Ten Things Every Feminist Should Know About the Song of Songs. Pages 24–35 in Brenner and Fontaine, eds., *The Song of Songs*.

———. 1993. Who's Afraid of "The Endangered Ancestress"? Pages 91–113 in *The New Literary Criticism and the Hebrew Bible*. Edited by J. Cheryl Exum and David J. A. Clines. Valley Forge, Pa.: Trinity Press International.

Feiner, Susan. 1986. Property Relations and Class Relations in Genovese and the Modes of Production Controversy. *Cambridge Journal of Economics* 10: 61–75.

Ferguson, J. Wesley. 2000. *What the Bible Teaches: Genesis*. Scotland: John Reitchie.

Ferry, Joëlle. 2008. *Isaïe: "comme les mots d'un livre scellé" (Is 29,11)*. Paris: Cerf.

Fiensy, David A. 1991. *The Social History of Palestine in the Herodian Period: The Land Is Mine*. Studies in the Bible and Early Christianity 20. Lewiston: Mellen.

Focus on the Family. N.d. Frequently Asked Questions About Same-Sex "Marriage." Cited 28 January 2002. Last updated 22 October 1999. Online: http://www.family.org/cforum/research/papers/a0008192.html.

Fontaine, C. R. 2000. Preface. Pages 13–15 in Brenner and Fontaine, eds., *The Song of Songs*.

Foster-Carter, Aidan. 1978. The Modes of Production Controversy. *New Left Review* 107:47–77.

Foucault, Michel. 1972. *The Archaeology of Knowledge and the Discourse on Language*. Translated by A. M. Sheridan Smith and Rupert Sawyer. New York: Harper & Row.

Fox, Ruth, OSB. 1996. Women in the Bible and the Lectionary. *Liturgy* 90. May/June. Cited 22 July 2008. No pages. Online: www.cta-usa.org/reprint6–96/fox.html.

Fraser, Nancy, 2009. Feminism, Capitalism and the Cunning of History. *New Left Review* 56:97–117.

Frazer, Jr., R. M. 1966. *Dares of Phrygia / Dictys of Crete, The Trojan War The Chronicles of Dictys of Crete and Dares the Phrygian: Translated with an Introduction and Notes*. Bloomington: Indiana University Press.

Freedman, Richard. 2001. *Commentary on the Torah*. New York: HarperCollins.

Fresno. 1982. *Victim Offender Restorative Program*. Fresno City.

Freyne, Sean. 1994. The Geography, Politics, and Economics of Galilee and the Quest for the Historical Jesus. Pages 75–121 in *Studying the Historical Jesus: Evaluations of the State of Current Research*. Edited by Bruce Chilton and Craig A. Evans. Leiden: Brill.

Frye, Northropp. 1957. *Anatomy of Criticism: Four Essays*. Princeton, N.J.: Princeton University Press.

Gaines, Janet Howe. 2003. *Forgiveness in a Wounded World: Jonah's Dilemma*. Atlanta: SBL.

Gamble, Harry Y. 1995. *Books and Readers in the Early Church*. New Haven: Yale University Press.

Garcia-Treto, Francisco O. 2009. Exile in the Hebrew Bible: A Postcolonial Look from the Cuban Diaspora. Pages 65–78 in Bailey, Liew and Segovia 2009.

Gaston, L. 1991. *Paul and Torah*. Vancouver: British Columbia University Press.

Gavrielides, T. 2007. *Restorative Justice Theory*. Helsinki: Criminal Justice.

Geering, L. 2010. *Such is Life: A Close Encounter with Ecclesiastes*. Wellington: Steele Roberts.

Geisler, Norman. 2003. *Systematic Theology*. Vol. 2, *God*. Bloomington: Bethany House.

Gesenius, Friedrich Wilhelm. 2006. *Gesenius' Hebrew Grammar*. Edited by E. Kautzsch. Translated by A. E. Cowley. Oxford: Clarendon, 1910. Repr. Mineola, N.Y.: Dover.

Ghosh, Suniti Kumar. 1984. Marx on India. *Monthly Review* 35:39–53.

Gibbs, M. 2009. Using Restorative Justice to Resolve Historical Injustices of Indigenous Peoples. *Contemporary Justice Review* 12:45–57.

Gibson, John C. L. 1981. *Genesis*, vol. 1. Edinburgh: Saint Andrews.

Gibson, Mel, dir. 2004. *The Passion of the Christ*. Newmarket Films.

Ginzberg, Louis. 1998. *The Legends of the Jews*, vol. 5. Baltimore: The Johns Hopkins University Press.

Goldingay, John. 2005. *The Message of Isaiah 40–55*. London: T&T Clark International.

Gottwald, Norman K. 1999. *The Tribes of Yahweh: A Sociology of Liberated Israel 1050–1250 BC*. Sheffield: Sheffield Academic.

———. 1993. *The Hebrew Bible in Its Social World and Ours*. Atlanta: Scholars Press.

———. 1992. Sociology of Ancient Israel. Pages 79–89 in *The Anchor Bible Dictionary*. Edited by D. N. Freedman. Garden City, N.Y.: Doubleday.

———. 1985. *The Hebrew Bible: A Socio-Literary Introduction*. Philadelphia: Fortress.

Goulder, M. D. 1986. *The Song of Fourteen Songs*. JSOTSup 36. Sheffield: Sheffield Academic.

Gowan, Donald E. 1988. *From Eden to Babel: Genesis 1–11*. Grand Rapids: Eerdmans.

Grabbe, L. L. 1998. *Ezra–Nehemiah*. London: Routledge.

Gray, James Comper. N.d. *Gray and Adams' Bible Commentary*. Grand Rapids: Zondervan.

Gregersen, N. 2006. Beyond Secularist Supersessionism: Risk, Religion and Technology. *Ecotheology* 11:137–58.

Grimké, Sarah Moore. 1838. *Letters on the Equality of the Sexes, and the Condition of Woman: Addressed to Mary S. Parker, President of the Boston Female Anti-Slavery Society*. Boston: Isaac Knapp.

Gruber, Mayer. 2004. Mordechai M. Kaplan and Abraham Joshua Heschel on Biblical Prophecy. *ZAW* 116:602–9.

Grudem, Wayne. 1994. *Systematic Theology*. Grand Rapids: Zondervan.

Guillaume, Philippe. 2009. Rhetorical Reading Redundant: A Response to Ehud Ben Zvi. *Journal of Hebrew Scriptures* 9, no. 6:2–9.

Gunkel, Herman. 1997. *Genesis*. Translated by Mark E. Biddle. Macon, Ga.: Mercer University Press.

Gunn, David M., and Danna Nolan Fewell. 1993. *Narrative in the Hebrew Bible*. Oxford: Oxford University Press.

Gutiérrez, Gustavo. 1983. *The Power of the Poor in History*. Maryknoll, N.Y.: Orbis.

———. 1969. *Theology of Liberation*. Maryknoll, N.Y.: Orbis.

Habel, Norman C. 2008. Introducing Ecological Hermeneutics. Pages 1–8 in *Exploring Ecological Hermeneutics*. Edited by Norman C. Habel and Peter Trudinger. Atlanta: SBL.

Hadley, M., ed. 2001. *The Spiritual Roots of Restorative Justice*. Albany: State University of New York Press.

Håkansson, Sigurd. 2003. *Weeds and Weed Management on Arable Land: An Ecological Approach*. Oxon: CABI.

Hallward, Peter. 2003. *Badiou: A Subject to Truth*. Minneapolis: University of Minnesota Press.

Halperin, D. 1990. *One Hundred Years of Homosexuality and Other Essays on Greek Love*. New York: Routledge.

Halton, Charles. 2008. How Big Was Nineveh? Literal Versus Figurative Interpretation of City Size. *Bulletin for Biblical Research* 18:193–207.

Hanson, K. C., and Douglas E. Oakman. 1998. *Palestine in the Time of Jesus: Social Structures and Social Conflicts*. Minneapolis: Fortress.

Haraway, Donna J. 1991. *Simians, Cyborgs, and Women: The Reinvention of Nature*. London: Free Association.

Harding, James. 2010. The Book of Job as Metaprophecy. *Studies in Religion* 39, no. 4:523–47.

Harrill, J. Albert. 2006. *Slaves in the New Testament: Literary, Social and Moral Dimensions*. Minneapolis: University of Minnesota Press.

Harrington, Daniel, J. SJ, and Anthony J. Saldarini. 1987. *Targum Jonathan of the Former Prophets: Introduction, Translation and Notes.* Wilmington, Del.: Glazier.

Hartenstein, Friedhelm. 1997. *Die Unzugänglichkeit Gottes im Heiligtum: Jesaja 6 und der Wohnort JHWHs in der Jerusalemer Kulttradition.* Neukirchen–Vluyn: Neukirchener Verlag.

Hartley, John. 2000. *Genesis.* NIBC. Peabody, Mass.: Hendrickson.

Haught, John F. 2006. *Is Nature Enough? Meaning and Truth in the Age of Science.* Cambridge: Cambridge University Press.

———. 2004. Christianity and Ecology. Pages 232–47 in *This Sacred Earth: Religion, Nature, Environment.* Edited by Roger S. Gottlieb. New York: Routledge.

Henry, Matthew. 1991. *Matthew Henry's Commentary on the Whole Bible.* Peabody, Mass.: Hendrickson.

Heschel, Abraham Joshua. 2001. *The Prophets.* New York: HarperCollins. 1st paperback ed, 1969/71.

Heschel, Susannah. 2005. Judaism, Dante, and the World Trade Center. *PMLA: Publications of the Modern Language Association of America* 120:877–79.

Hesse, Franz. 1955. *Das Verstockungsproblem im Alten Testament. Ein frömmigkeitsgeschichtliche Untersuchung.* Berlin: Töpelmann.

Hildegard. 1990. *Scivias.* Translated by Columba Hart and Jane Bishop. New York: Paulist.

Hillel, Daniel. 2006. *The Natural History of the Bible: An Environmental Exploration of the Hebrew Scriptures.* New York: Columbia University Press.

Hindess, Barry, and Paul Q. Hirst. 1975. *Precapitalist Modes of Production.* London: Routledge & Kegan Paul.

Holladay, William. 1986–89. *Jeremiah: A Commentary on the Book of the Prophet Jeremiah.* 2 vols. Minneapolis: Fortress.

Horst, Pieter W. van der. 1996. Sarah's Seminal Emission: Hebrews 1.11 in the Light of Ancient Embryology. Pages 112–34 In *The Feminist Companion to the Hebrew Bible in the New Testaments.* Edited by Athalya Brenner. Feminist Companion to the Bible 10. Sheffield: Sheffield Academic.

Horton Jr., Fred L. 1976. *The Melchizedek Tradition: A Critical Examination of the Sources to the Fifth Century A.D. and in the Epistle to the Hebrews.* Cambridge: Cambridge University Press.

Howard, Robert E. 2003. A Witch Shall Be Born. Pages 255–301 in *The Bloody Crown of Conan.* Edited by Patrice Louinet. New York: Ballantine.

Hoyle, C., and R. Young. 2002. Restorative Justice: Assessing the Prospects and Pitfalls. Pages 525–48 in McConville and Wilson, eds., *The Handbook of the Criminal Justice Process.*

Hubmaier, Balthasar. 1989. Theses Against Eck XXIll. In *Balthasar Hubmaier: Theologian of Anabaptism.* Edited by H. Wayne Pipkin and John H. Yoder. Scottdale: Herald.

Husserl, Edmund. 1962. *Ideas.* Translated by W. R. Boyce Gibson. New York: Macmillan.

Irigaray, L. 1993. *An Ethics of Sexual Difference.* Translated by C. Burke and G. C. Gill. Ithaca: Cornell University Press.

———. 1991. *Marine Lover of Friedrich Nietzsche.* Translated by Gillian C. Hill. New York: Columbia University Press.

———. 1985. *This Sex Which Is Not One.* Translated by Catherine Porter with Carolyn Burke. Ithaca: Cornell University Press.

Isaac, J. 1971. *Jesus and Israel*. New York: Holt, Reinhart & Winston.

Jackson, Melissa, 2002. Lot's Daughters and Tamar as Tricksters and the Patriarchal Narratives as Feminist Theology. *JSOT* 26:29–46.

Jameson, Fredric. 2005. *Archaeologies of the Future: The Desire Called Utopia and Other Science Fictions*. London: Verso.

———. 1992. *The Geopolitical Aesthetic: Cinema and Space in the World System*. Bloomington: Indiana University Press.

———. 1991. *Postmodernism, or, the Cultural Logic of Late Capitalism*. Durham, N.C.: Duke University Press.

———. 1988. *The Ideologies of Theory, Essays 1971–1986*. Vol. 2, *Syntax of History*. Minneapolis: University of Minnesota Press.

———. 1984. Rimbaud and the Spatial Text. Pages 66–88 in *Rewriting Literary History*. Edited by T.-W. Wong and M. A. Abbas. Hong Kong: Hong Kong University Press.

———. 1981. *The Political Unconscious: Narrative as a Socially Symbolic Act*. Ithaca: Cornell University Press.

———. 1971. *Marxism and Form: Twentieth-Century Dialectical Theories of Literature*. Princeton, N.J.: Princeton University Press.

———. 1969. Walter Benjamin, or Nostalgia. *Salmagundi* 11:52–68.

Jantzen, Grace M. 1995. *Power, Gender and Christian Mysticism*. Cambridge: Cambridge University Press.

Janzen, W. 1994. *Old Testament Ethics*. Louisville, Ky.: John Knox.

Jeanrond, W. G. 1974. *Theological Hermeneutics: Development and Significance*. Basingstoke: Macmillan.

Jehle, A., and M. Miller. 2006. My God I am Sorry: The Role of Religion in Restorative Justice Programs. Paper presented to the Law and Society Association Conference.

Jerome. 1983. *Against Jovinianus*. In *A Select Library of Nicene and Post-Nicene Fathers of the Christian Church*. Second Series 6. Edited Philip Schaff and Henry Wace. Translated by W. H. Fremantle. Grand Rapids: Eerdmans.

Jobling, David. 1998. *1 Samuel*. Collegeville: Liturgical.

———. 1992b. Deconstruction and the Political Analysis of Biblical Texts. *Semeia* 59: 95–127.

———. 1992a. "Forced Labor": Solomon's Golden Age and the Question of Literary Representation. *Semeia* 54:57–76.

———. 1991. Feminism and "Mode of Production" in Israel: Search for a Method. Pages 239–51 in *The Bible and the Politics of Exegesis*. Edited by D. Jobling, Peggy L. Day, and Gerald Sheppard. Cleveland, Ohio: Pilgrim.

Johnstone, G., ed. 2003. *A Restorative Justice Reader*. Abingdon: Willan.

———. 1999. Restorative Justice, Shame and Forgiveness. *Liverpool Law Review* 21, no. 2/3:197–216.

Justin Martyr. 2003. *Dialogue with Trypho*. Washington, D.C.: Catholic University of America Press.

Kaiser, Otto. 1983. *Isaiah 1–12*. Translated by John Bowden. 2d ed. OTL. London: SCM.

Kaplan, Mordechai M. 1926. Isaiah 6 1–11. *JBL* 45:251–59.

Kapleau, Philip. 1966. *The Three Pillars of Zen: Teaching, Practice, and Enlightenment*. New York: Harper & Row.

Katz, J. N. 1995. *The Invention of Heterosexuality*. New York: Dutton/Penguin.

Kautsky, Karl. 2007. *Foundations of Christianity*. Translated by H. F. Mins. London: IMG.

Keel, Othmar. 1977. *Jahwe-Visionen und Siegelkunst*. Stuttgarter Bibelstudien 84/85. Stuttgart: Katholisches Bibelwerk.

Kelso, Julie. 2003. Reading the Silence of Women in Genesis 34. Pages 85–109 in Boer and Conrad 2003.

Kim, Hyun Chül Paul. 2010. Review of Olof Bäckersten, *Isaiah's Political Message: An Appraisal of His Alleged Social Critique*. *Biblical Interpretation* 10:267–69.

Klawans, J. 2006. *Purity, Sacrifice, and the Temple: Symbolism and Supersessionism in the Study of Ancient Judaism*. New York: Oxford University Press.

Knoppers, Gary N. 1994. *Two Nations Under God: The Deuteronomistic History of Solomon and the Dual Monarchies*. Vol. 2, *The Reign of Jereboam, the Fall of Israel, and the Reign of Josiah*. HSM 52. Atlanta: Scholars Press.

Kreitzer, Larry J. 2002. *Gospel Images in Fiction and Film*. London: Continuum/ Sheffield Academic.

Kristeva, Julia. 1984. *Revolution in Poetic Language*. Translated by Margaret Waller. New York: Columbia University Press.

Laato, Antti. 1998. *"About Zion I Will Not Be Silent": The Book of Isaiah as an Ideological Unity*. Coniectanea biblica 44. Stockholm: Almqvist & Wiksell.

Lack, Rémi. 1973. *La symbolique du livre d'Isaïe*. Analecta Biblica 69. Rome: Pontifical Biblical Institute.

Landy, Francis. 2011. The Book that Cannot Be Read. In *A Critical Engagement: Essays in Honor of J. Cheryl Exum*. Edited by J. Ellen van Wolde and David J.A. Clines. Sheffield: Sheffield Phoenix.

———. 2010. Exile in the Book of Isaiah. Pages 251–56 in *The Concept of Exile in Ancient Israel and Its Historical Contexts*. Edited by Ehud Ben Zvi and Christoph Levin. Berlin: de Gruyter.

———. 2002. Ghostwriting Isaiah. Pages in 93–114 in *First Person: Essays in Biblical Autobiography*. Edited by Philip R. Davies. The Biblical Seminar 81. London: Sheffield Academic.

———. 2001. *Beauty and the Enigma and Other Essays in the Hebrew Bible*. JSOTSup 306. Sheffield: Sheffield Academic.

———. 2000. Vision and Voice in Isaiah. *JSOT* 88:19–36. Repr. pages 371–91 in Landy 2001.

———. 1999. Strategies of Concentration and Diffusion in Isaiah 6. *Biblical Interpretation* 7:59–86. Repr. pages 298–327 in Landy 2001.

———. 1995. *Hosea*. Readings. Sheffield: Sheffield Academic.

Leith, Mary Joan Winn. 2001. Women: Ancient Near East and Israel. Pages 325–30 in *The Oxford Guide to People & Places of the Bible*. Edited by Bruce M. Metzger and Michael D. Coogan. Oxford: Oxford University Press.

Leupold, H. C. 1942. *Exposition of Genesis*. Columbus, Ohio: Wartburg.

Levinas, Emmanuel. 2003. *Die Unerhöhrte Prophetie: Kommunikative Strukturen prophetische Rede im Buch Yesha'yahu*. Leipzig: Evangelische Verlagsanstalt.

———. 1998. *Otherwise than Being or Beyond Essence*. Translated by Alphonse Lingis. Pittsburgh: Duquesne University Press, 1st ed. 1981.

———. 1989. Ethics as First Philosophy. Pages 75–87 in *The Levinas Reader*. Edited by Seán Hand. Oxford: Blackwell.

Liebman, Matt, Charles L. Mohler, and Charles P. Staver, eds. 2001. *Ecological Management of Agricultural Weeds*. Cambridge: Cambridge University Press.

Liebreich, Leon J. 1955–56. The Compilation of the Book of Isaiah. *JQR* 46:259–77.

Liew, Tat-siong Benny. 1999. *Politics of Parousia: Reading Mark Inter(Con)Textually*. Biblical Interpretation Series 42. Leiden: Brill.

Lim, Johnson T. K. 2009. What's the Big Fuss Over an Apple? Pages 171–96 in *Take Root Downward, Bear Fruit Upward: A Festschrift Presented to Lien-Hwa Chow On the Occasion of His Eighty-Eighth Birthday*. Edited by Johnson T. K. Lim. Hong Kong: ABGTS.

———. 2006. The Empowered Reader and the Elusive Text. *Mission Today* 8:145–58

———. 2002b. *A Strategy for Reading Biblical Texts*. Studies in Biblical Literature 29. New York: Lang.

———. 2002a. How Then Shall We Read? *Church and Society* 5, no. 3:85–92.

———. 2001. Theological Hermeneutics: A Reading Strategy. *Asia Journal of Theology* 15:2–13.

Liss, Hanna. 2002. Undisclosed Speech: Patterns of Communication in the Book of Isaiah. *JHS* 4, no. 4. No pages. Online: http://www.arts.ualberta.ca/JHS/Articles/article_26.pdf.

Love, Mark C. 1999. *The Evasive Text: Zechariah 1–8 and the Frustrated Reader*. JSOTSup 296. Sheffield: Sheffield Academic.

Lundbom, Jack R. 1999–2004 *Jeremiah: A New Translation with Introduction and Commentary*. 3 vols. New York: Doubleday.

Luther, Martin. 1973. Lectures on 1 Timothy. Pages 217–384 in *Luther's Works*, vol. 28. Translated by Richard J. Dinda. St. Louis, Miss.: Concordia.

———. 1961. *Lectures on Genesis, Chapters 15–20*. In *Works*, vol. 3. Translated by George V. Schick. Edited by Jaroslav Pelikan and Helmut T. Lehmann. St. Louis: Concordia.

———. 1959. Misuse of the Mass. In *Luther's Works*, vol. 36. Philadelphia: Muhlenburg.

———. 1958b. Infiltrating and Clandestine Preachers. Pages 383–94 in *Luther's Works*, vol. 40. Translated by Conrad Bergendoff. Philadelphia: Muhlenberg.

———. 1958a. Lectures on Genesis Chapters 1–5. In *Luther's Works*, vol. 1. Translated by George V. Schick. St. Louis: Concordia.

Luxemburg, Rosa. 1970. Socialism and the Churches. Translated by Juan Punto. Pages 131–52 in *Rosa Luxemburg Speaks*. Edited by Mary-Alice Waters. New York: Pathfinder.

Lyotard, Jean-François. 1984. *The Postmodern Condition: A Report on Knowledge*. Translated by Geoff Bennington and Brian Massumi. Minneapolis: University of Minnesota Press.

MacHaffie, Barbara, ed. 1992. *Readings in Her Story*. Minneapolis: Fortress.

Mackendrick, K. 1999. *Counterpleasures*. SUNY Series in Postmodern Culture. New York: State University of New York Press.

Madden, Frederic W. 1967. *History of Jewish Coinage and of Money in the Old and New Testament*. Library of Biblical Studies. New York: KTAV.

Magonet, Jonathan. 1991. *A Rabbi's Bible*. London: SCM.

———. 1985. The Structure of Isaiah 6. Pages 91–97 in *Proceedings of the Ninth World Congress of Jewish Studies: Division A (The Period of the Bible)*. Jerusalem: World Union of Jewish Studies.

Maher, Michael, trans. 1992b. *Targum Neofiti 1: Genesis.* Collegeville: Glazier.

———. 1992a. *Targum Pseudo–Jonathan: Genesis.* Collegeville: Glazier.

———. 1988. *Targum Onqelos to Genesis.* Collegeville: Glazier.

Marin, L. 1984. *Utopics: Spatial Play.* Translated by R. A. Vollrath. Atlantic Highlands, N.J.: Humanities.

Marx, Karl, and Friedrich Engels. 1976. *Marx Engels Collected Works (MECW)*, vol. 5. Moscow: Progress.

———. 1975. *Marx Engels Collected Works (MECW)*, vol. 2. Moscow: Progress.

———. 1973. *Grundrisse: Foundations of the Critique of Political Economy (Rough Draft).* Translated by M. Nicolaus. Harmondsworth: Penguin in association with New Left.

Matheson, Peter. 1995. *Argula von Grumbach: A Woman's Voice in the Reformation.* Edinburgh: T. & T. Clark.

Matthews, Kenneth. 1996. *Genesis 1–11.* Nashville: Broadman & Holman.

Maxwell, G., and A. Morris. 2000. Restorative Justice and Reoffending. Pages 93–103 in Strang and Braithwaite 2000.

May, Jon, and Nigel Thrift. 2001. Introduction. Pages 1–46 In *Timespace: Geographies of Temporality.* Edited by Jon May and Nigel Thrift. London: Routledge.

McCold, P. 2004. Paradigm Muddle. *Contemporary Justice Review* 7:13–35.

McConville, M., and G. Wilson, eds. 2002. *The Handbook of the Criminal Justice Process.* Oxford: Oxford University Press.

McIvor, Robert K. 1995. The Parable of the Weeds Among the Wheat (Matt 13:24–30, 36–43) and the Relationship Between the Kingdom and the Church as Portrayed in the Gospel of Matthew. *JBL* 114, no. 4:643–59.

McKane, William. 1986–96. *Jeremiah.* 2 vols. ICC. Edinburgh: T. & T. Clark.

McKinlay, Judith. 2005b. Gazing at Huldah. *The Bible and Critical Theory* 1, no. 3. No pages. Online: www.epress.monash.edu.au.

———. 2005a. Huldah Speaks Again and Again. Paper Presented at the Association of Biblical Studies (NZ), Dunedin, November.

Mellor, Mary. 1997. *Feminism and Ecology.* Cambridge: Polity.

Melugin, Roy F. 2009. Poetic Imagination, Intertextuality, and Life in a Symbolic World. Pages 7–15 in *The Desert Will Bloom: Poetics Visions in Isaiah.* Edited by A. Joseph Everson and Hyun Chul Paul Kim. Atlanta: SBL.

———. 1996. Figurative Speech and the Reading of Isaiah 1. Pages 282–305 in Melugin and Sweeney 1996.

———. 1976. *The Formation of Isaiah 40–55.* BZAW 141. Berlin: de Gruyter.

Melugin, Roy F., and Marvin A. Sweeney, eds. 1996. *New Visions of Isaiah.* JSOTSup 214. Sheffield: JSOT.

Merkle, S. 1994. Telling the True Story of the Trojan War: The Eyewitness Account of Dictys of Crete. Pages 183–96 in *The Search for the Ancient Novel.* Edited by J. Tatum. Baltimore: The Johns Hopkins University Press.

Meyer, E. 1896. *Entstehung des Judentums.* Halle: Niemeyer.

Meyers, Eric M. 2003. The Problems of Gendered Space in Syro-Palestinian Domestic Architecture: The Case of Roman-Period Galilee. Pages 44–69 in *Early Christian Families in Context: An Interdisciplinary Dialogue.* Edited by David L. Balch and Carolyn Osiek. Grand Rapids: Eerdmans.

Midrash Rabbah: Genesis. 1939. Translated into English with notes, glossary and indices under the editorship of Rabbi Dr. Harry Freedman and Maurice Simon, with a foreword by Rabbi Dr. I. Epstein. London: Soncino.

Miles, Jack. 1996. *God: A Biography.* New York: Vintage.

Milgrom, Jacob. 1964. Did Isaiah Prophecy During the Reign of Uzziah? *VT* 14:164–82.

Milich, Klaus J. 2005. The Divine Comedy of Terror. *PMLA: Publications of the Modern Language Association of America* 120:879–81.

Milius, John, dir. 1982. *Conan the Barbarian.* Screenplay by John Milius, Robert E Howard, and Oliver Stone. Universal City, CA: MCA/Universal Pictures and Dino de Laurentiis Corporation.

Miranda, José P. 1982. *Communism in the Bible.* Translated by R. R. Barr. Maryknoll, N.Y.: Orbis.

———. 1974. *Marx and the Bible: A Critique of the Philosophy of Oppression.* Translated by J. Eagleson. Maryknoll, N.Y.: Orbis.

Miscall, Peter. 1993. *Isaiah.* Readings; Sheffield: Sheffield Academic Press.

Moberly, R. W. L. 2008. Did the Interpreters Get it Right? Genesis 2–3 Reconsidered. *Journal of Theological Studies* 59:22–40.

———. 1998. "God Is not a Human that He Should Repent" (Num. 23:19 and 1 Sam. 15:29). Pages 112–26 in *God in the Fray: A Tribute to Walter Brueggemann.* Edited by Tod Linafelt and Timothy K. Beal. Minneapolis: Fortress.

———. 1988. Did the Serpent Get It Right? *Journal of Theological Studies* 39:1–27.

Moldenke, Harold N., and Alma L. Moldenke. 2002. *Plants of the Bible.* The Kegan Paul Library of Religion and Mysticism. London: Kegan Paul.

Mollenkott, Virginia Ramey. 2000. God's Daughters Have Always Prophesied: The Past, Present, and Future of Feminist Theologies. *EEWC Update* 24, no. 2 (Summer). No pages. Cited 22 July 2008. Online: www.eewc.com/Update/Summer2000Daughter.html.

Montagu, Rachel. 1994. *Pirke Imot:* Women as Role Models in the Hebrew Bible. Pages 40–55 in *Hear Our Voice: Women Rabbis Tell Their Stories.* Edited by Sybil Sheridan. London: SCM.

Moreiras, Alberto. 2004. Children of Light: Neo-Paulinism and the Cathexis of Difference. *Bible and Critical Theory* 1. No pages. Online: www.epress.monash.edu.au/bc.

Morgan, J. R. 1985. Lucian's True Histories and the Wonders Beyond Thule of Antonius Diogenes. *Classical Quarterly* 35:475–90.

Morris, P. 2006. Secular Supersessionism, Geering, Jews and Judaism. Pages 165–76 in *A Religious Atheist?* Edited by R. Pelly and P. Stuart. Dunedin: Otago University Press.

Morton, Timothy. 2007. *Ecology without Nature: Rethinking Environmental Aesthetics.* Cambridge, Mass.: Harvard University Press.

Mosala, Itumeleng J. 1989. *Biblical Hermeneutics and Black Theology in South Africa.* Grand Rapids: Eerdmans.

Muessig, Carolyn. 1998. Prophecy and Song: Teaching and Preaching by Medieval Women. Pages 146–58 in *Women Preachers and Prophets Through Two Millennia of Christianity.* Edited by Beverley Mayne Kienzle and Pamela J. Walker. Berkeley: University of California Press.

Muffs, Yochanan. 1992. *Love & Joy: Law, Language and Religion in Ancient Israel.* New York: Jewish Theological Society of America.

Müller, Hans-Peter. 1992. Sprachliche und religionsgeschichtliche Beobachtungen zu Jesaja 6. *ZAH* 5:163–85.

Muyebe, Stanslaus. 2009. *Restorative Justice Reform in the Catholic Church: Its Risks and Its Benefits*. Cape Town: New Voices.

Myers, Carol. 1988. *Discovering Eve*. New York: Oxford University Press.

Myers, C., and E. Enns. 2009. *Ambassadors of Reconciliation: New Testament Reflections on Restorative Justice and Peacemaking*. Maryknoll, N.Y.: Orbis.

Neevel, Teddi. 1988. Huldah. *Titus 2 Men and Women*. No pages. Cited 16 August 2005. www.titus2menandwomen.org/Articles/TeddiNeevel/WomenInBible/Huldah.

Neiman, Rachel. 2008. Women in Judaism: The Prophetess Huldah: Her Message of Hope. No pages. Cited 22 July 2008. Online: www.torah.org/learning/women/class51.html.

Nelson, Stephanie A. 1998. *God and the Land: The Metaphysics of Farming in Hesiod and Vergil*. New York: Oxford University Press.

Ness, D. van. 1986. *Crime and Its Victims*. Downers Grove, Ill.: Intervarsity.

Ness, D. van, and K. Strong. 1997. *Restoring Justice*. Cincinnati, Ohio: Anderson.

Nida, Eugene, and Charles R. Taber. 1982. *The Theory and Practice of Translation*. Leiden: Brill.

Nielsen, Kirsten. 1986. Is 6:1–8:18 as Dramatic Writing. *StTh* 40:1–16.

Norris, Richard A. 2003. *The Song of Songs: Interpreted by Early Christian and Medieval Commentators*. Grand Rapids: Eerdmans.

Norton, David. 2000. *A History of the English Bible as Literature*. Cambridge: Cambridge University Press.

Novak, D. 2004. The Covenant in Rabbinic Thought. Pages 65–80 in *Two Faiths, One Covenant? Jewish and Christian Identity in the Presence of the Other*. Edited by E. Korn. Lanham, Md.: Rowman & Littlefield.

Nunberg, Geoffrey, ed. 1996. *The Future of the Book*. Berkeley: University of California Press.

Oliva, P. 1971. *Sparta and Her Social Problems*. Amsterdam: Hakkert.

Orlov, Andrei A. 2003. On the Polemical Nature of 2 (Slavonic) Enoch: A Reply to C. Böttrich. *Journal for the Study of Judaism in the Persian, Hellenistic and Roman Period* 34:274–303.

———. 2000. Melchizedek Legend of 2 (Slavonic) Enoch. *Journal for the Study of Judaism in the Persian, Hellenistic and Roman Period* 31:23–38.

Ostriker, A. 2000. A Holy of Holies: The Song of Songs as Countertext. Pages 36–54 in Brenner and Fontaine, eds., *The Song of Songs*.

Otto, Rudolf, and John W. Harvey. 1923. *The Idea of the Holy: An Inquiry into the Non-rational Factor in the Idea of the Divine and Its Relation to the Rational*. Oxford: Oxford University Press.

Paley, W. 1790. *Horae Paulinae*. London: Faulder.

Parrish, John W. 2010. Speaking With Tongues, Dancing with Ghosts: Redescription, Translation, and the Language of Resurrection. *Studies in Religion* 39:25–45.

Parunak, H. Van Dyke, 1975. A Semantic Survey of NHM. *Biblica* 56:512–32.

Pateman, C. 1988. *The Sexual Contract*. Stanford: Stanford University Press.

Pavlich, G. 2005. *Governing Paradoxes of Restorative Justice*. London: Glasshouse.

PCIB. 2009. *Supersessionism*. Committee Church Doctrine, Presbyterian Church in Canada. No pages. Cited 1 October 2010. Online: http://www.presbyterian.ca/webfm_send/5040.

Pearson, L. 1962. The Pseudo-history of Messenia and its authors. *Historia* 11:397–426.

Peperzak, Adriaan T., ed. 1995. *Ethics as First Philosophy: The Significance of Emmanuel Levinas*. New York: Routledge.

Philo of Alexandria. 1929–1962. *Philo*. Translated by F. H. Colson. 10 vols. and 2 supplementary vols. LCL. London: William Heinemann; Cambridge, Mass.: Harvard University Press.

Pixley, Jorge. 1987. *On Exodus: A Liberation Perspective*. Translated by R. R. Barr. Maryknoll, N.Y.: Orbis.

Plaskow, Judith. 1990. *Standing Again at Sinai: Judaism from a Feminist Perspective*. New York: HarperSanFrancisco.

Plaut, Gunther W. 1974. *The Torah: A Modern Commentary*. New York: Union of American Hebrew Congregations.

Pliny. 1971. *Natural History*. Vol. 5, *Books 17–19*. Cambridge, Mass.: Harvard University Press.

Plumwood, Val. 1993. *Feminism and the Mastery of Nature*. London: Routledge.

Pomeroy, Sarah B. 1994. *Xenophon, Oeconomicus : A Social and Historical Commentary, with a New English Translation*. Oxford: Clarendon.

Praetorius, Ina. 2006. Speaking of God as a Woman Since the Enlightenment. *Feminist Theology* 15:84–97.

Pranis, K. 2004. The Practice and Efficacy of Restorative Justice. *Journal of Religion & Spirituality in Social Work: Social Thought* 23:133–57.

Prouser, Ora Horn. 1991. The Phenomenology of the Lie in Biblical Narrative. Ph.D. diss., The Jewish Theological Seminary of America.

Rad, Gerhard von. 1972. *Genesis: A Commentary*. Translated by John H. Marks. Philadelphia: Westminster.

Rashkow, Ilona N. 1998. Daddy-Dearest and the "Invisible Spirit of Wine". Pages 82–107 in *Genesis*. Edited by Athalya Brenner. A Feminist Companion to the Bible (second series) 1. Sheffield: Sheffield Academic.

Rendtorff, Rolf. 1993. Jesaja 6 im Rahmen der Komposition des Jesajabuches. Pages 73–82 in *The Book of Isaiah*. Leuven, 1989. ET, "Isaiah 6 in the Framework of the Composition of the Book." Pages 170–79 in Rendtorff and Kohl 1993.

Rendtorff, Rolf, and Margaret Kohl 1993. *Canon and Theology: Overtures to an Old Testament Theology*. OBT. Minneapolis: Fortress.

Ricoeur, Paul. 2000. Experience and Language in Religious Discourse. Pages 127–46 in *Phenomenology and the "Theological Turn": The French Debate*. Edited by D. Janicaud et al. New York: Fordham University Press.

Rigby, Kate. 2004. Earth, World, Text: On the (Im)Possibility of Ecopoiesis. *New Literary History* 35, no. 3:427–42.

Robbins, Vernon K. 1996. *Exploring the Texture of Texts: A Guide to Socio-Rhetorical Interpretation*. Valley Forge, Pa.: Trinity Press International.

Roberts, Alexander, and James Donaldson, eds. 1985. The Constitutions of the Holy Apostles. In *The Ante-Nicene Fathers*, vol. 7. Grand Rapids: Eerdmans.

Roberts, J. J. M. 2002. *The Bible and the Ancient Near East: Collected Essays*. Winona Lake: Eisenbrauns.

———. 1992. Double Entendre in First Isaiah. *CBQ* 54:39–48.

Robinson, S. E. 1987. The Apocryphal Story of Melchizedek. *Journal for the Study of Judaism in the Persian, Hellenistic and Roman Period* 18:26–39.

Roche, D. 2003. *Accountability in Restorative Justice*. Oxford: Oxford University Press.

Rosenberg, A. J., trans. 1993. *Genesis: A New English Translation of Text, Rashi and Other Commentaries*, vol. 1. New York: Judaica.

Rossing, Barbara R. 2005. Prophets, Prophetic Movements, and the Voices of Women. Pages 261–86 in *Christian Origins*. Edited by Richard R. Horsley. Minneapolis: Fortress.

Ruether, R. 1974. *Faith and Fratricide*. New York: Seabury.

Sahlins, Marshall. 1972. *Stone Age Economics*. New York: Aldine de Gruyter.

———. 1968. *Tribesmen*. Englewood Cliffs, N.J.: Prentice–Hall.

Sarna, Nahum. 1989. *The JPS Torah Commentary Genesis*. New York: The Jewish Publication Society.

Schenker, Adrian. 1986. Gerichtsverkündigung und Verblendung be den vorexilischen Propheten. *Revue Biblique* 93–94:563–80.

Schmid, D. 2001. *Restorative Justice in New Zealand: A Model for US Criminal Justice*. Wellington: Institute for Policy Studies.

Schüssler Fiorenza, Elisabeth. 2001. *Wisdom Ways: Introducing Feminist Biblical Interpretation*. Maryknoll, N.Y.: Orbis.

———. 1992. *In Memory of Her: A Feminist Theological Reconstruction of Christian Origins*. Rev. ed. New York: Crossroad.

Segal, Allan F. 1991. Matthew's Jewish Voice. Pages 3–37 in *Social History of the Matthean Community*. Edited by David L. Balch. Louisville, Ky.: Westminster John Knox.

Segundo, Juan Luis. 1985. *The Historical Jesus of the Synoptics*. Maryknoll, N.Y.: Orbis.

———. 1976. *The Liberation of Theology*. Maryknoll, N.Y.: Orbis.

Seitz, Christopher R. 1998. *Word without End: The Old Testament as Abiding Theological Witness*. Grand Rapids: Eerdmans.

———. 1991. *Zion's Final Destiny: The Development of the Book of Isaiah*. Minneapolis: Fortress.

Selvidge, Marla J. 1996. *Notorious Voices: Feminist Biblical Interpretation 1500–1920*. New York: Continuum.

Shero, L. R. 1938. Aristomenes the Messenian. *Transactions and Proceedings of the American Philological Association* 17:500–531.

Sherwood, Yvonne. 2004. *Derrida's Bible*. New York: Routledge.

———. 2000. *A Biblical Text and Its Afterlives: The Survival of Jonah in Western Culture*. Cambridge: Cambridge University Press.

Simkins, Ronald A. 2004. Family in the Political Economy of Monarchic Israel. *Bible and Critical Theory* 1. No pages. Online: www.epress.monash.edu.au/bc.

———. 1999. Patronage and the Political Economy of Ancient Israel. *Semeia* 87:123–44.

Skinner, John. 1930. *Genesis*. ICC. Edinburgh: T. & T. Clark. Latest impression 1994.

Smith, F. Lagard. 1993. *Sodom's Second Coming*. Eugene, Ore.: Harvest House.

Smith, Jonathan Z. 1978. *Map Is Not Territory*. Chicago: University of Chicago Press.

Smith, Linda Tuhiwai. 1999. *Decolonizing Methodologies: Research and Indigenous Peoples*. Dunedin: University of Otago Press.

Sneed, Mark. 2004. Qohelet and his "Vulgar" Critics: A Jamesonian Reading. *Bible and Critical Theory*. No pages. Online: www.epress.monash.edu.au/bc.

Sölle, D. 1975. *Suffering*. Minneapolis: Fortress.

Sommer, Benjamin D. 1998. *A Prophet Reads Scripture: Allusion in Isaiah 40–66*. Contraversions. Stanford: Stanford University Press.

Sonnet, Jean-Pierre. 1992. Le Motif de l'endurcissement (Is 6,9–10) et la lecture d'Isaïe. *Biblica* 73:208–39.

Soulen, R. K. 1996. *The God of Israel and Christian Theology*. Minneapolis: Fortress.

Souza, K. 2004. Examining the Role of Volunteers in Community Based Restorative Justice Programs. M.A. diss., University of Victoria, Canada.

Speiser, E. A. 1981. *Genesis*. New York: Doubleday.

Spinoza, Baruch. 1883. *Ethics*. Translated by R. H. M. Elwes. No pages. Cited 3 August 2009. Online: http://frank.mtsu.edu/~rbombard/RB/Spinoza/ethica-front.html.

Spuy, E. van der, et al., eds. 2007. *Restorative Justice: Politics, Policies and Prospects*. Cape Town: Juta & Co.

Stanton, Elizabeth Cady. 1898. *The Woman's Bible*, part 2. New York: European Publishing.

Ste. Croix, G. E. M. de. 1981. *The Class Struggle in the Ancient Greek World: From the Archaic Age to the Arab Conquest*. London: Duckworth.

Stigers, Harold. 1976. *A Commentary on Genesis*. Grand Rapids: Zondervan.

Stott, K. M. 2008. *Why Did They Write This Way? Reflections on References to Written Documents in the Hebrew Bible and Ancient Literature*. New York: T&T Clark International.

———. 2005. "Book-Find Reports" in Antiquity: A Re-examination of Wolfgang Speyer with Insights from Biblical Studies. *Ancient History Bulletin* 19, no. 3:105–30.

———. 2002. Herodotus and the Old Testament: A Comparative Reading of the Ascendancy Stories of King Cyrus and David. *Scandinavian Journal of the Old Testament* 16:52–78.

Strang, H., and J. Braithwaite, eds. 2000. *Restorative Justice*. Farnham: Ashgate.

Sweeney, Marvin A. 1997. Prophetic Exegesis in Isaiah 65–66. Pages 455–74 in Broyles and Evans 1997.

———. 1996. *Isaiah 1–39 with an Introduction to Prophetic Literature*. Grand Rapids: Eerdmans.

———. 1988. *Isaiah 1–4 and the Post-Exilic Understanding of the Isaiah Tradition*. BZAW 171. Berlin: de Gruyter.

Tamez, Elsa. 1982. *Bible of the Oppressed*. Translated by M. J. O'Connell. Maryknoll, N.Y.: Orbis.

Tate, M. E. 1996. The Book of Isaiah in Recent Study. Pages 22–56 in *Forming Prophetic Literature: Essays on Isaiah and the Twelve in Honor of John D. W. Watts*. Edited by James W. Watts and Paul R. House. JSOTSup 235. Sheffield: Sheffield Academic.

Tertullian. 1956. *Early Latin Theology*. Translated by S. L. Greenslade. The Library of Christian Classics 5. London: SCM.

Theophrastus. 1916. *Enquiry into Plants and Minor Works on Odours and Weather Signs*. Translated by Arthur Hort. 2 vols. London: Heinemann.

Tiedemann, Rolf. 1991. Dialectics at a Standstill: Approaches to the *Passagen-Werk*. Pages 260–91 in *On Walter Benjamin: Critical Essays and Recollections*. Edited by G. Smith. Cambridge, Mass.: MIT.

Timmer, Daniel. 2009. The Intertextual Israelite Jonah *face à l'empire:* The Post-colonial Significance of the Book's Cotexts and Purported Neo-Assyrian Context. *Journal of Hebrew Scriptures* 9, no. 9:2–22.

Torrey, C. C. 1970. *Ezra Studies*. 1910. New York: KTAV.

Trapp, John. 1649. *A Clavis to the Bible, or a New Commentary Upon the Pentateuch: Or Five Books of Moses*. London.

Trible, Phyllis. 1992. Genesis 22: The Sacrifice of Sarah. Pages 170–91 in *Not in Heaven: Coherence and Complexity in Biblical Narrative*. Edited by Jason P. Rosenblatt and Joseph C. Sitterson. Bloomington: Indiana University Press.

———. 1985. Huldah's Holy Writ: On Women and Biblical Authority. *Touchstone* 3 (January):6–13.

———. 1978. *God and the Rhetoric of Sexuality*. OBT. Philadelphia: Fortress.

Tsevat, Mattiteyahu. 1980. The Vision of Isaiah. Pages 155–76 in *The Meaning of the Book of Job and Other Biblical Studies*. New York: KTAV.

Varro, Marcus Terentius. 1999. *On Agriculture*. LCL 283. Translated by William Davis Hooper. Cambridge, Mass.: Harvard University Press.

Vermeylen, Jacques. 1977. *Du Prophète Isaïe à L'apocalyptique: Isaïe, I–XXXV, miroir d'un demi-millenaire d'experience religieuse en Israël*, vol. 1. Paris: Gabalda.

Vlach, M. 2010. *Has the Church Replaced Israel? A Theological Evaluation*. Nashville: B. & H. Academic.

Voaden, Rosalynn. 1999. *God's Words, Women's Voices: The Discernment of Spirits in the Writing of Late-Medieval Women Visionaries*. York: York Medieval.

Walker, Michelle Boulous. 1998. *Philosophy and the Maternal Body: Reading Silence*. London: Routledge.

Waltke, Bruce K., and Cathi J. Fredricks. 2001. *Genesis*. Grand Rapids: Zondervan.

Walton, John. 2001. *Genesis: The NIV Application Bible*. Grand Rapids: Zondervan.

Watts, John D. W. 2005. *Isaiah 1–33/34–66*. WBC 24/25. Nashville: Thomas Nelson.

Webb, Barry G. 1990. Zion in Transformation: A Literary Approach to Isaiah. Pages 65–84 in *the Bible in Three Dimensions: Essays in Celebration of Forty Years of Biblical Studies in the University of Sheffield*. Edited by David J. A. Clines, Stephen E. Fowl and Stanley E. Porter. Sheffield: Sheffield Academic.

Weems, Renita J. 2003. Huldah the Prophet: Reading a (Deuteronomistic) Woman's Identity. Pages 321–39 in *A God So Near: Essays on Old Testament Theology in Honor of Patrick D. Miller*. Edited by Brent A. Strawn and Nancy R. Brown. Winona Lake, Ind.: Eisenbrauns.

Wenham, Gordon. 1987. *Genesis 1–15*. WBC 1. Waco, Tex.: Word.

Westermann, Claus. 1984. *Genesis 1–11*. Translated by J. J. Scullion. London: SPCK; Minneapolis: Augsburg.

Whatmore, Sarah. 1999. Hybrid Geographies: Rethinking the "Human" in Human Geography. Pages 22–45 in *Human Geography Today*. Edited by Doreen Massey, John Allen and Philip Sarre. Cambridge: Polity.

Whitford, M. 1991. *Luce Irigaray: Philosophy in the Feminine*. London: Routledge.

Wilcox, Aidan (with Carolyn Hoyle). 2004. *The National Evaluation of the Youth Justice Board's Restorative Justice Projects*. London: Youth Justice Board.

Wilder, Amos H. 1974. The Parable of the Sower: Naivete and Method in Interpretation. *Semeia* 2:134–51.

Willet, Andrew. 1633. *Hexapla in Genesin & Exodum: That is a Sixfold Commentary Upon the Two First Bookes of Moses Being Genesis and Exodus*. London.

Williamson, H. G. M. 2009. Recent Issues in the Study of Isaiah. Pages 21–39 in *Interpreting Isaiah: Issues and Approaches*. Edited by David G. Firth and H. G. M. Williamson. Downers Grove: IVP.

———. 2006. *Isaiah 1–5*. ICC. London: T&T Clark International.

———. 2005. Temple and Worship in Isaiah 6. Pages 122–44 in *Temple and Worship in Biblical Israel*. Edited by John Day. Proceedings of the Oxford Bible Seminar. London: T&T Clark International.

————. 1994. *The Book Called Isaiah: Deutero-Isaiah's Role in Composition and Redaction.* Oxford: Oxford University Press.

————. 1987. *Ezra–Nehemiah.* Sheffield: Sheffield Academic.

Wilson, N. G. 1994. *Photius: The Bibliotecha.* London: Duckworth.

Wire, Antoinette Clark. 1990. *The Corinthian Women Prophets: A Reconstruction Through Paul's Rhetoric.* Minneapolis: Fortress.

Wittfogel, Karl. 1963. *Oriental Despotism.* New Haven: Yale University Press.

Wohlfarth, Irving. 1997. Walter Benjamin and the "German–Jewish Parnassus." *New German Critique* 70:3–86.

Wolfson, Elliot R. 2005. *Language, Eros, Being: Kabbalistic Hermeneutics and Poetic Imagination.* New York: Fordham University Press.

Wright, Abraham, 1662. *A Practical Commentary or Exposition Upon the Pentateuch: viz: These Five Books of Moses Genesis, Exodus, Leviticus, Numbers, Deuteronomy.* London.

Wright, N. T. 2006. *Evil and the Justice of God.* Downers Grove, Ill.: Inter-Varsity.

Xenophon. 1994. *Oeconomicus/A Social and Historical Commentary, with a New English Translation by Sarah B. Pomeroy.* Oxford: Clarendon.

Xie, Shaobo. 1996. History and Utopian Desire: Fredric Jameson's Dialectical Tribute to Northrop Frye. *Cultural Critique* 34:115–42.

Yee, Gale A. 2003. *Poor Banished Children of Eve: Woman as Evil in the Hebrew Bible.* Minneapolis: Fortress.

Zapff, Burkhard M. 2006. *Jesaja 56–66.* Würzburg: Echter.

Zehr, H. *The Little Book of Restorative Justice.* Intercourse, Pa.: Good Books.

————. 1999. Interview with Howard Zehr. *Peacework* (April):9–12.

————. 1990. *Changing Lenses.* Scottsdale, Pa.: Herald.

————. 1985. *Retributive Justice, Restorative Justice.* Akron, Pa.: Mennonite Central Committee.

Zehr, H., and H. Mikra. 1998. Fundamental Concepts of Restorative Justice. *Contemporary Justice Review* 1:47–55.

Zehr, H., and B. Toews, eds. 2004. *Critical Issues in Restorative Justice.* Monsey, N.Y. Criminal Justice.

Žižek, Slavoj. 2003. *The Puppet and the Dwarf: The Perverse Core of Christianity.* Cambridge, Mass.: MIT.

————. 2001. *On Belief.* London: Routledge.

————. 2000. *The Fragile Absolute, or, Why is the Christian Legacy Worth Fighting For?* London: Verso.

————. 1999. *The Ticklish Subject: The Absent Centre of Political Ontology.* London: Verso.

Zlotowitz, M., trans. and Commentary. 1986. *Bereishis: Genesis / A New Translation with a Commentary Anthologized from Talmudic, Midrashic and Rabbinic Sources.* With Overviews by N. Scherman. Brooklyn, N.Y.: Mesorah.

Zohar. 1984. Translated Harry Sperling and Maurice Simon. Introduction by J. Abelson. London: Soncino.

Zohary, Michael. 1982. *Plants of the Bible: A Complete Handbook to All the Plants with 200 Full-Color Plates Taken in the Natural Habitat.* Cambridge: Cambridge University Press.

Zornberg, Avivah Gottlieb. 1995. *The Beginning of Desire: Reflections on Genesis.* New York: Doubleday.

INDEXES

INDEX OF REFERENCES

INDEX OF AUTHORS

Wissenschaftliche Untersuchungen
zum Neuen Testament

Herausgegeben von
Martin Hengel und Otfried Hofius

129